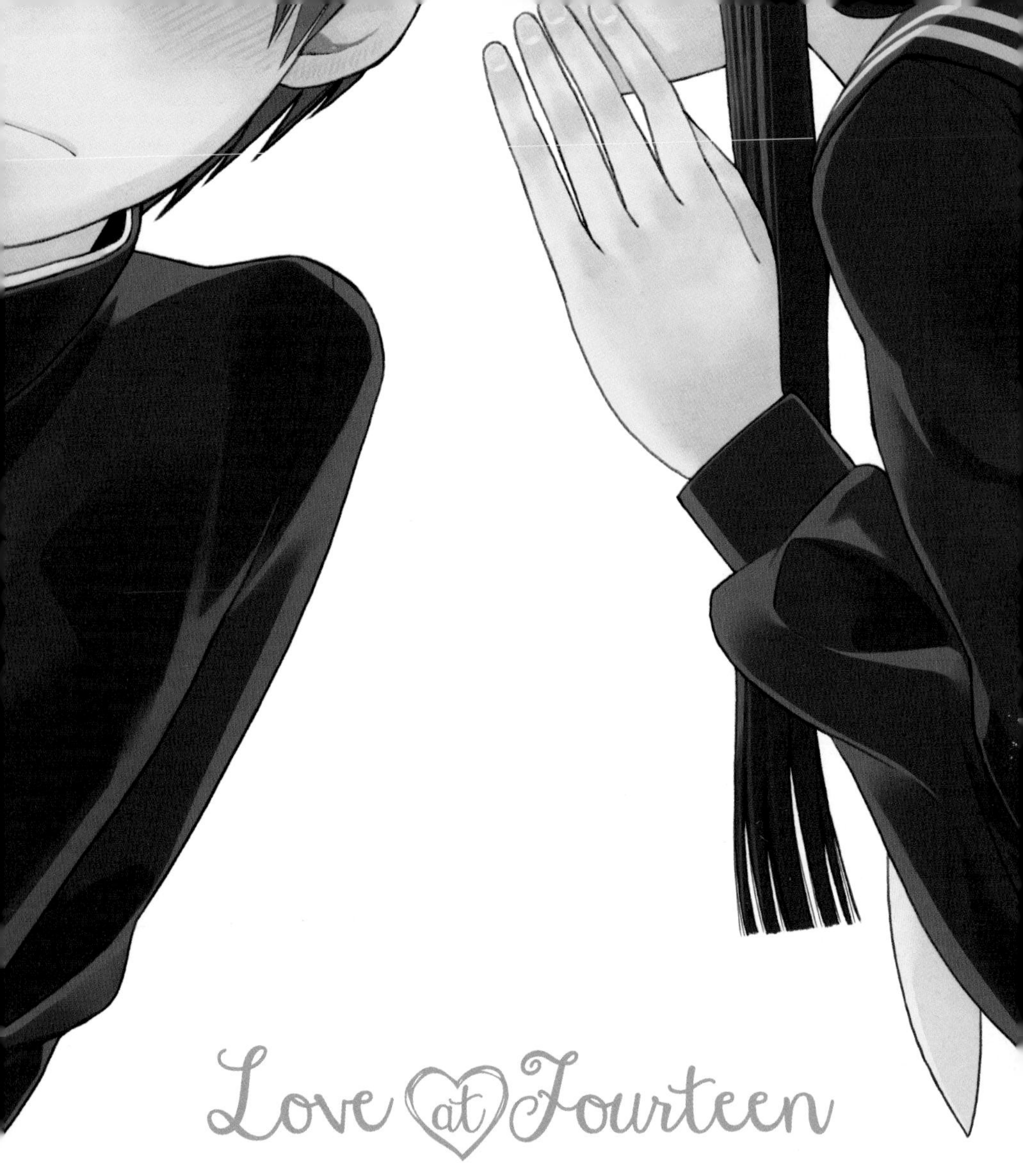

Love at Fourteen

Fuka Mizutani

8

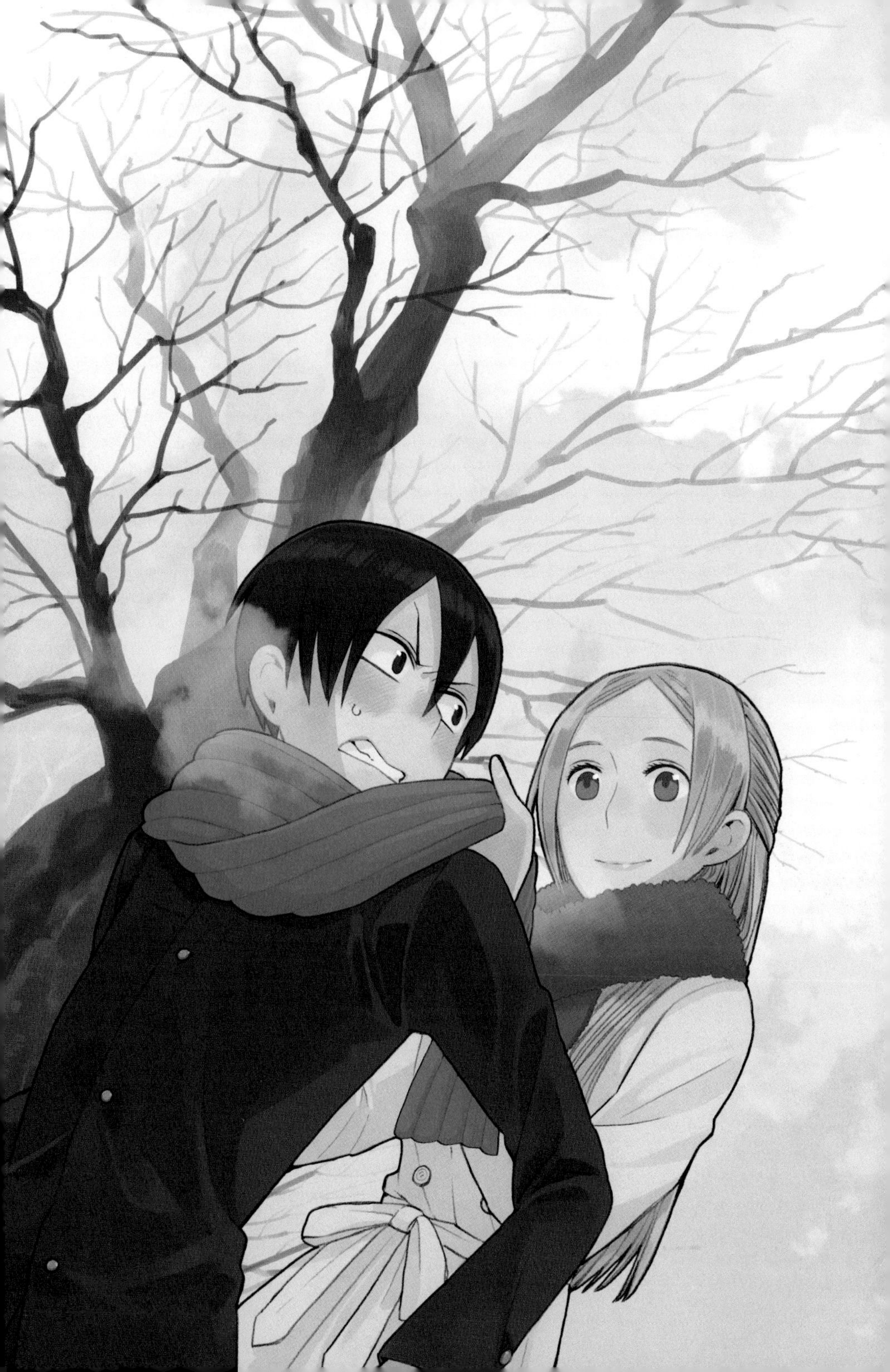

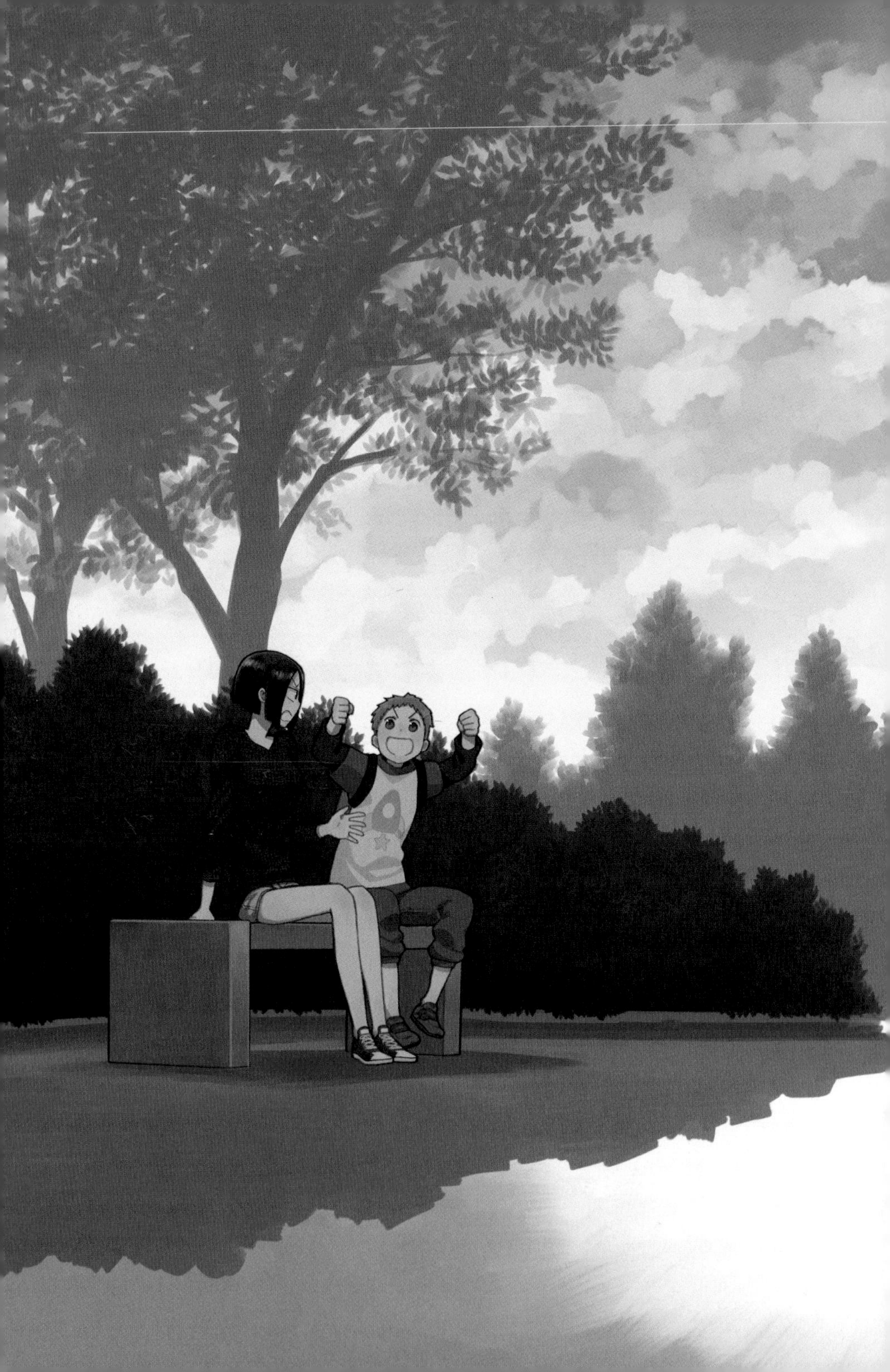

C o n t e n t s

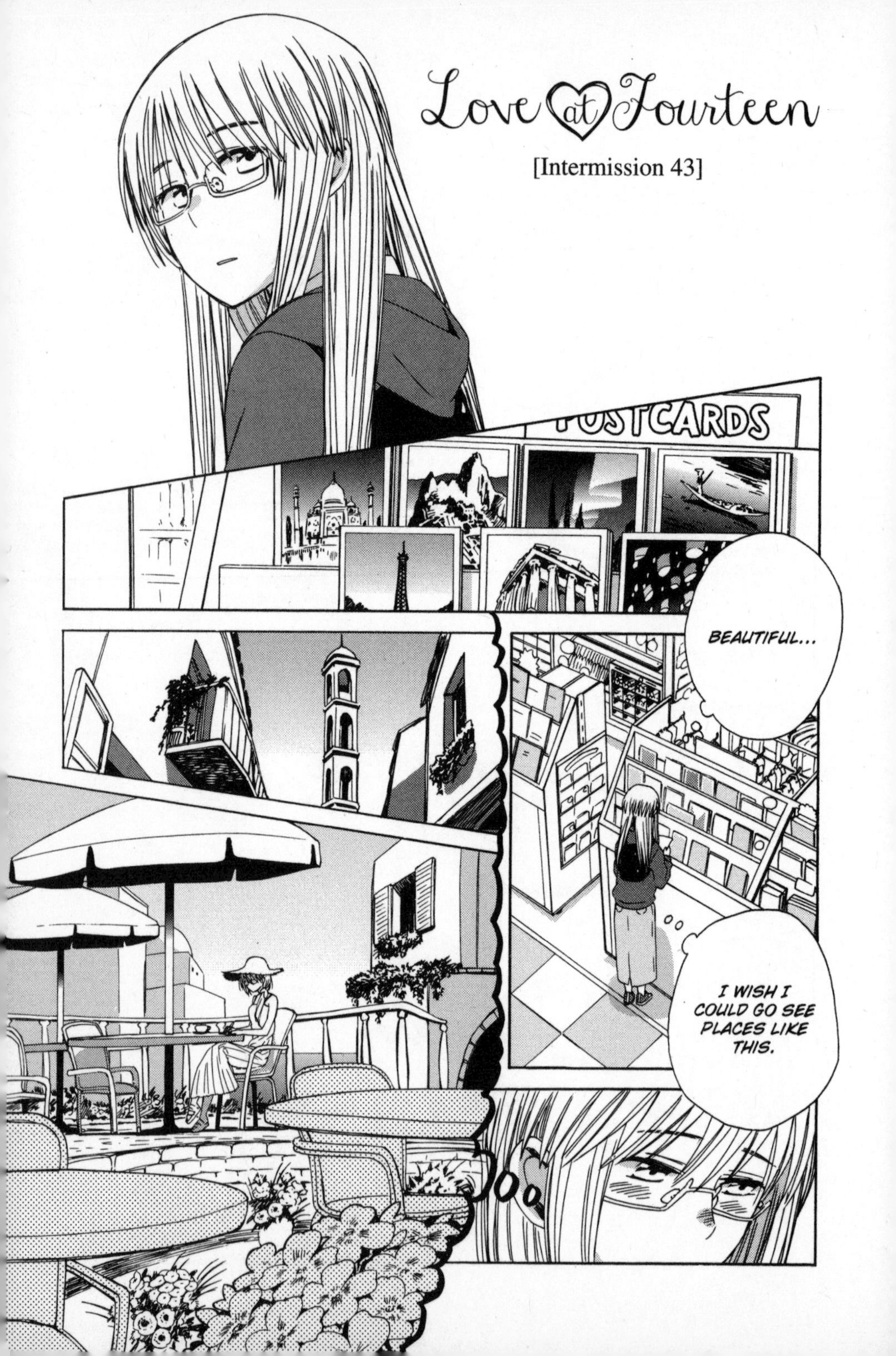
Love at Fourteen
[Intermission 43]
POSTCARDS
BEAUTIFUL...
I WISH I COULD GO SEE PLACES LIKE THIS.

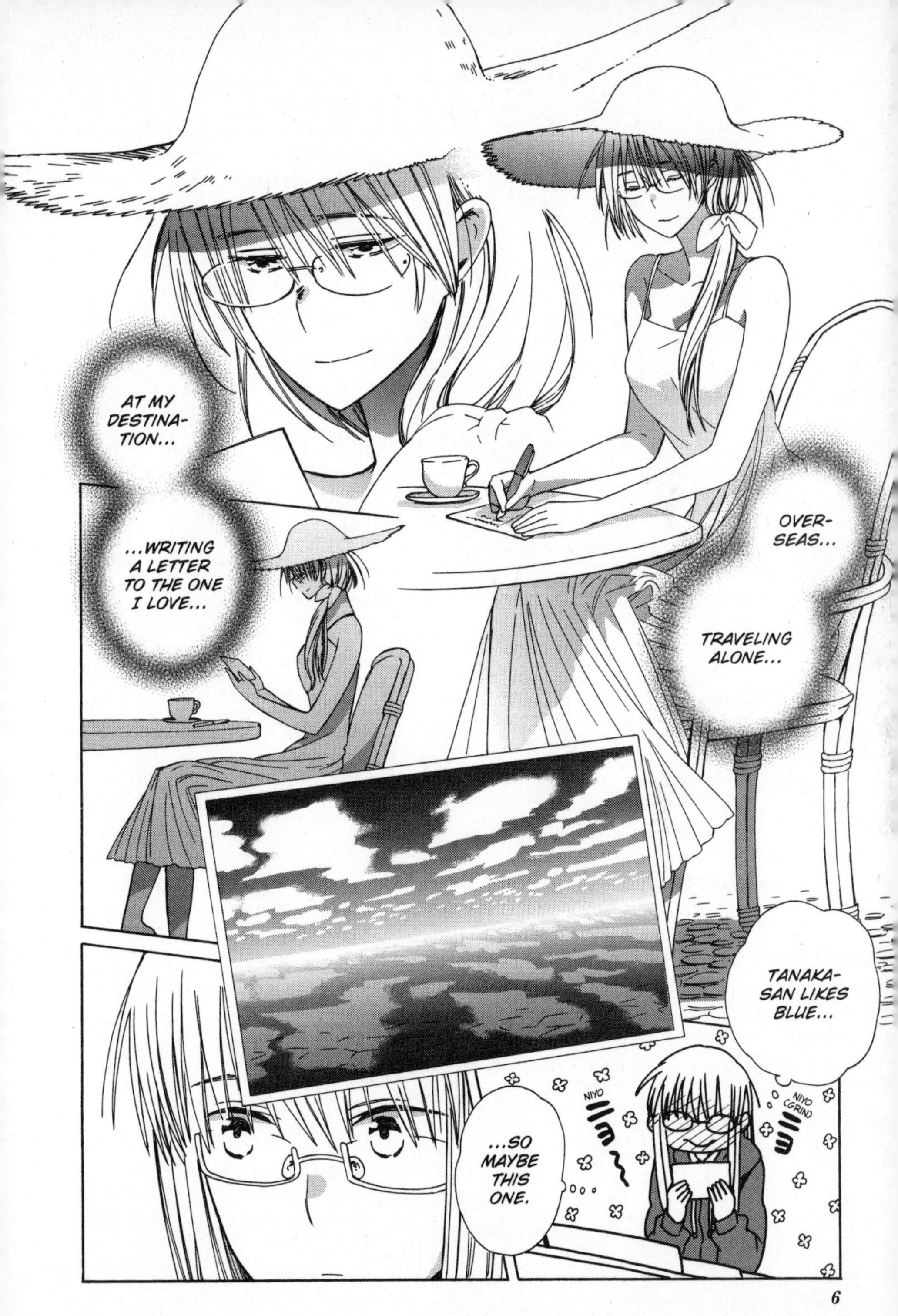
OVER-SEAS...
TRAVELING ALONE...
AT MY DESTINATION...
...WRITING A LETTER TO THE ONE I LOVE...
TANAKA-SAN LIKES BLUE...
NIYO (GRIN)
NIYO
...SO MAYBE THIS ONE.

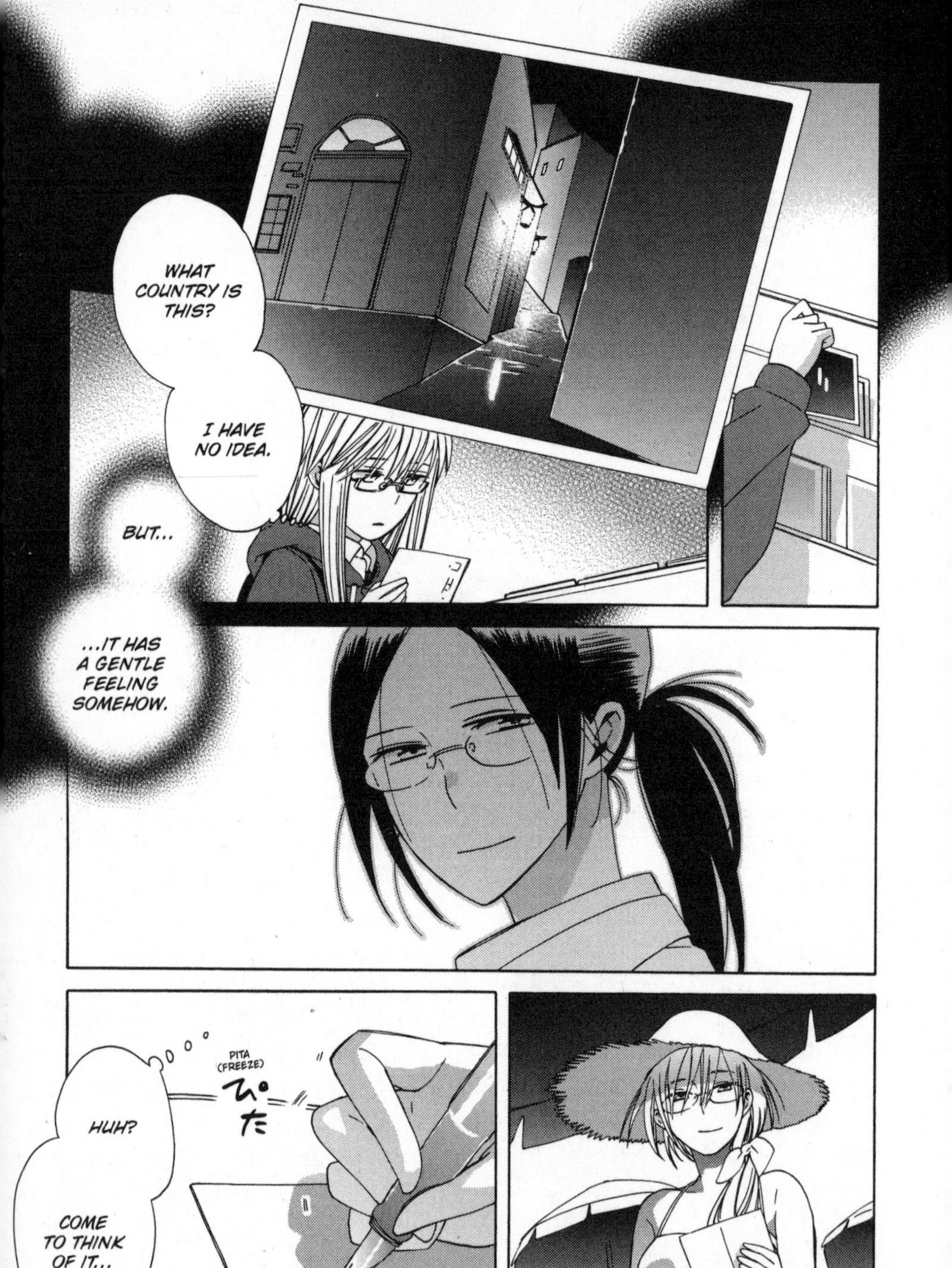
WHAT COUNTRY IS THIS?
I HAVE NO IDEA.
BUT...
...IT HAS A GENTLE FEELING SOMEHOW.
PITA (FREEZE)
ぴた
HUH?
COME TO THINK OF IT...

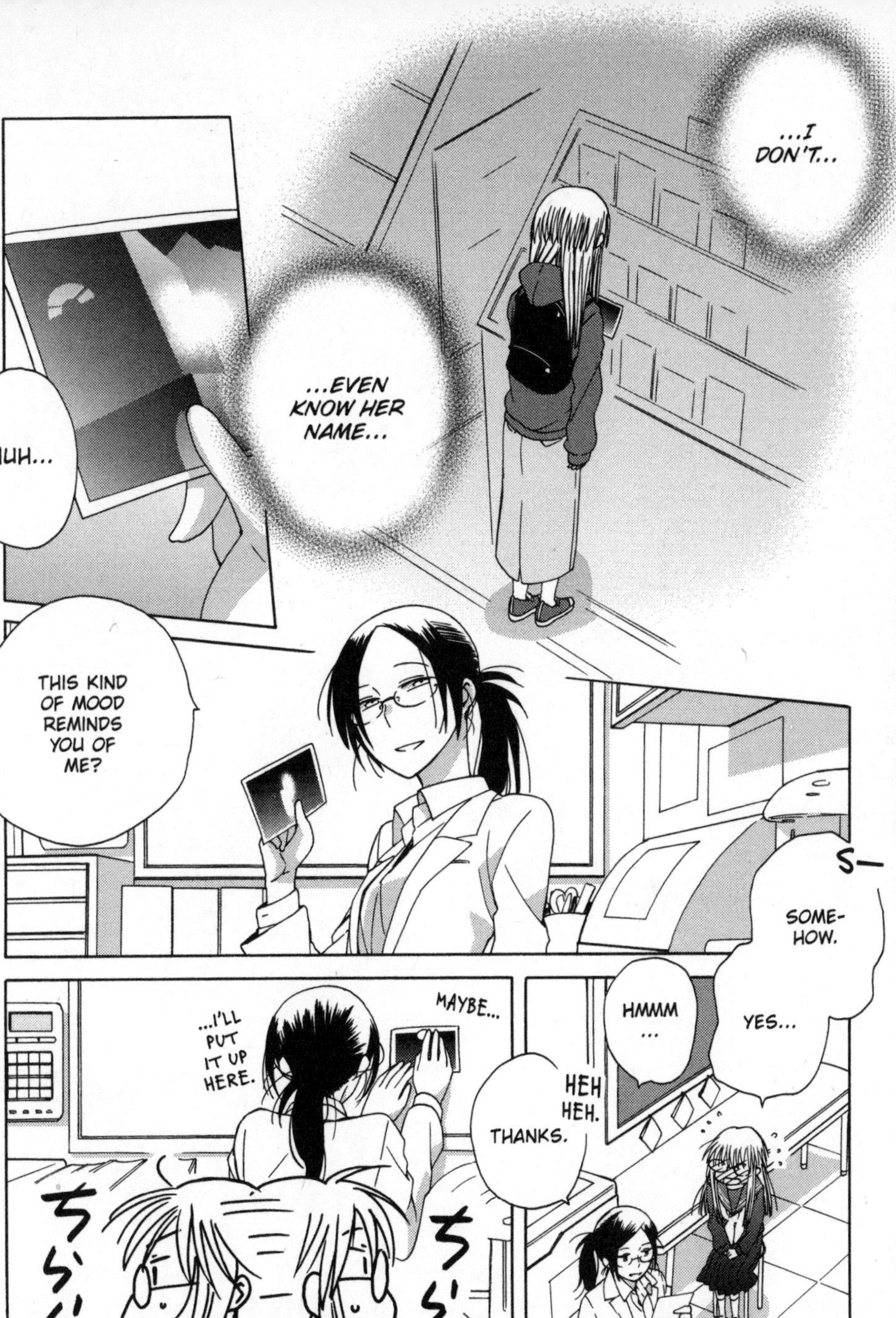
...I DON'T...
...EVEN KNOW HER NAME...
HUH...
THIS KIND OF MOOD REMINDS YOU OF ME?
S— SOME-HOW.
YES...
HMMM ...
HEH HEH.
THANKS.
MAYBE...
...I'LL PUT IT UP HERE.
ちらっ
CHIRA (GLANCE)
ちららっ
CHIRARA

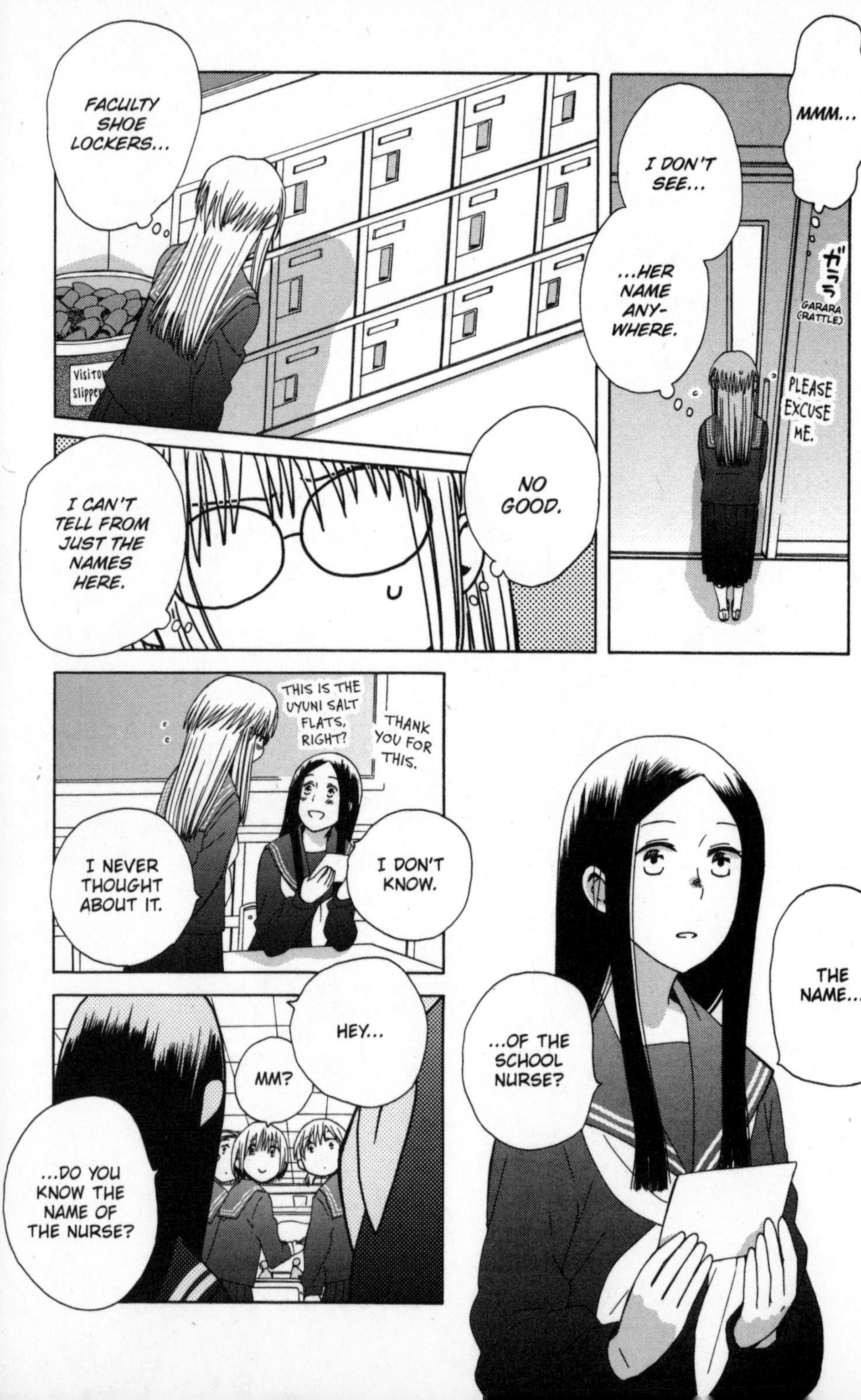
MMM...
I DON'T SEE...
...HER NAME ANYWHERE.
ガラ
GARARA (RATTLE)
PLEASE EXCUSE ME.
FACULTY SHOE LOCKERS...
Visitor Slipper
NO GOOD.
I CAN'T TELL FROM JUST THE NAMES HERE.
THE NAME...
...OF THE SCHOOL NURSE?
THANK YOU FOR THIS.
THIS IS THE UYUNI SALT FLATS, RIGHT?
I DON'T KNOW.
I NEVER THOUGHT ABOUT IT.
HEY...
MM?
...DO YOU KNOW THE NAME OF THE NURSE?

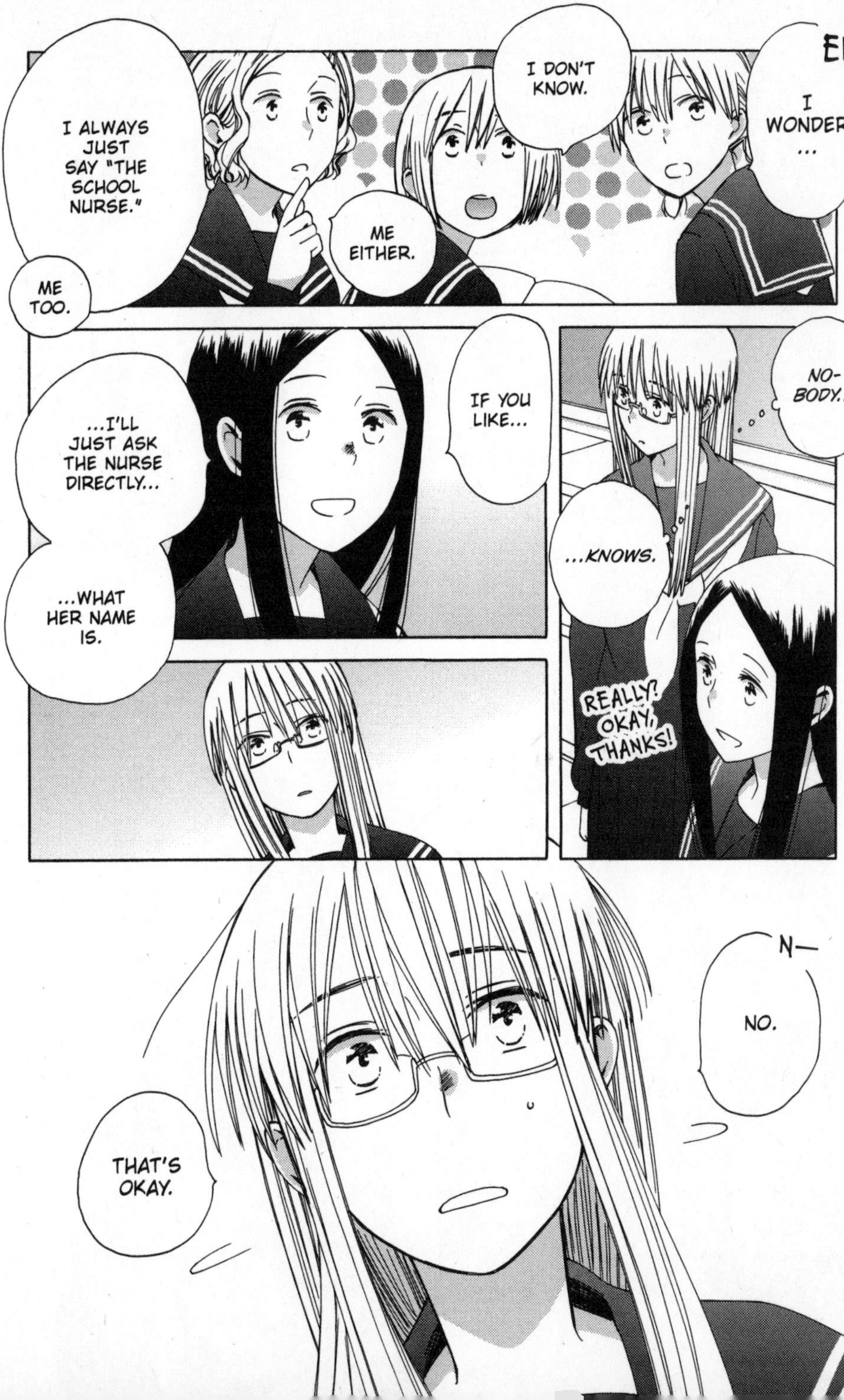
EH?
I WONDER...
I DON'T KNOW.
ME EITHER.
I ALWAYS JUST SAY "THE SCHOOL NURSE."
ME TOO.
NO-BODY...
...KNOWS.
REALLY? OKAY, THANKS!
IF YOU LIKE...
...I'LL JUST ASK THE NURSE DIRECTLY...
...WHAT HER NAME IS.
N—
NO.
THAT'S OKAY.

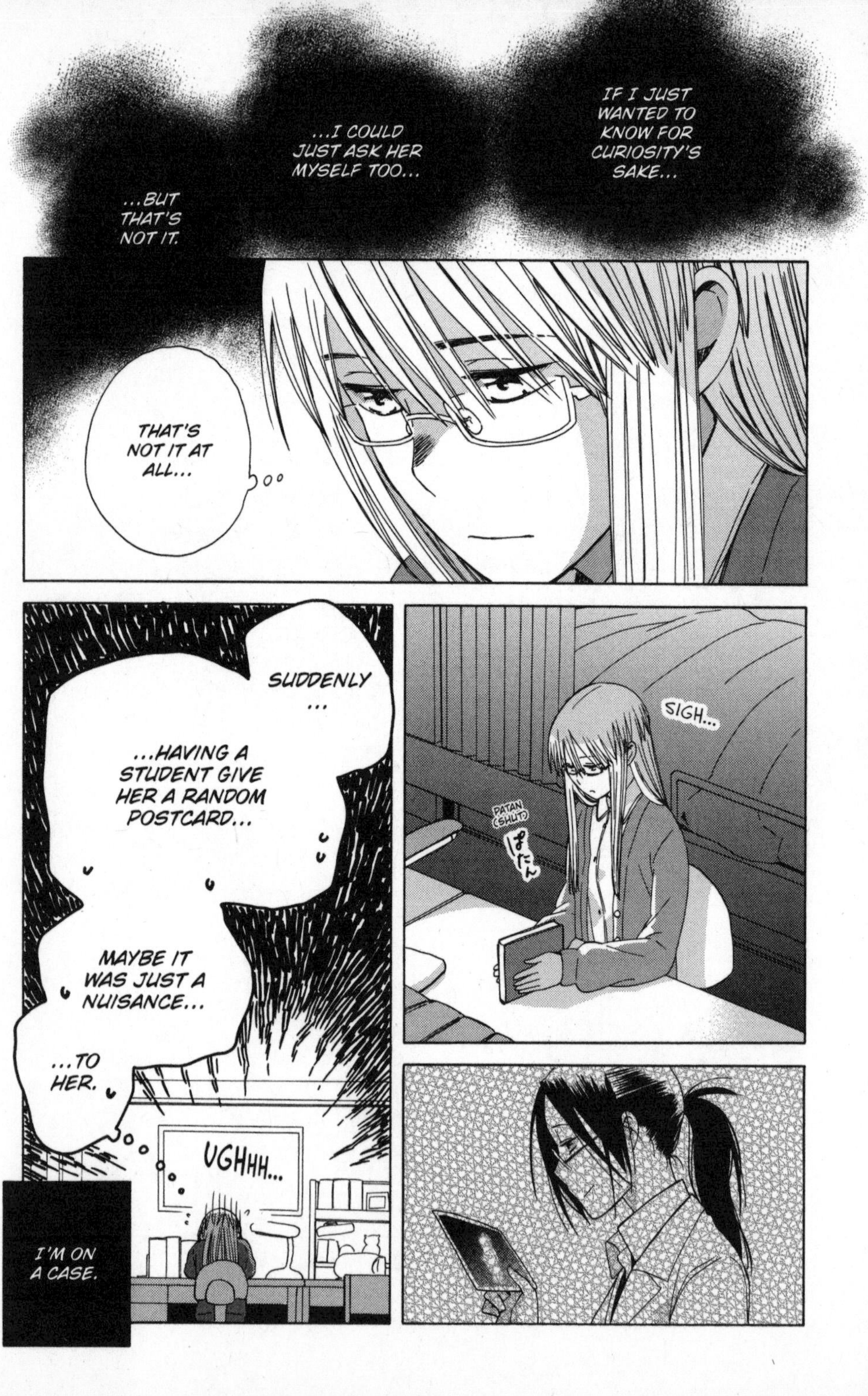
IF I JUST WANTED TO KNOW FOR CURIOSITY'S SAKE...
...I COULD JUST ASK HER MYSELF TOO...
...BUT THAT'S NOT IT.
THAT'S NOT IT AT ALL...
SIGH...
PATAN (SHUT)
ぱたん
SUDDENLY...
...HAVING A STUDENT GIVE HER A RANDOM POSTCARD...
MAYBE IT WAS JUST A NUISANCE...
...TO HER.
UGHHH...
I'M ON A CASE.

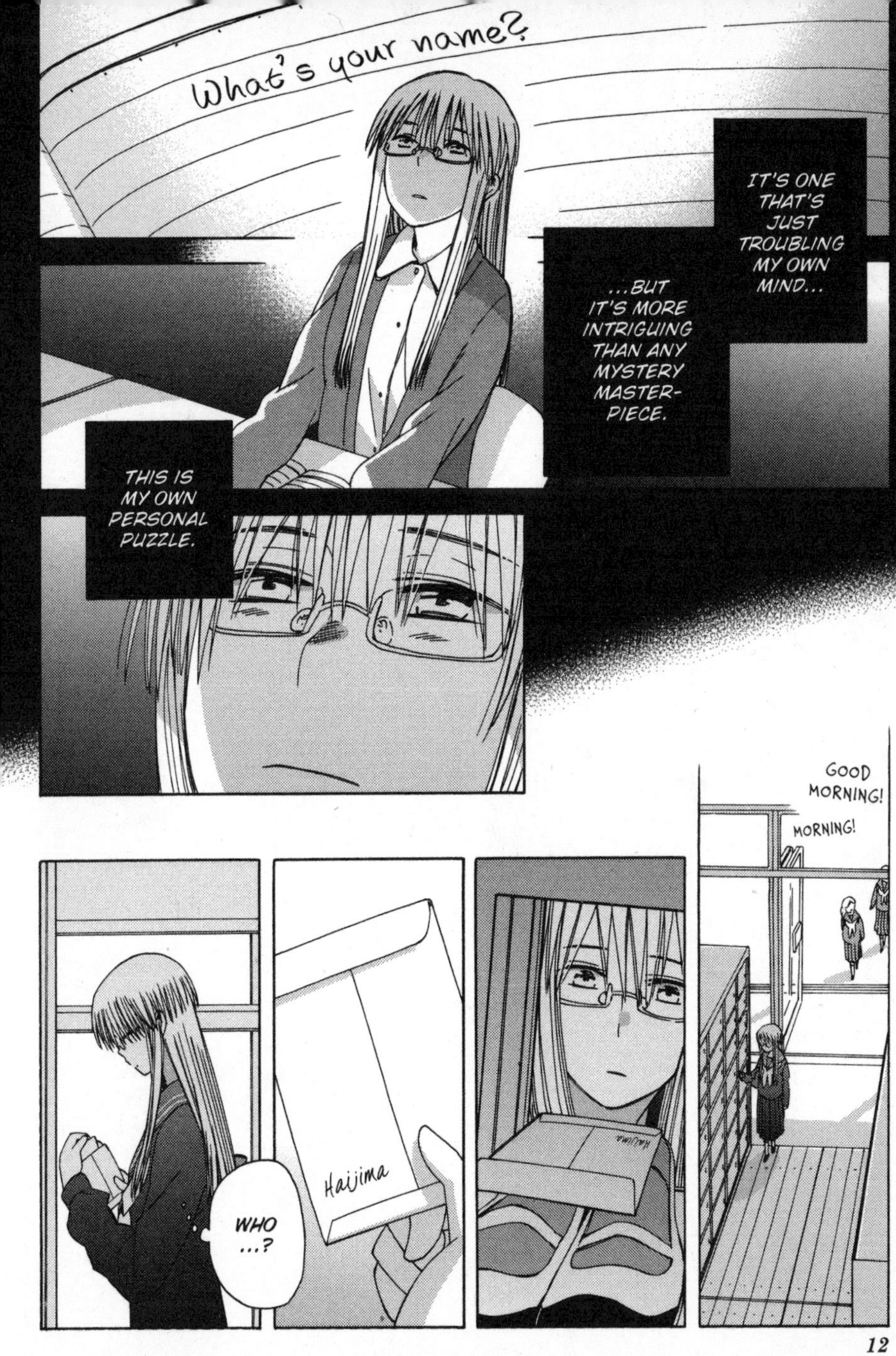

What's your name?
IT'S ONE THAT'S JUST TROUBLING MY OWN MIND...
...BUT IT'S MORE INTRIGUING THAN ANY MYSTERY MASTER-PIECE.
THIS IS MY OWN PERSONAL PUZZLE.
GOOD MORNING!
MORNING!
Haijima
WHO ...?

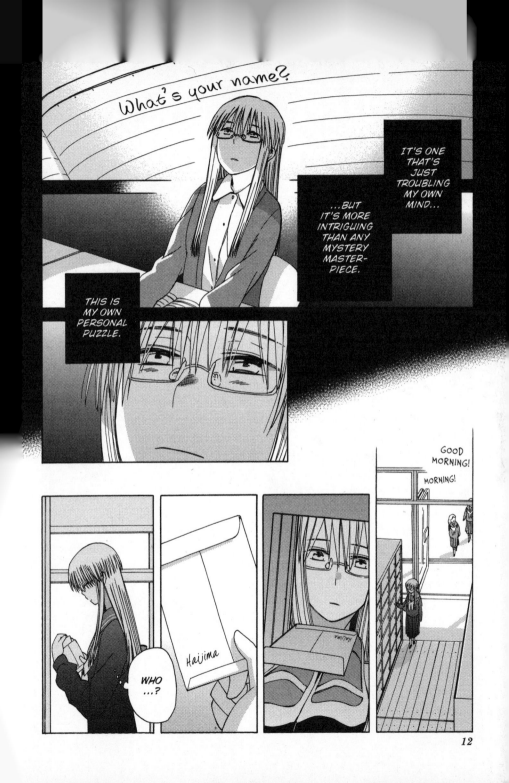

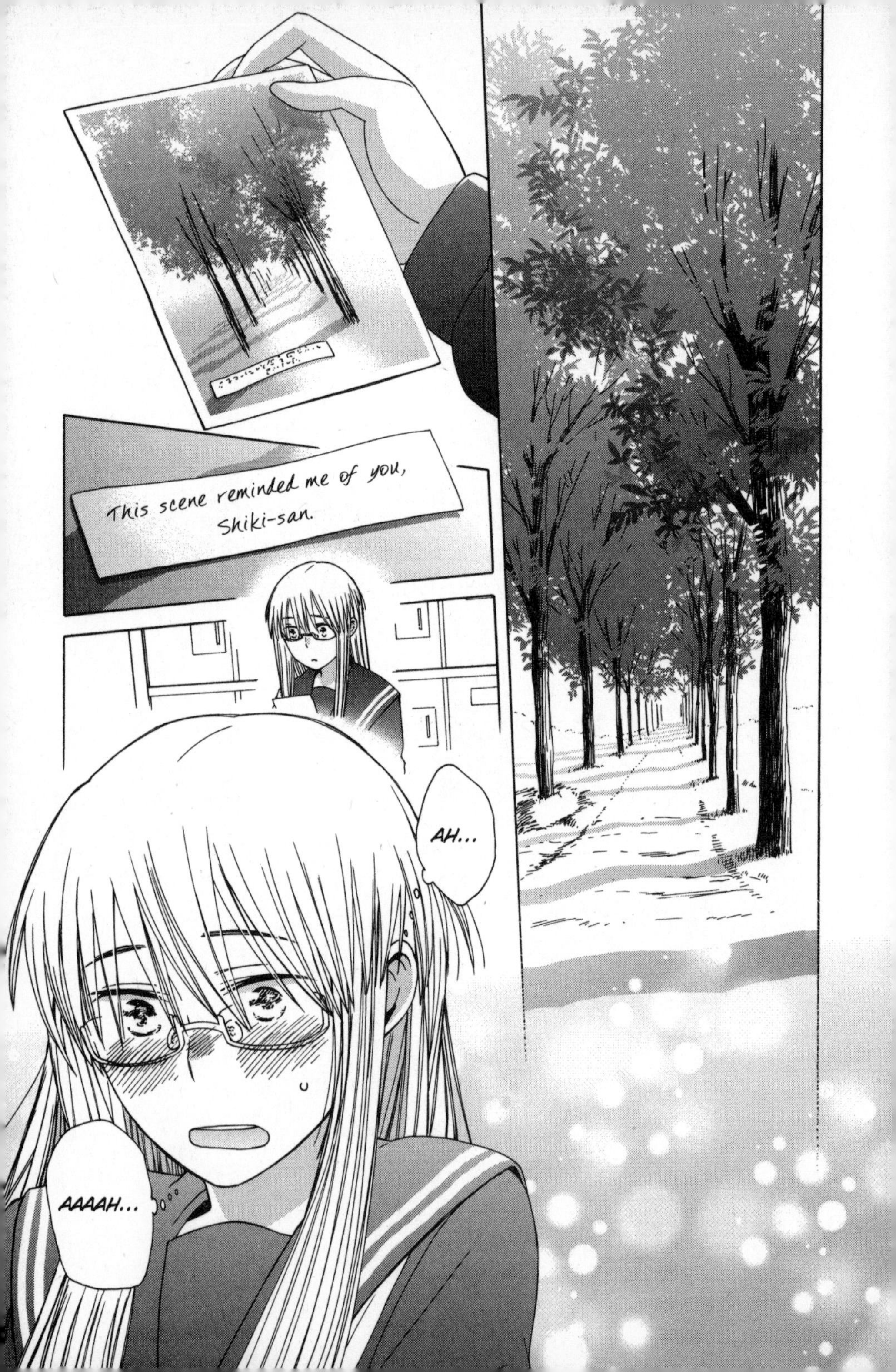
This scene reminded me of you, Shiki-san.
AH...
AAAAH...

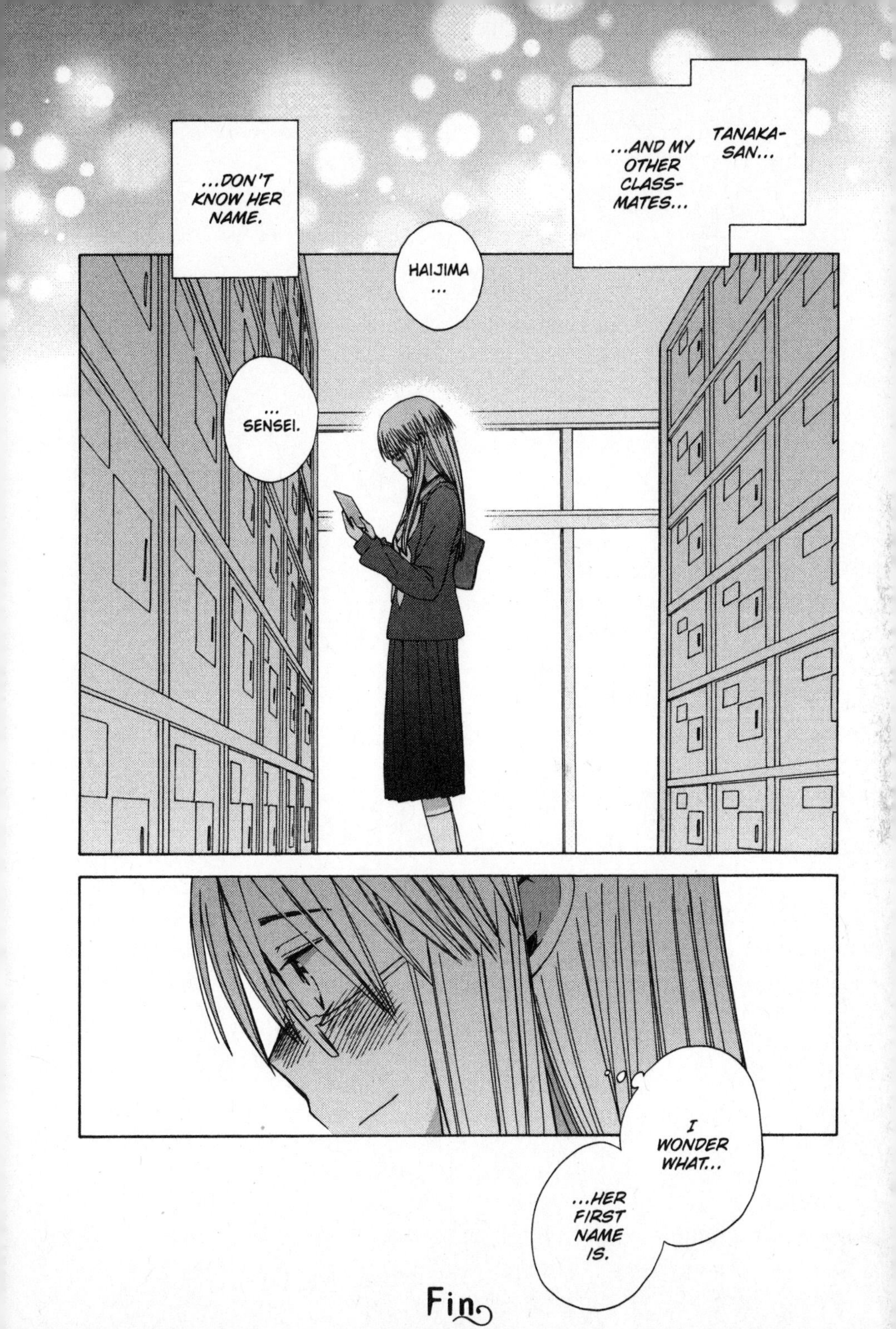
TANAKA-SAN...
...AND MY OTHER CLASSMATES...
...DON'T KNOW HER NAME.
HAIJIMA...
...SENSEI.
I WONDER WHAT...
...HER FIRST NAME IS.

Fin

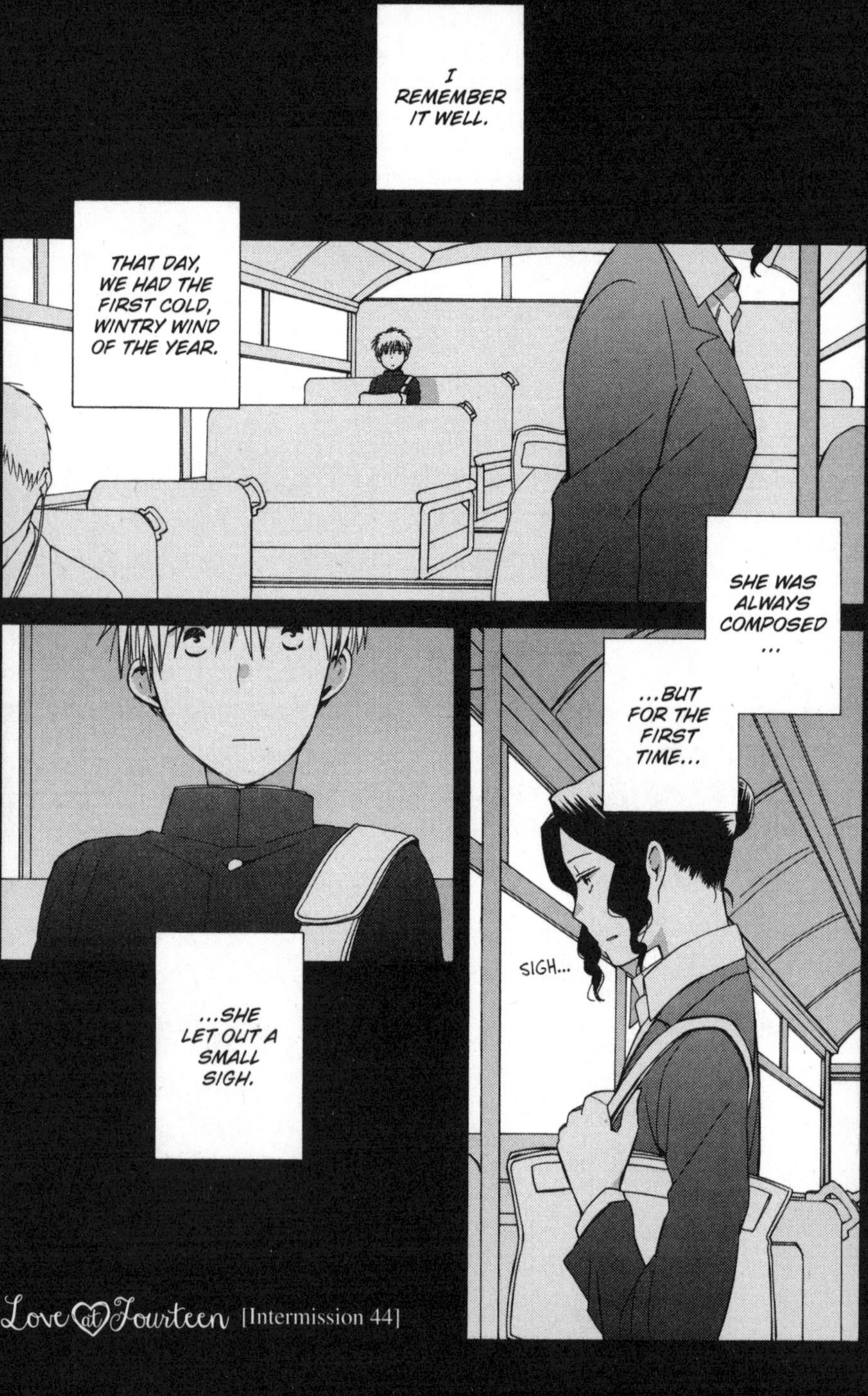
I REMEMBER IT WELL.
THAT DAY, WE HAD THE FIRST COLD, WINTRY WIND OF THE YEAR.
SHE WAS ALWAYS COMPOSED ...
...BUT FOR THE FIRST TIME...
SIGH...
...SHE LET OUT A SMALL SIGH.

Love at Fourteen

[Intermission 44]

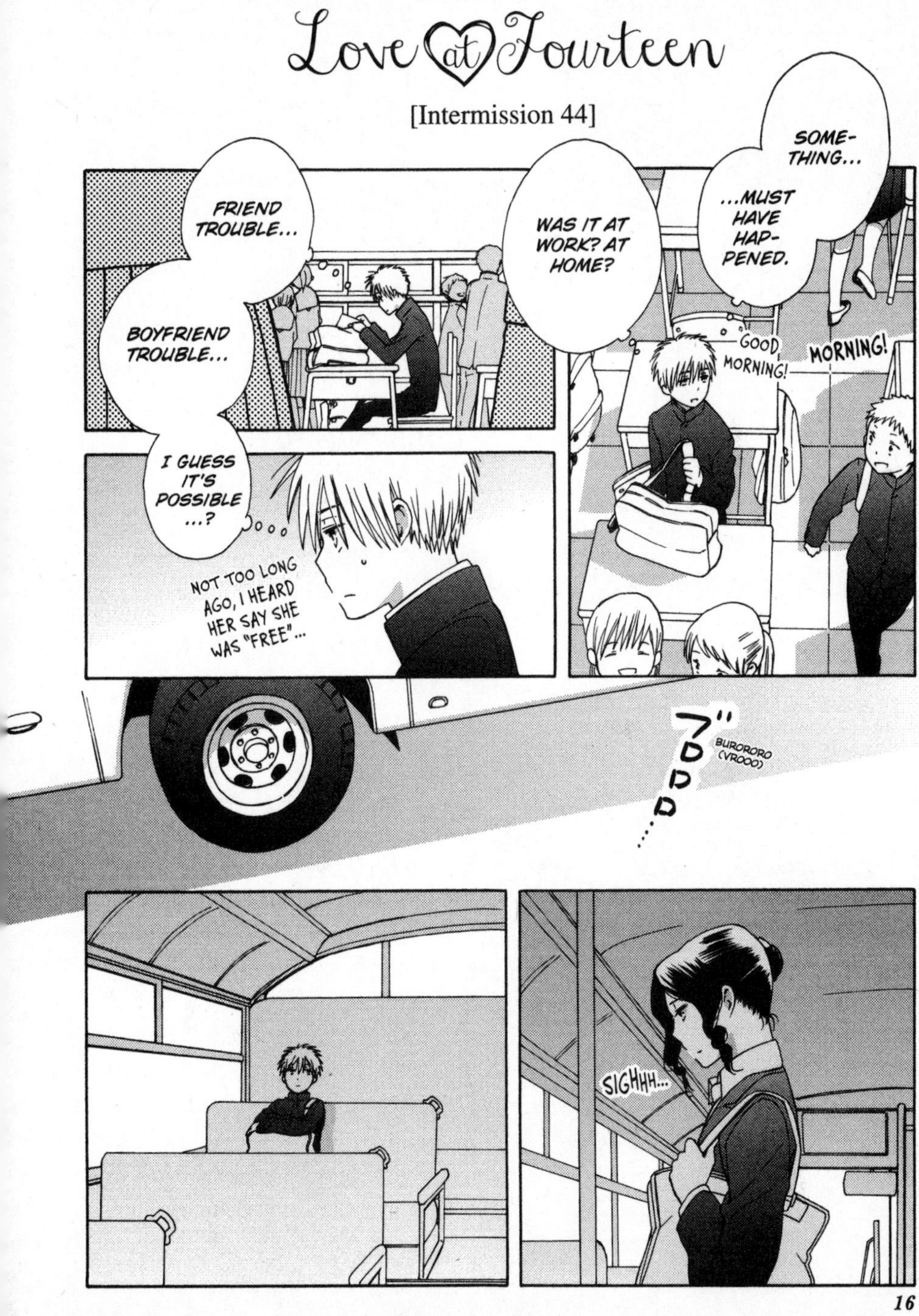
SOME-THING...
...MUST HAVE HAP-PENED.
WAS IT AT WORK? AT HOME?
MORNING!
GOOD MORNING!
FRIEND TROUBLE...
BOYFRIEND TROUBLE...
I GUESS IT'S POSSIBLE ...?
NOT TOO LONG AGO, I HEARD HER SAY SHE WAS "FREE"...
ブロロロ...
BURORORO (VROOO)
SIGHHH...

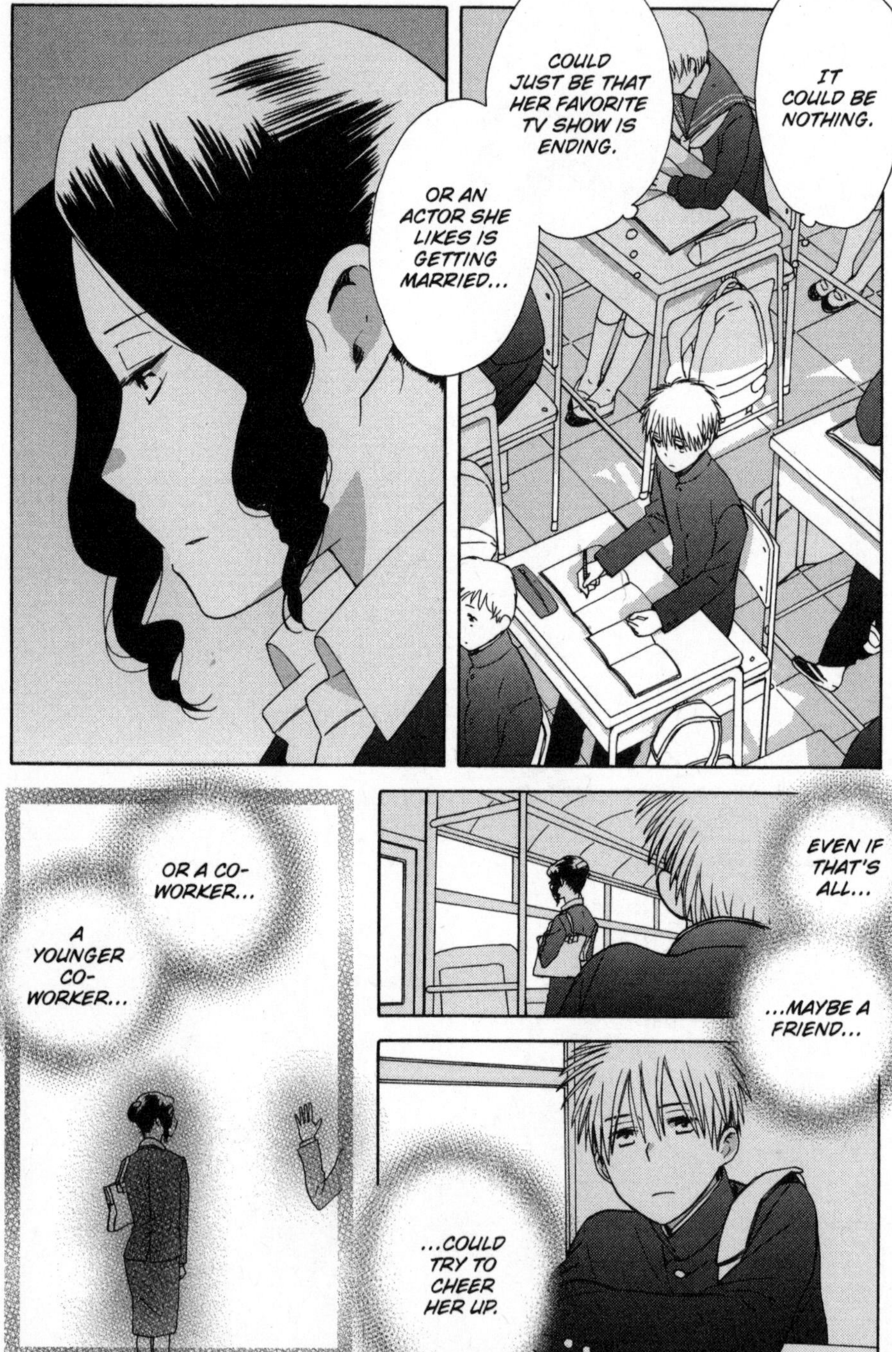
IT COULD BE NOTHING.
COULD JUST BE THAT HER FAVORITE TV SHOW IS ENDING.
OR AN ACTOR SHE LIKES IS GETTING MARRIED...
EVEN IF THAT'S ALL...
...MAYBE A FRIEND...
...COULD TRY TO CHEER HER UP.
OR A CO-WORKER...
A YOUNGER CO-WORKER...

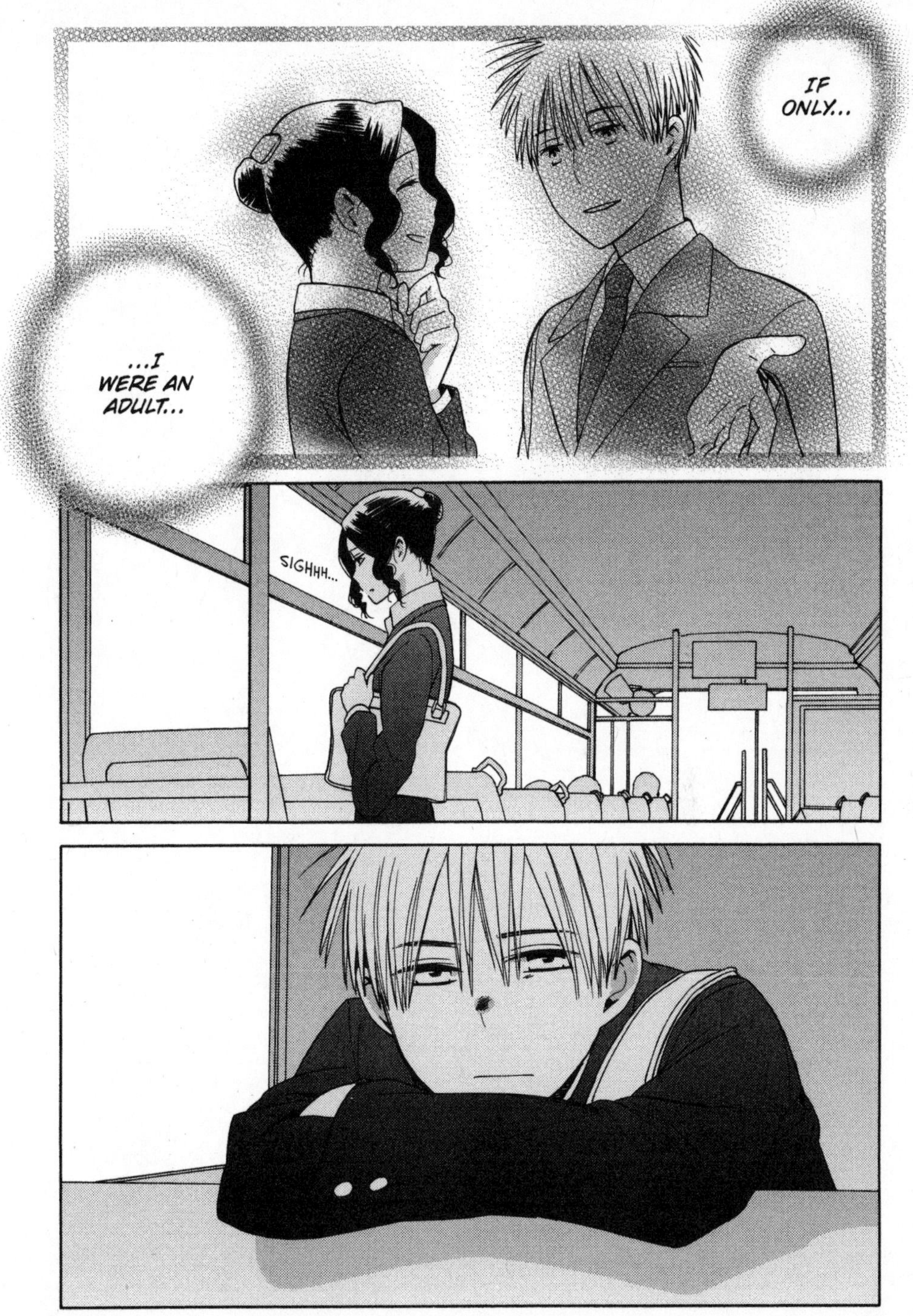
IF ONLY...
...I WERE AN ADULT...
SIGHHH...

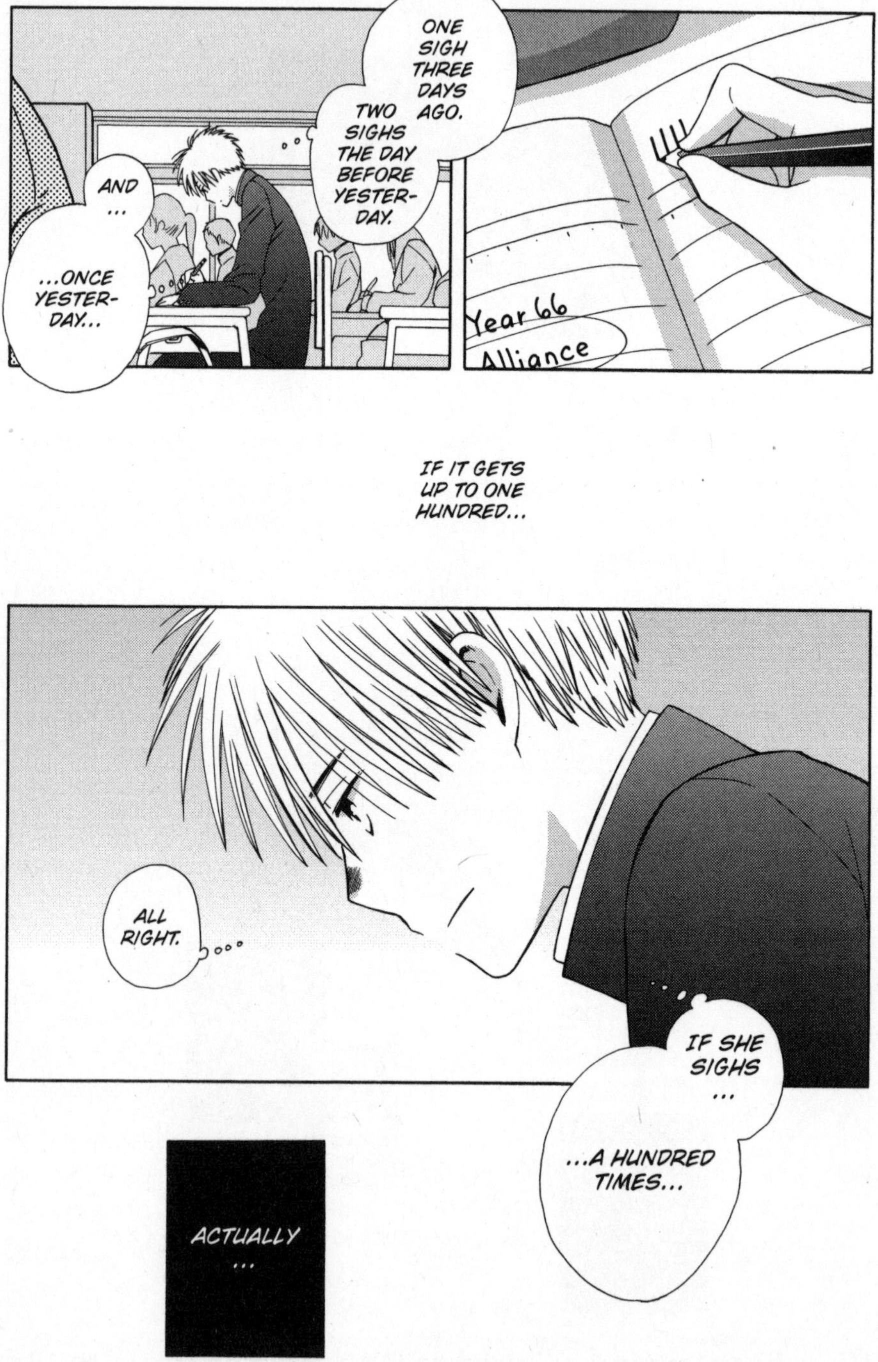
Year 66 Alliance
ONE SIGH THREE DAYS AGO.
TWO SIGHS THE DAY BEFORE YESTER-DAY.
AND ...
...ONCE YESTER-DAY...
IF IT GETS UP TO ONE HUNDRED...
IF SHE SIGHS ...
...A HUNDRED TIMES...
ALL RIGHT.
ACTUALLY ...

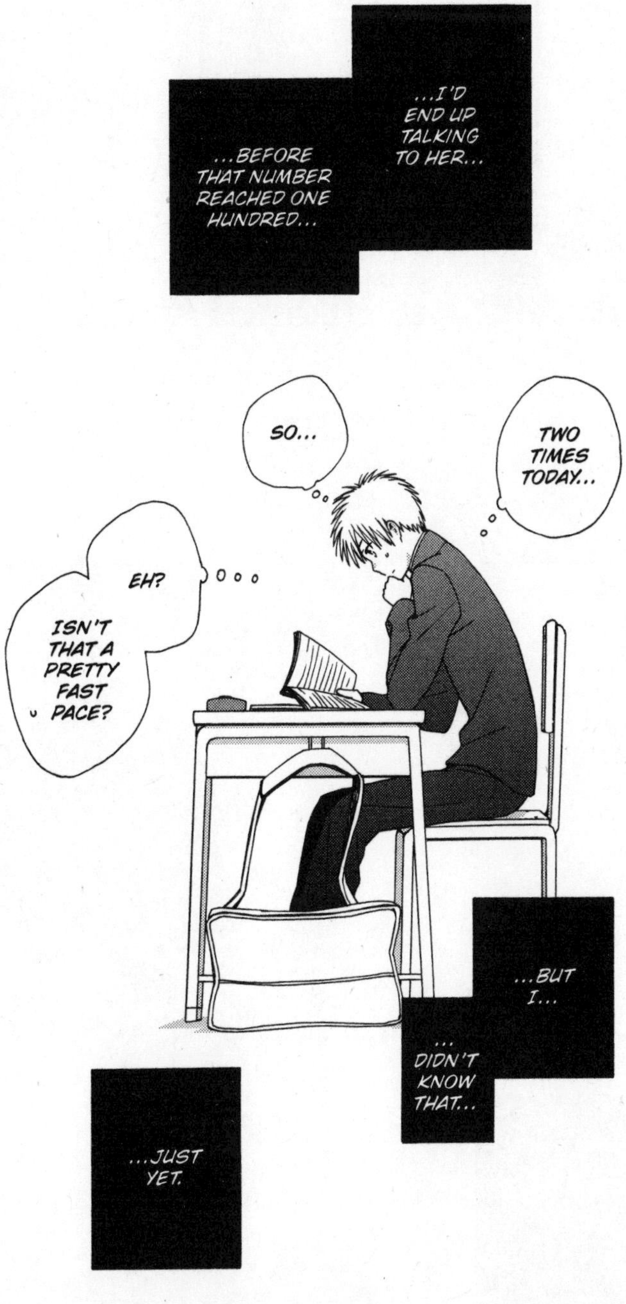
...I'D END UP TALKING TO HER...
...BEFORE THAT NUMBER REACHED ONE HUNDRED...
TWO TIMES TODAY...
SO...
EH?
ISN'T THAT A PRETTY FAST PACE?
...BUT I...
...DIDN'T KNOW THAT...
...JUST YET.
Fin

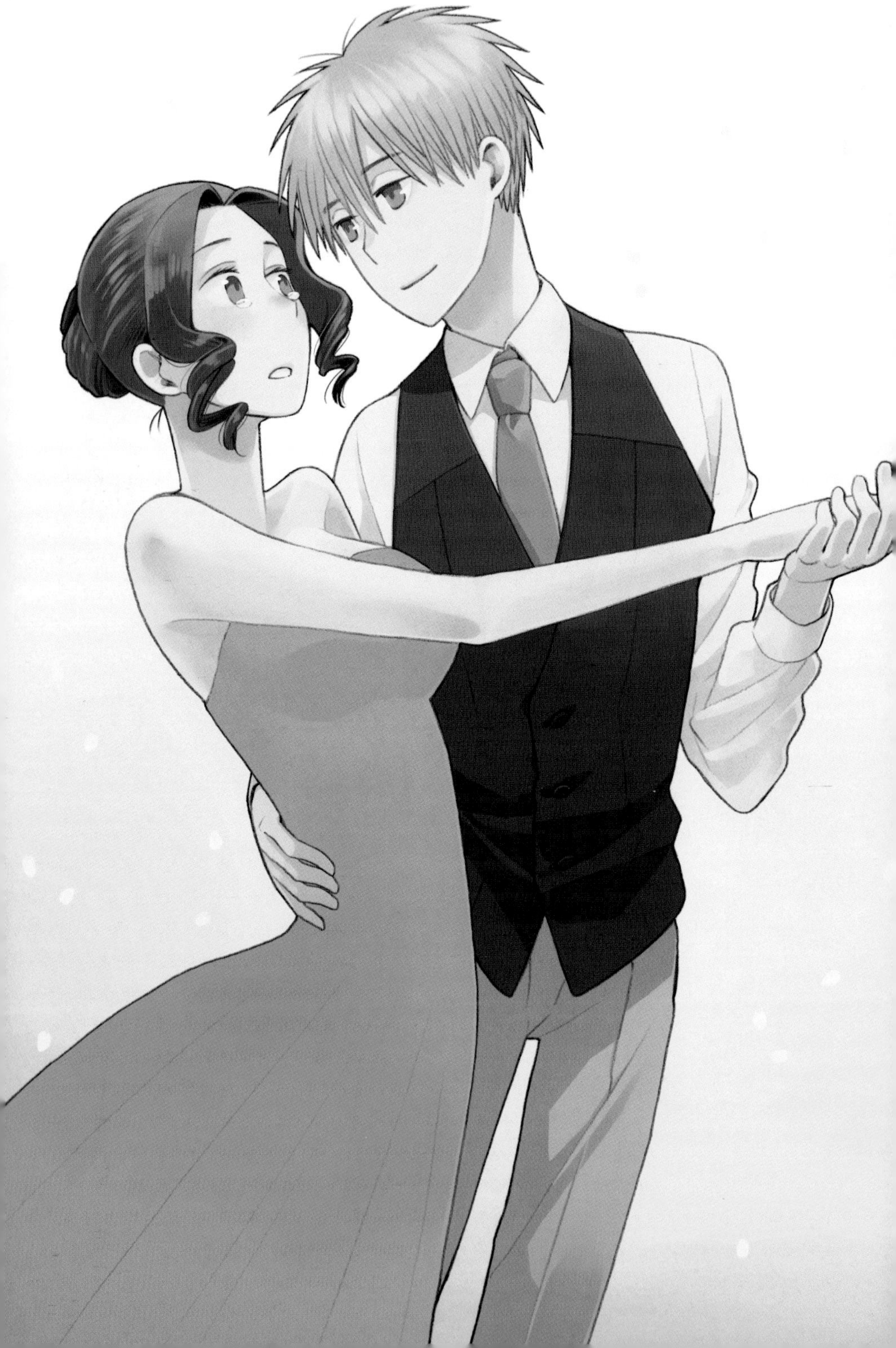

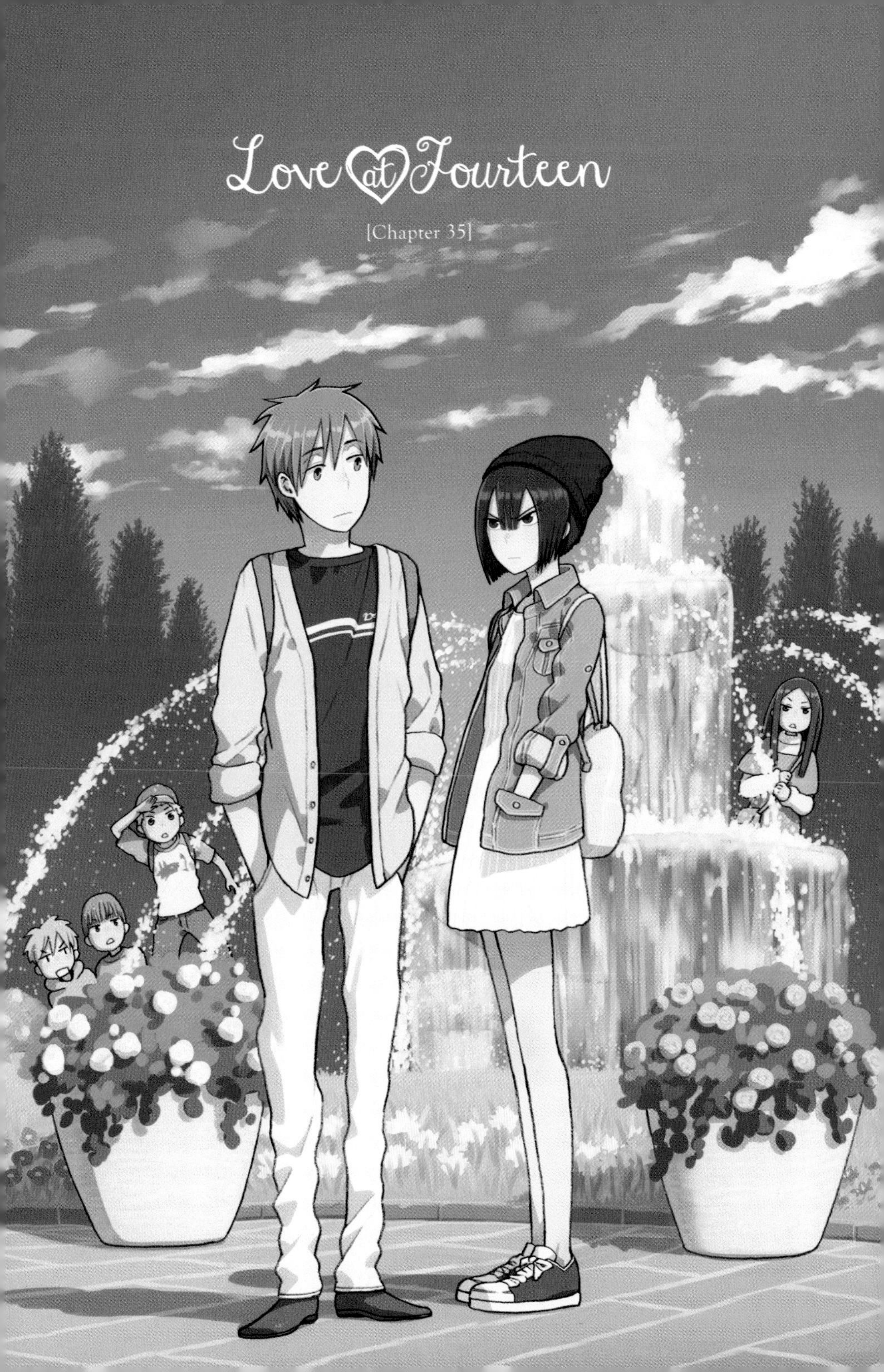
Love at Fourteen
[Chapter 35]

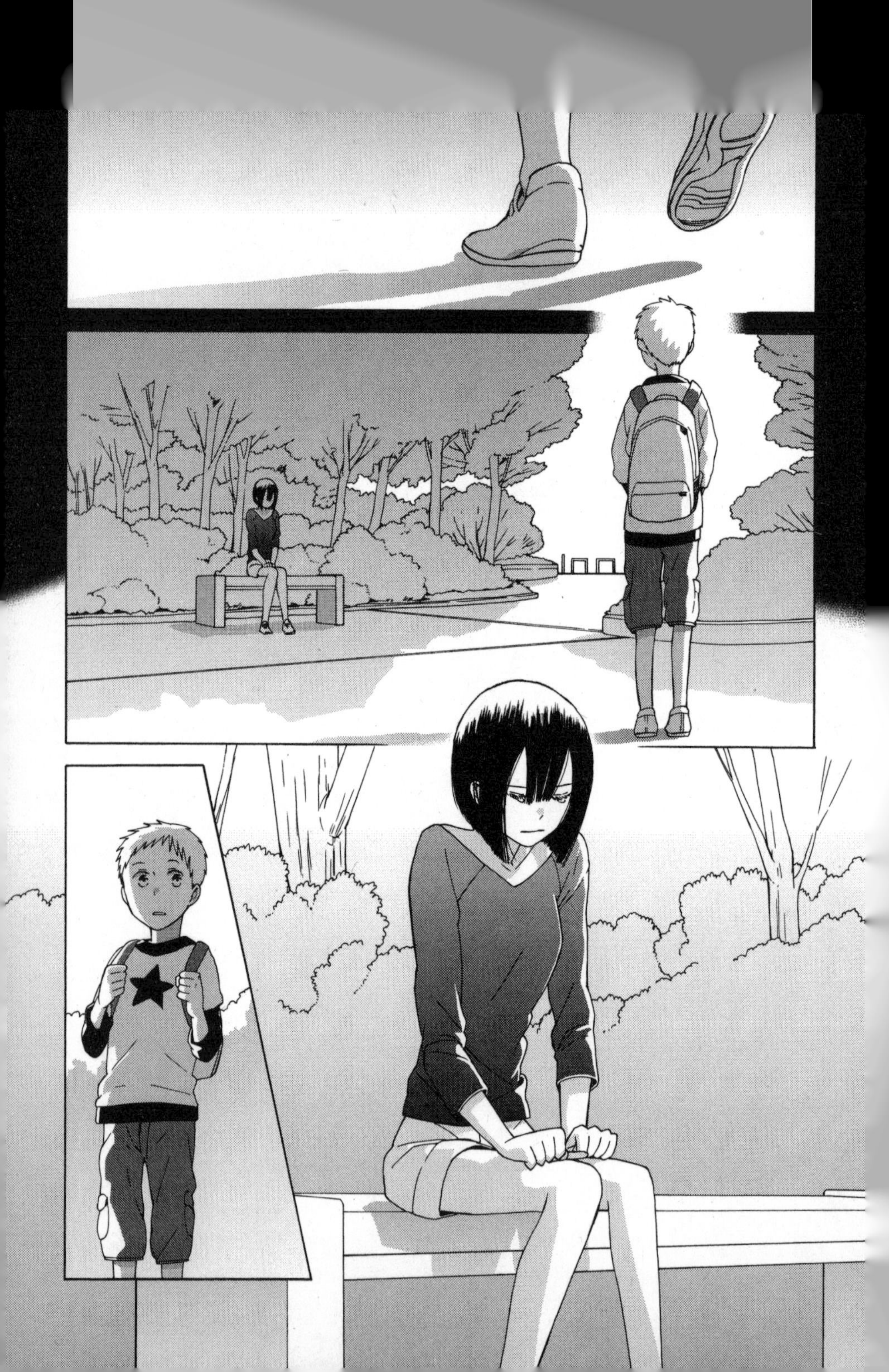

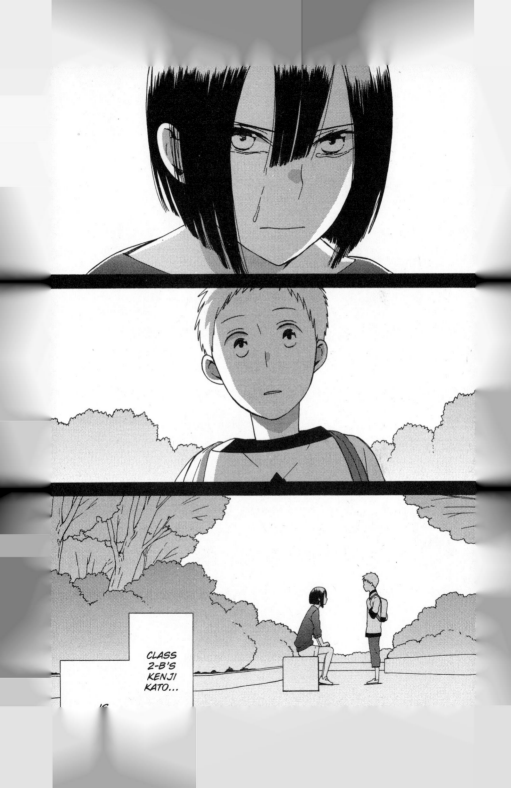

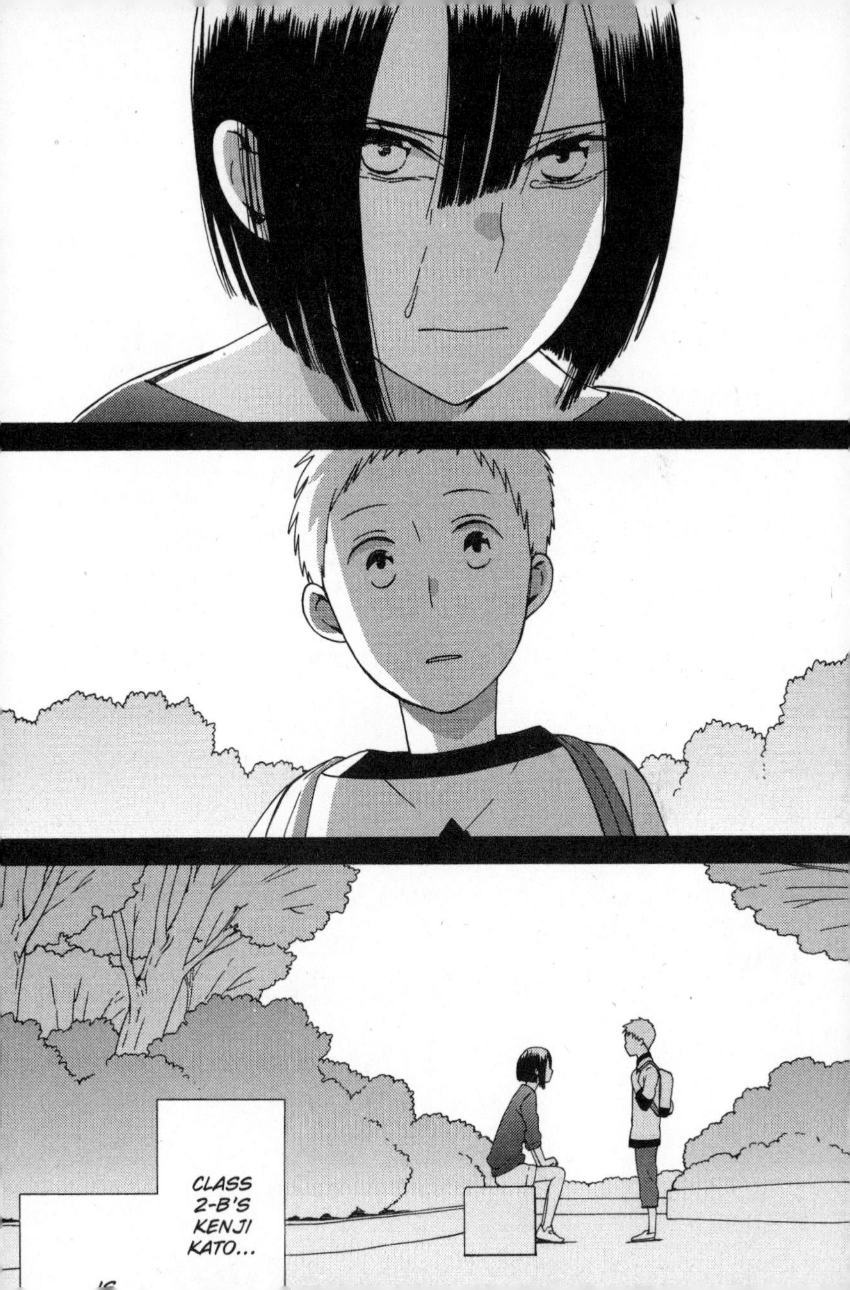
CLASS 2-B'S KENJI KATO...

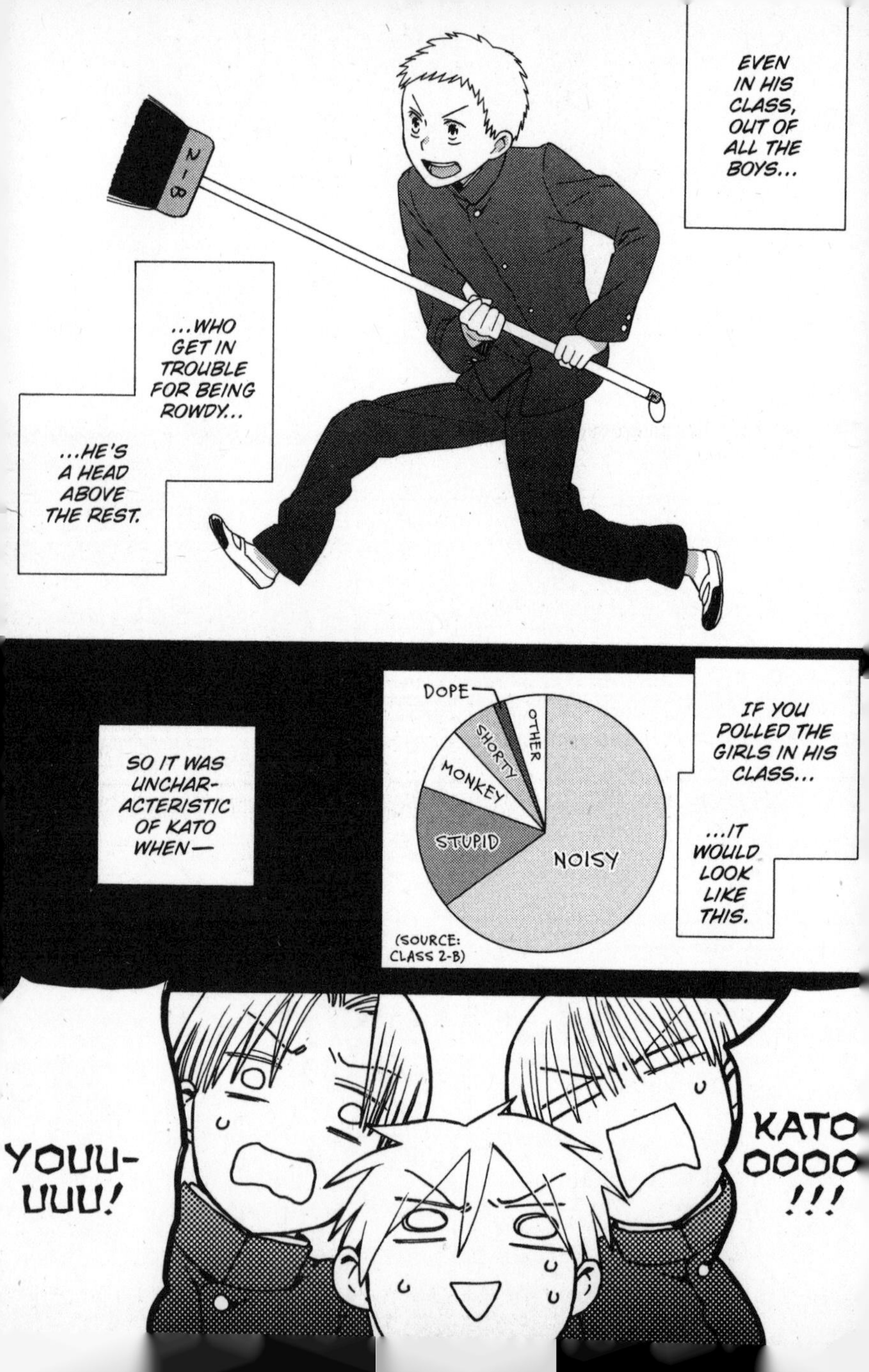
EVEN IN HIS CLASS, OUT OF ALL THE BOYS...
2-B
...WHO GET IN TROUBLE FOR BEING ROWDY...
...HE'S A HEAD ABOVE THE REST.
IF YOU POLLED THE GIRLS IN HIS CLASS...
...IT WOULD LOOK LIKE THIS.
DOPE
OTHER
SHORTY
MONKEY
STUPID
NOISY
(SOURCE: CLASS 2-B)
SO IT WAS UNCHAR-ACTERISTIC OF KATO WHEN—
KATOOOOO!!!
YOUU-UUU!

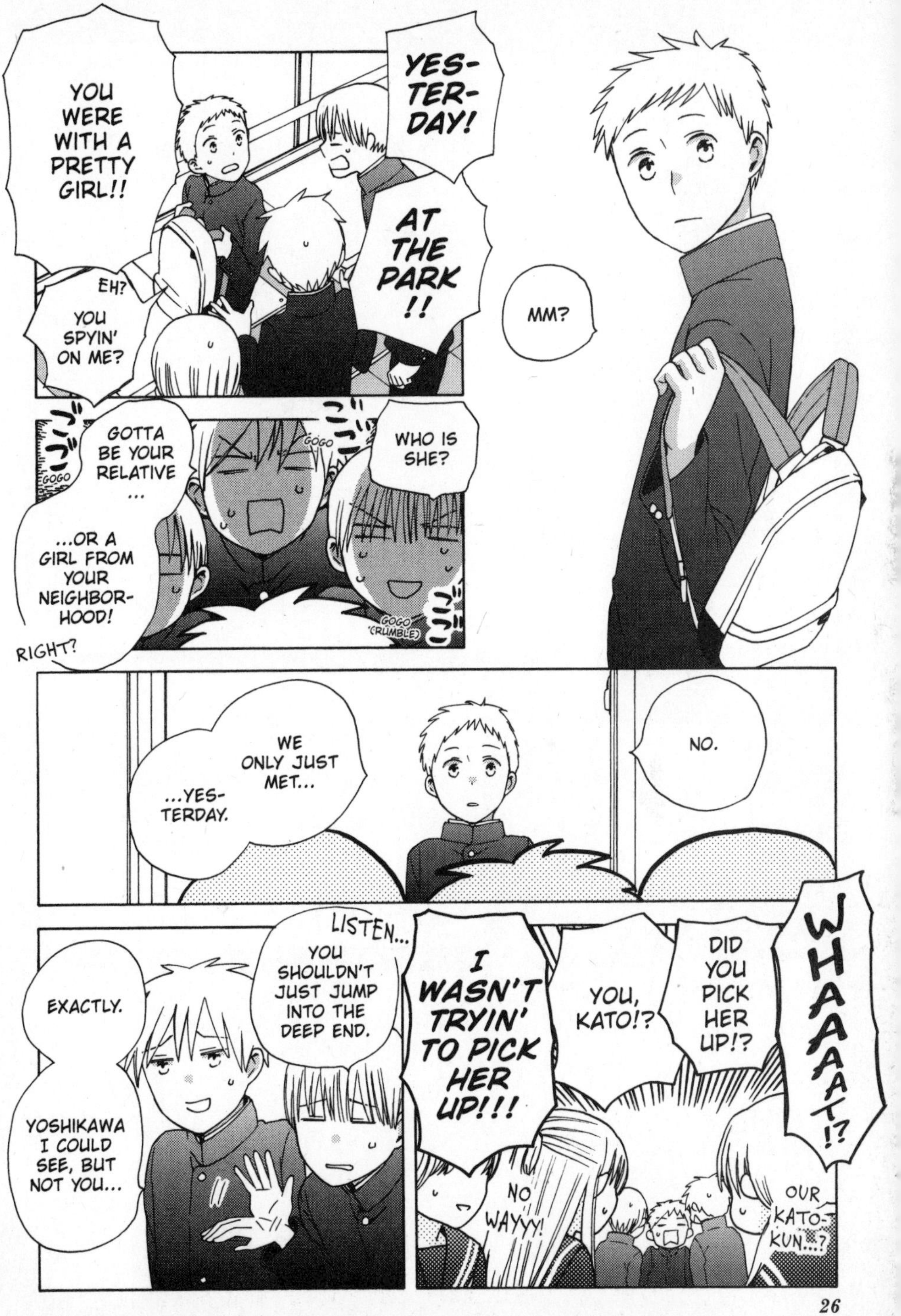
MM?
YES-TER-DAY!
AT THE PARK!!
YOU WERE WITH A PRETTY GIRL!!
EH? YOU SPYIN' ON ME?
WHO IS SHE?
GOGO
GOGO (CRUMBLE)
GOTTA BE YOUR RELATIVE...
GOGO
...OR A GIRL FROM YOUR NEIGHBOR-HOOD!
RIGHT?
NO.
WE ONLY JUST MET...
...YES-TERDAY.
WHAAAAT!?
DID YOU PICK HER UP!?
YOU, KATO!?
OUR KATO-KUN...?
NO WAYYY!
I WASN'T TRYIN' TO PICK HER UP!!!
LISTEN...
YOU SHOULDN'T JUST JUMP INTO THE DEEP END.
EXACTLY.
YOSHIKAWA I COULD SEE, BUT NOT YOU...

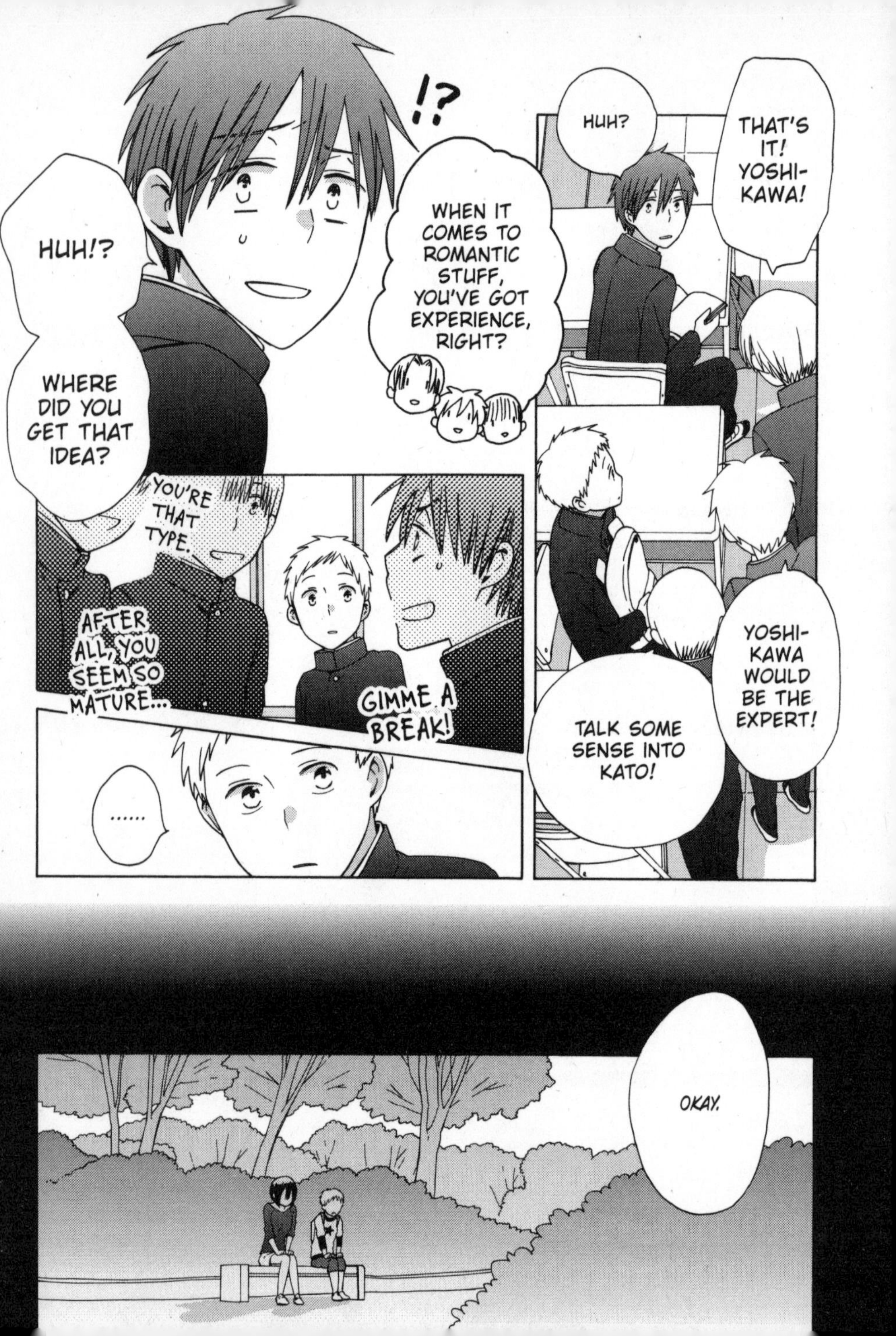
THAT'S IT! YOSHI-KAWA!
HUH?
YOSHI-KAWA WOULD BE THE EXPERT!
TALK SOME SENSE INTO KATO!
WHEN IT COMES TO ROMANTIC STUFF, YOU'VE GOT EXPERIENCE, RIGHT?
!?
HUH!?
WHERE DID YOU GET THAT IDEA?
YOU'RE THAT TYPE.
AFTER ALL, YOU SEEM SO MATURE...
GIMME A BREAK!
......
OKAY.

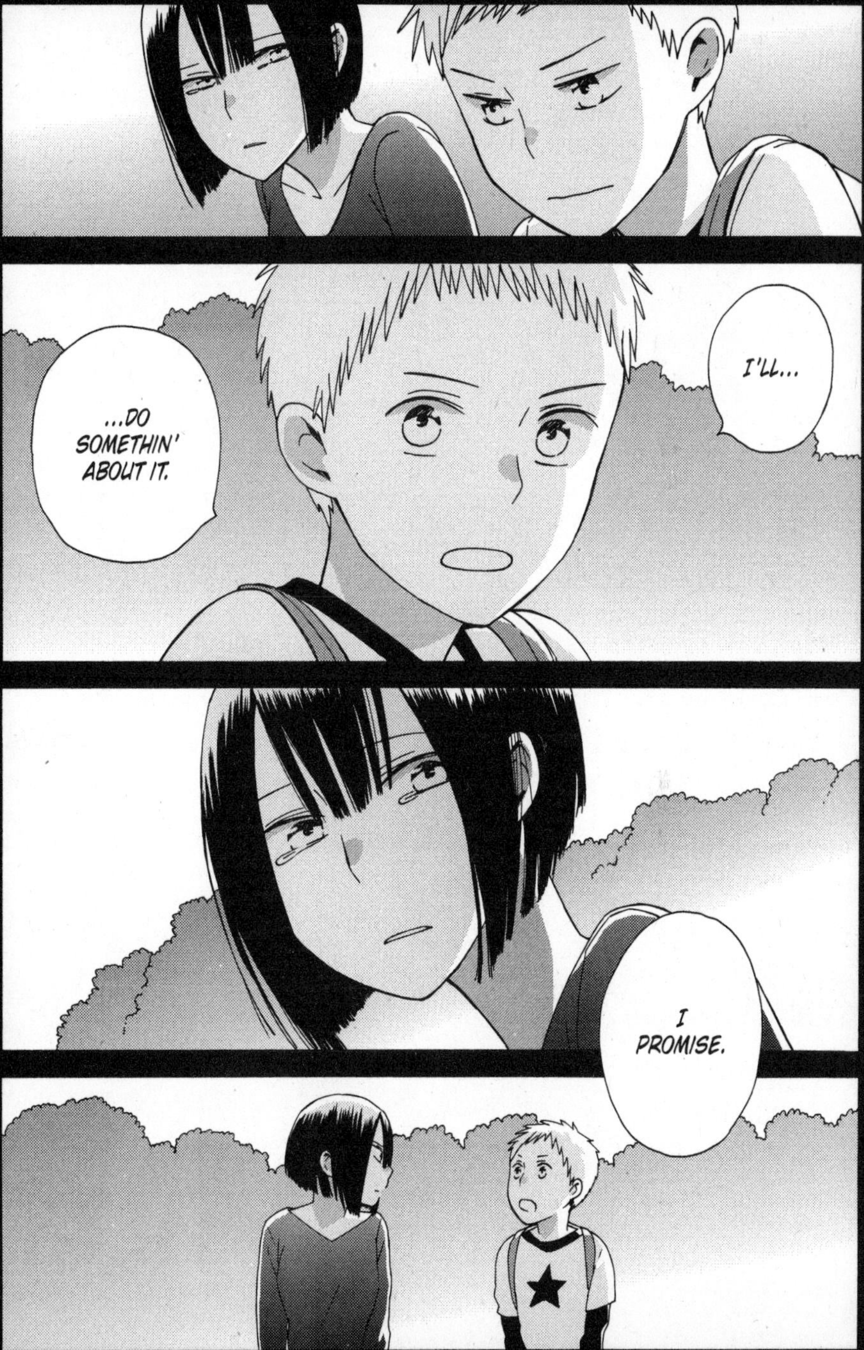
I'LL...
...DO SOMETHIN' ABOUT IT.
I PROMISE.

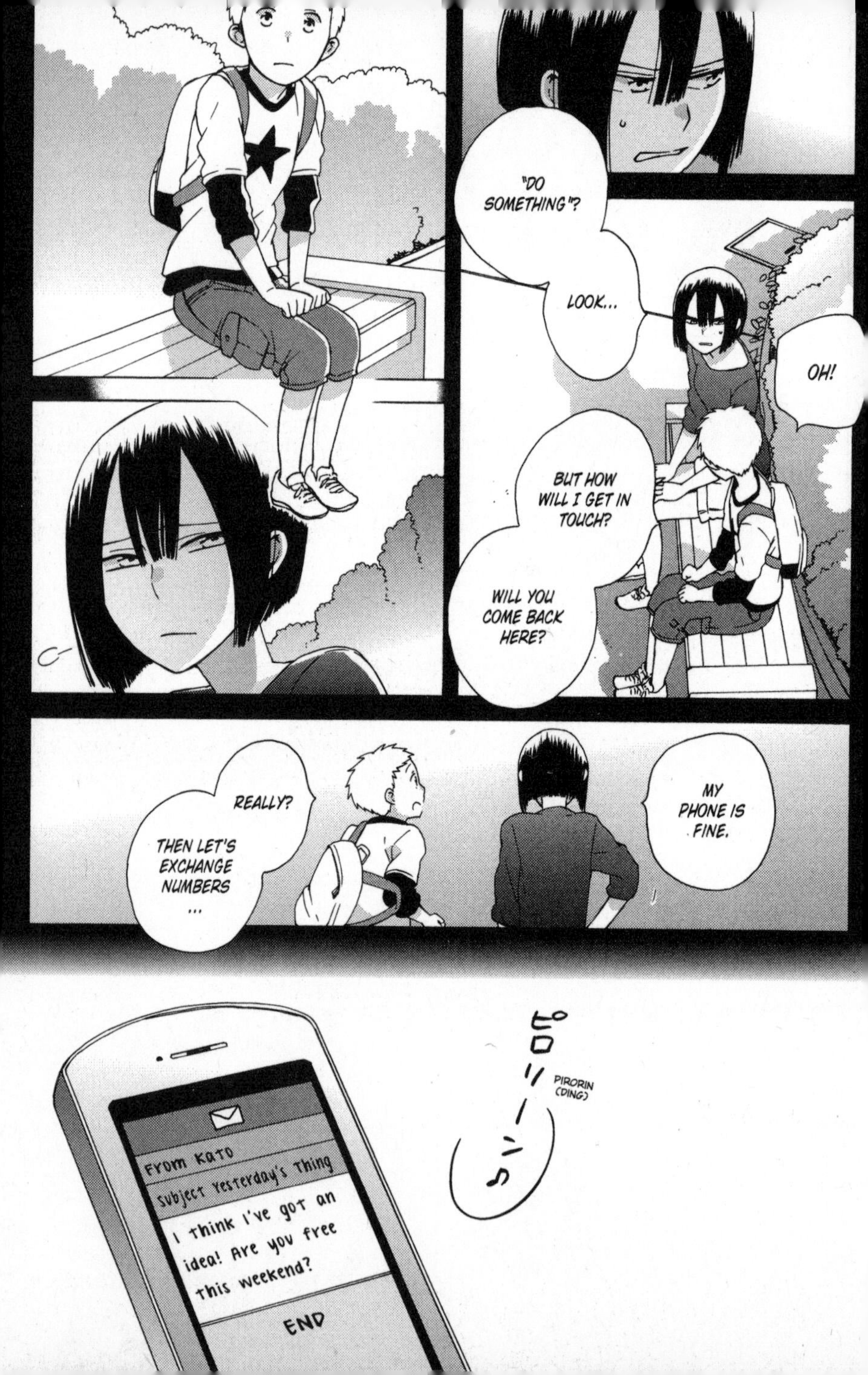
"DO SOMETHING"?
LOOK...
OH!
BUT HOW WILL I GET IN TOUCH?
WILL YOU COME BACK HERE?
MY PHONE IS FINE.
REALLY?
THEN LET'S EXCHANGE NUMBERS ...
ピロリーン♪
PIRORIN (DING)
From Kato
Subject Yesterday's Thing
I think I've got an idea! Are you free this weekend?
END

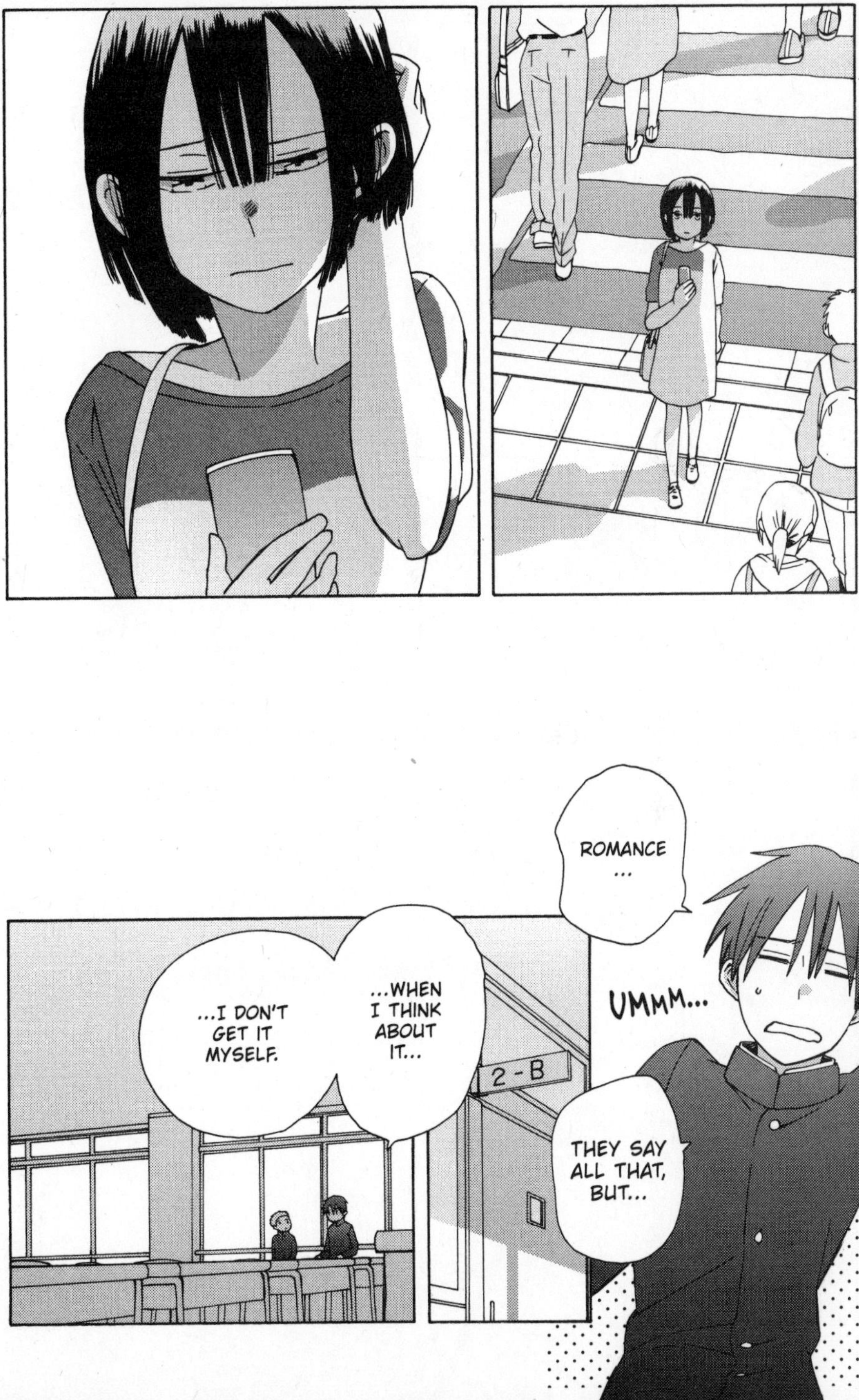
ROMANCE ...
UMMM...
THEY SAY ALL THAT, BUT...
...WHEN I THINK ABOUT IT...
...I DON'T GET IT MYSELF.
2-B

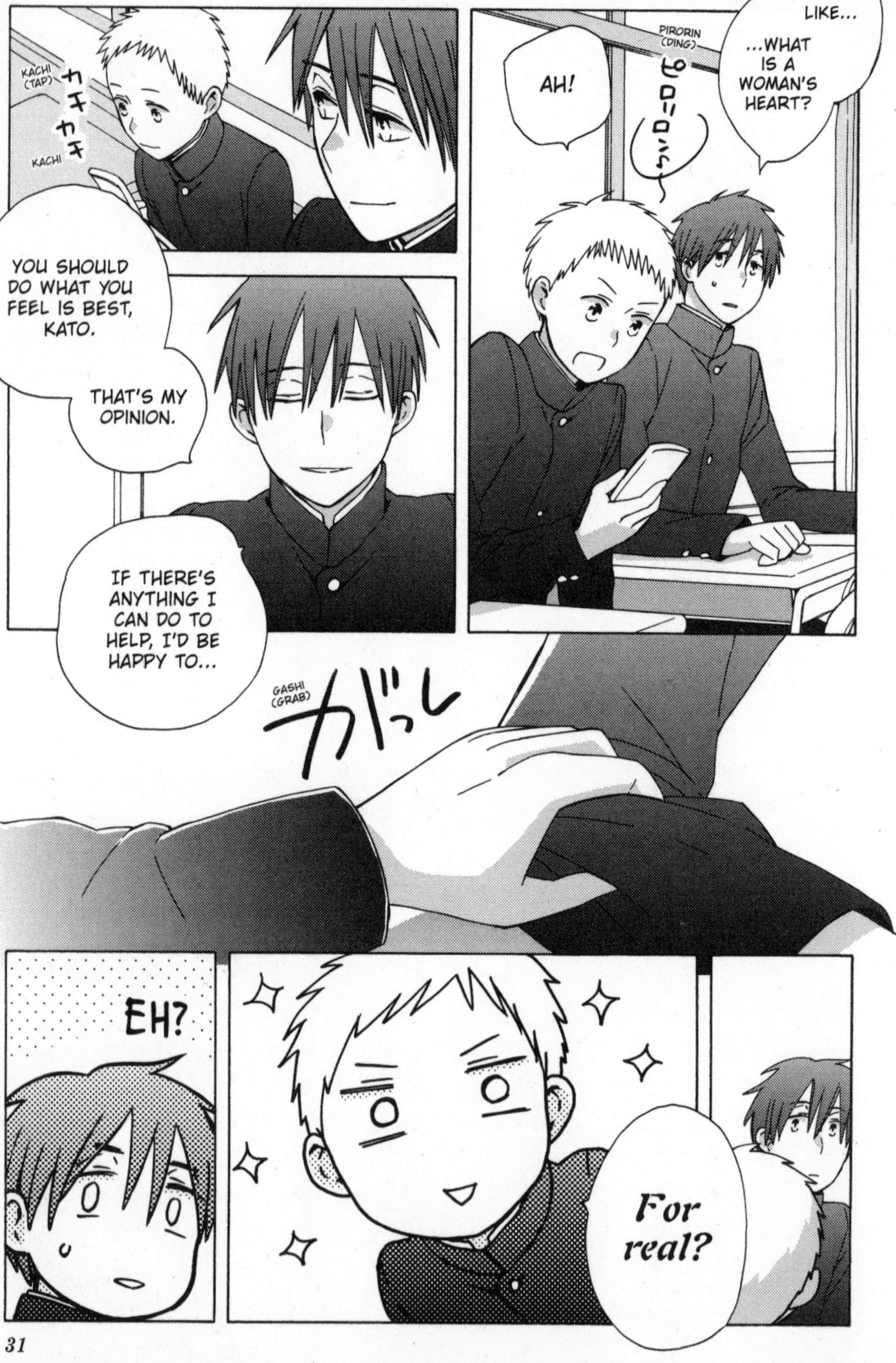
LIKE... ...WHAT IS A WOMAN'S HEART?
PIRORIN (DING)
AH!
KACHI (TAP)
KACHI
YOU SHOULD DO WHAT YOU FEEL IS BEST, KATO.
THAT'S MY OPINION.
IF THERE'S ANYTHING I CAN DO TO HELP, I'D BE HAPPY TO...
GASHI (GRAB)
For real?
EH?

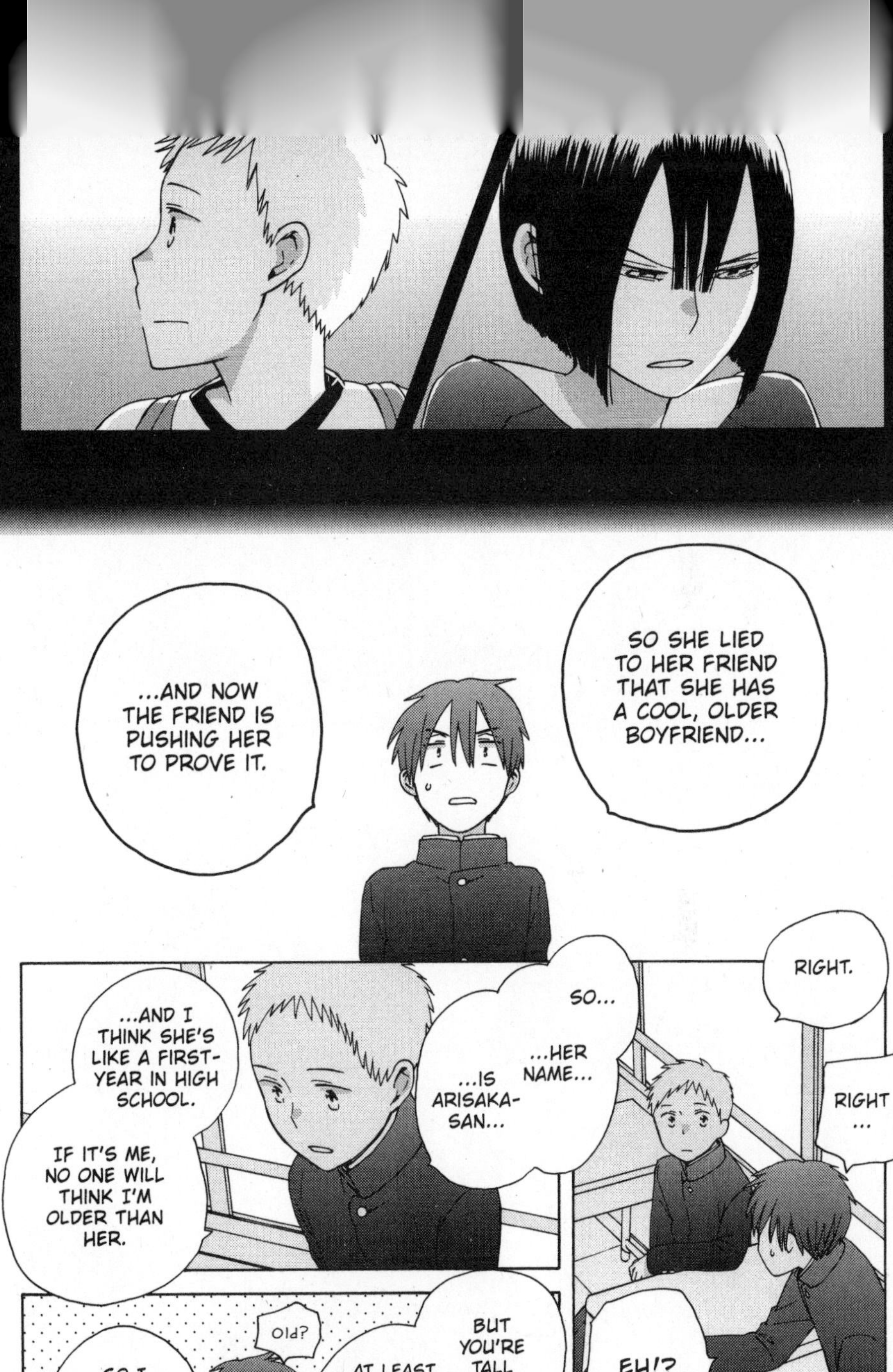

SO SHE LIED TO HER FRIEND THAT SHE HAS A COOL, OLDER BOYFRIEND...
...AND NOW THE FRIEND IS PUSHING HER TO PROVE IT.
RIGHT.
RIGHT ...
EH!?
SO...
...HER NAME...
...IS ARISAKA-SAN...
...AND I THINK SHE'S LIKE A FIRST-YEAR IN HIGH SCHOOL.
IF IT'S ME, NO ONE WILL THINK I'M OLDER THAN HER.
BUT YOU'RE TALL AND YOU LOOK OLD...
...AT LEAST, OLDER THAN A MIDDLE SCHOOL SECOND-YEAR.
Old?
SO I THINK IT WOULD WORK.

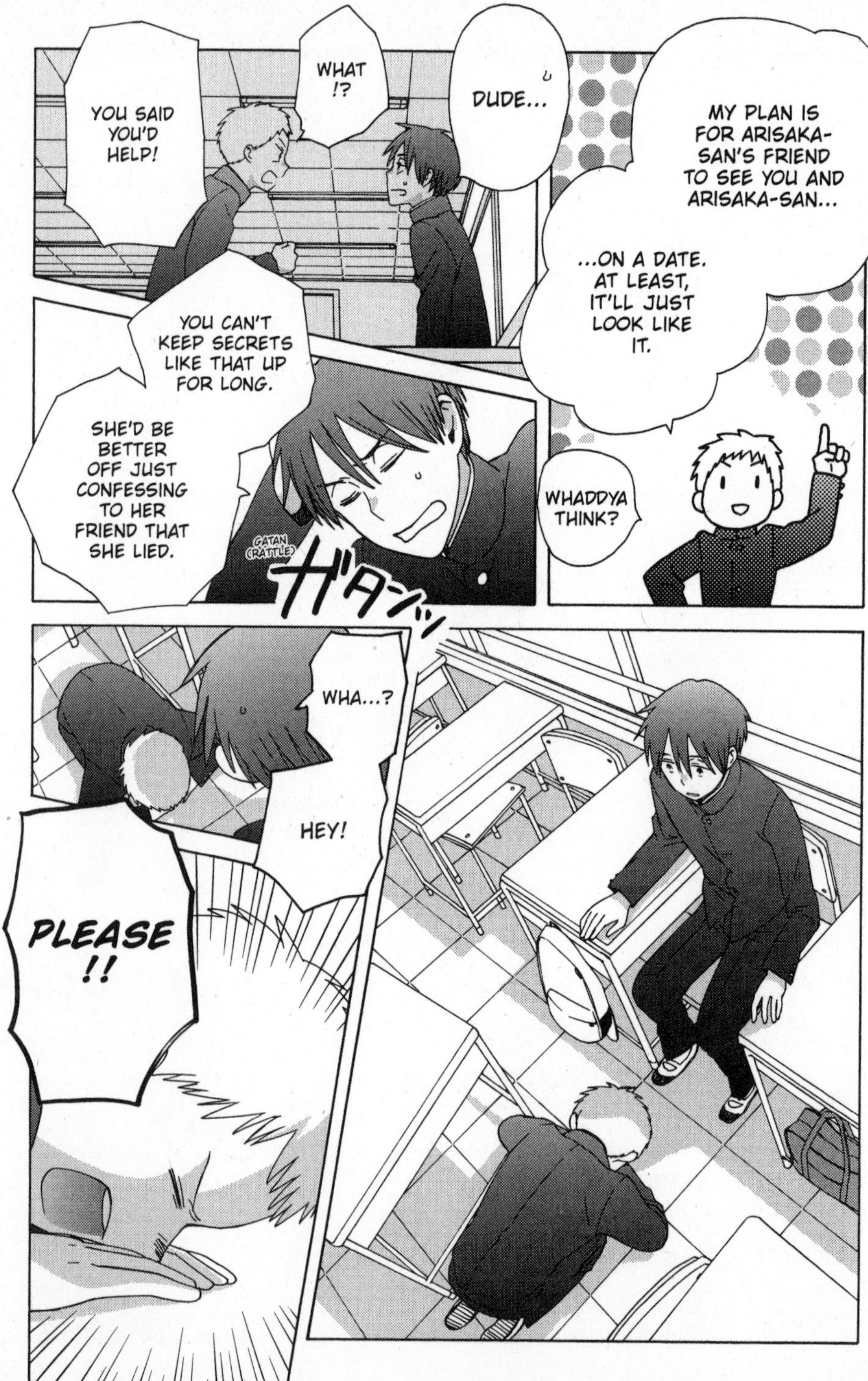
MY PLAN IS FOR ARISAKA-SAN'S FRIEND TO SEE YOU AND ARISAKA-SAN...
...ON A DATE. AT LEAST, IT'LL JUST LOOK LIKE IT.
WHADDYA THINK?
DUDE...
WHAT !?
YOU SAID YOU'D HELP!
YOU CAN'T KEEP SECRETS LIKE THAT UP FOR LONG.
SHE'D BE BETTER OFF JUST CONFESSING TO HER FRIEND THAT SHE LIED.
GATAN (RATTLE)
ガタンッ
WHA...?
HEY!
PLEASE !!

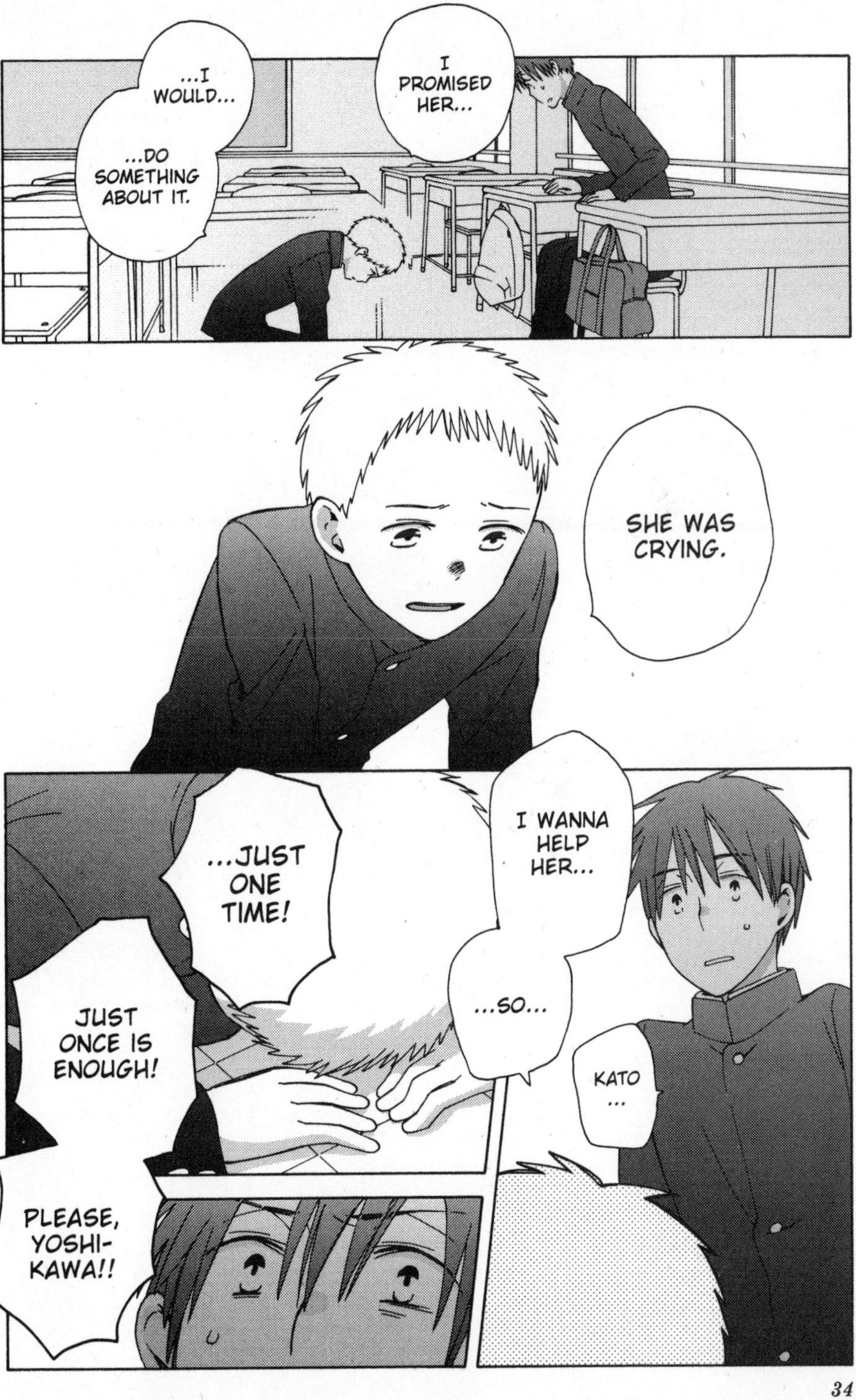
I PROMISED HER...
...I WOULD...
...DO SOMETHING ABOUT IT.
SHE WAS CRYING.
I WANNA HELP HER...
...SO...
KATO ...
...JUST ONE TIME!
JUST ONCE IS ENOUGH!
PLEASE, YOSHI-KAWA!!

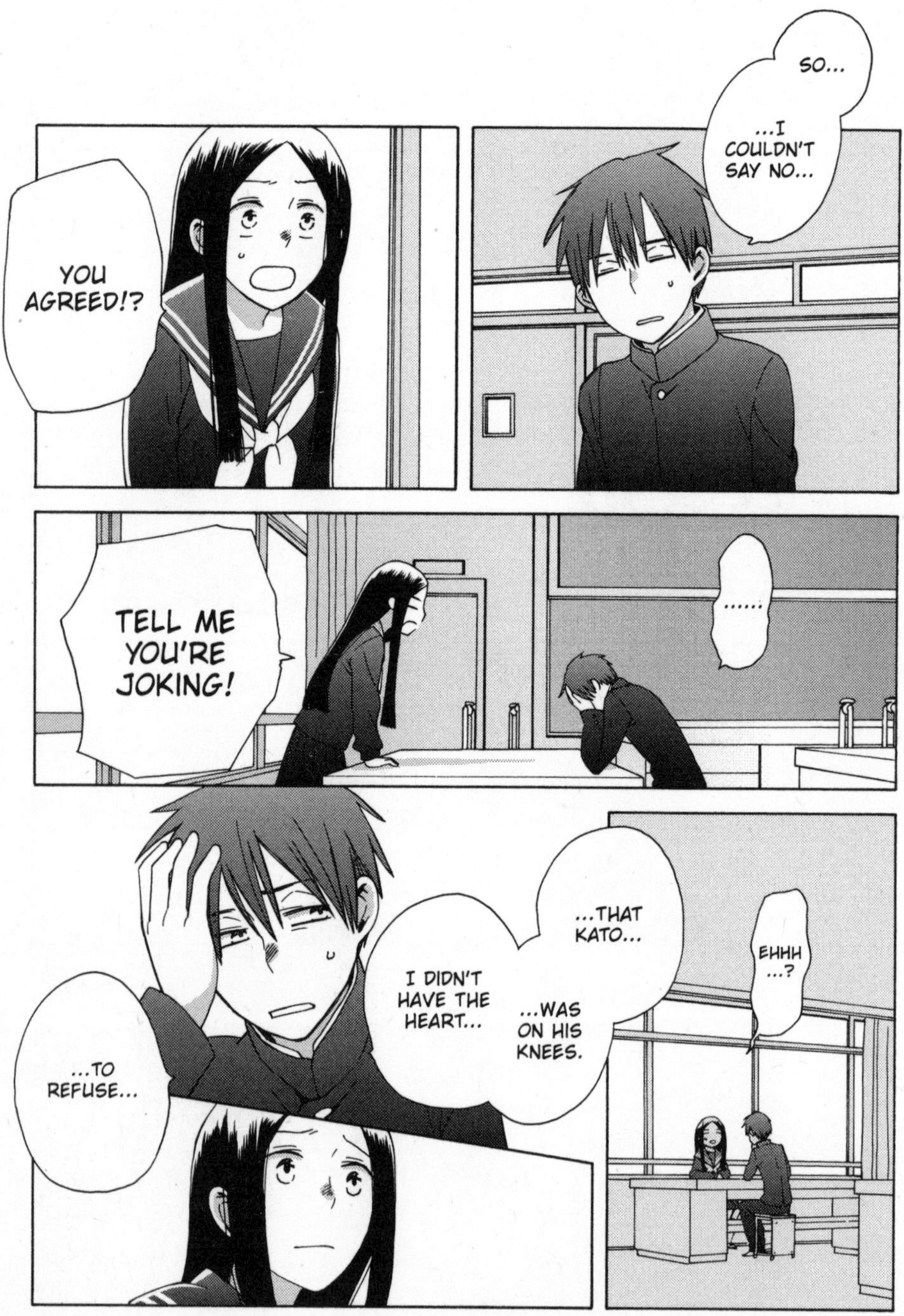
SO...
...I COULDN'T SAY NO...
YOU AGREED!?
......
TELL ME YOU'RE JOKING!
EHHH ...?
...THAT KATO...
...WAS ON HIS KNEES.
I DIDN'T HAVE THE HEART...
...TO REFUSE...

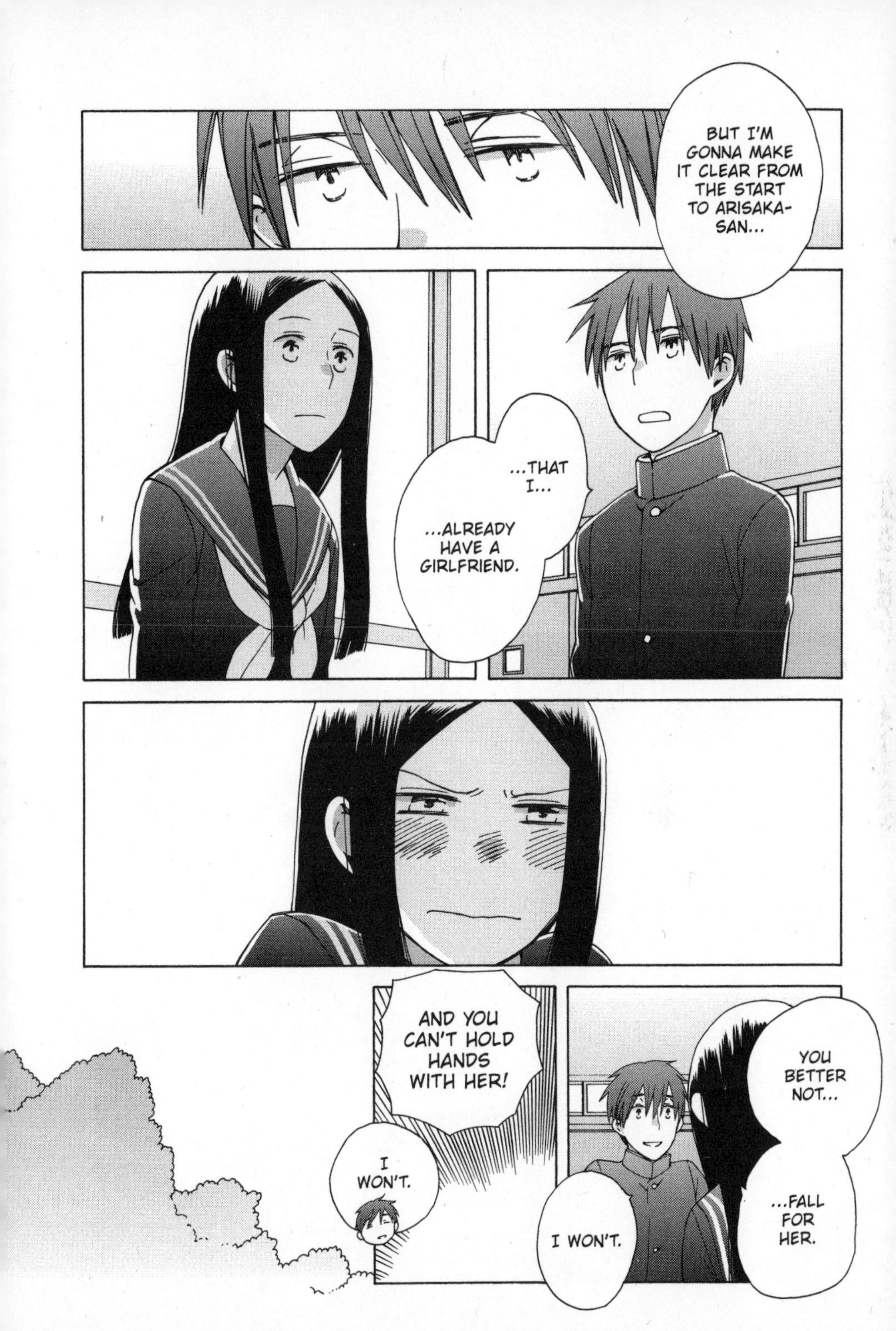
BUT I'M GONNA MAKE IT CLEAR FROM THE START TO ARISAKA-SAN...
...THAT I...
...ALREADY HAVE A GIRLFRIEND.
YOU BETTER NOT...
...FALL FOR HER.
I WON'T.
AND YOU CAN'T HOLD HANDS WITH HER!
I WON'T.

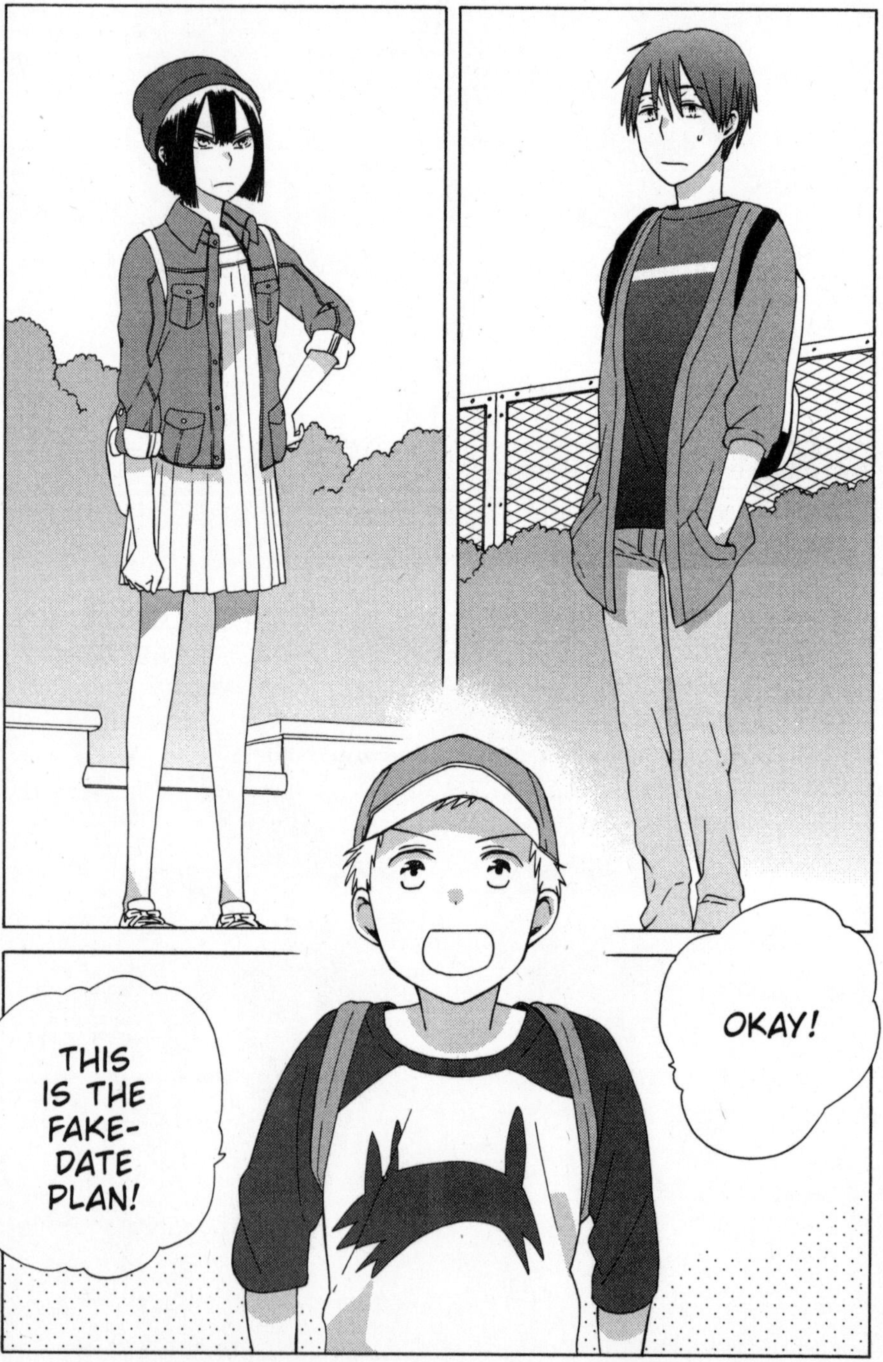
OKAY!
THIS IS THE FAKE-DATE PLAN!

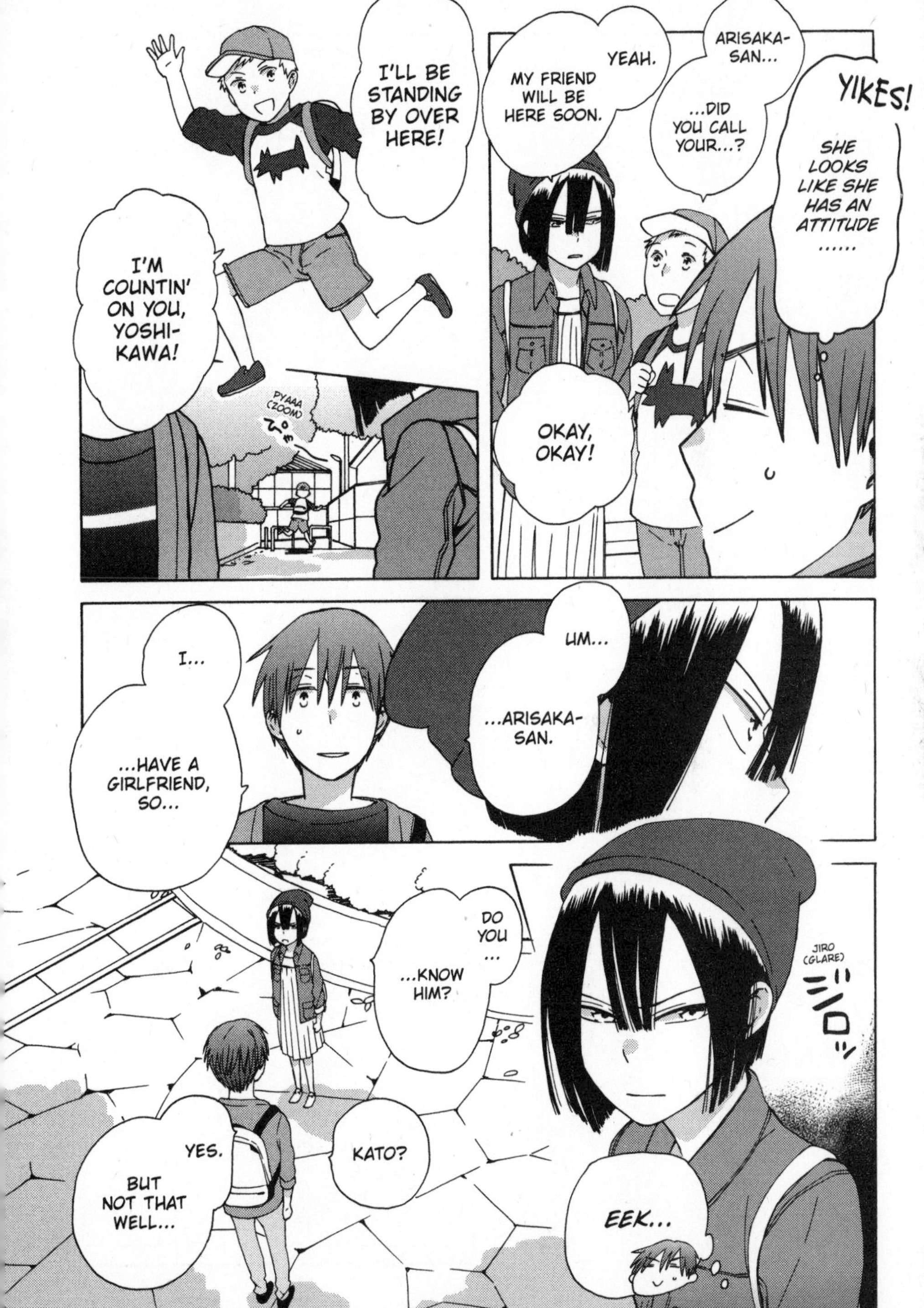
ARISAKA-SAN...
...DID YOU CALL YOUR...?
YEAH.
MY FRIEND WILL BE HERE SOON.
YIKES!
SHE LOOKS LIKE SHE HAS AN ATTITUDE ......
OKAY, OKAY!
I'LL BE STANDING BY OVER HERE!
I'M COUNTIN' ON YOU, YOSHI-KAWA!
PYAAA (ZOOM)
UM...
...ARISAKA-SAN.
I...
...HAVE A GIRLFRIEND, SO...
JIRO (GLARE)
EEK...
KATO?
DO YOU ...
...KNOW HIM?
YES.
BUT NOT THAT WELL...

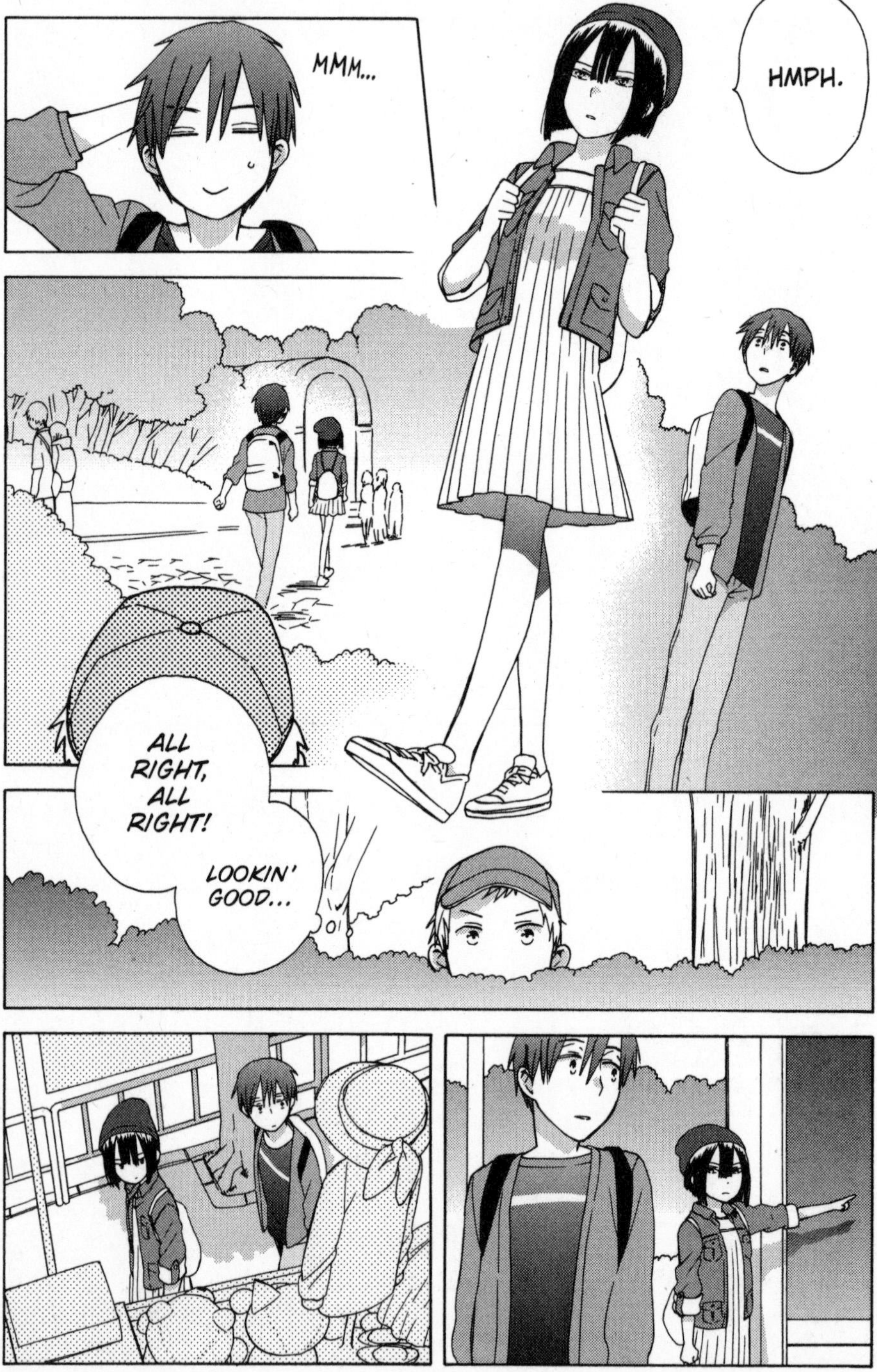
HMPH.
MMM...
ALL RIGHT, ALL RIGHT!
LOOKIN' GOOD...

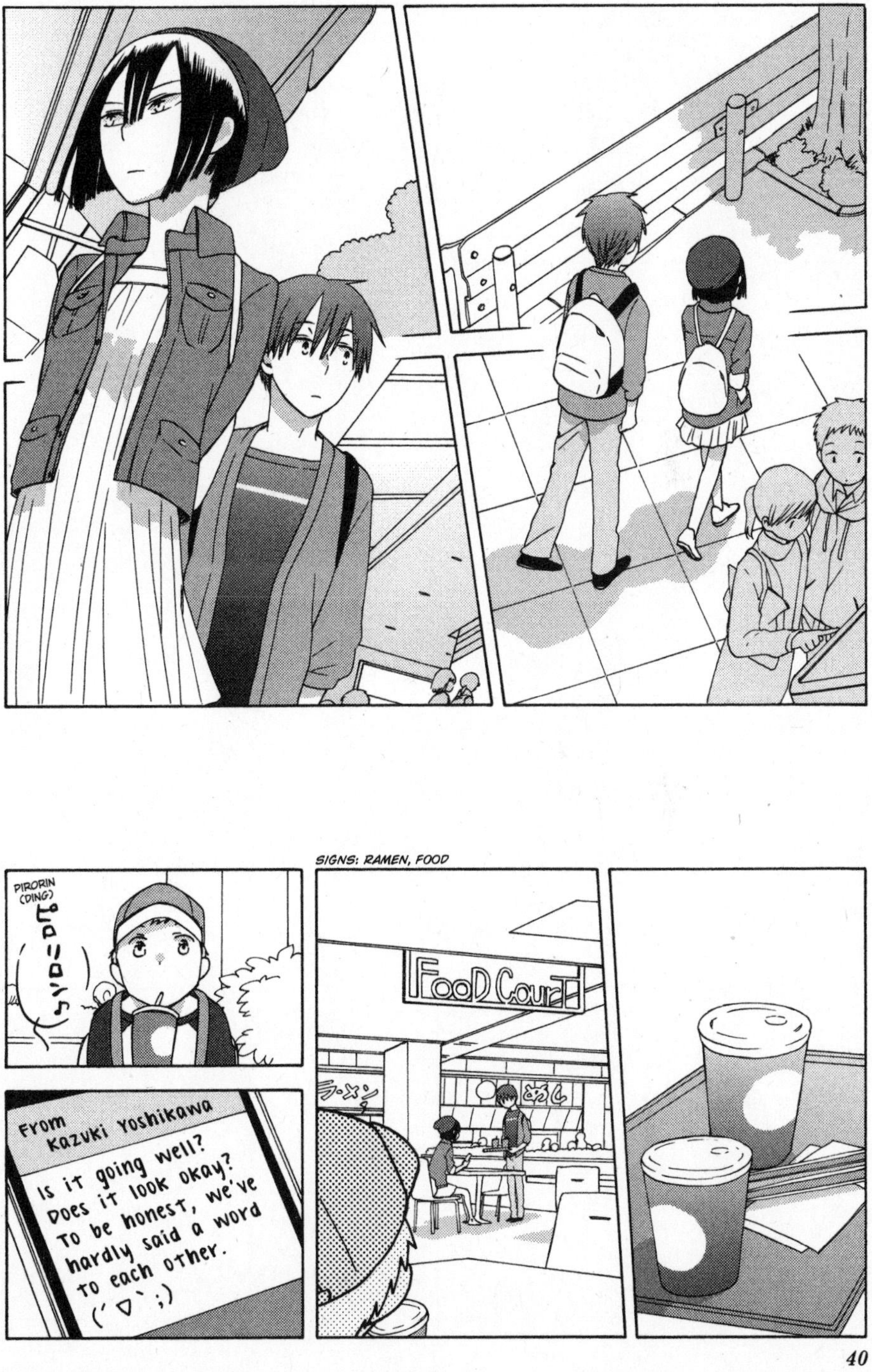
SIGNS: RAMEN, FOOD
FOOD COURT
PIRORIN (DING)
From Kazuki Yoshikawa
Is it going well? Does it look okay? To be honest, we've hardly said a word to each other. (´▽`;)

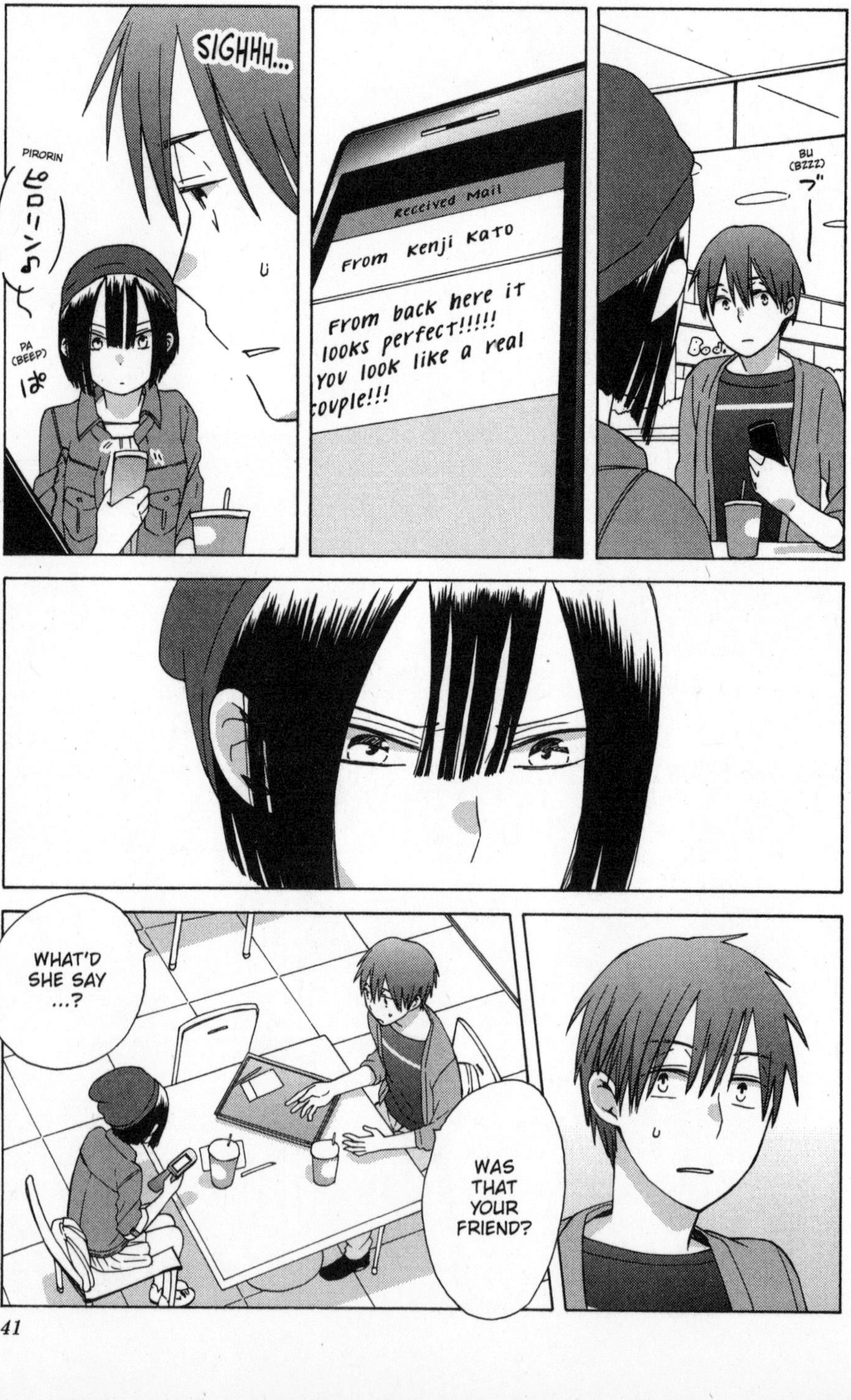
BU
(BZZZ)
ブー
Received Mail
From Kenji Kato
From back here it looks perfect!!!!! You look like a real couple!!!
SIGHHH...
PIRORIN
ピロリン♪
PA
(BEEP)
ぱ
WAS THAT YOUR FRIEND?
WHAT'D SHE SAY ...?

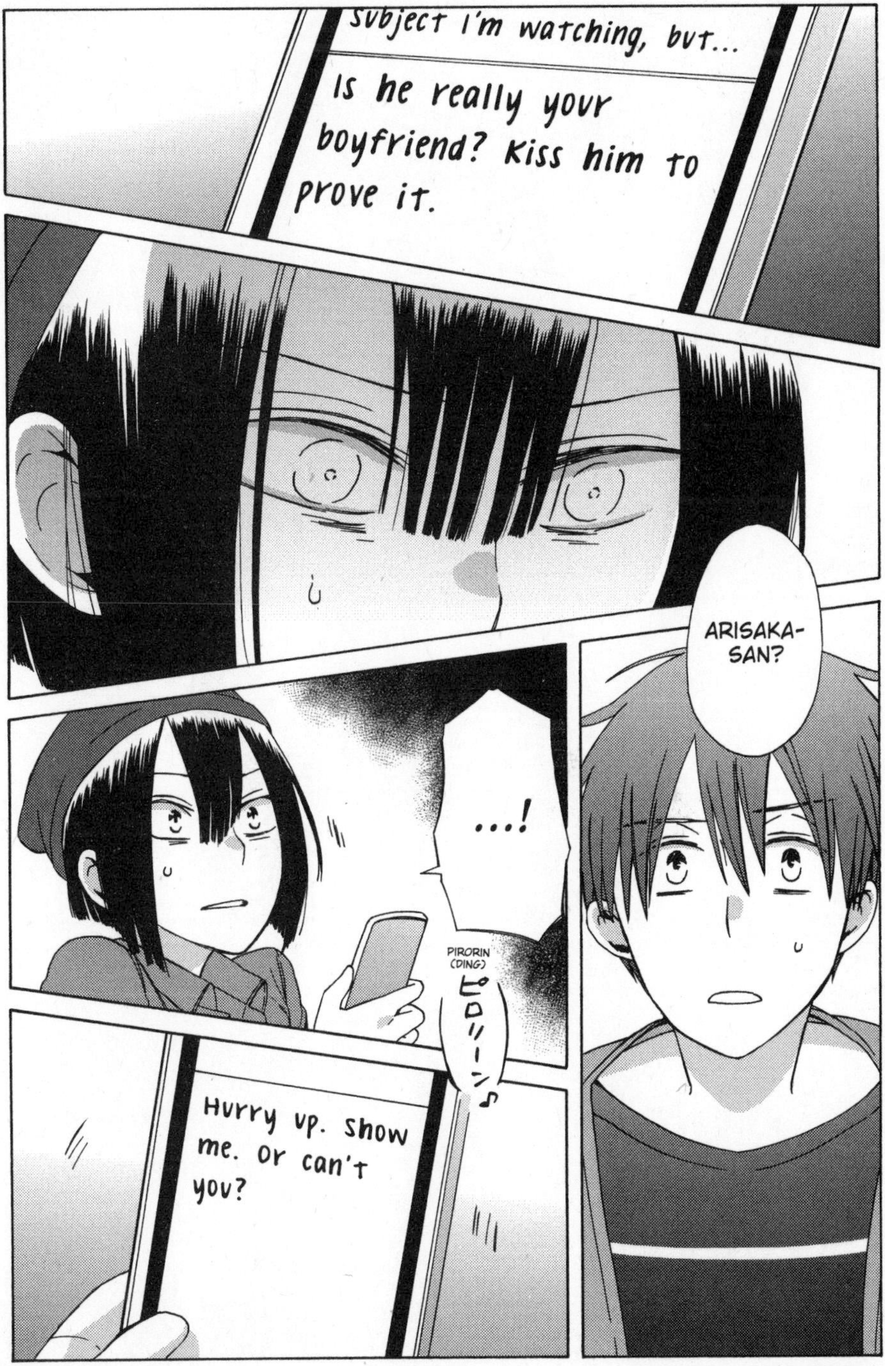
subject I'm watching, but...
Is he really your boyfriend? Kiss him to prove it.
ARISAKA-SAN?
...!
PIRORIN (DING)
ピロリーン♪
Hurry up. show me. or can't you?

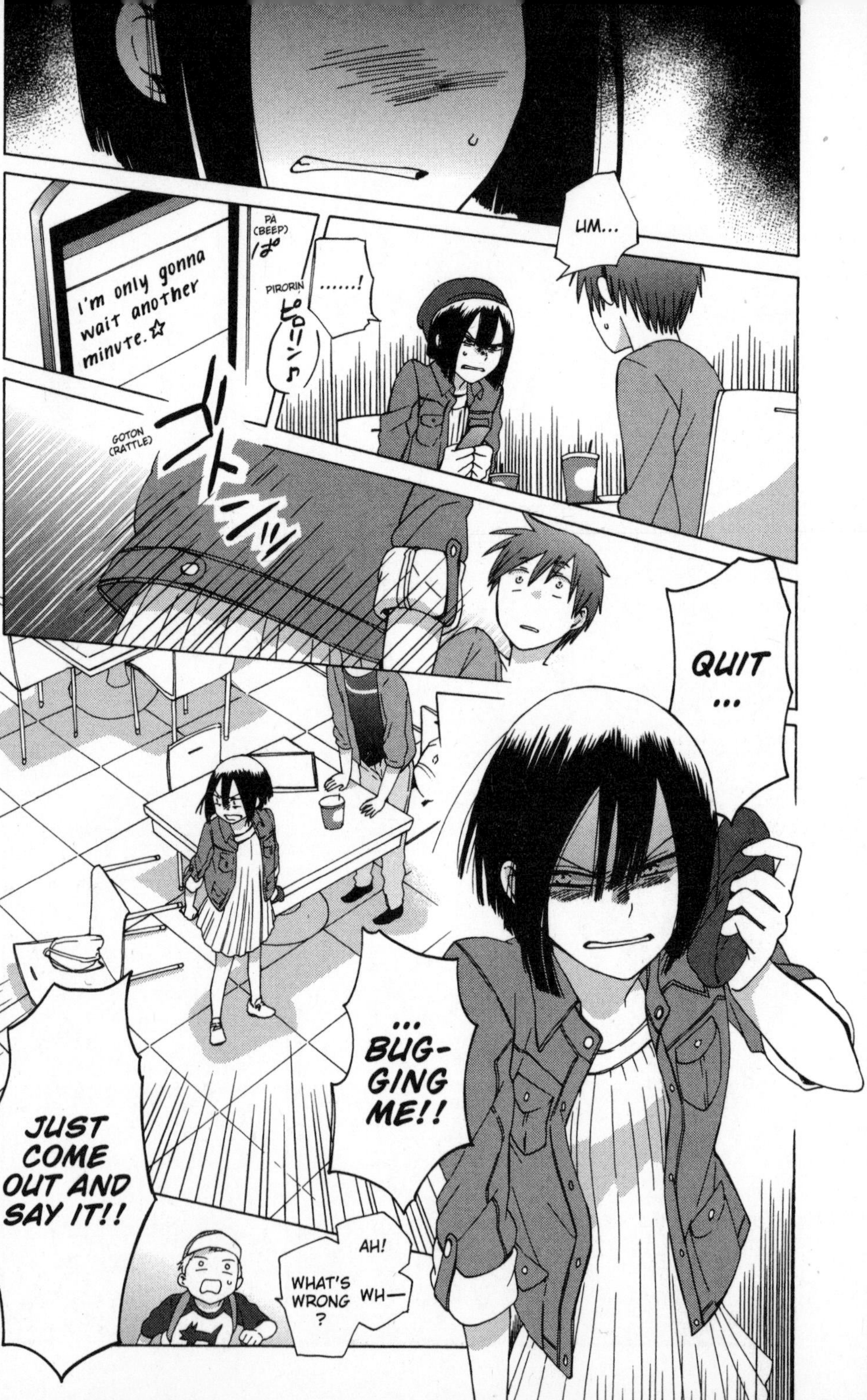
UM...
......!
PIRORIN
ピロリン♪
I'm only gonna wait another minute.☆
PA (BEEP)
ぱ
GOTON (RATTLE)
ゴトンッ
QUIT...
...BÜG-GING ME!!
JUST COME OUT AND SAY IT!!
AH!
WHAT'S WRONG WH—?

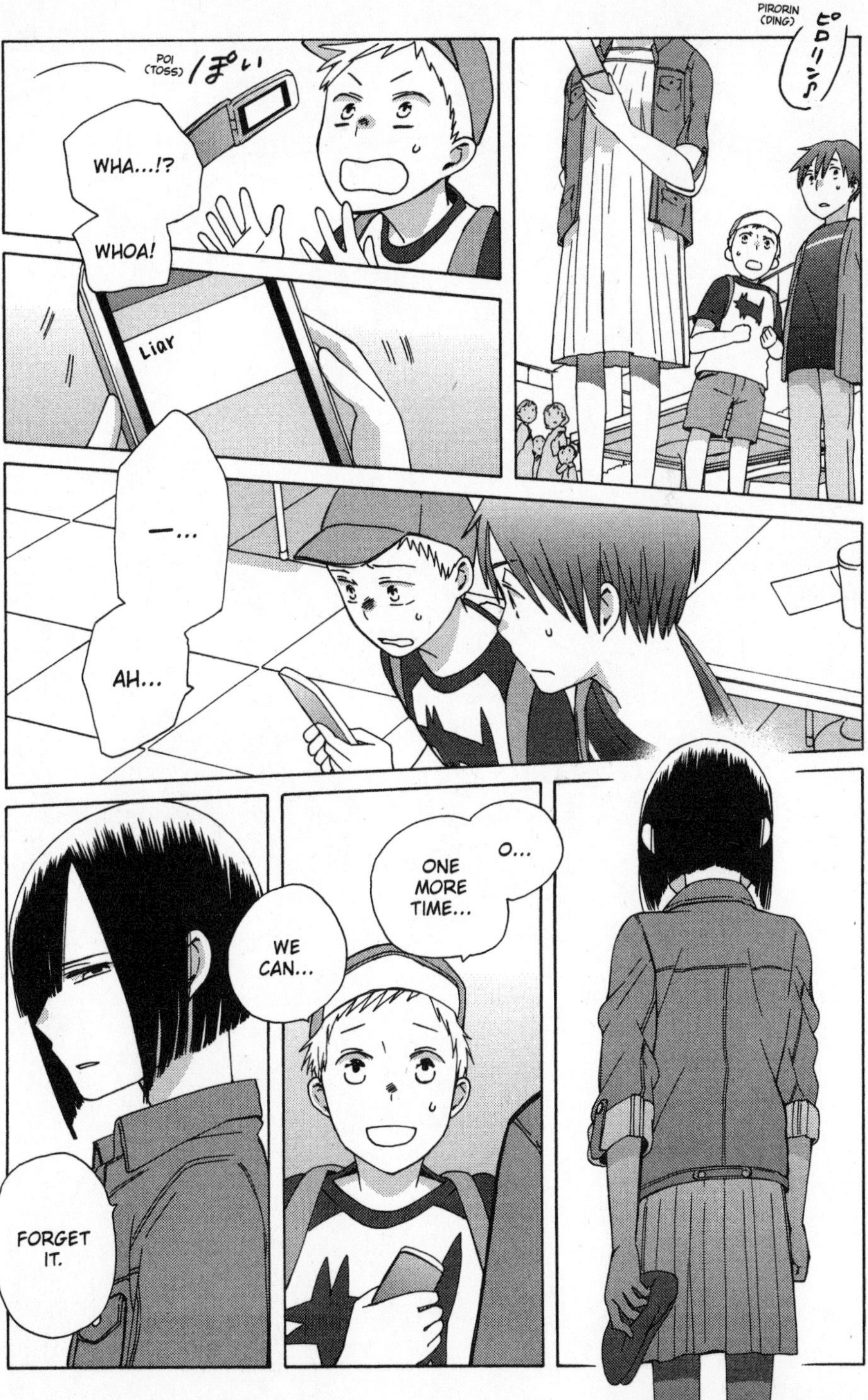
PIRORIN (DING)
ピロリン♪
POI (TOSS)
ぽい
WHA...!?
WHOA!
Liar
—...
AH...
O...
ONE MORE TIME...
WE CAN...
FORGET IT.

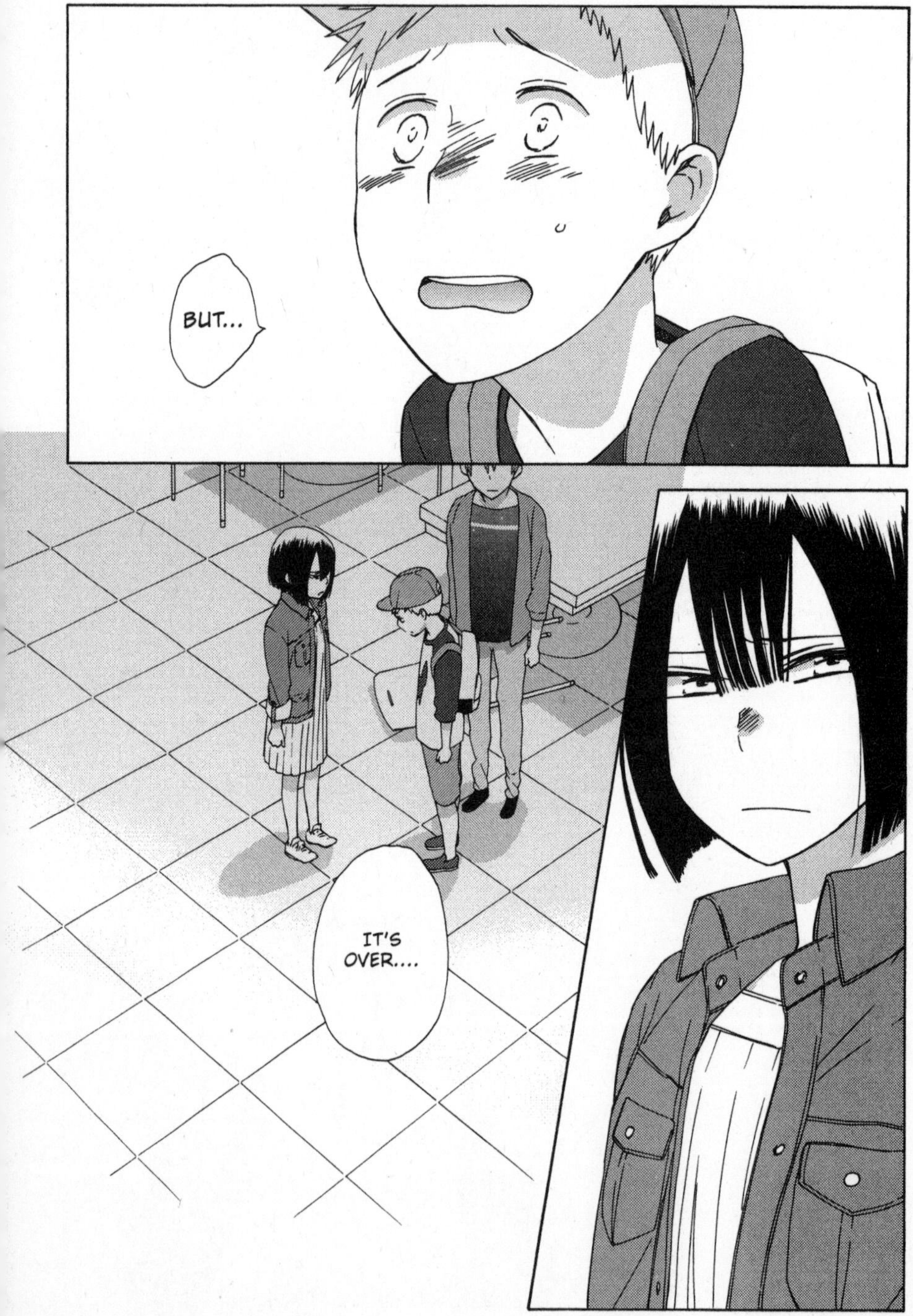
BUT...
IT'S OVER....

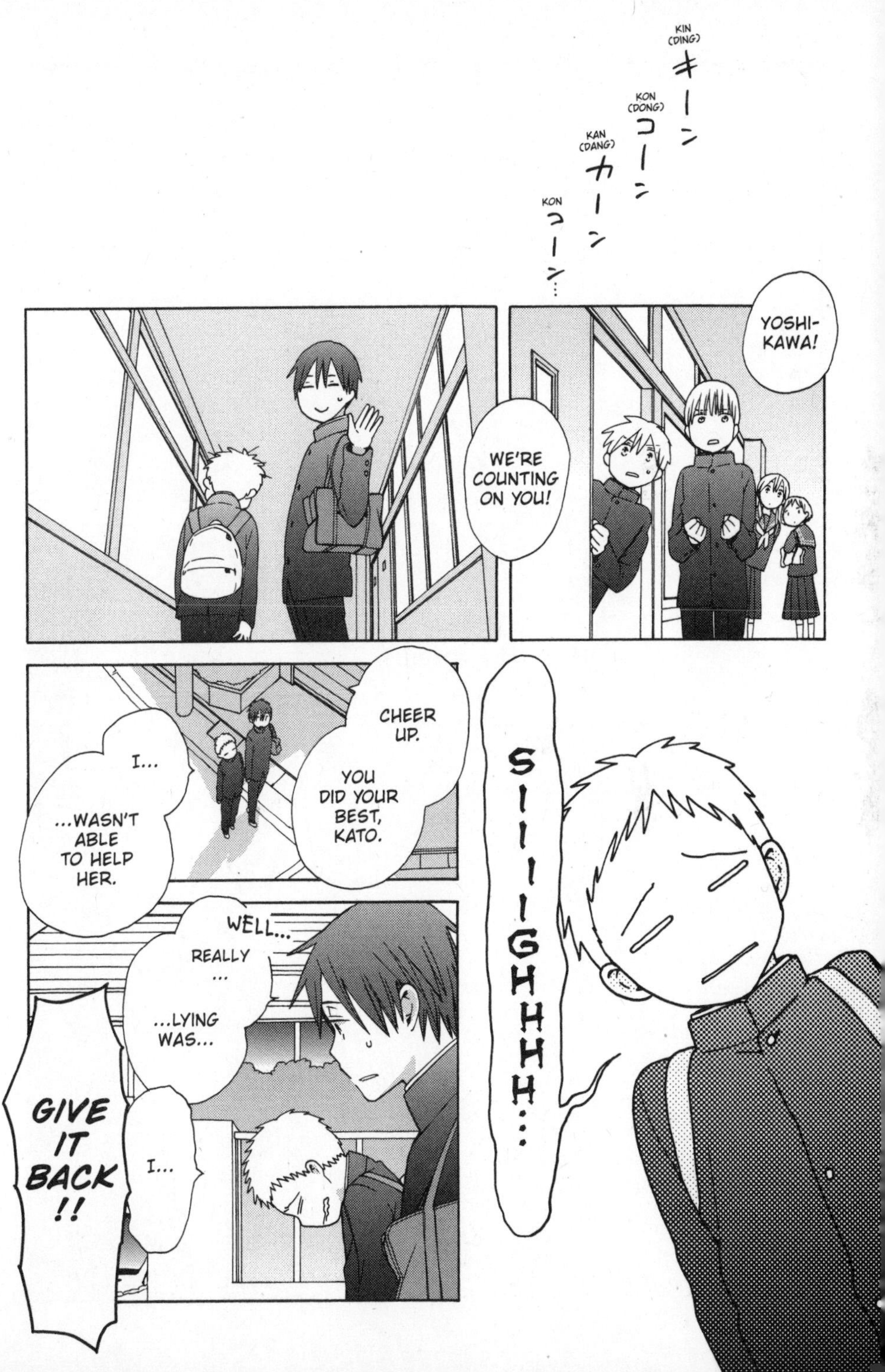
KIN (DING) キーン
KON (DONG) コーン
KAN (DANG) カーン
KON コーン…
YOSHI-KAWA!
WE'RE COUNTING ON YOU!
SIIIIGHHHH...
CHEER UP.
YOU DID YOUR BEST, KATO.
I...
...WASN'T ABLE TO HELP HER.
WELL...
REALLY ...
...LYING WAS...
I...
GIVE IT BACK!!

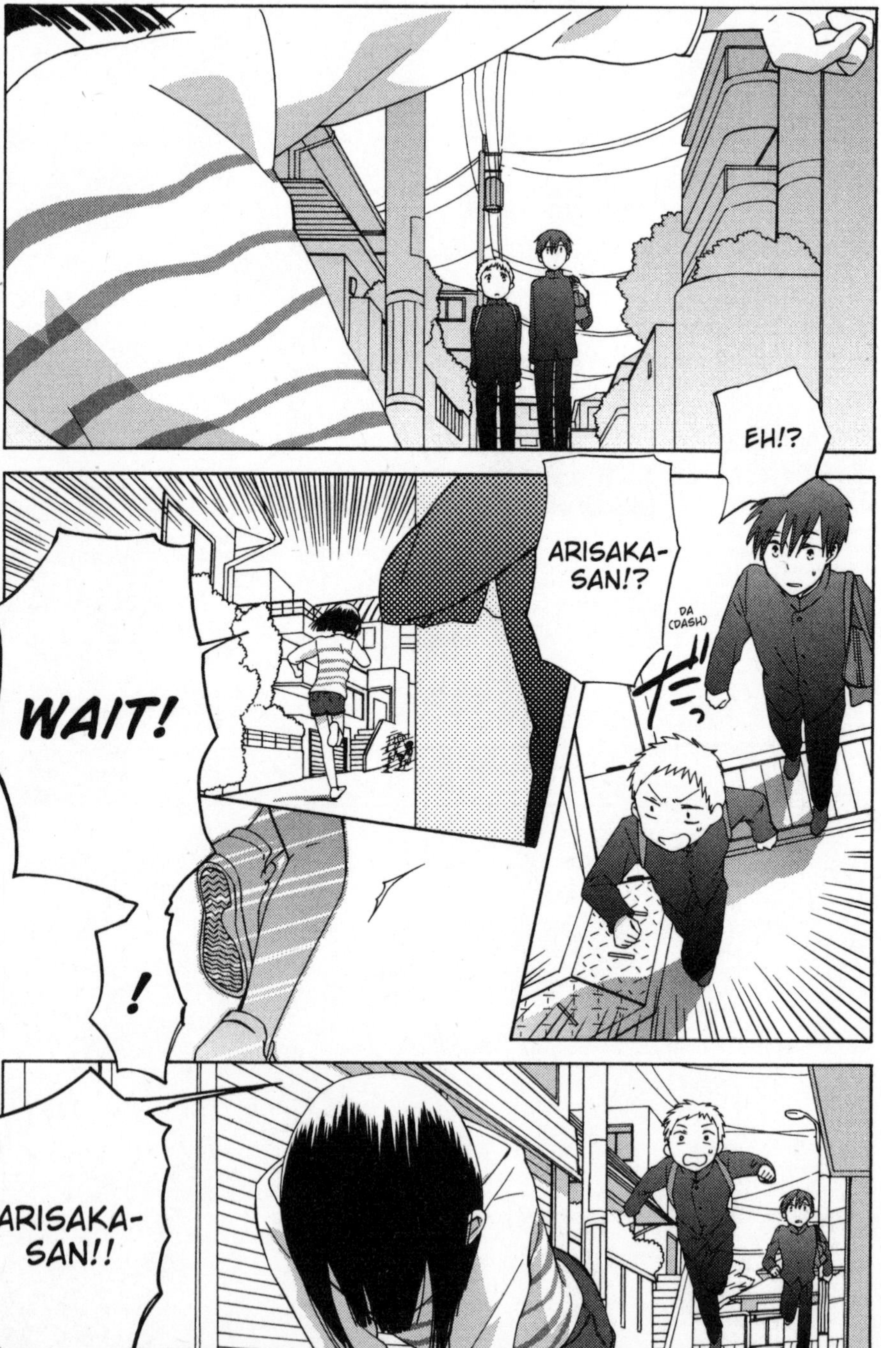

EH!?
ARISAKA-SAN!?
DA (DASH)
WAIT!
!
ARISAKA-SAN!!

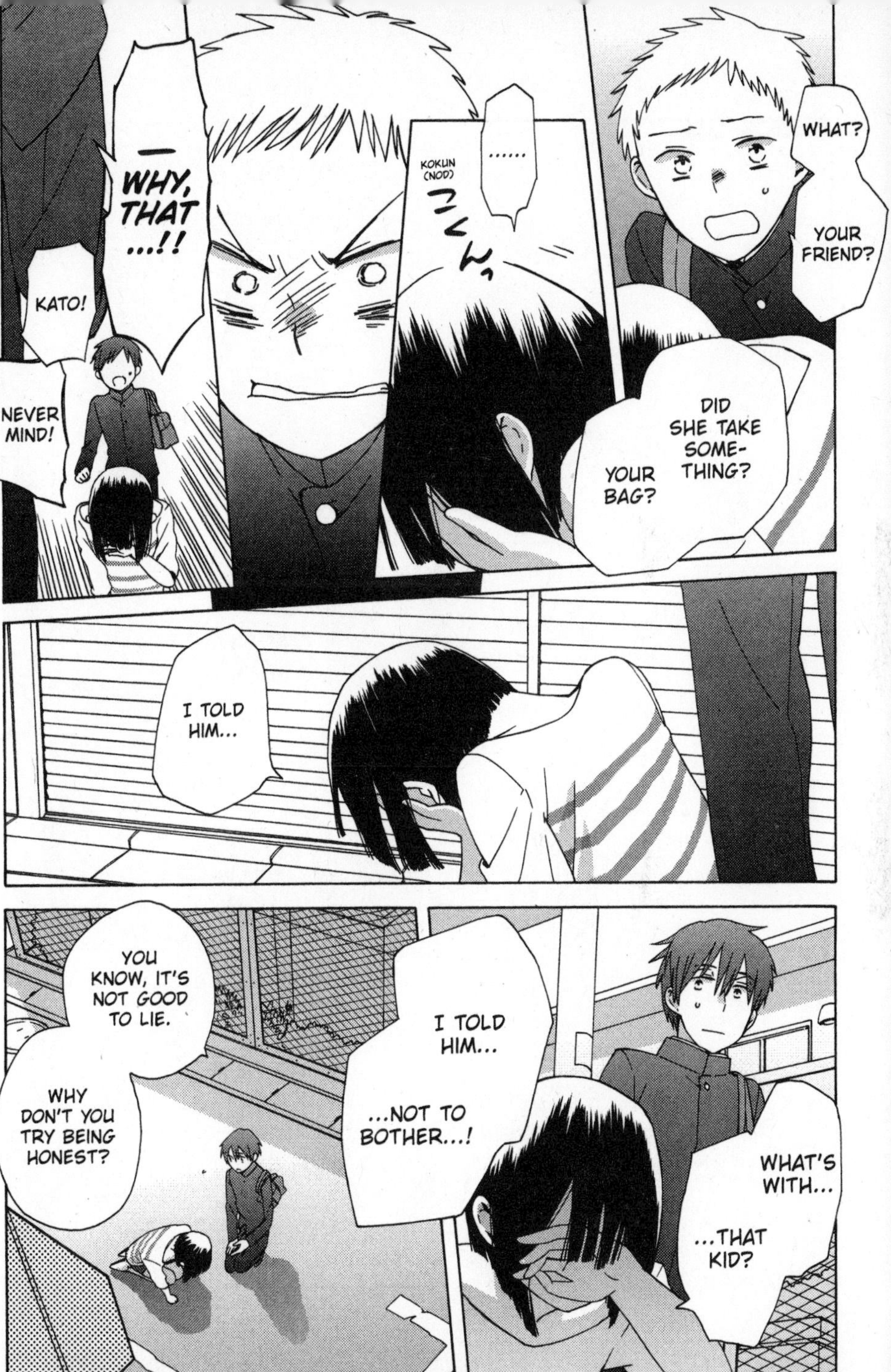
WHAT?
YOUR FRIEND?
DID SHE TAKE SOME-THING?
YOUR BAG?
KOKUN (NOD)
こくん
......
—WHY, THAT...!!
KATO!
NEVER MIND!
I TOLD HIM...
I TOLD HIM...
...NOT TO BOTHER...!
WHAT'S WITH...
...THAT KID?
YOU KNOW, IT'S NOT GOOD TO LIE.
WHY DON'T YOU TRY BEING HONEST?

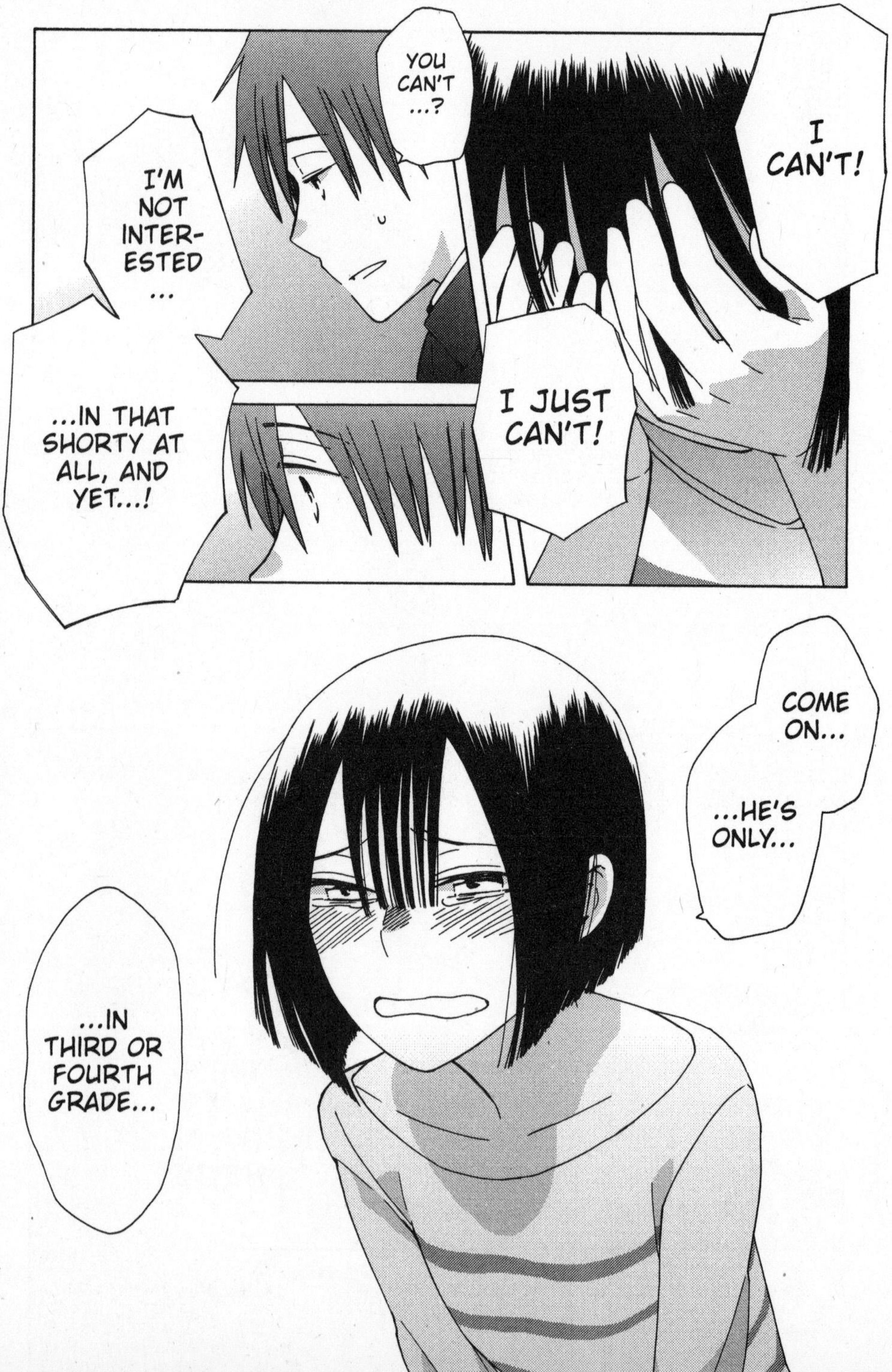
I CAN'T!
I JUST CAN'T!
YOU CAN'T ...?
I'M NOT INTER-ESTED ...
...IN THAT SHORTY AT ALL, AND YET...!
COME ON...
...HE'S ONLY...
...IN THIRD OR FOURTH GRADE...

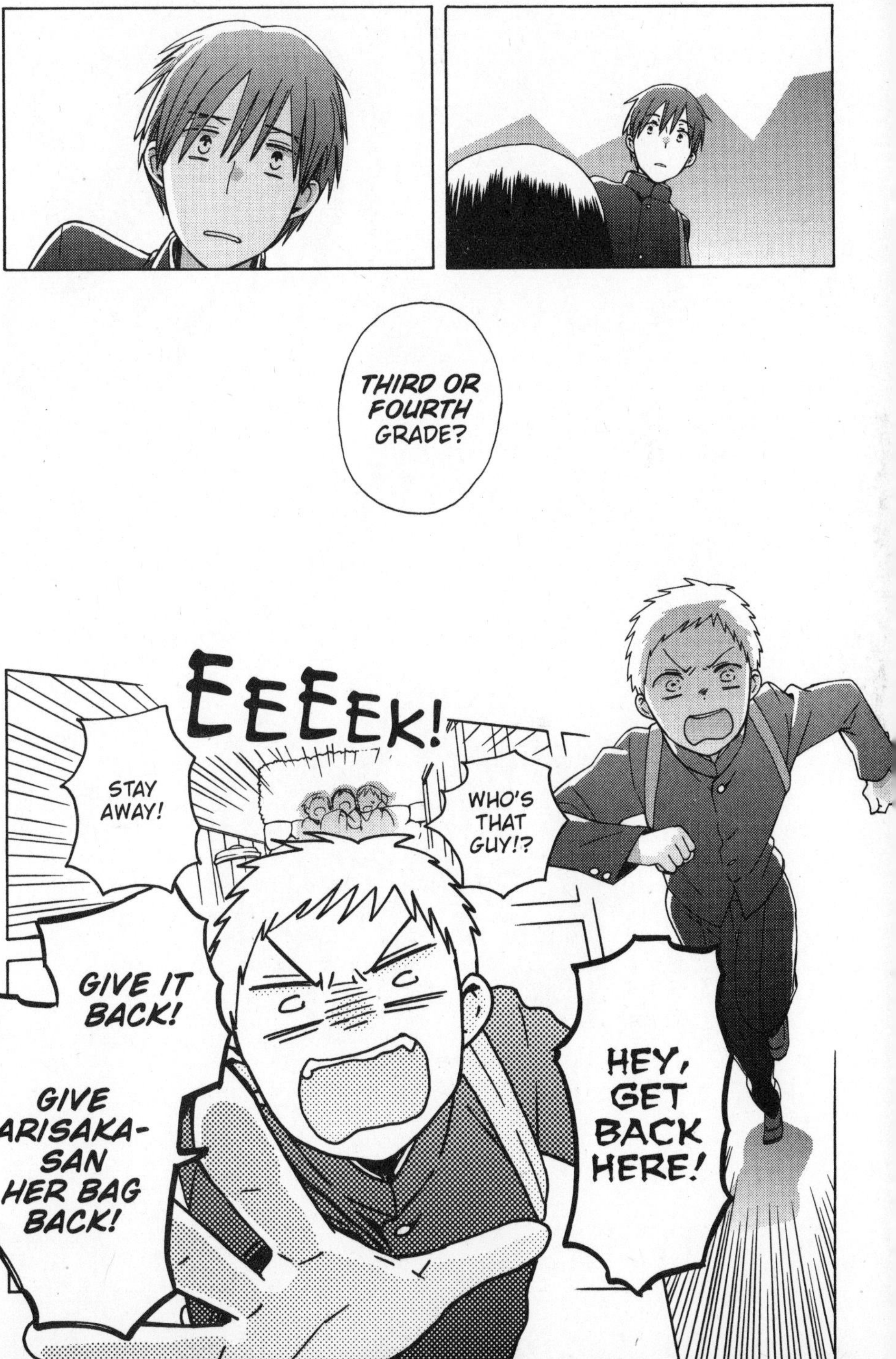
THIRD OR FOURTH GRADE?
EEEEK!
WHO'S THAT GUY!?
STAY AWAY!
HEY, GET BACK HERE!
GIVE IT BACK!
GIVE ARISAKA-SAN HER BAG BACK!

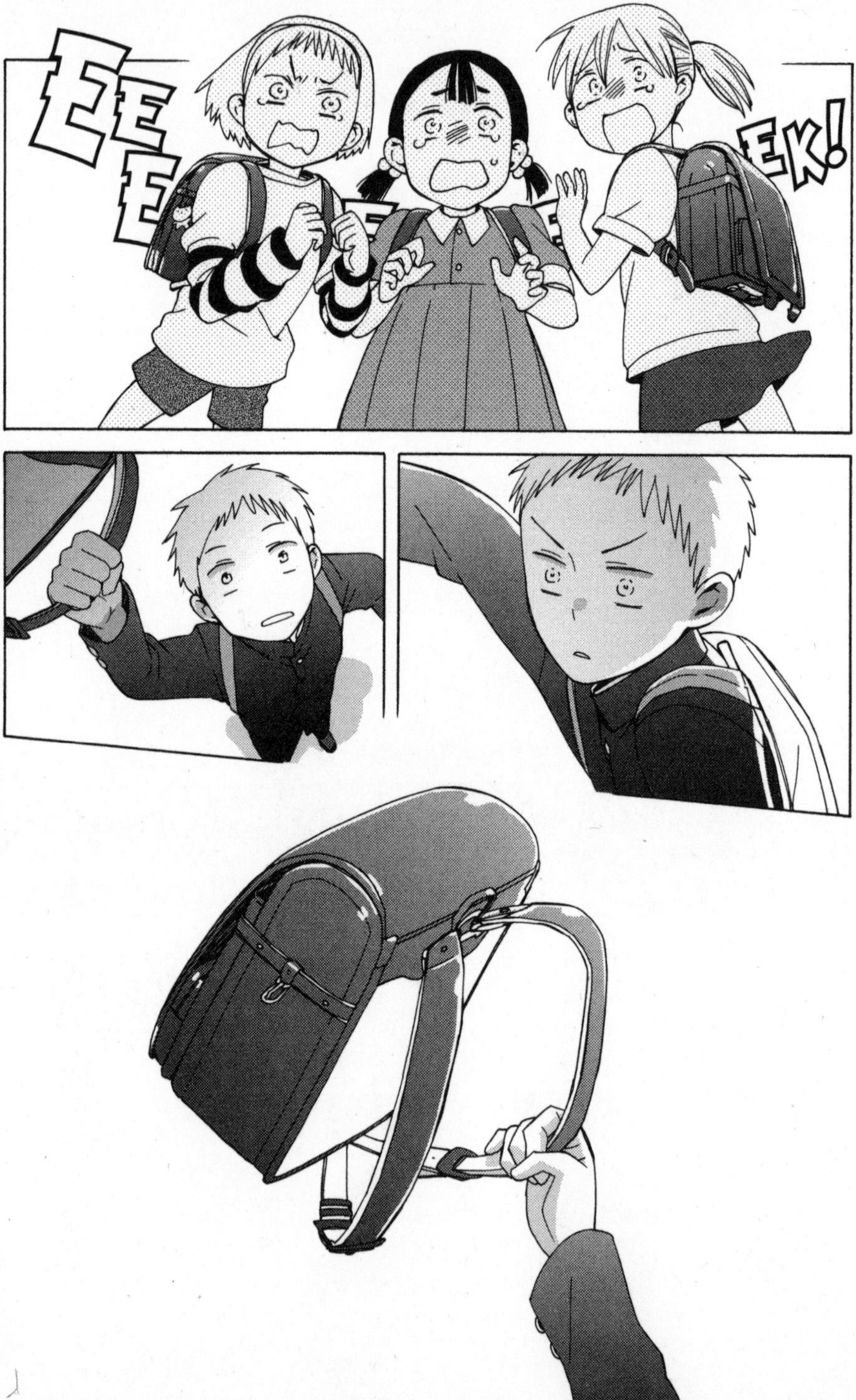
EEEEEEEK!

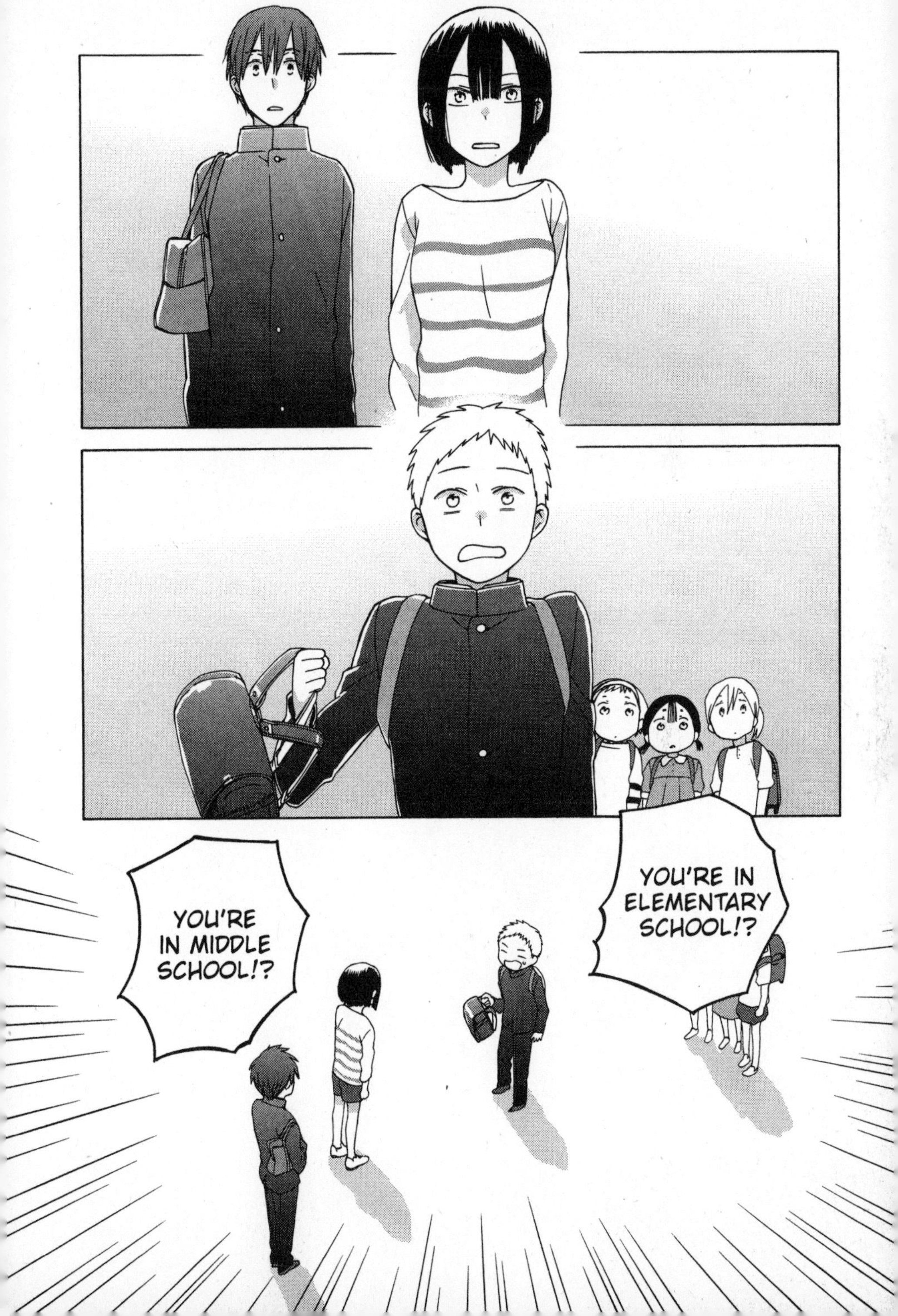
YOU'RE IN ELEMENTARY SCHOOL!?
YOU'RE IN MIDDLE SCHOOL!?

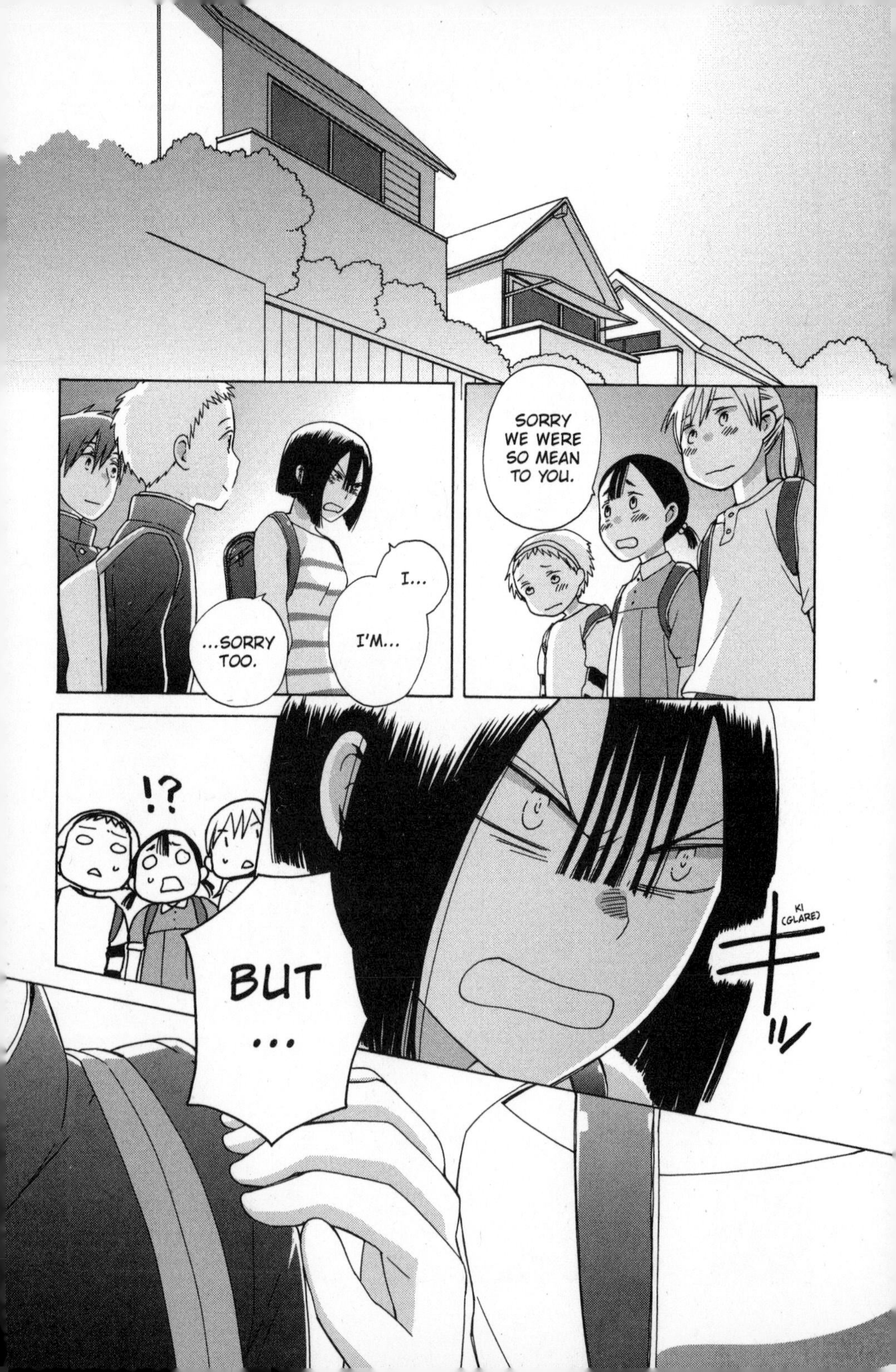
SORRY WE WERE SO MEAN TO YOU.
I...
I'M...
...SORRY TOO.
KI (GLARE)
BUT ...
!?

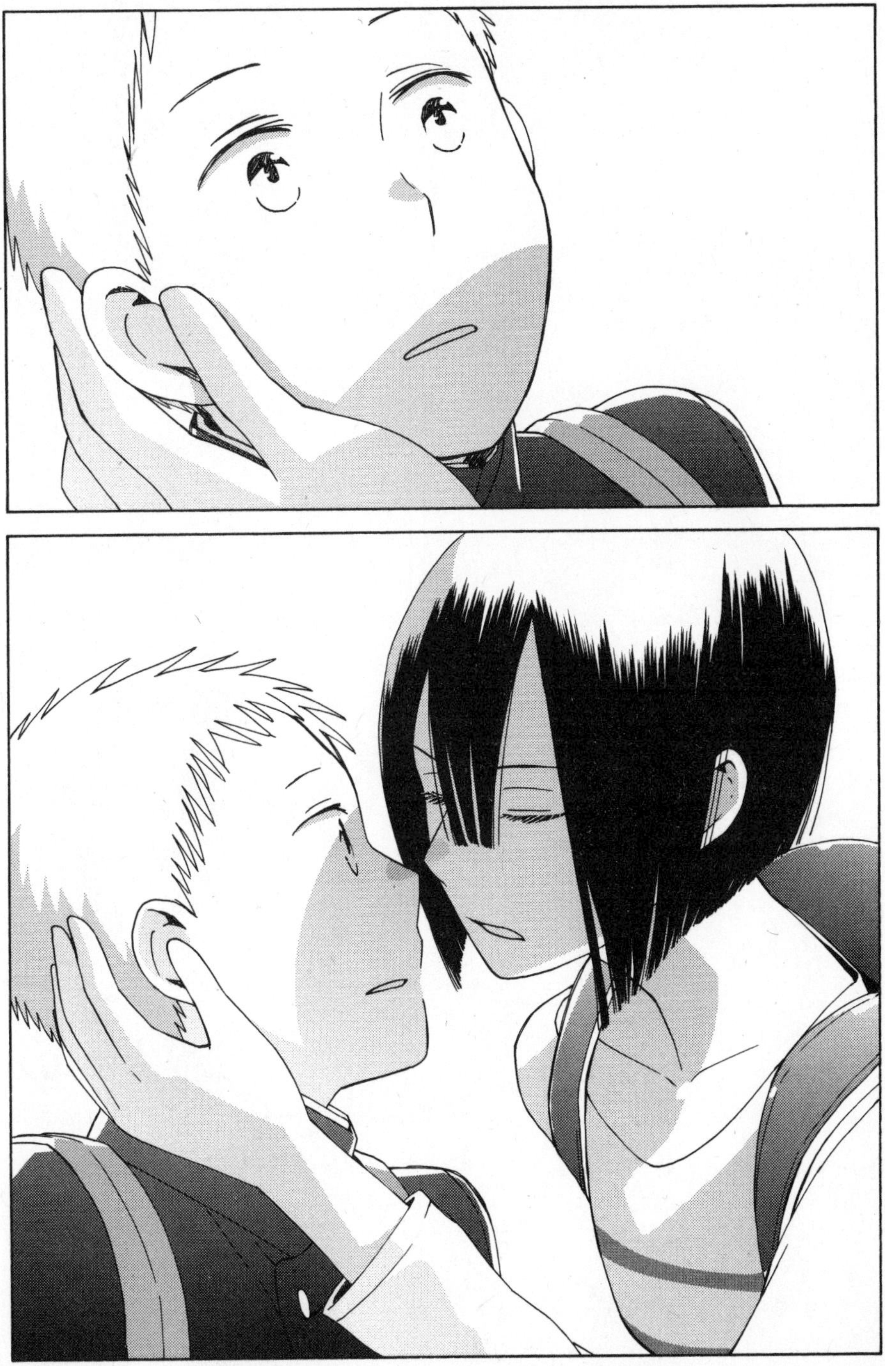

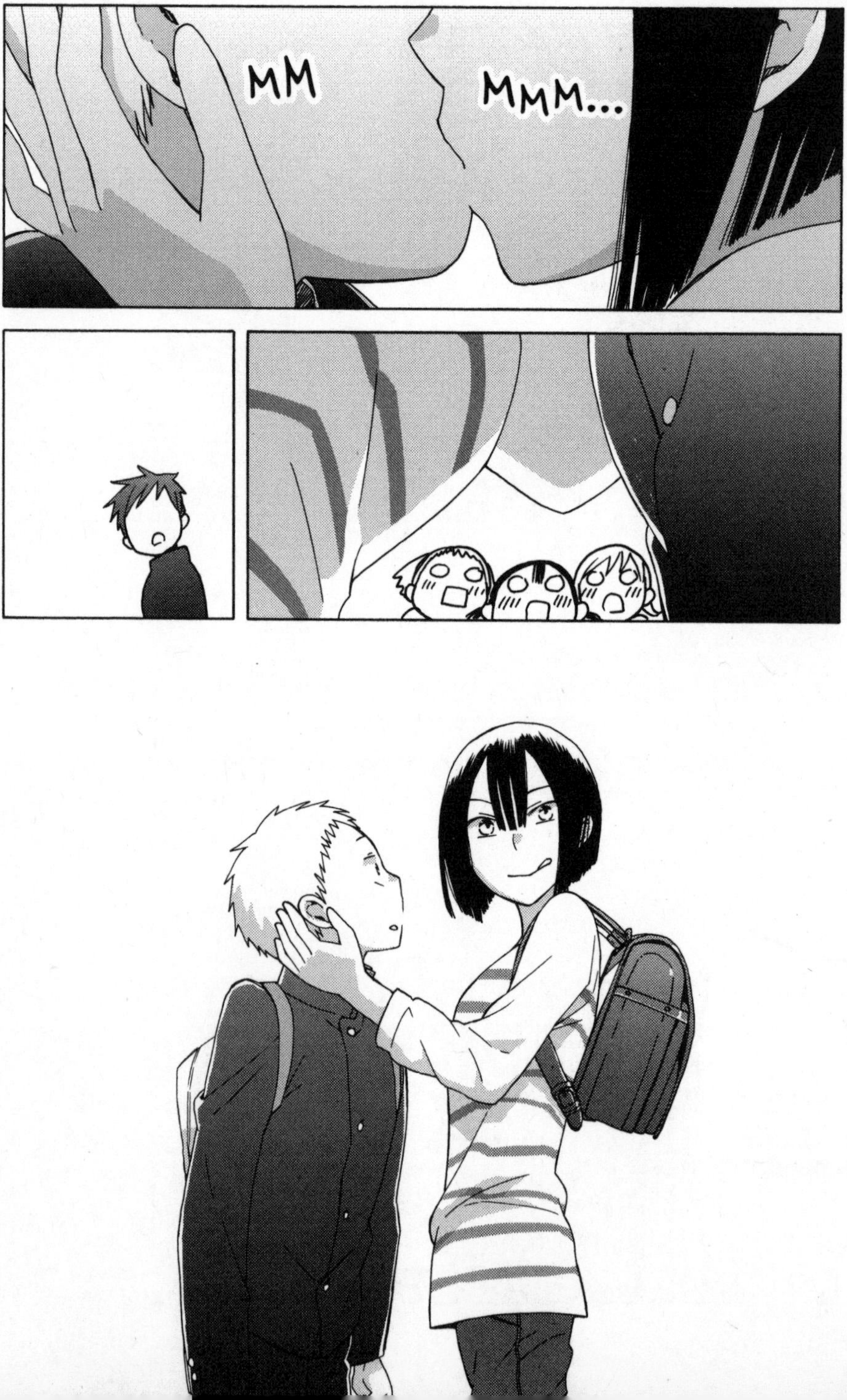
MMM...
MM

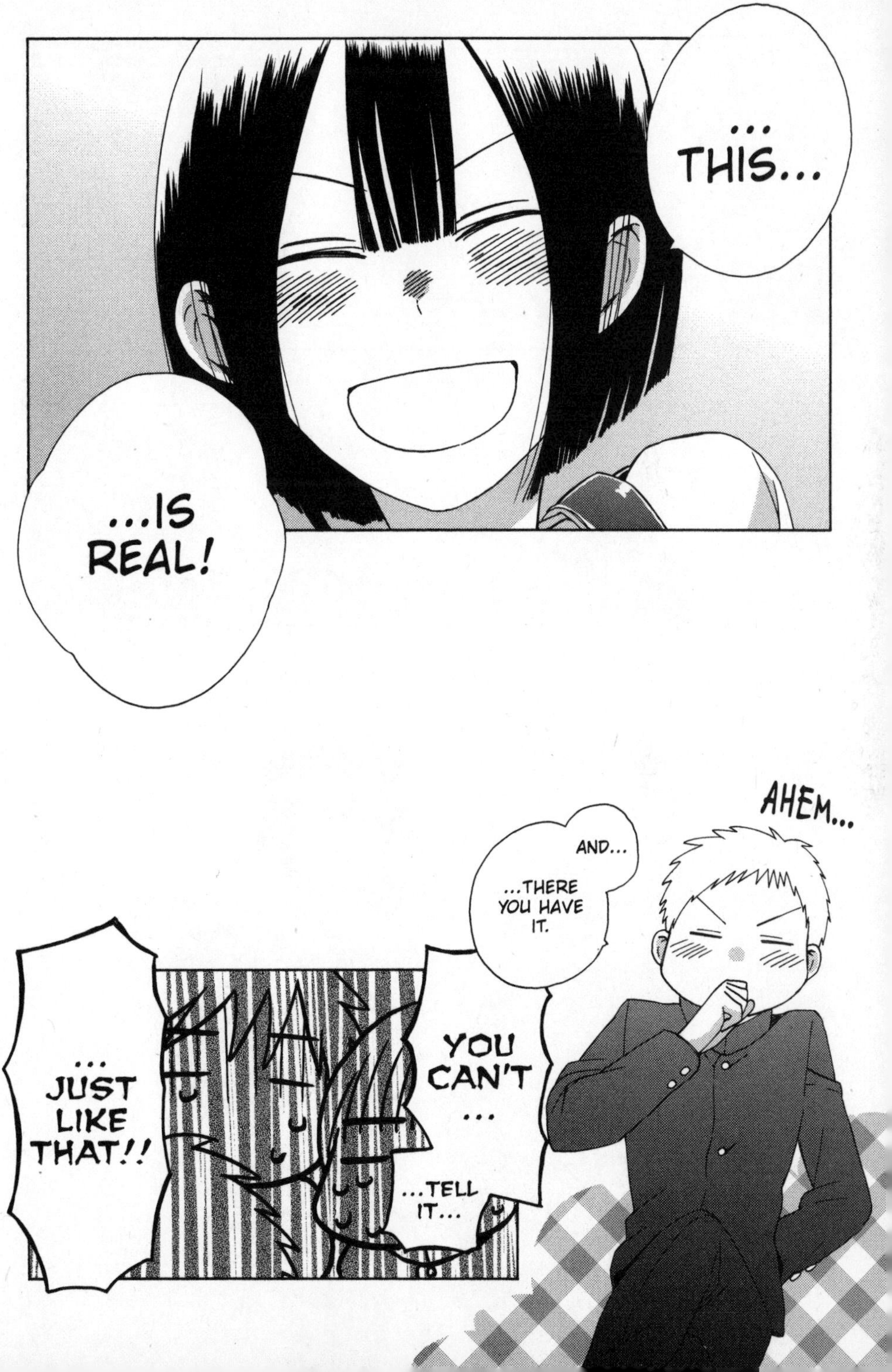
... THIS...
...IS REAL!
AHEM...
AND...
...THERE YOU HAVE IT.
YOU CAN'T ...
...TELL IT...
... JUST LIKE THAT!!

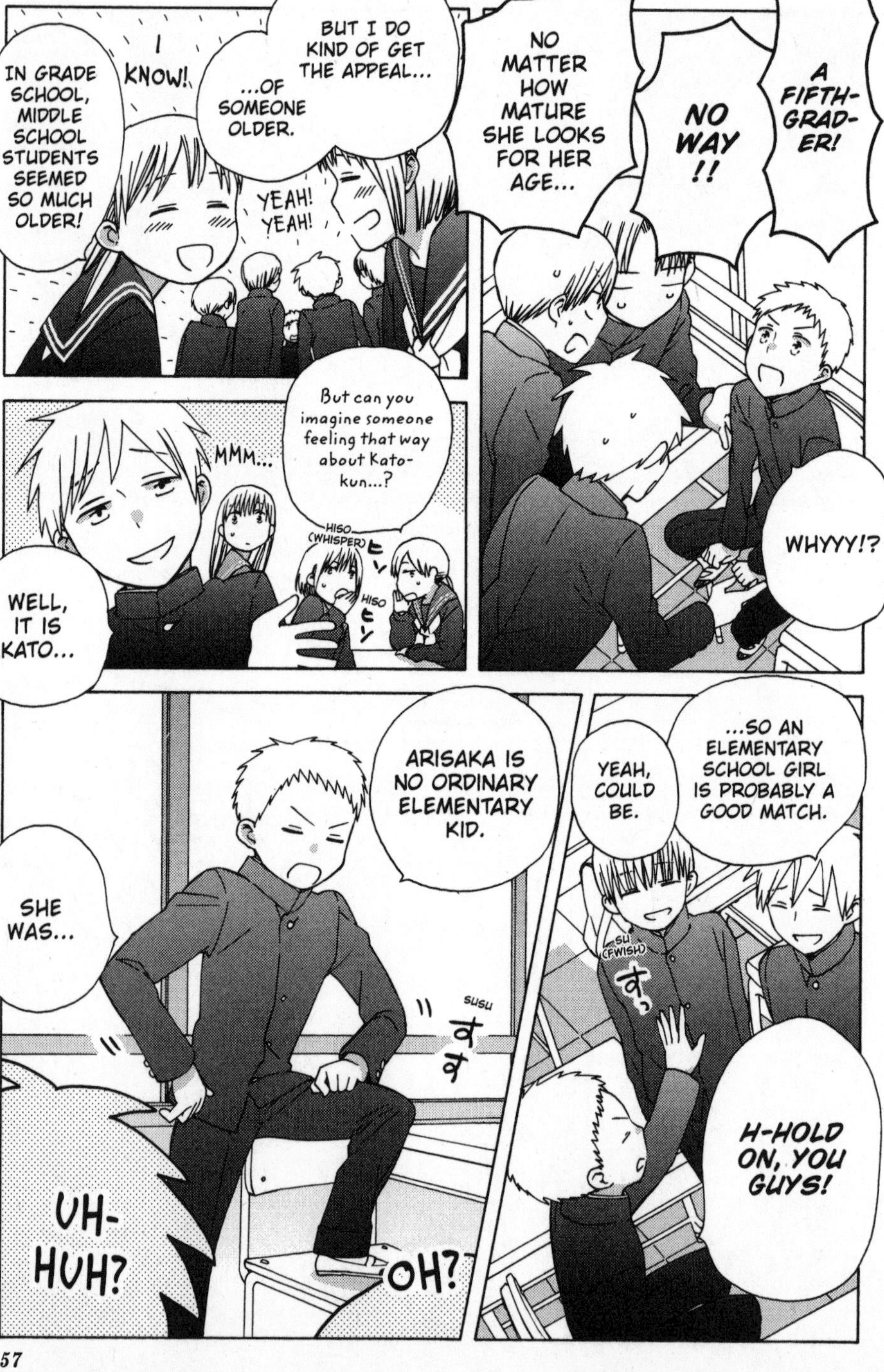

A FIFTH-GRADER!
NO WAY!!
NO MATTER HOW MATURE SHE LOOKS FOR HER AGE...
WHYYY!?
BUT I DO KIND OF GET THE APPEAL...
...OF SOMEONE OLDER.
I KNOW!
YEAH! YEAH!
IN GRADE SCHOOL, MIDDLE SCHOOL STUDENTS SEEMED SO MUCH OLDER!
But can you imagine someone feeling that way about Kato-kun...?
MMM...
HISO (WHISPER) ヒソ
HISO ヒソ
WELL, IT IS KATO...
...SO AN ELEMENTARY SCHOOL GIRL IS PROBABLY A GOOD MATCH.
YEAH, COULD BE.
SU (FWISH) すっ
H-HOLD ON, YOU GUYS!
ARISAKA IS NO ORDINARY ELEMENTARY KID.
SHE WAS...
SUSU すす
OH?
UH-HUH?

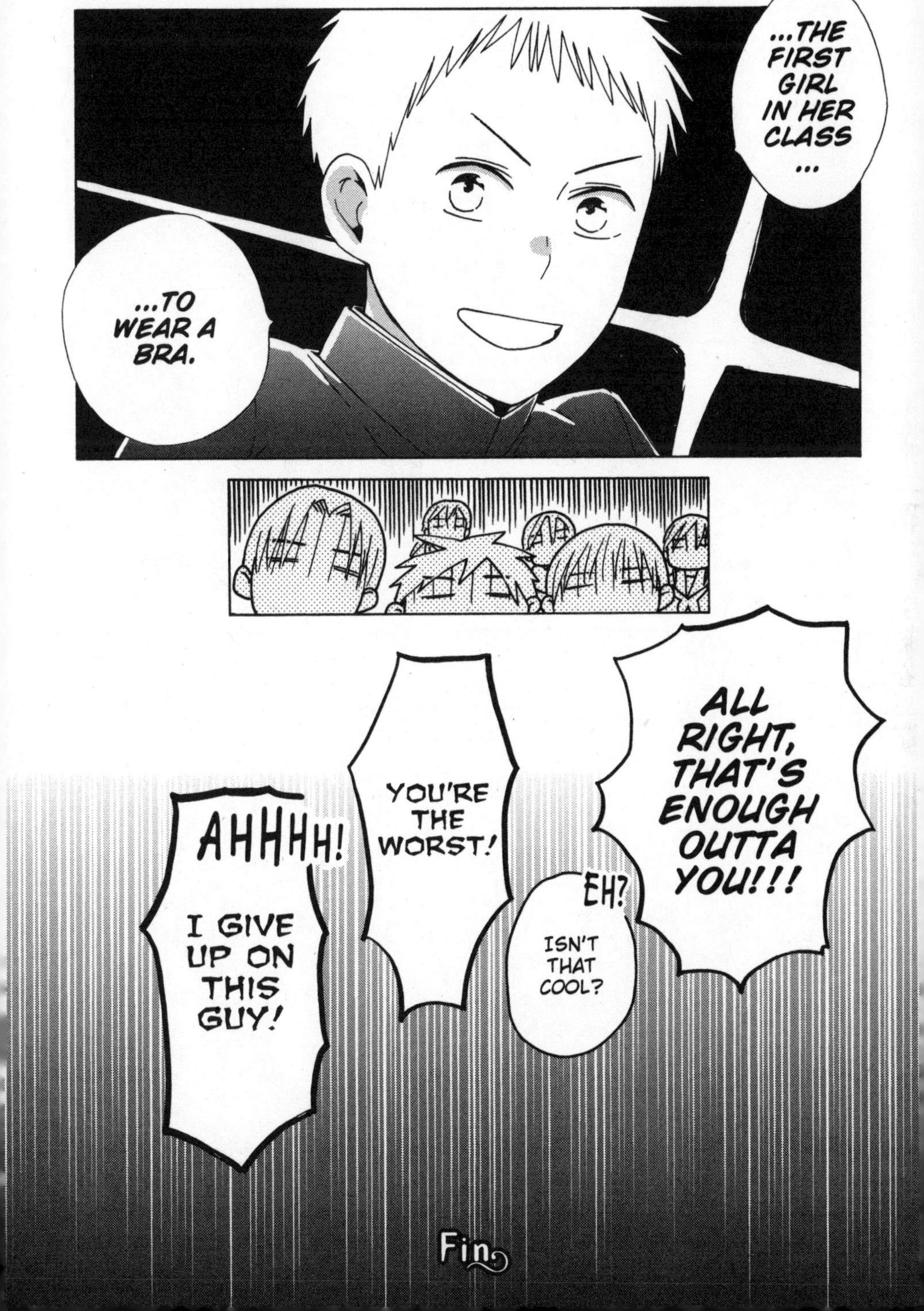
...THE FIRST GIRL IN HER CLASS ...
...TO WEAR A BRA.
ALL RIGHT, THAT'S ENOUGH OUTTA YOU!!!
EH?
ISN'T THAT COOL?
YOU'RE THE WORST!
AHHHH!
I GIVE UP ON THIS GUY!
Fin

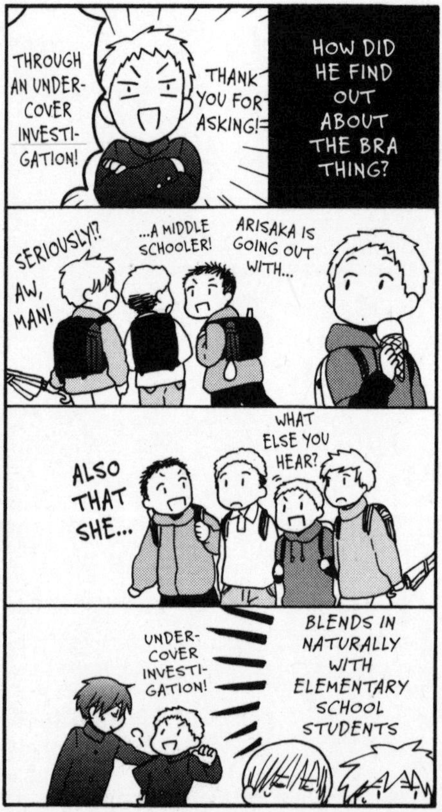
HOW DID HE FIND OUT ABOUT THE BRA THING?
THANK YOU FOR ASKING!
THROUGH AN UNDER-COVER INVESTI-GATION!
ARISAKA IS GOING OUT WITH...
...A MIDDLE SCHOOLER!
SERIOUSLY!?
AW, MAN!
WHAT ELSE YOU HEAR?
ALSO THAT SHE...
BLENDS IN NATURALLY WITH ELEMENTARY SCHOOL STUDENTS
UNDER-COVER INVESTI-GATION!

Love at Fourteen

Fuka Mizutani

Love at Fourteen

[Intermission 45]

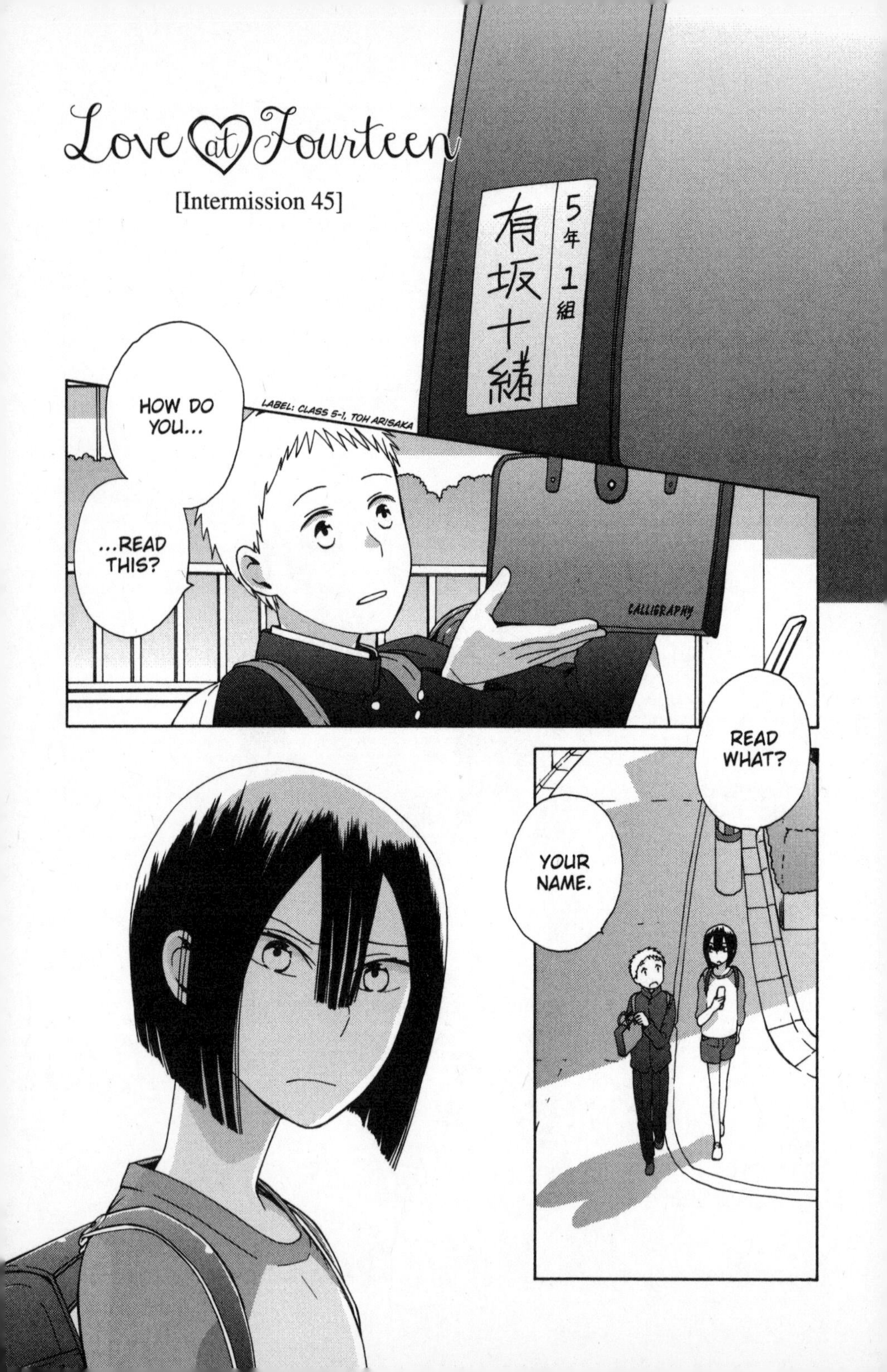
5年1組
有坂十緒
LABEL: CLASS 5-1, TOH ARISAKA
HOW DO YOU...
...READ THIS?
CALLIGRAPHY
READ WHAT?
YOUR NAME.

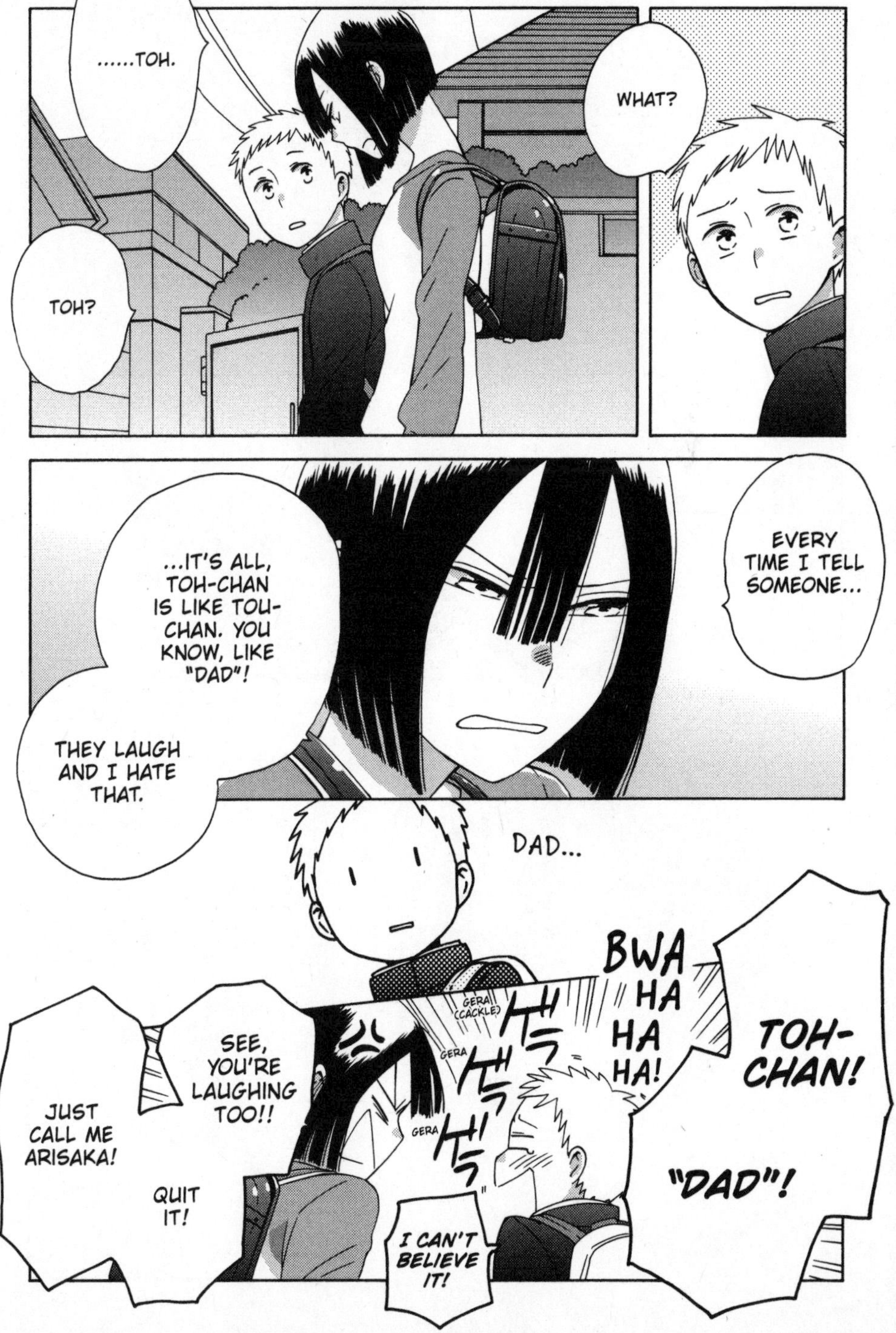
WHAT?
......TOH.
TOH?
EVERY TIME I TELL SOMEONE...
...IT'S ALL, TOH-CHAN IS LIKE TOU-CHAN. YOU KNOW, LIKE "DAD"!
THEY LAUGH AND I HATE THAT.
DAD...
TOH-CHAN! "DAD"!
BWA HA HA HA!
GERA (CACKLE)
GERA
GERA
ゲラ ゲラ ゲラ
I CAN'T BELIEVE IT!
SEE, YOU'RE LAUGHING TOO!!
JUST CALL ME ARISAKA!
QUIT IT!

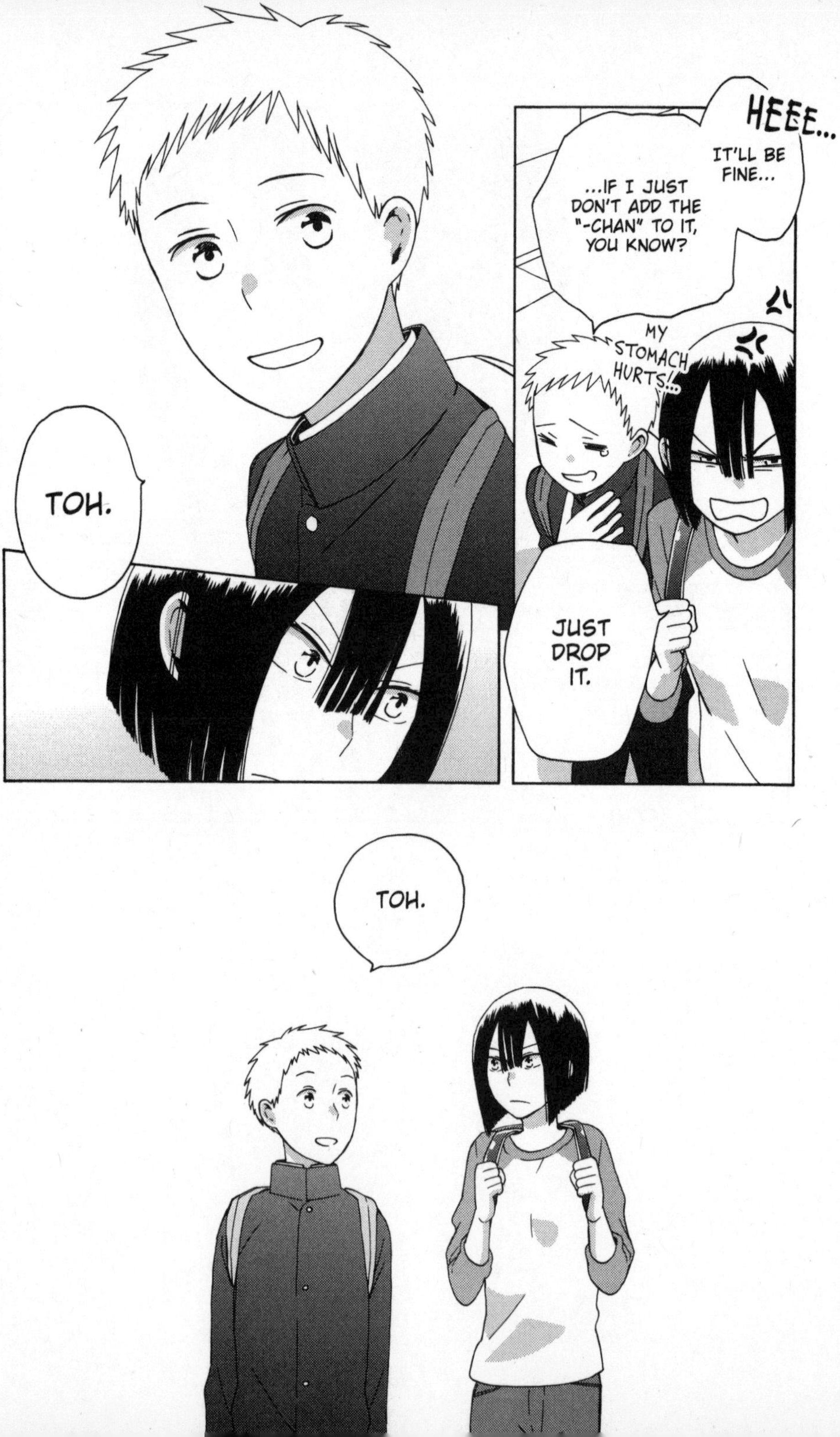
HEEE...
IT'LL BE FINE...
...IF I JUST DON'T ADD THE "-CHAN" TO IT, YOU KNOW?
MY STOMACH HURTS!...
JUST DROP IT.
TOH.
TOH.

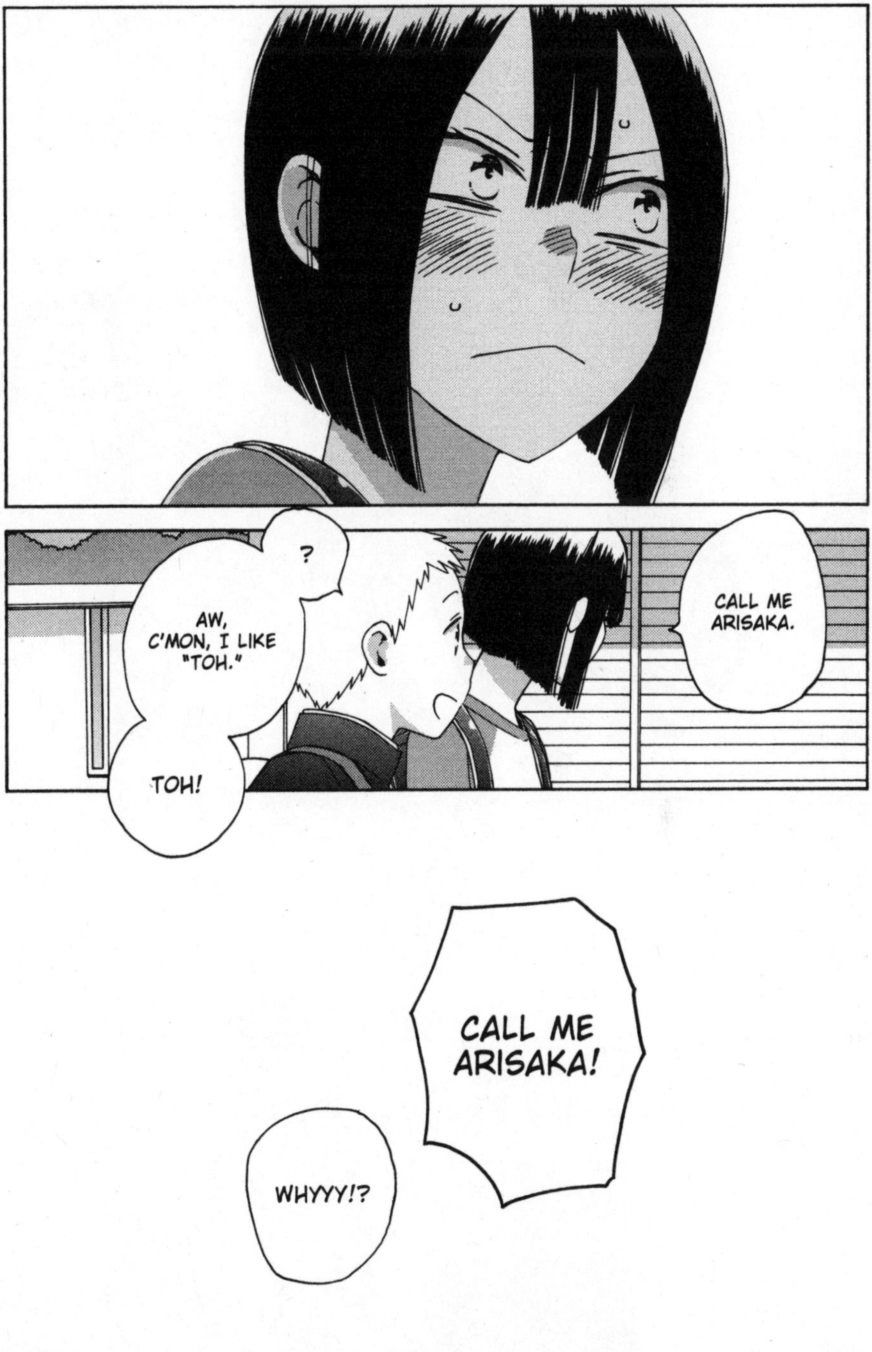
CALL ME ARISAKA.
?
AW, C'MON, I LIKE "TOH."
TOH!
CALL ME ARISAKA!
WHYYY!?

Fin

Love at Fourteen

[Intermission 46]

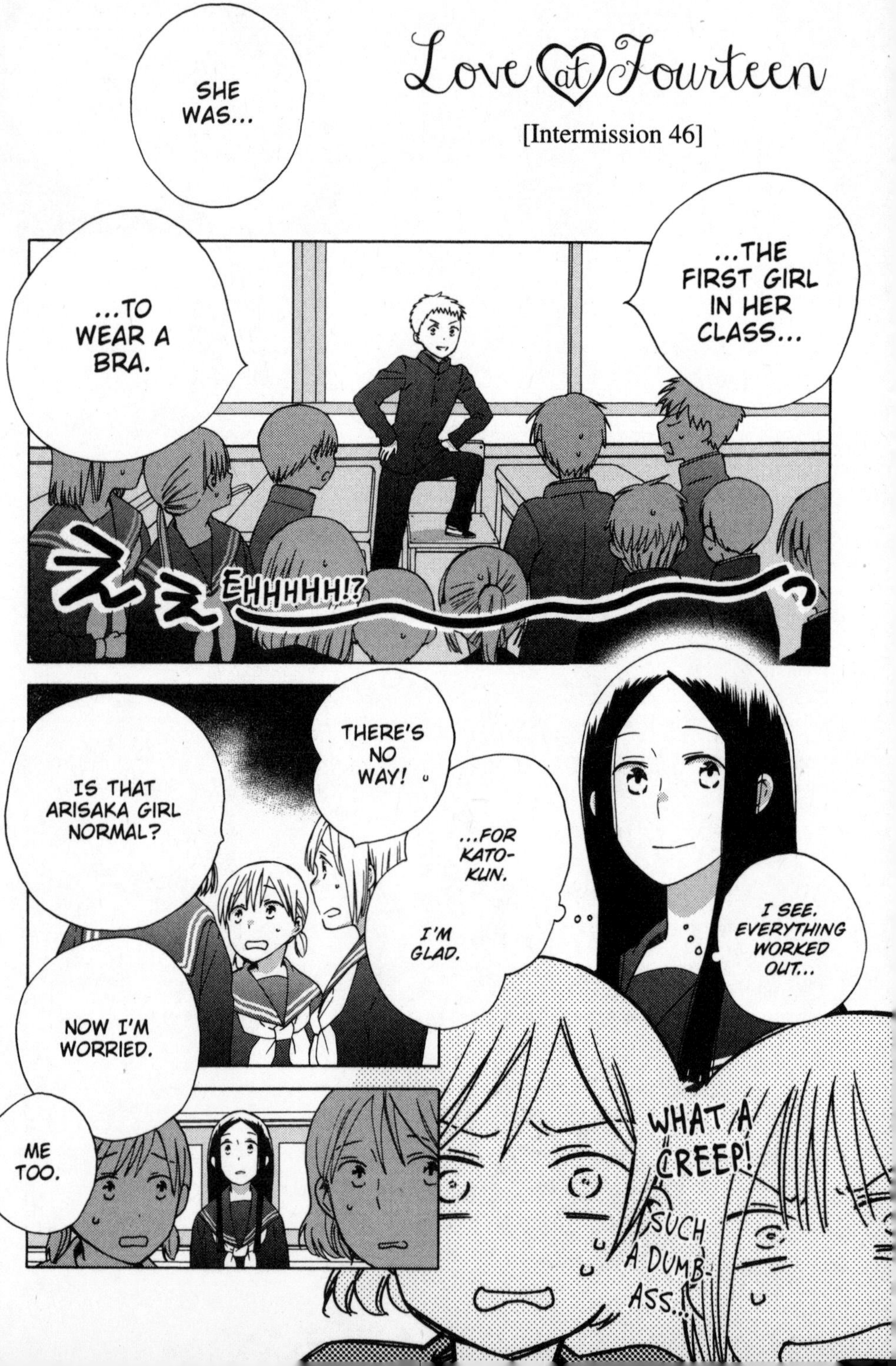
SHE WAS...
...THE FIRST GIRL IN HER CLASS...
...TO WEAR A BRA.
ええ EHHHHH!?
I SEE. EVERYTHING WORKED OUT...
...FOR KATO-KUN.
I'M GLAD.
THERE'S NO WAY!
IS THAT ARISAKA GIRL NORMAL?
WHAT A CREEP!
SUCH A DUMB-ASS..!
NOW I'M WORRIED.
ME TOO.

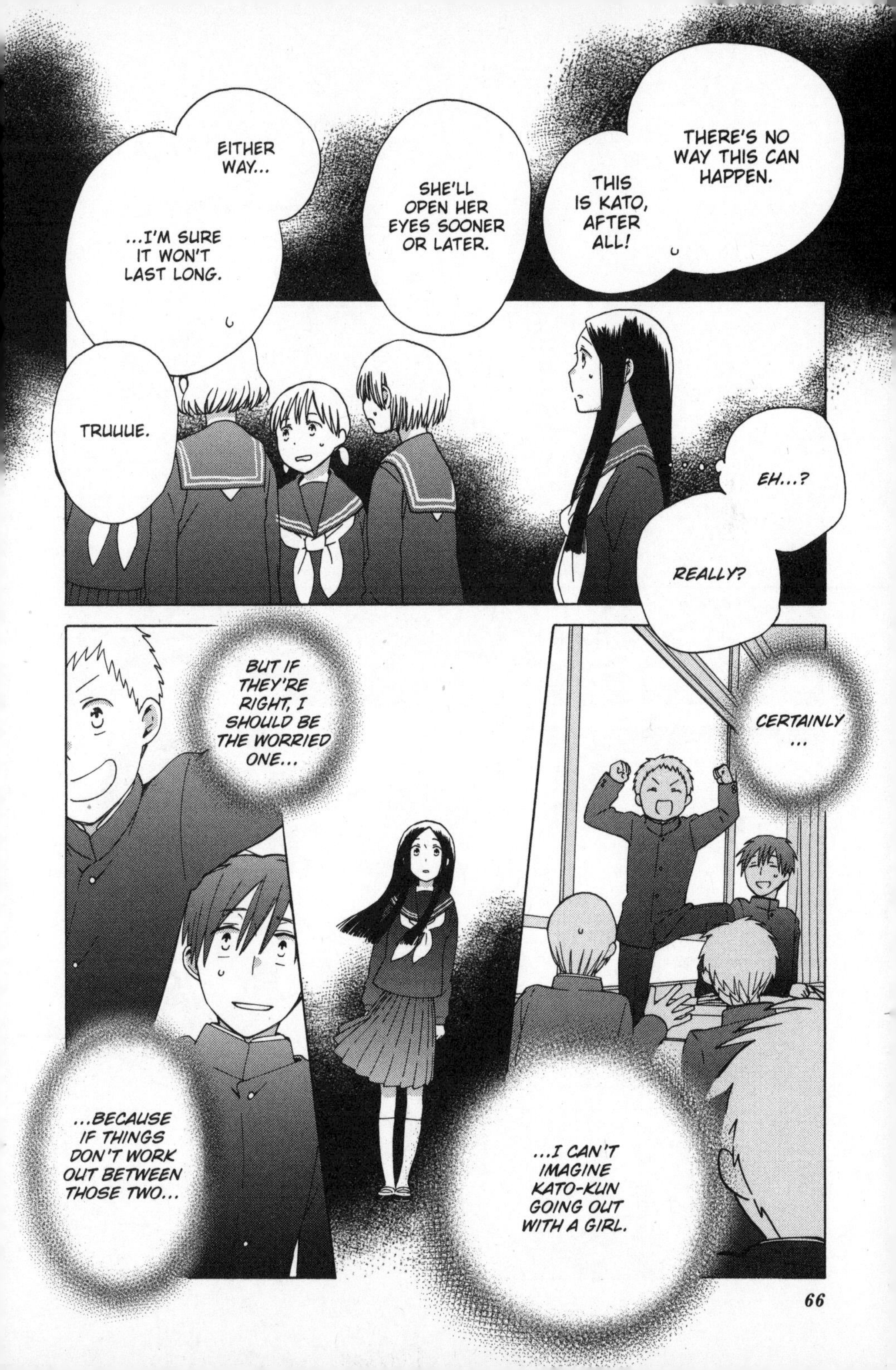
THERE'S NO WAY THIS CAN HAPPEN.
THIS IS KATO, AFTER ALL!
SHE'LL OPEN HER EYES SOONER OR LATER.
EITHER WAY...
...I'M SURE IT WON'T LAST LONG.
TRUUUE.
EH...?
REALLY?
CERTAINLY...
...I CAN'T IMAGINE KATO-KUN GOING OUT WITH A GIRL.
BUT IF THEY'RE RIGHT, I SHOULD BE THE WORRIED ONE...
...BECAUSE IF THINGS DON'T WORK OUT BETWEEN THOSE TWO...

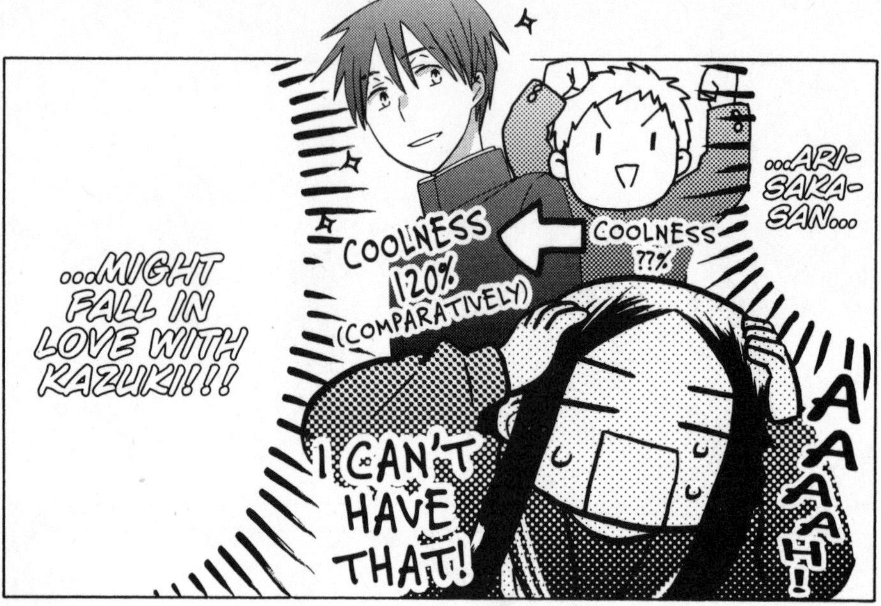
...ARI-SAKA-SAN...
AAAAH!
COOLNESS ??%
COOLNESS 120% (COMPARATIVELY)
I CAN'T HAVE THAT!
...MIGHT FALL IN LOVE WITH KAZUKI!!!

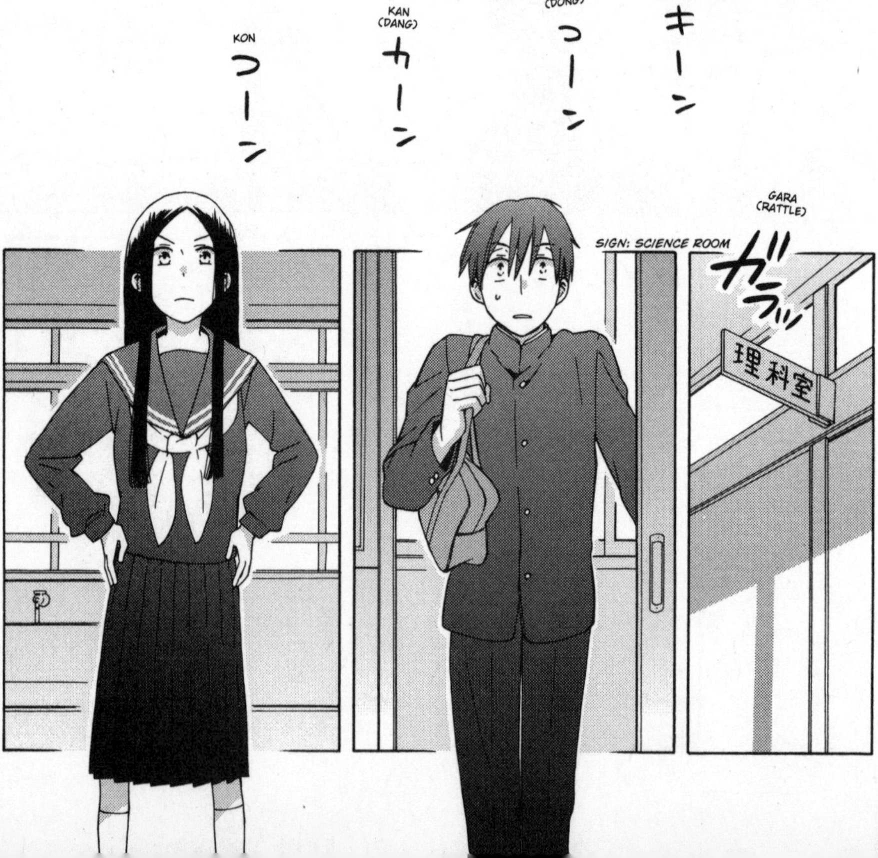
KIN (DING)
キーン
KON (DONG)
コーン
KAN (DANG)
カーン
KON
コーン
GARA (RATTLE)
ガラッ
SIGN: SCIENCE ROOM
理科室

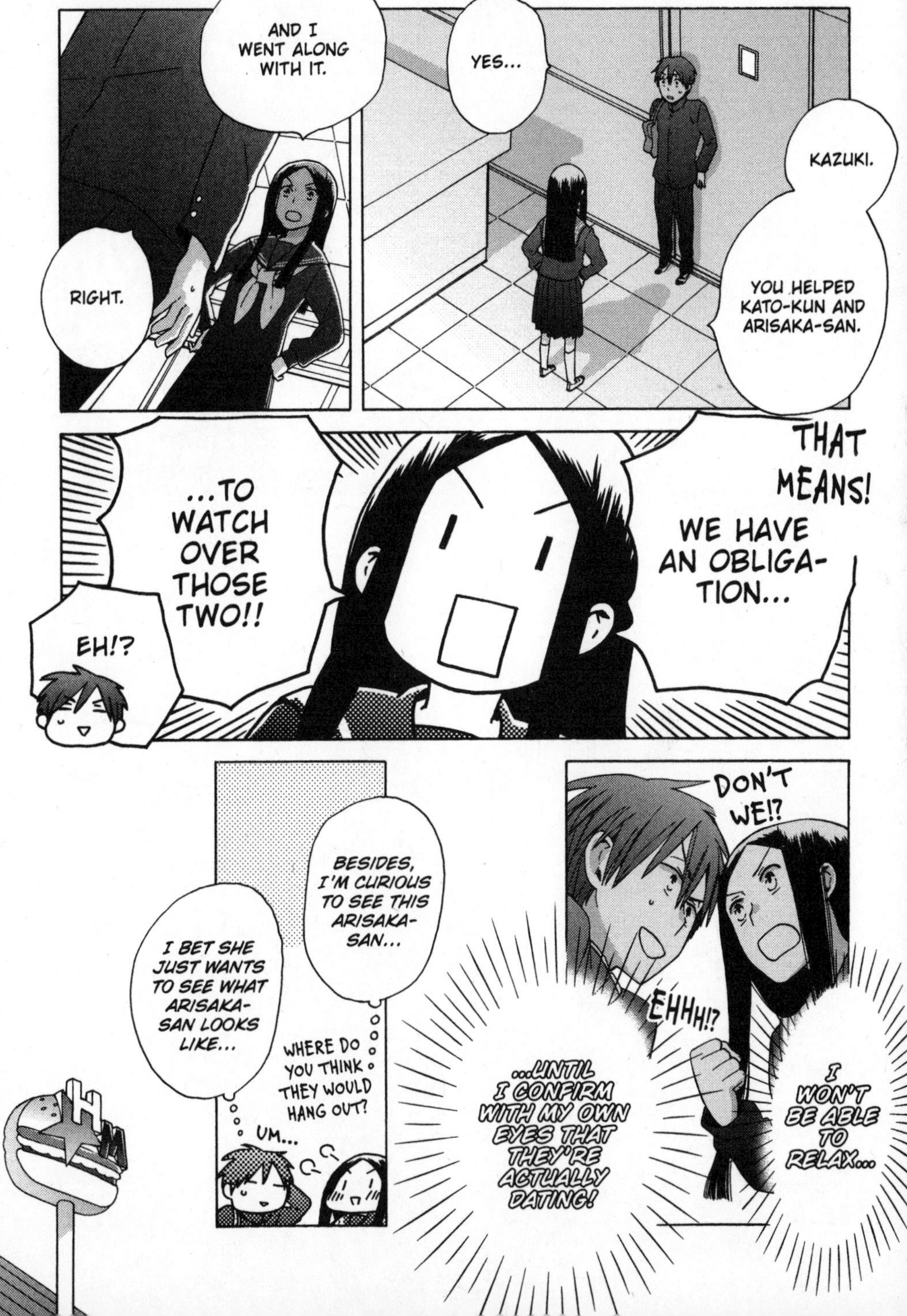
KAZUKI.
YOU HELPED KATO-KUN AND ARISAKA-SAN.
YES...
AND I WENT ALONG WITH IT.
RIGHT.
THAT MEANS!
WE HAVE AN OBLIGA-TION...
...TO WATCH OVER THOSE TWO!!
EH!?
DON'T WE!?
EHHH!?
I WON'T BE ABLE TO RELAX...
...UNTIL I CONFIRM WITH MY OWN EYES THAT THEY'RE ACTUALLY DATING!
BESIDES, I'M CURIOUS TO SEE THIS ARISAKA-SAN...
I BET SHE JUST WANTS TO SEE WHAT ARISAKA-SAN LOOKS LIKE...
WHERE DO YOU THINK THEY WOULD HANG OUT?
UM...

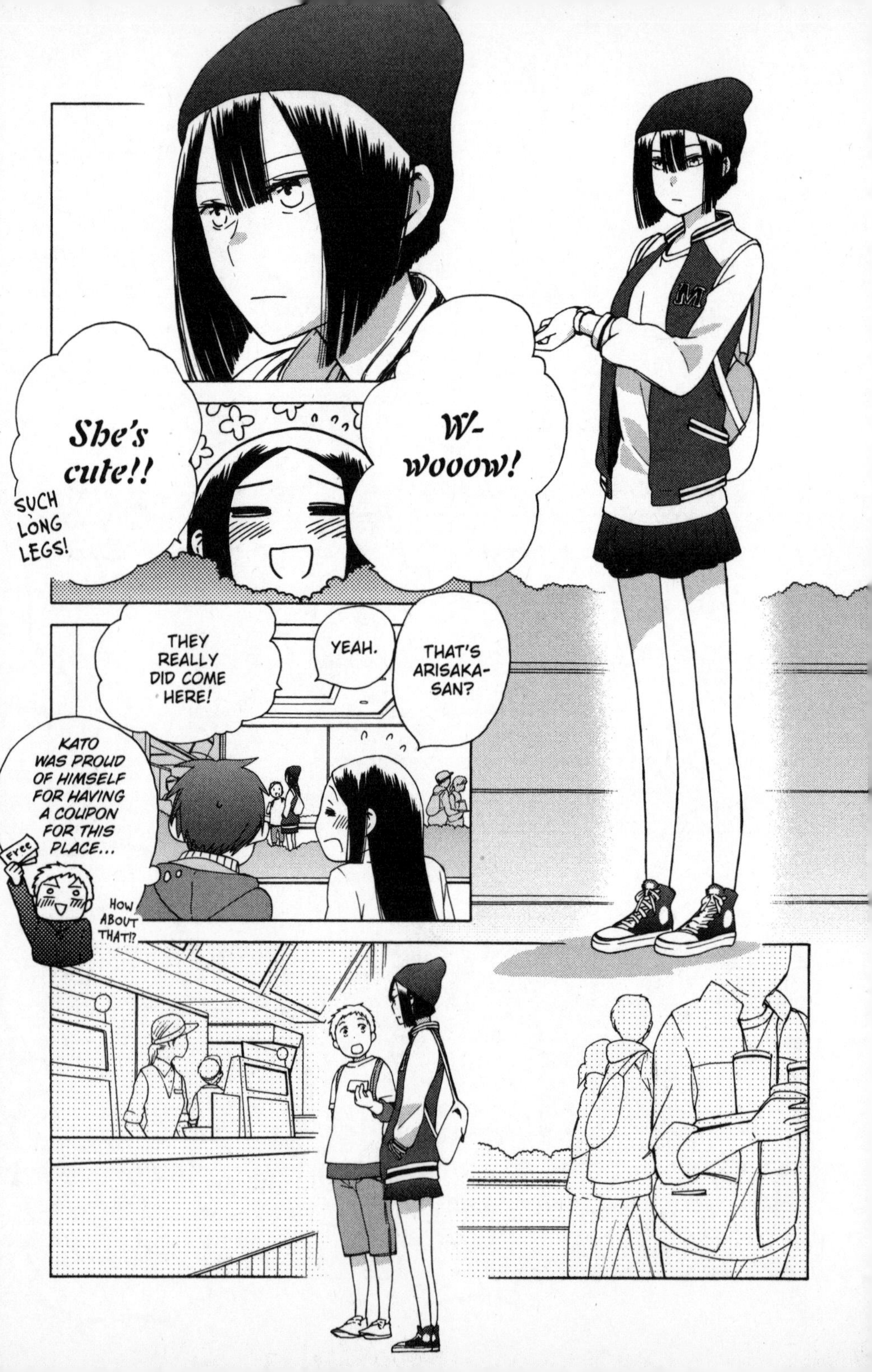
W-wooow!
She's cute!!
SUCH LONG LEGS!
THAT'S ARISAKA-SAN?
YEAH.
THEY REALLY DID COME HERE!
KATO WAS PROUD OF HIMSELF FOR HAVING A COUPON FOR THIS PLACE...
Free
HOW ABOUT THAT!?

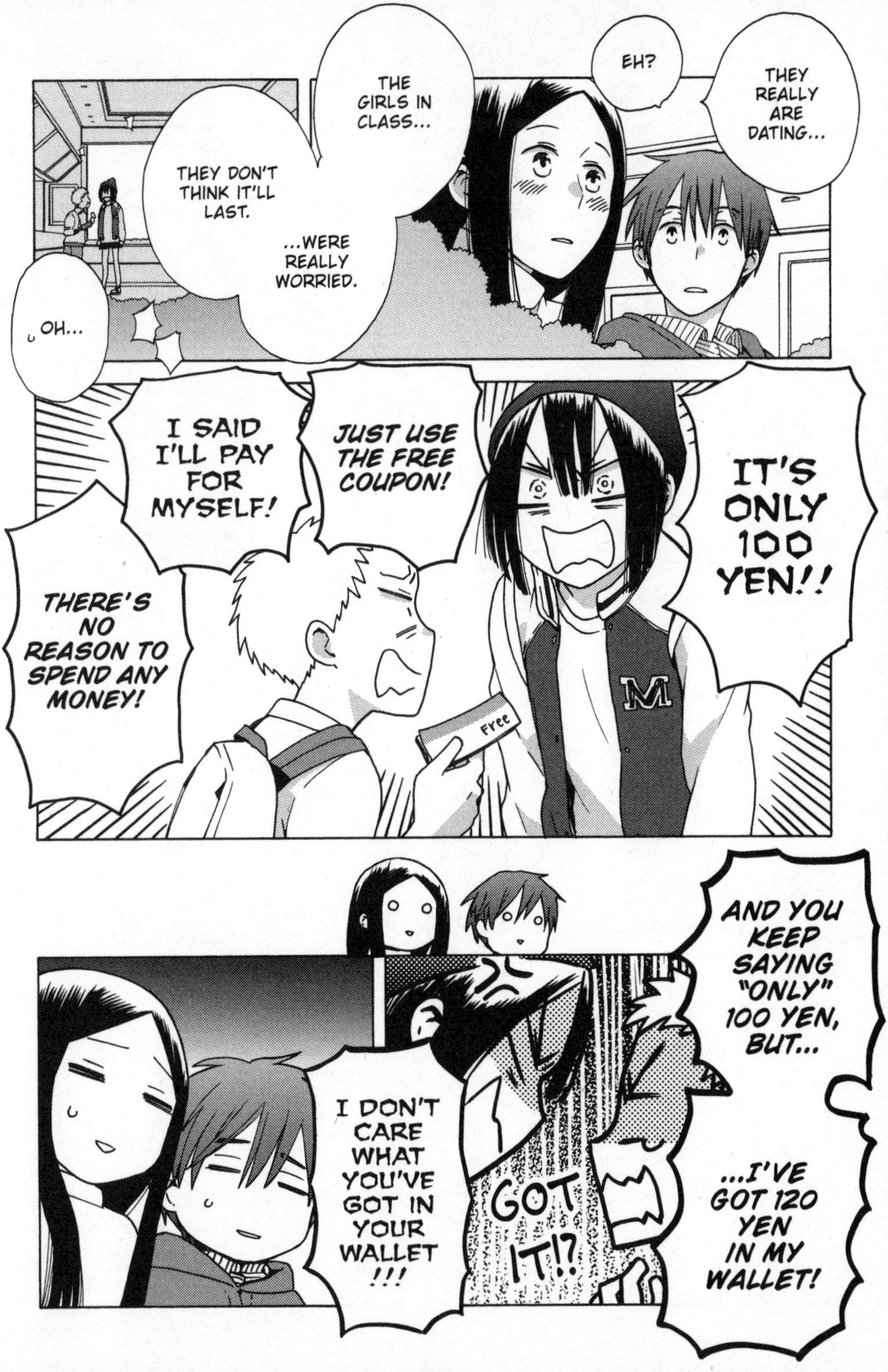
THEY REALLY ARE DATING...
EH?
THE GIRLS IN CLASS...
...WERE REALLY WORRIED.
THEY DON'T THINK IT'LL LAST.
OH...
IT'S ONLY 100 YEN!!
JUST USE THE FREE COUPON!
I SAID I'LL PAY FOR MYSELF!
THERE'S NO REASON TO SPEND ANY MONEY!
Free
AND YOU KEEP SAYING "ONLY" 100 YEN, BUT...
...I'VE GOT 120 YEN IN MY WALLET!
GOT IT!?
I DON'T CARE WHAT YOU'VE GOT IN YOUR WALLET!!!

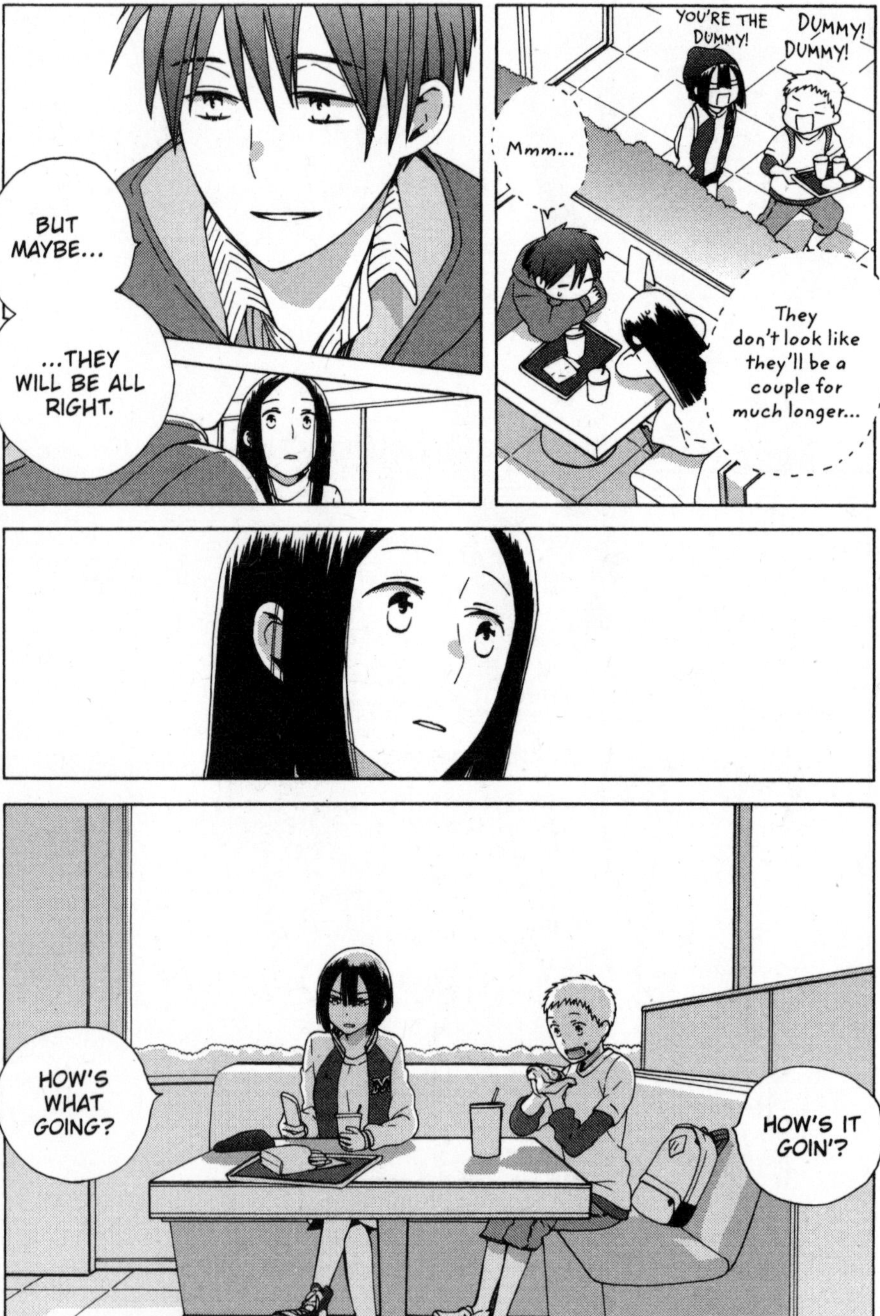
DUMMY! DUMMY!
YOU'RE THE DUMMY!
Mmm...
They don't look like they'll be a couple for much longer...
BUT MAYBE...
...THEY WILL BE ALL RIGHT.
HOW'S IT GOIN'?
HOW'S WHAT GOING?

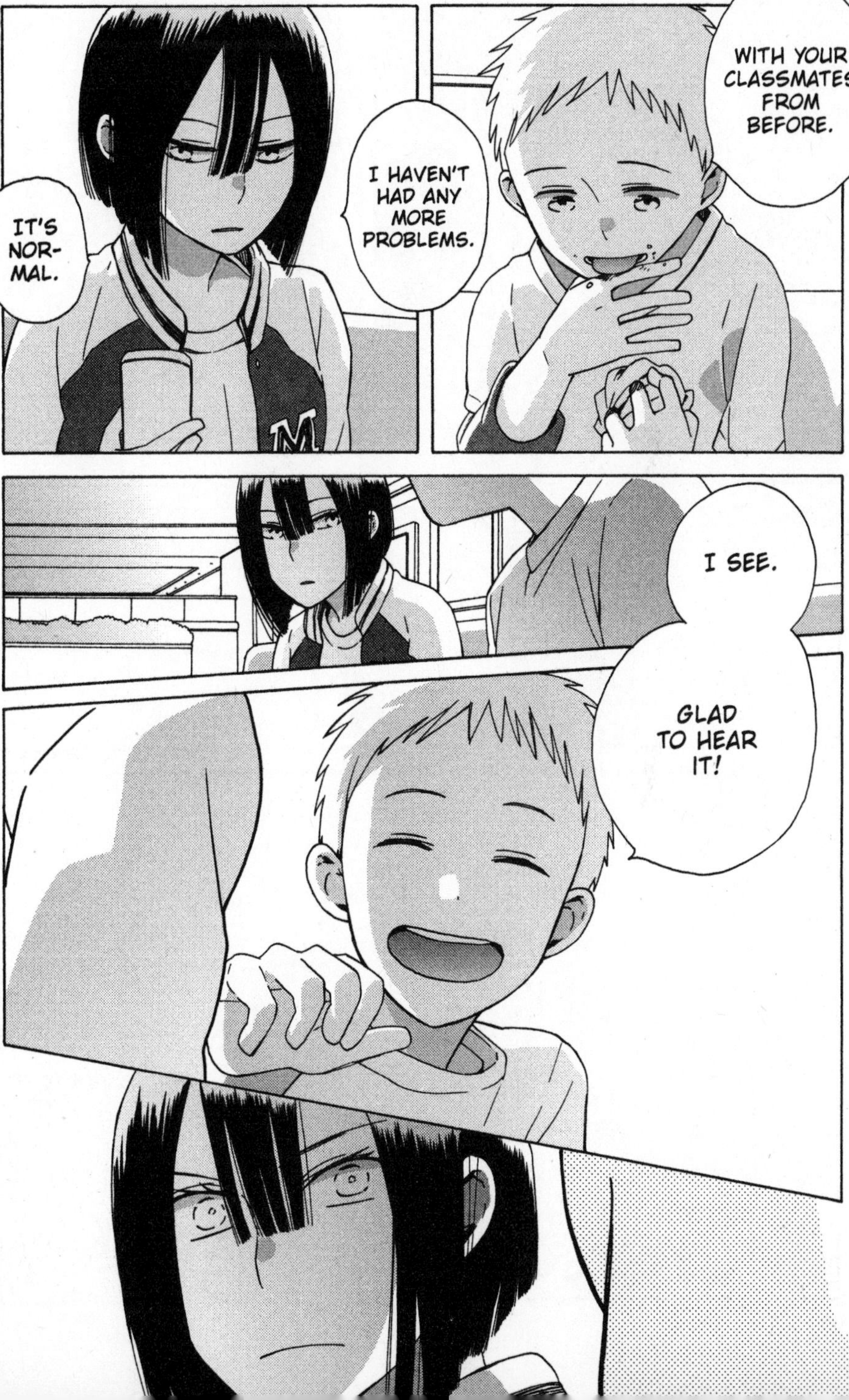
WITH YOUR CLASSMATES FROM BEFORE.
I HAVEN'T HAD ANY MORE PROBLEMS.
IT'S NOR-MAL.
I SEE.
GLAD TO HEAR IT!

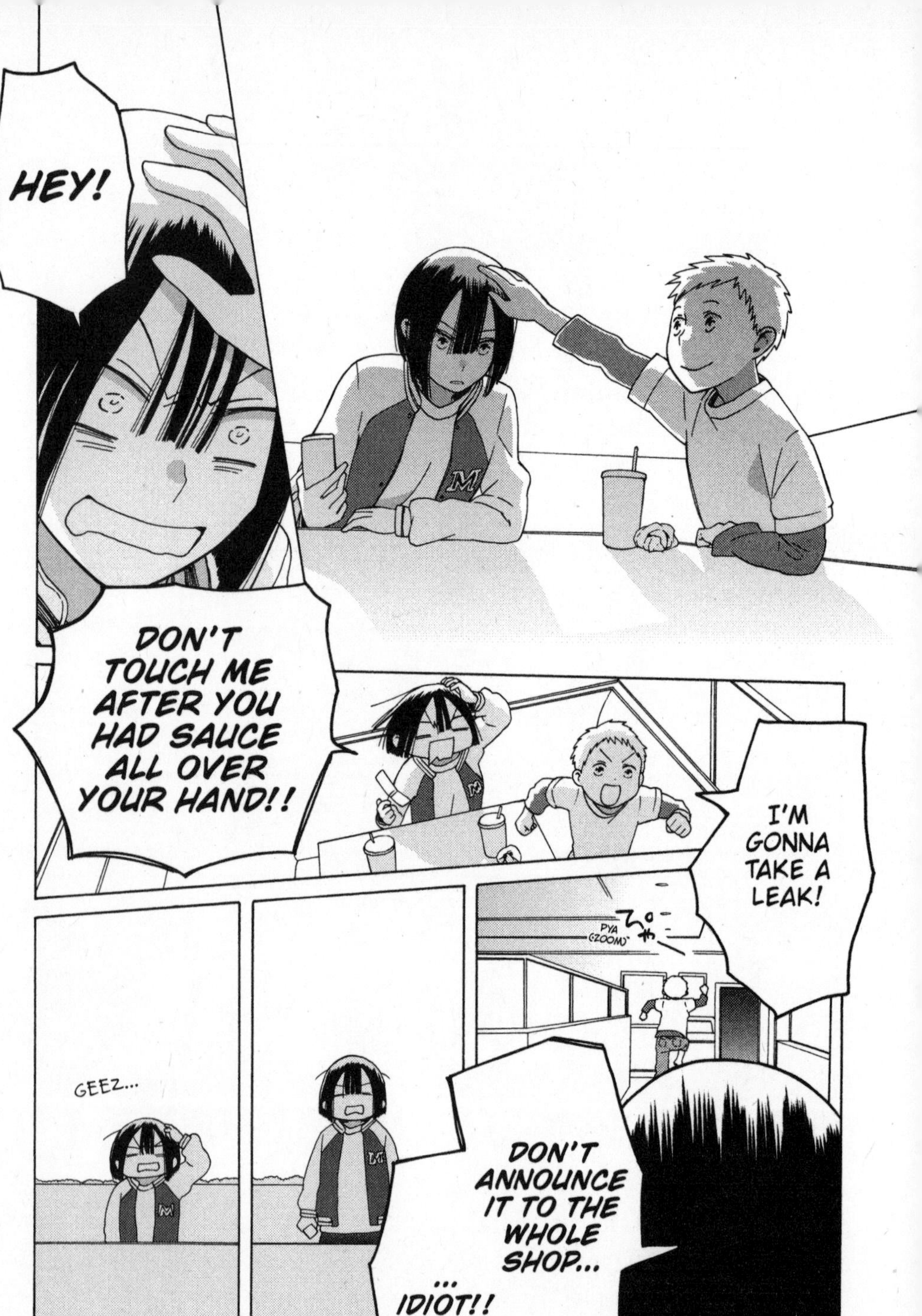
HEY!
DON'T TOUCH ME AFTER YOU HAD SAUCE ALL OVER YOUR HAND!!
I'M GONNA TAKE A LEAK!
PYA (ZOOM)
DON'T ANNOUNCE IT TO THE WHOLE SHOP...
... IDIOT!!
GEEZ...

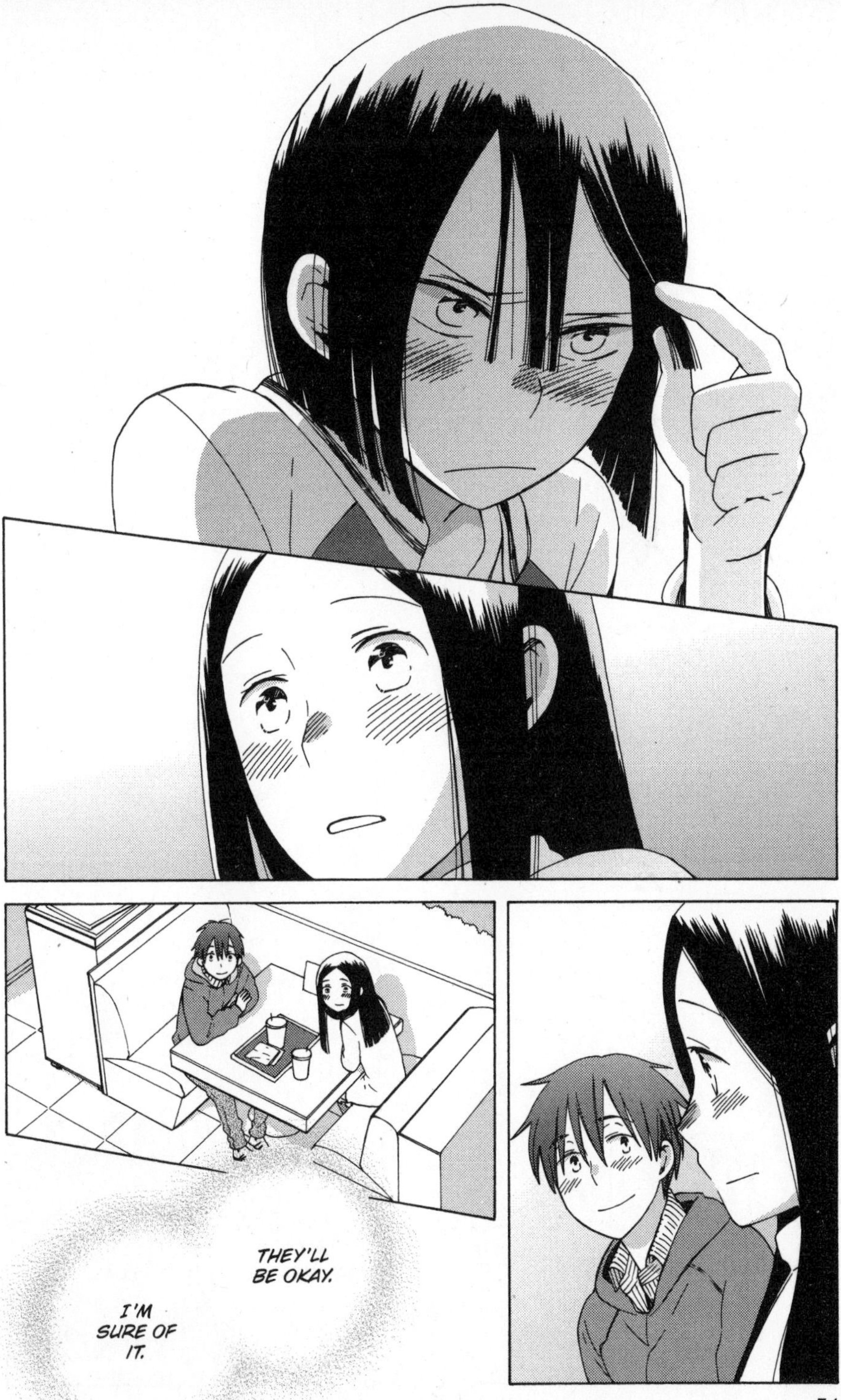
THEY'LL BE OKAY.
I'M SURE OF IT.

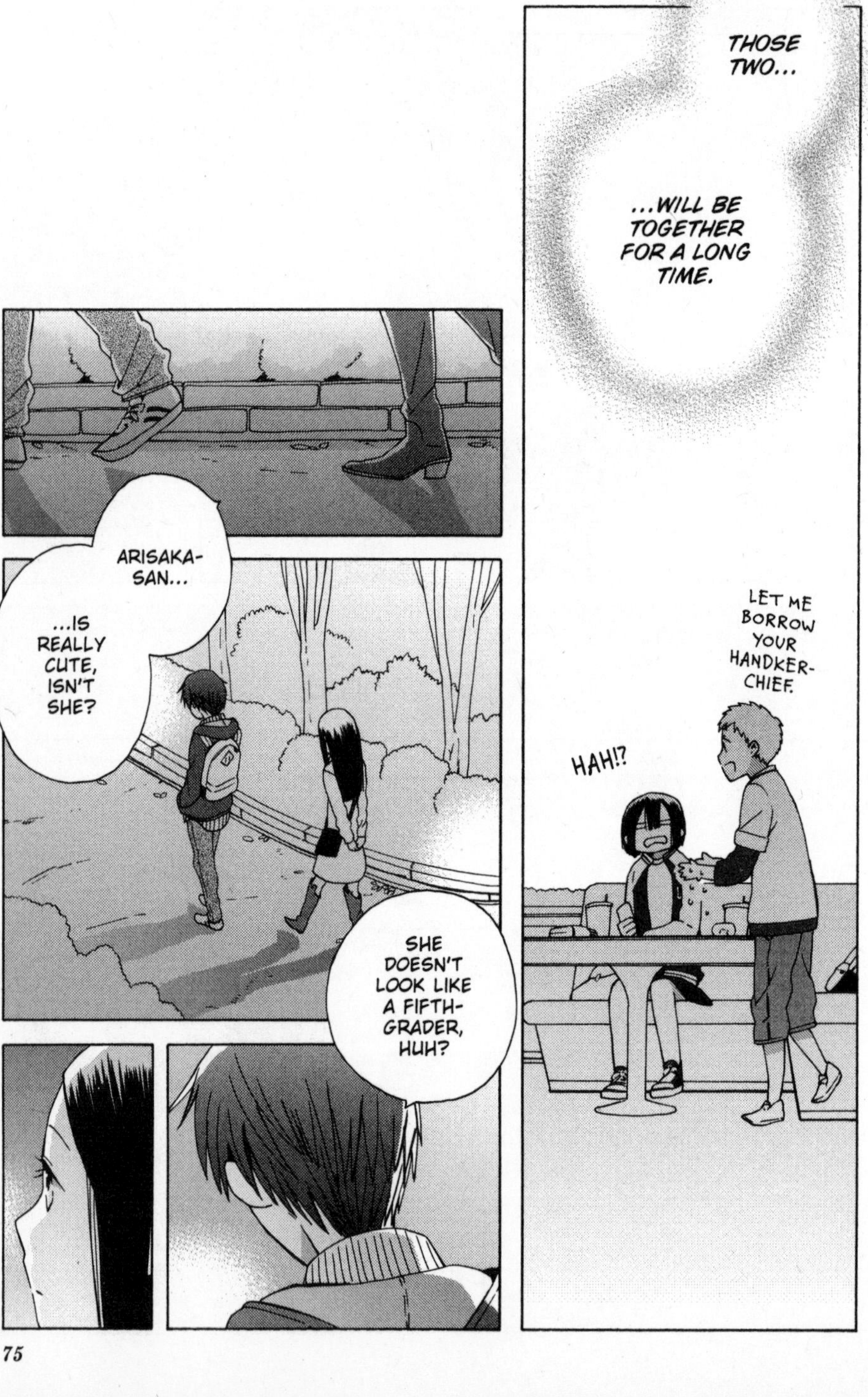
THOSE TWO...
...WILL BE TOGETHER FOR A LONG TIME.
LET ME BORROW YOUR HANDKER-CHIEF.
HAH!?
ARISAKA-SAN...
...IS REALLY CUTE, ISN'T SHE?
SHE DOESN'T LOOK LIKE A FIFTH-GRADER, HUH?

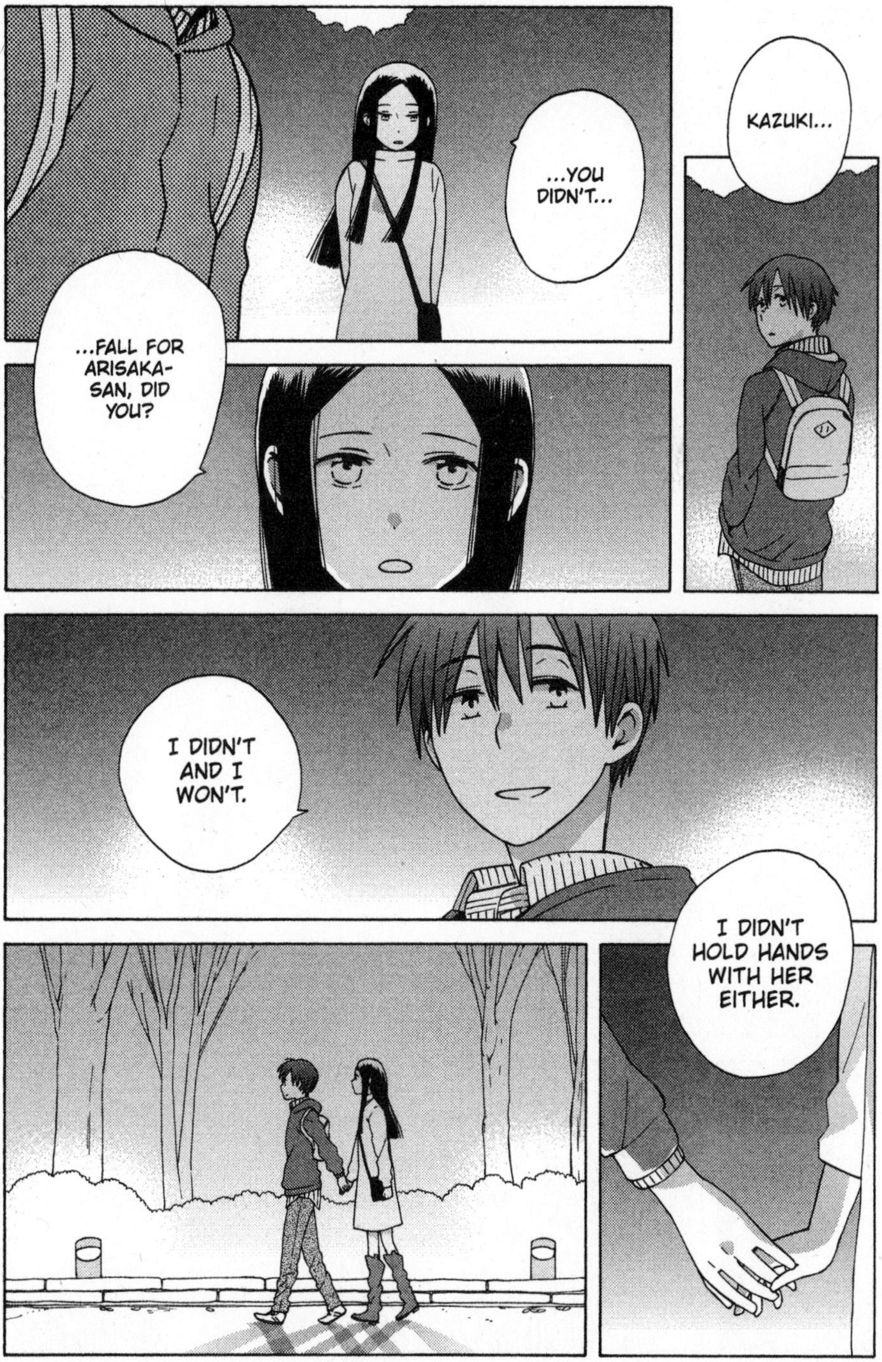
KAZUKI...
...YOU DIDN'T...
...FALL FOR ARISAKA-SAN, DID YOU?
I DIDN'T AND I WON'T.
I DIDN'T HOLD HANDS WITH HER EITHER.

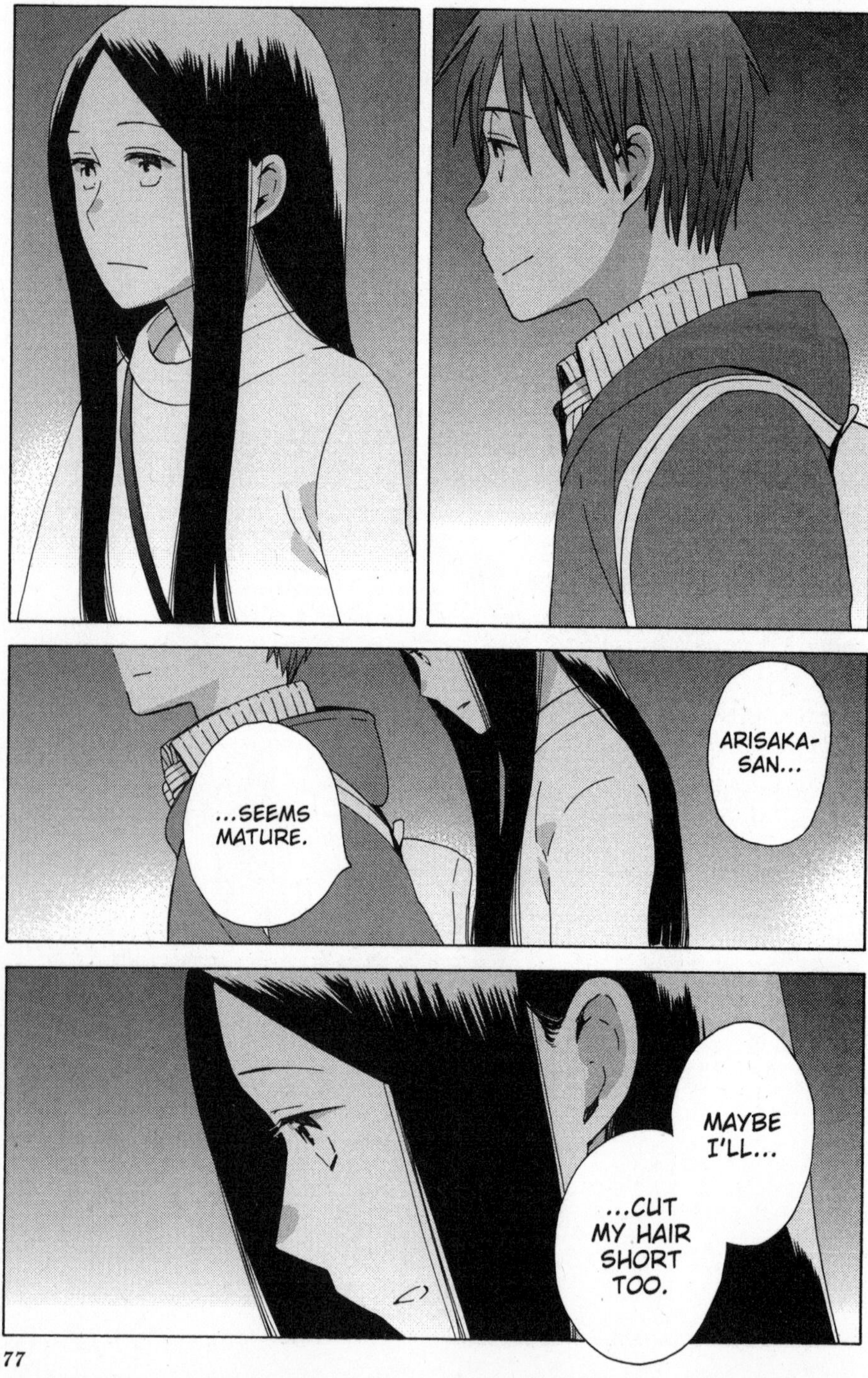
ARISAKA-SAN...
...SEEMS MATURE.
MAYBE I'LL...
...CUT MY HAIR SHORT TOO.

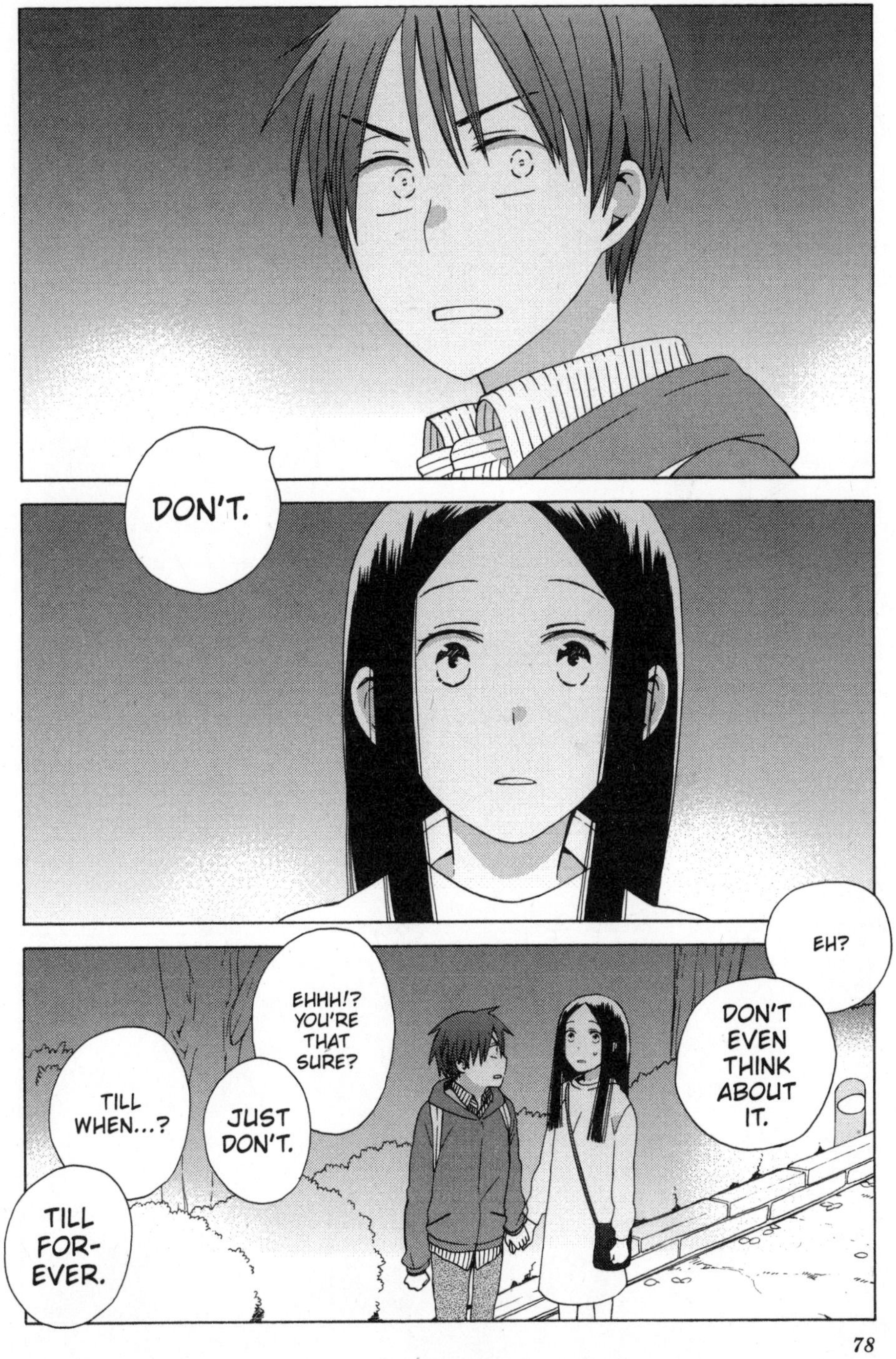
DON'T.
EH?
DON'T EVEN THINK ABOUT IT.
EHHH!? YOU'RE THAT SURE?
JUST DON'T.
TILL WHEN...?
TILL FOR-EVER.

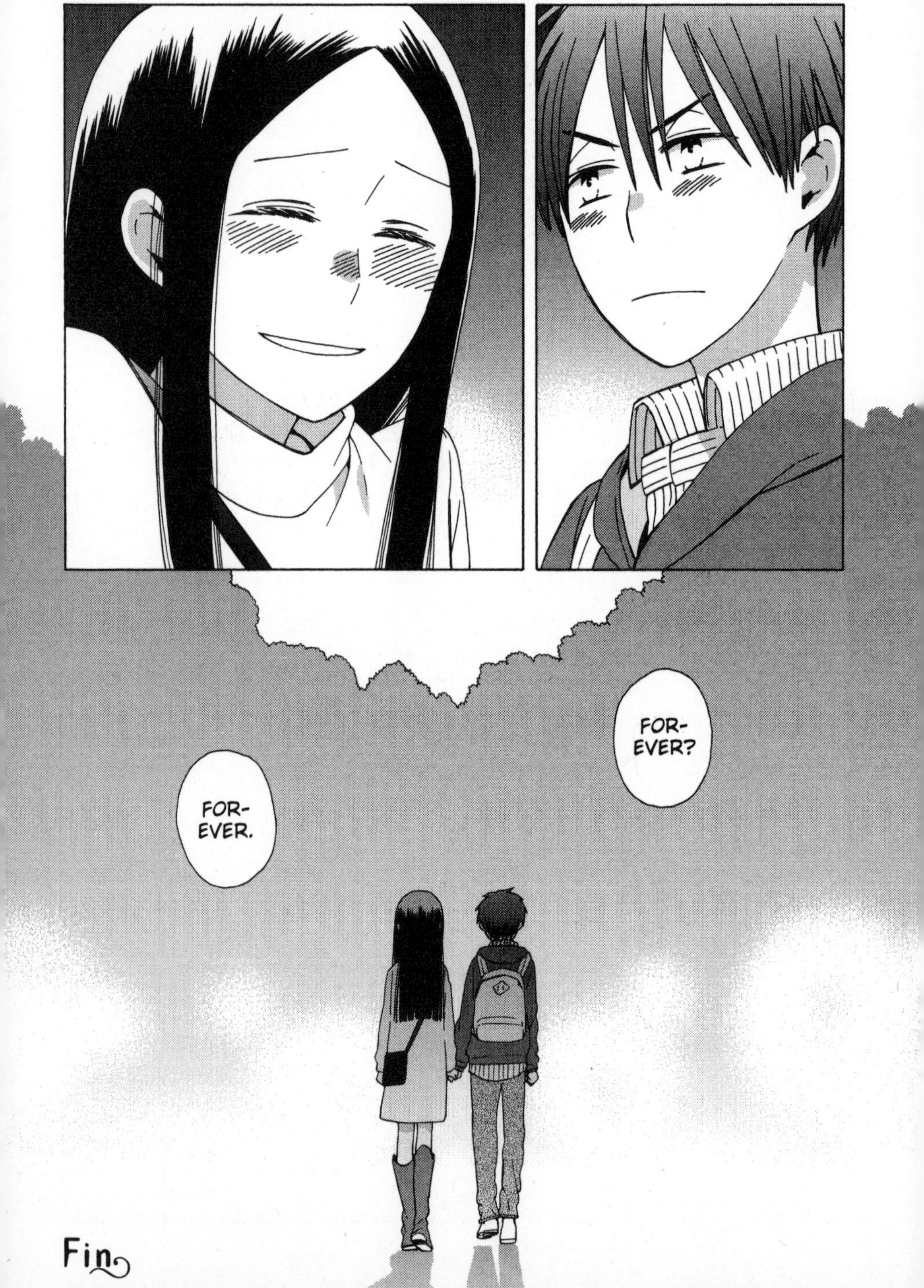
FOR-EVER?
FOR-EVER.
Fin

Love at Fourteen

Fuka Mizutani

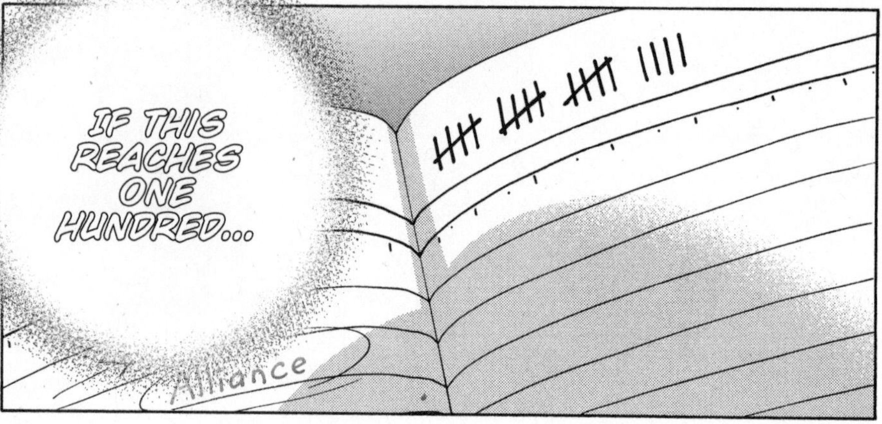
IF THIS REACHES ONE HUNDRED...
Alliance

Love at Fourteen

[Intermission 47]

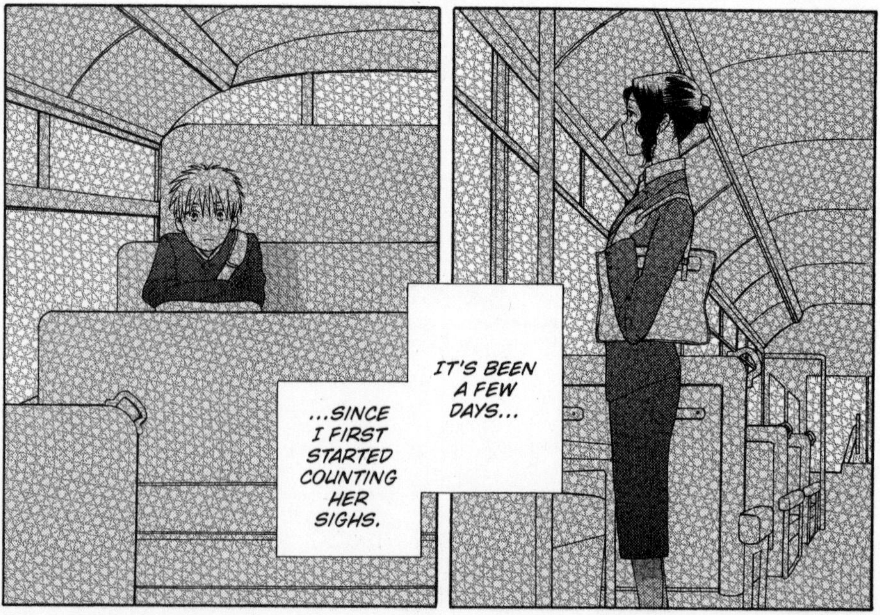
IT'S BEEN A FEW DAYS...
...SINCE I FIRST STARTED COUNTING HER SIGHS.

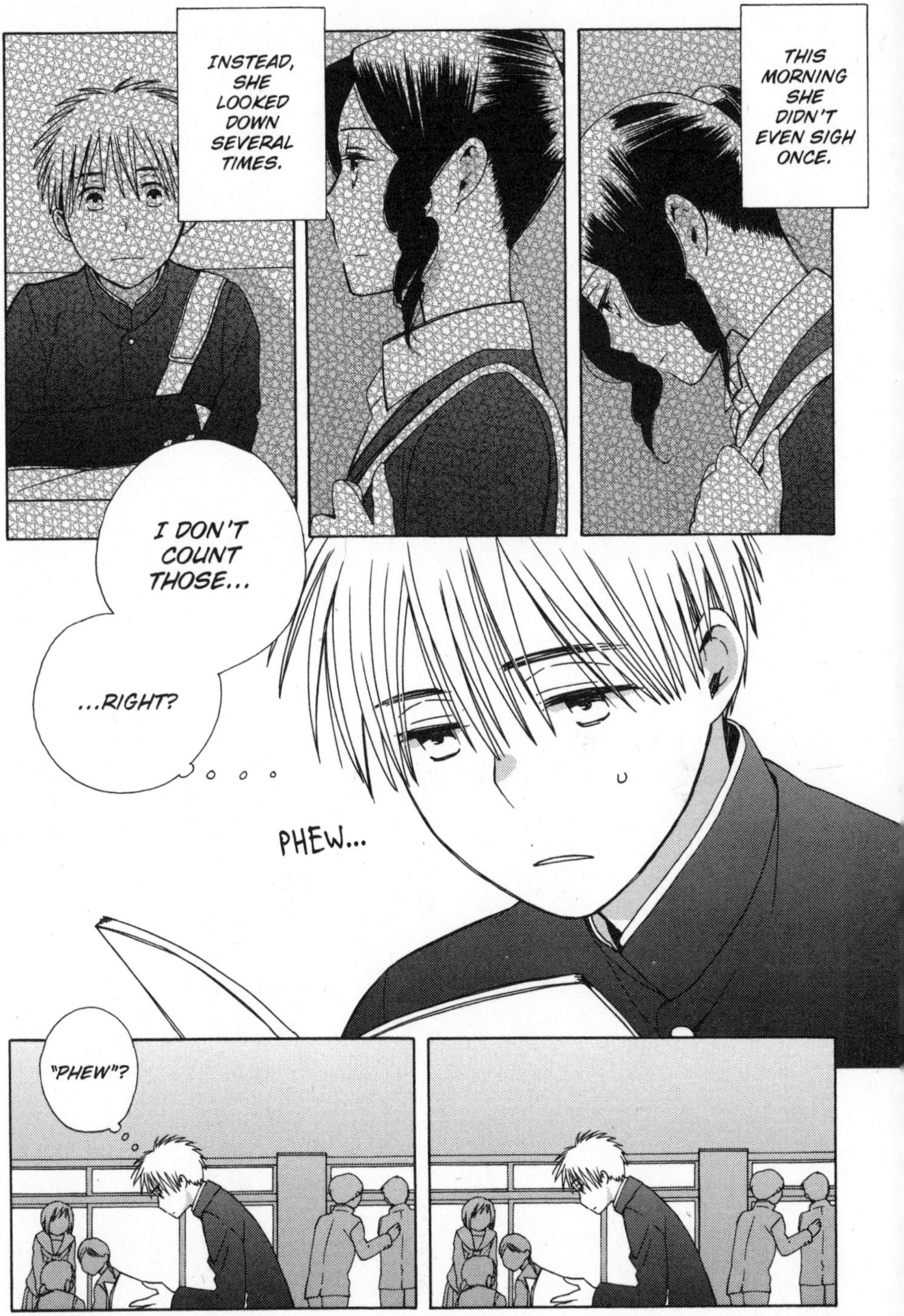
THIS MORNING SHE DIDN'T EVEN SIGH ONCE.
INSTEAD, SHE LOOKED DOWN SEVERAL TIMES.
I DON'T COUNT THOSE...
...RIGHT?
PHEW...
"PHEW"?

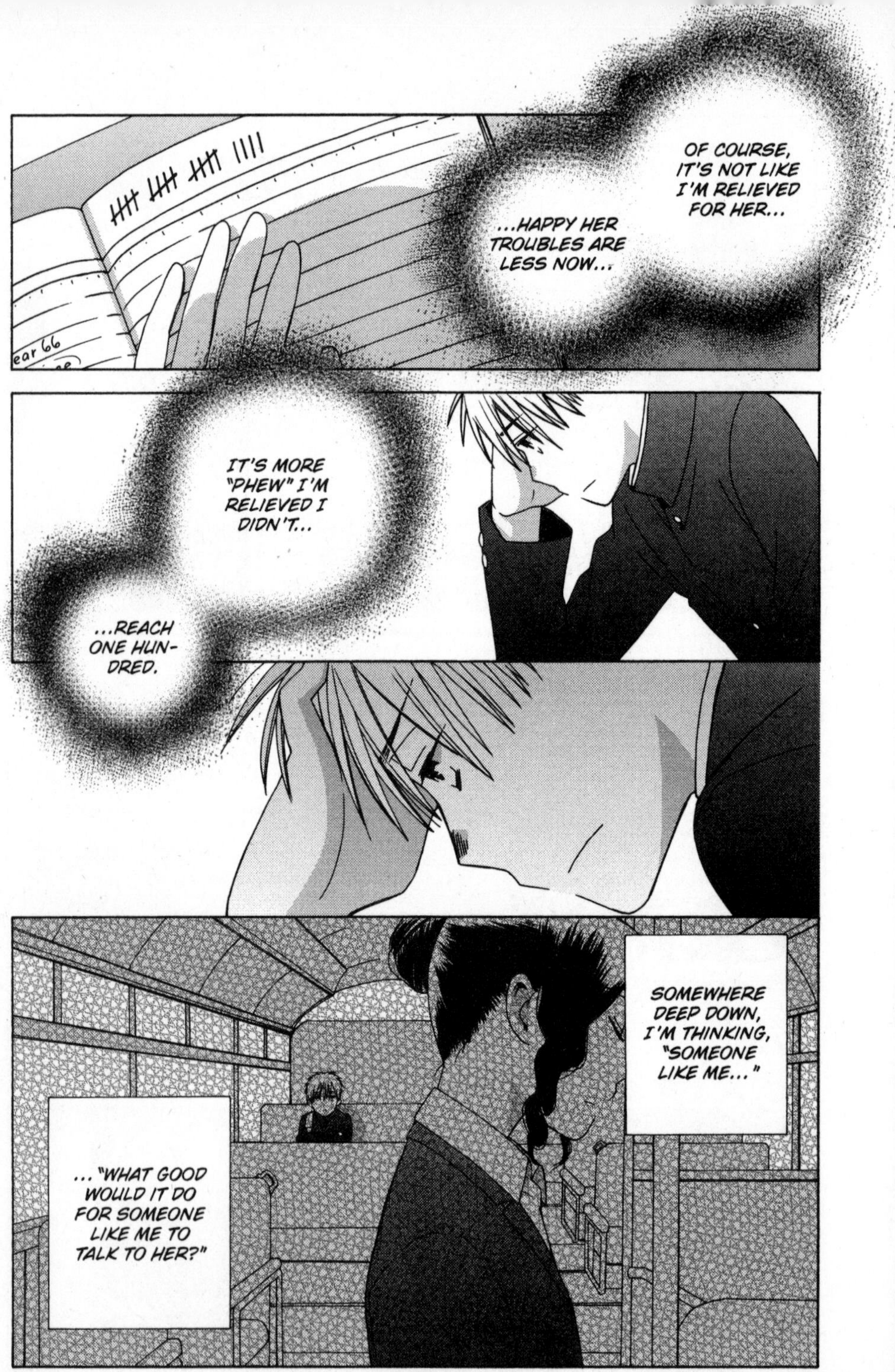
OF COURSE, IT'S NOT LIKE I'M RELIEVED FOR HER...
...HAPPY HER TROUBLES ARE LESS NOW...
IT'S MORE "PHEW" I'M RELIEVED I DIDN'T...
...REACH ONE HUNDRED.
SOMEWHERE DEEP DOWN, I'M THINKING, "SOMEONE LIKE ME..."
..."WHAT GOOD WOULD IT DO FOR SOMEONE LIKE ME TO TALK TO HER?"

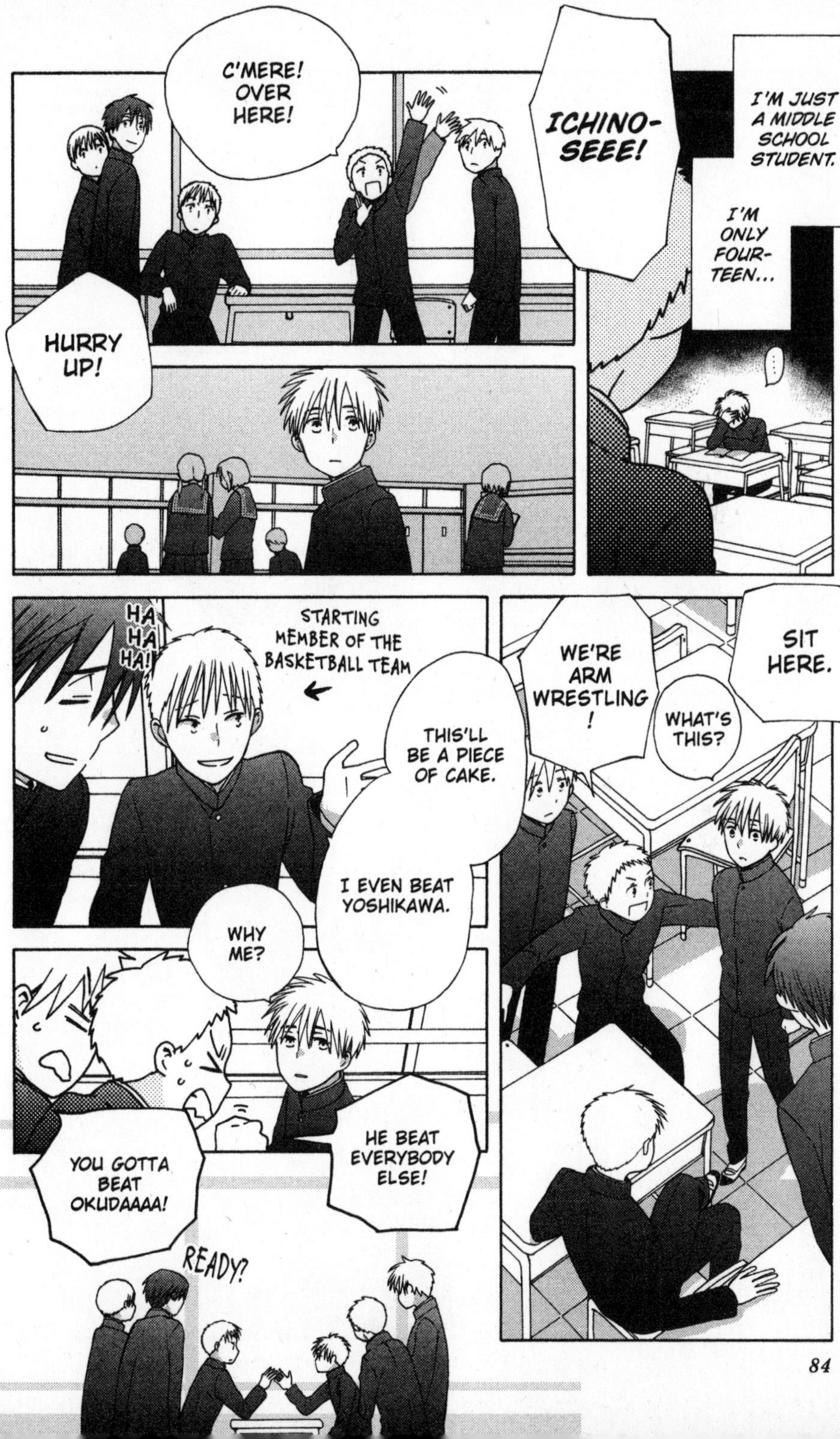
I'M JUST A MIDDLE SCHOOL STUDENT.
I'M ONLY FOURTEEN...
ICHINO-SEEE!
...
C'MERE! OVER HERE!
HURRY UP!
SIT HERE.
WHAT'S THIS?
WE'RE ARM WRESTLING!
STARTING MEMBER OF THE BASKETBALL TEAM
HA HA HA!
THIS'LL BE A PIECE OF CAKE.
I EVEN BEAT YOSHIKAWA.
WHY ME?
HE BEAT EVERYBODY ELSE!
YOU GOTTA BEAT OKUDAAAA!
READY?

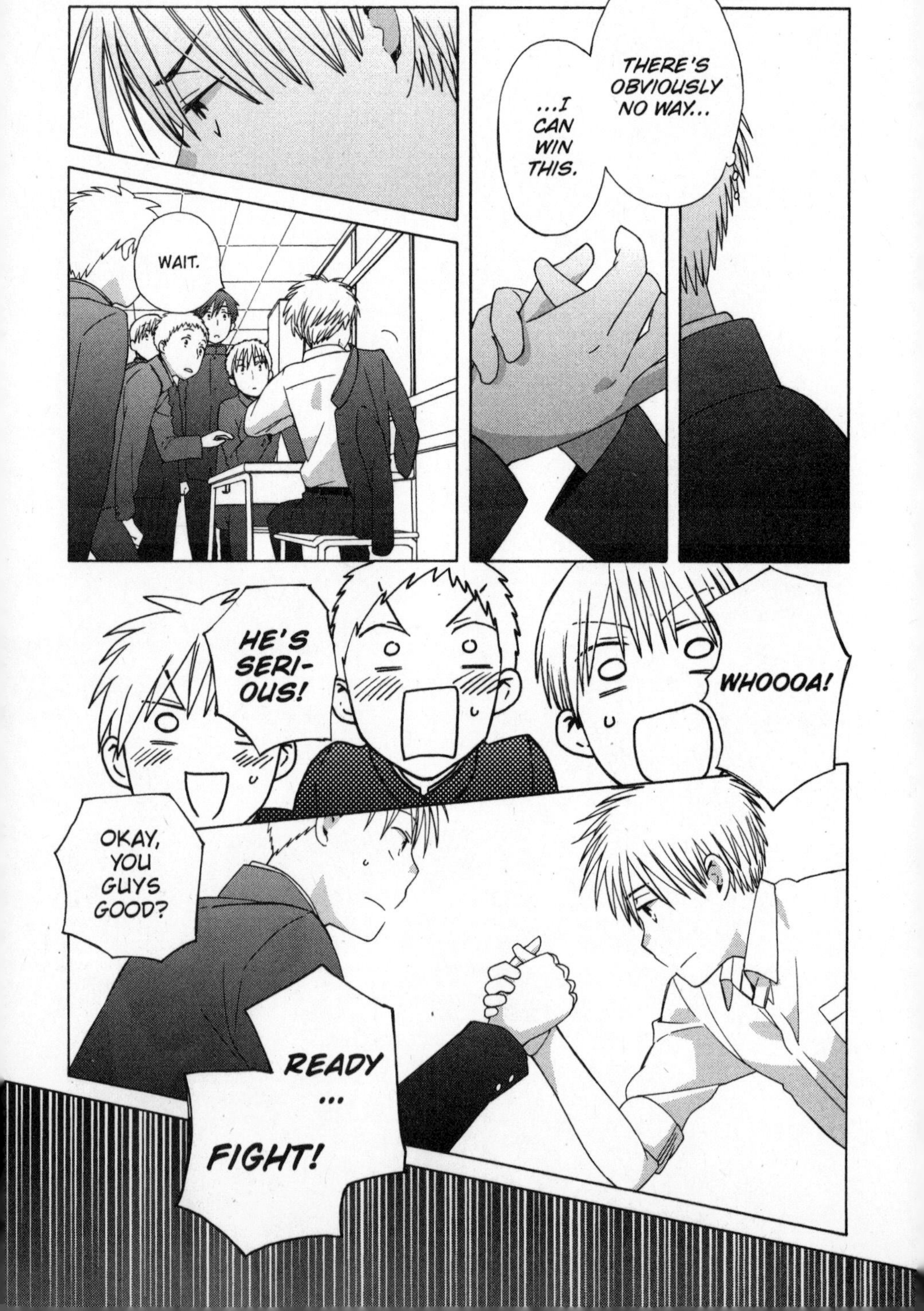
THERE'S OBVIOUSLY NO WAY...
...I CAN WIN THIS.
WAIT.
WHOOOA!
HE'S SERI-OUS!
OKAY, YOU GUYS GOOD?
READY ...
FIGHT!

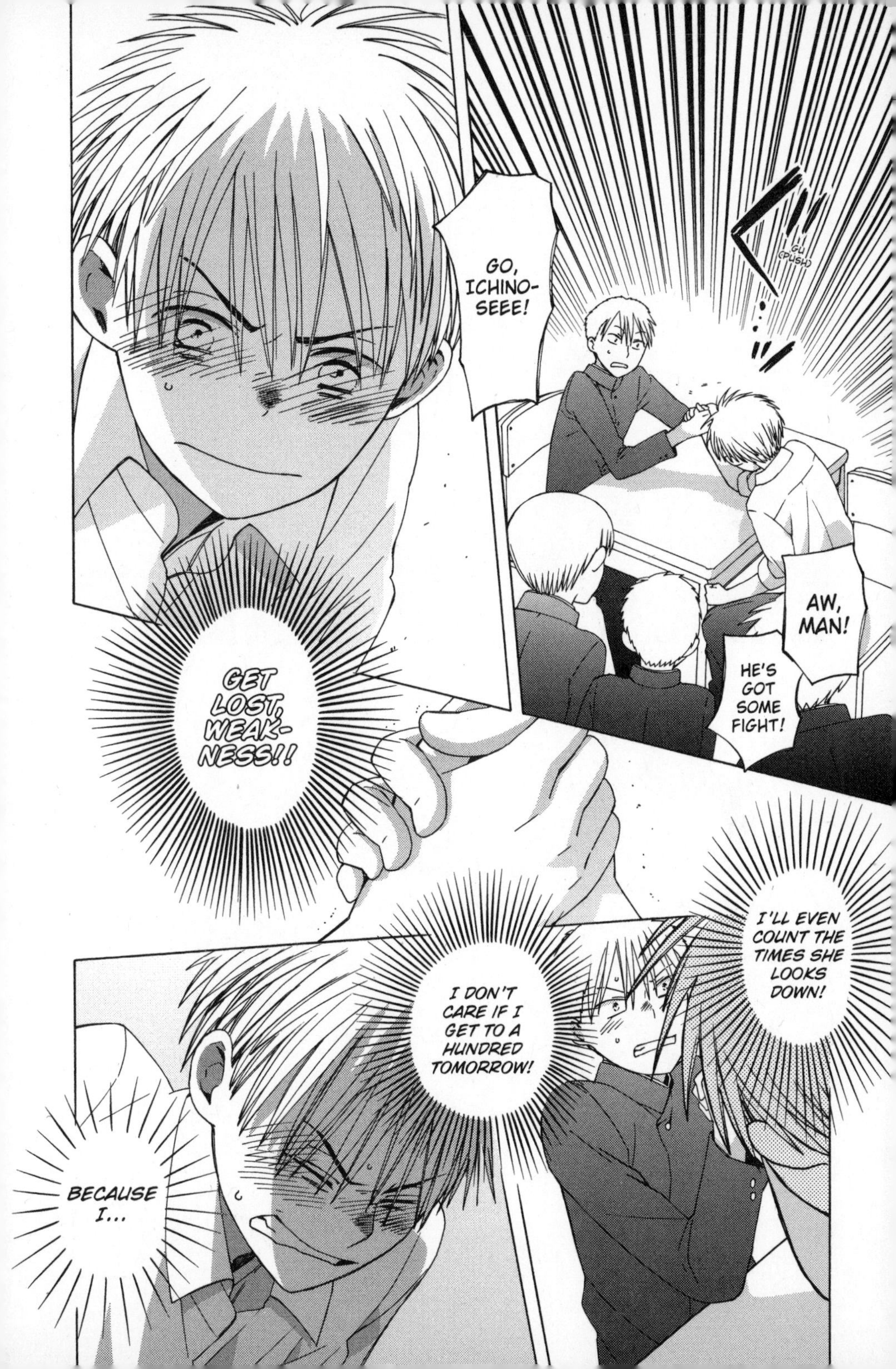
GU (PUSH)
GO, ICHINO-SEEE!
AW, MAN!
HE'S GOT SOME FIGHT!
GET LOST, WEAK-NESS!!
I'LL EVEN COUNT THE TIMES SHE LOOKS DOWN!
I DON'T CARE IF I GET TO A HUNDRED TOMORROW!
BECAUSE I...

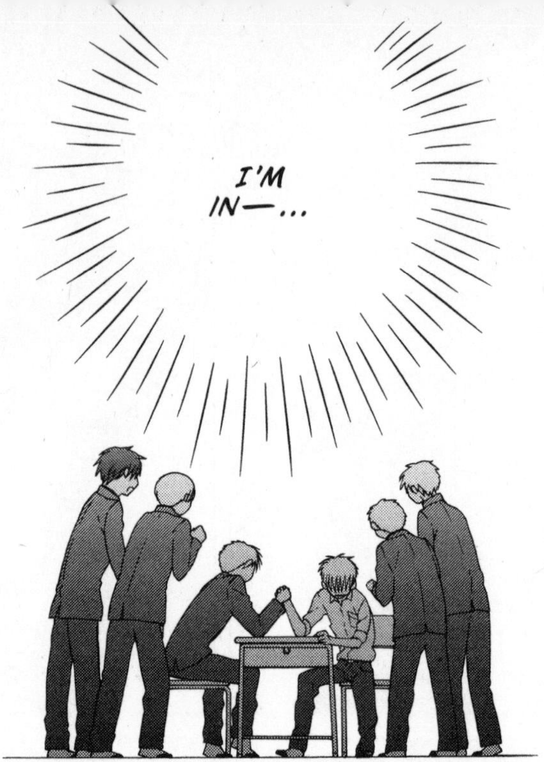
I'M IN—...

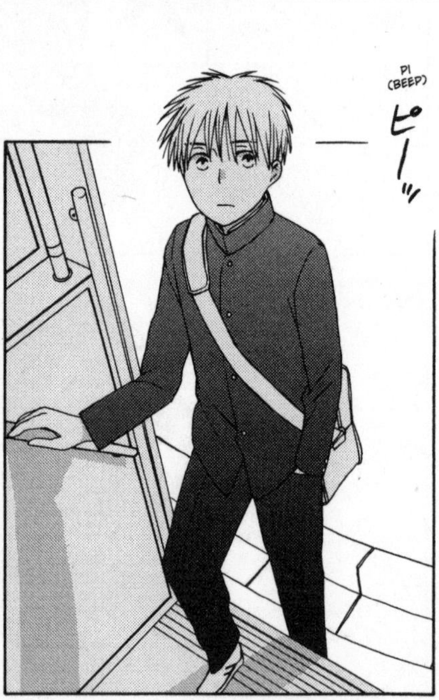
PI (BEEP)
ピーッ

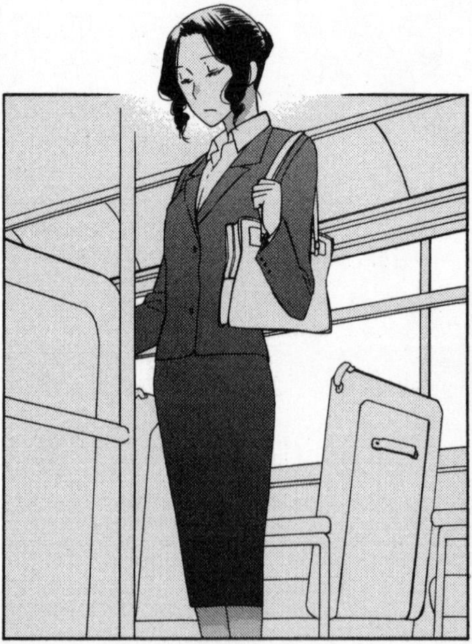

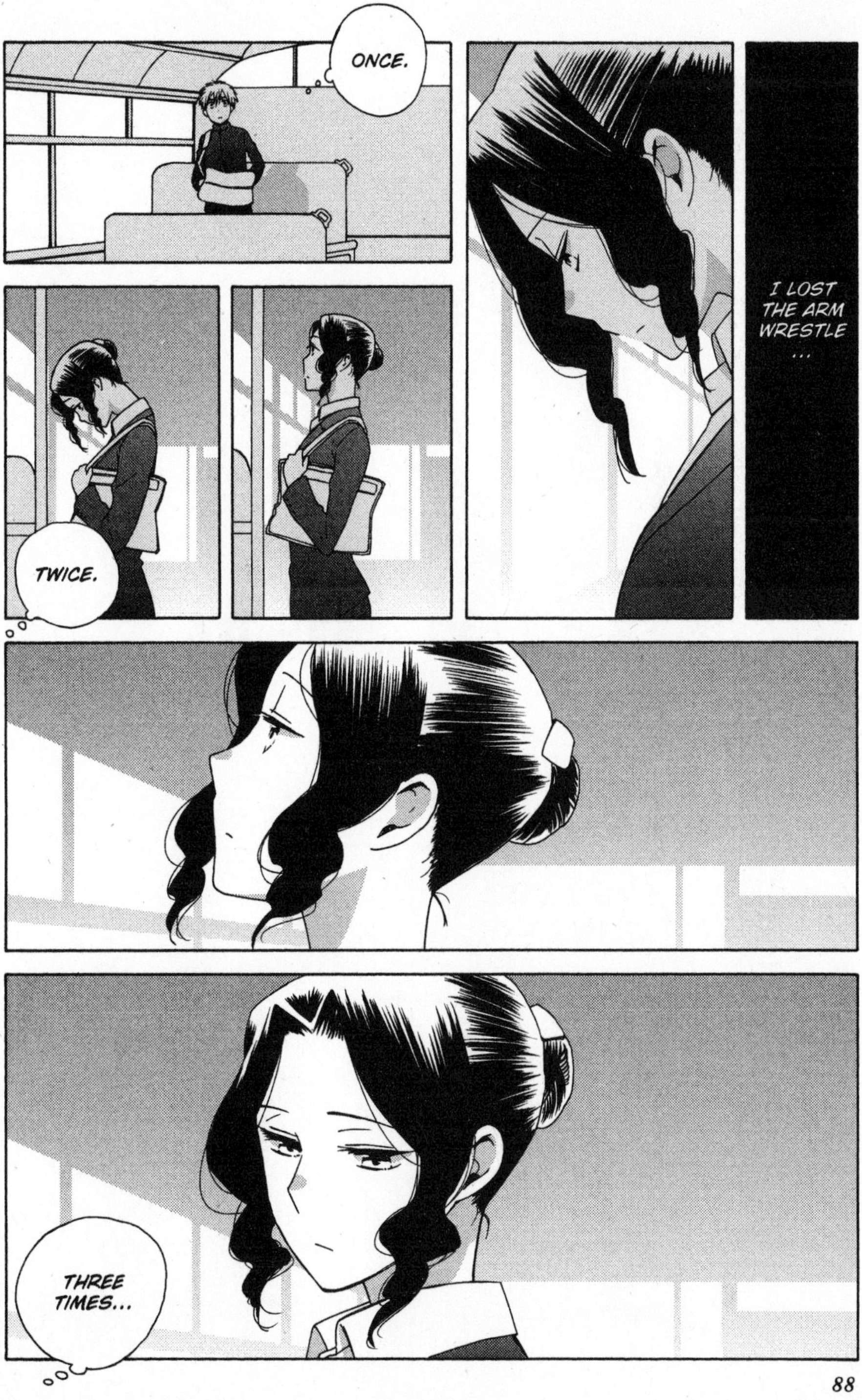
I LOST THE ARM WRESTLE ...
ONCE.
TWICE.
THREE TIMES...

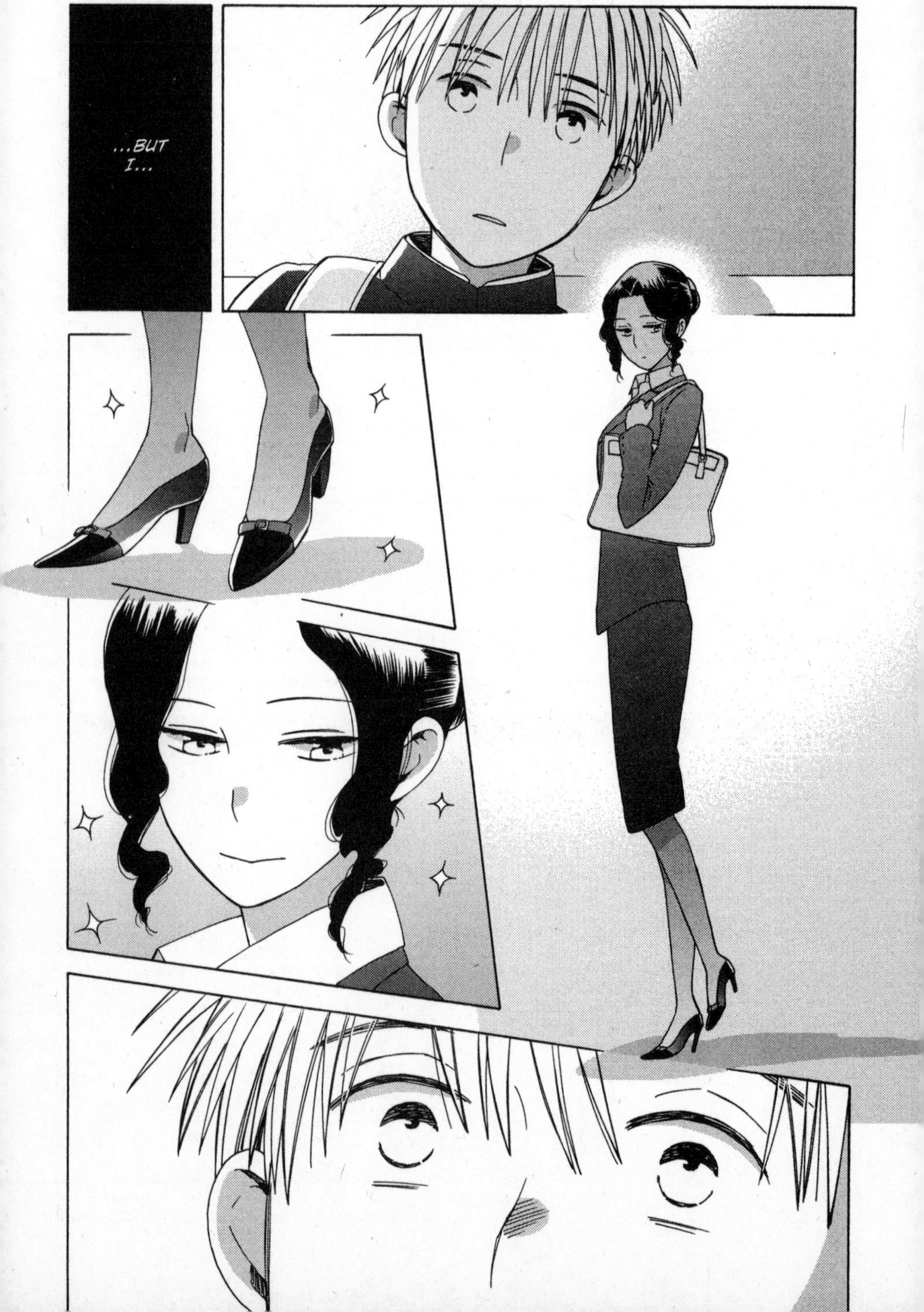
...BUT I...

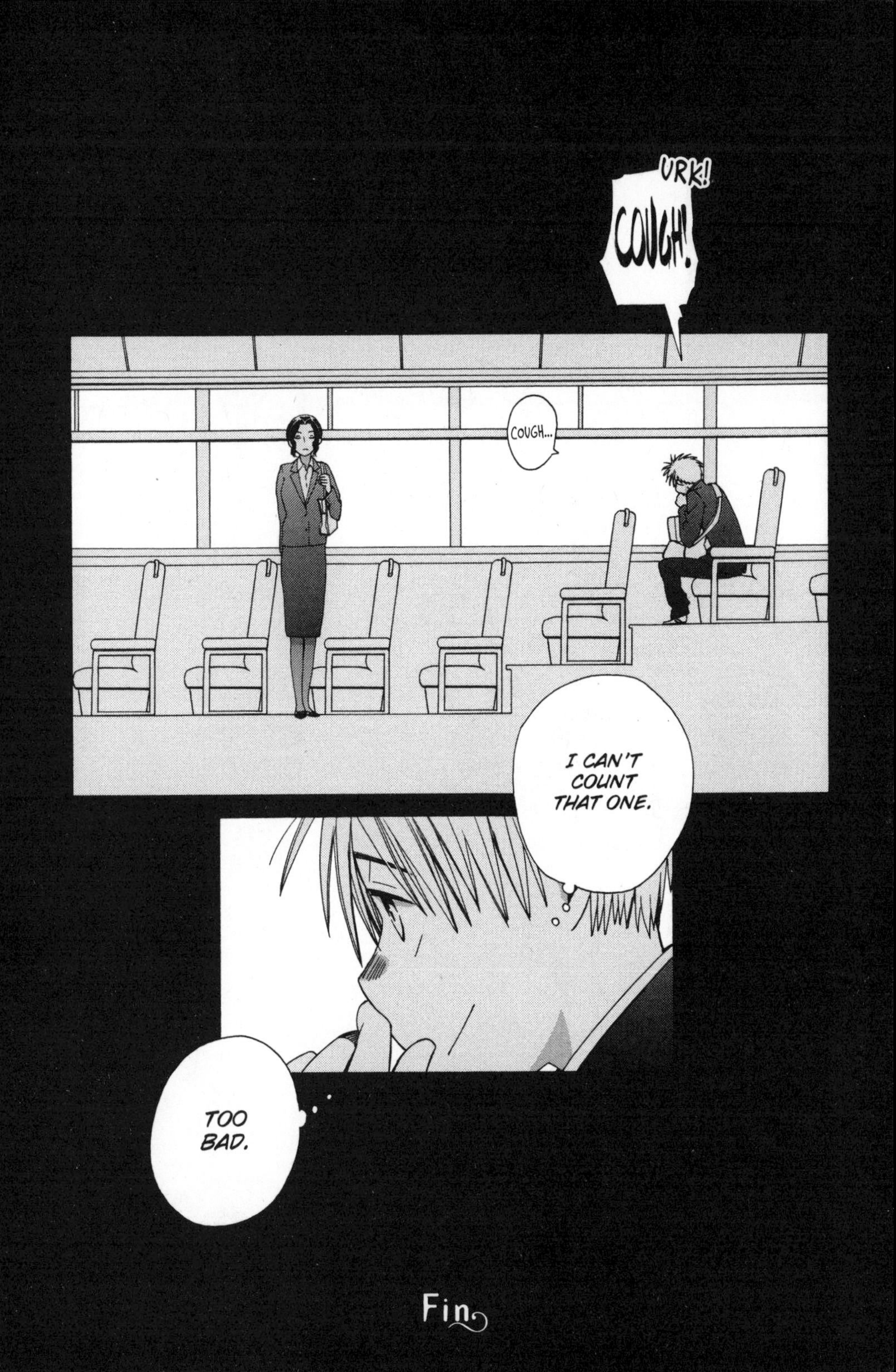
URK!
COUGH!
COUGH...
I CAN'T COUNT THAT ONE.
TOO BAD.

Fin

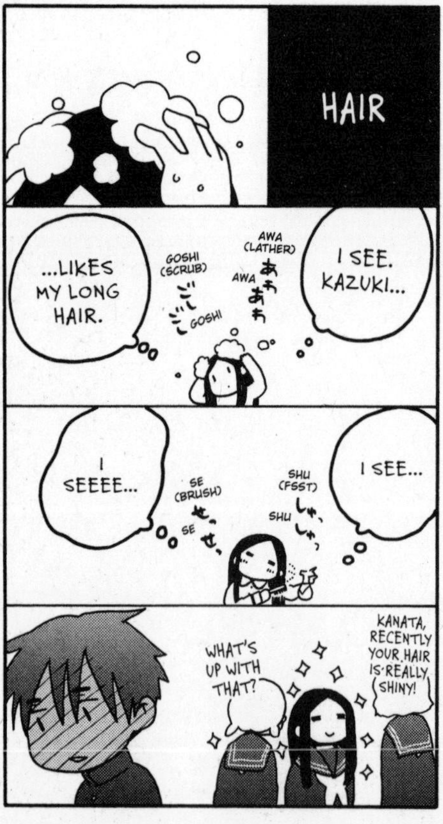
HAIR
I SEE. KAZUKI...
AWA (LATHER)
AWA
GOSHI (SCRUB)
GOSHI
...LIKES MY LONG HAIR.
I SEE...
SHU (FSST)
SHU
SE (BRUSH)
SE
I SEEEE...
KANATA, RECENTLY YOUR HAIR IS REALLY SHINY!
WHAT'S UP WITH THAT?

Love at Fourteen

Fuka Mizutani

Love ♡ at Fourteen

[Chapter 36]

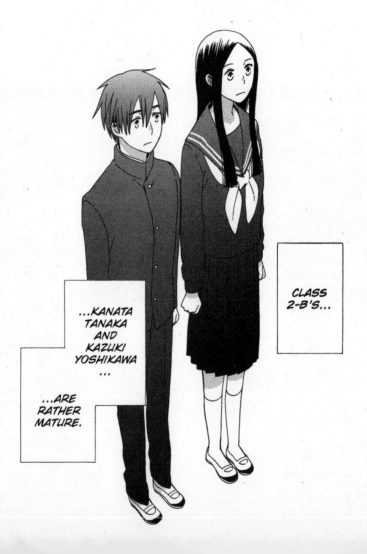

...KANATA
TANAKA
AND
KAZUKI
YOSHIKAWA
...

...ARE
RATHER
MATURE.

CLASS
2-B'S...

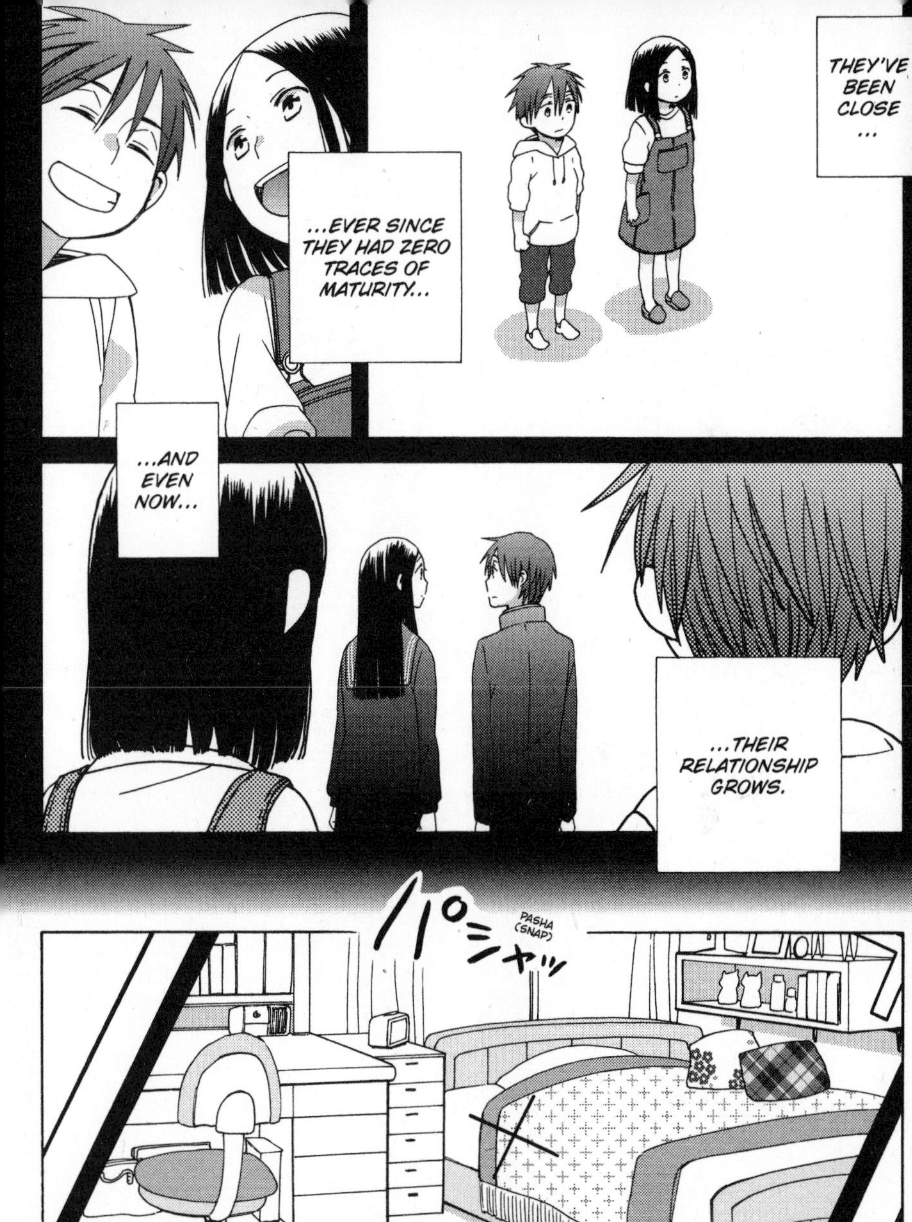
THEY'VE BEEN CLOSE ...
...EVER SINCE THEY HAD ZERO TRACES OF MATURITY...
...AND EVEN NOW...
...THEIR RELATIONSHIP GROWS.
パシャッ
PASHA (SNAP)

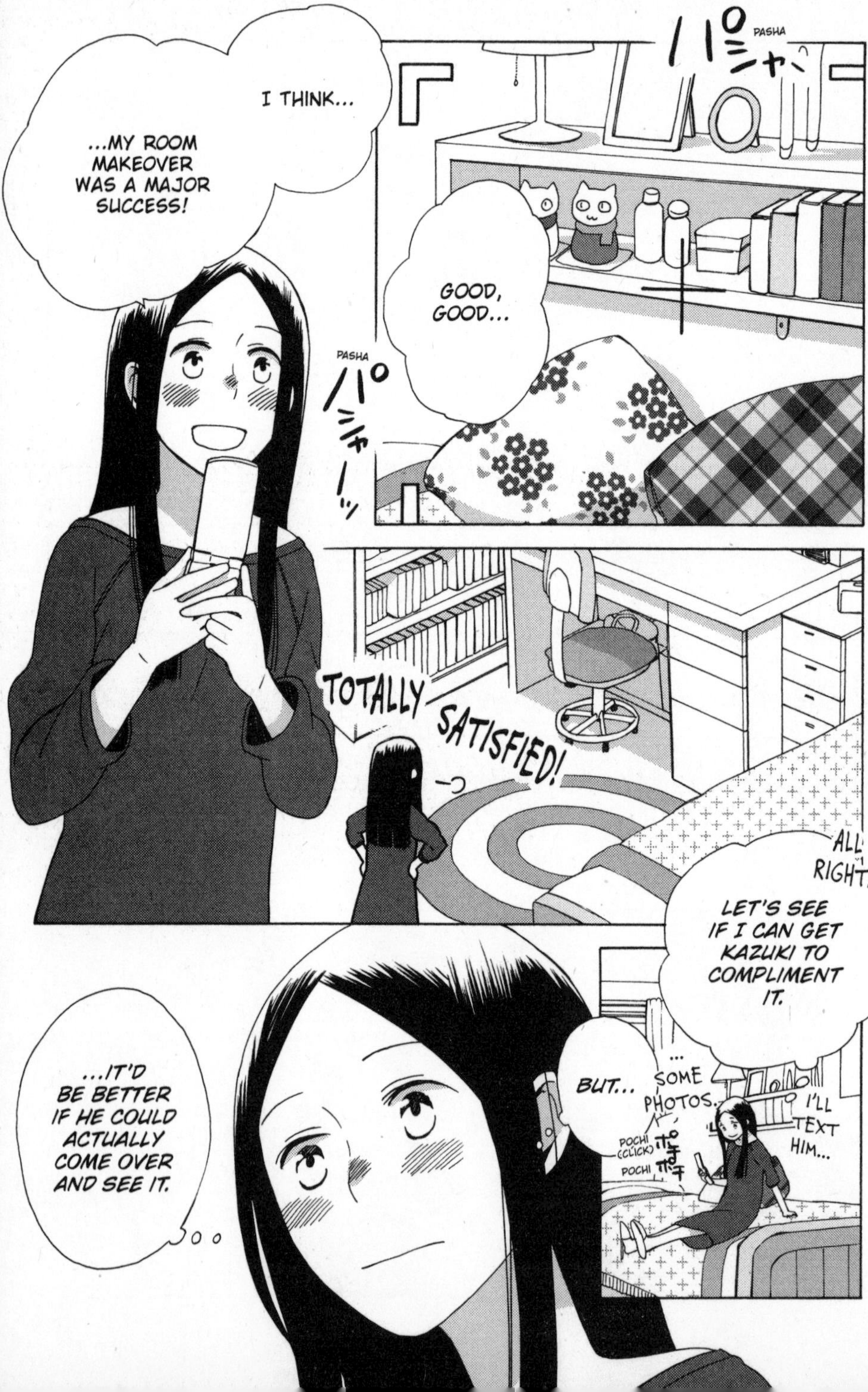
PASHA
GOOD, GOOD...
PASHA
TOTALLY SATISFIED!
I THINK...
...MY ROOM MAKEOVER WAS A MAJOR SUCCESS!
ALL RIGHT!
LET'S SEE IF I CAN GET KAZUKI TO COMPLIMENT IT.
I'LL TEXT HIM...
...SOME PHOTOS...
POCHI (CLICK)
POCHI
BUT...
...IT'D BE BETTER IF HE COULD ACTUALLY COME OVER AND SEE IT.

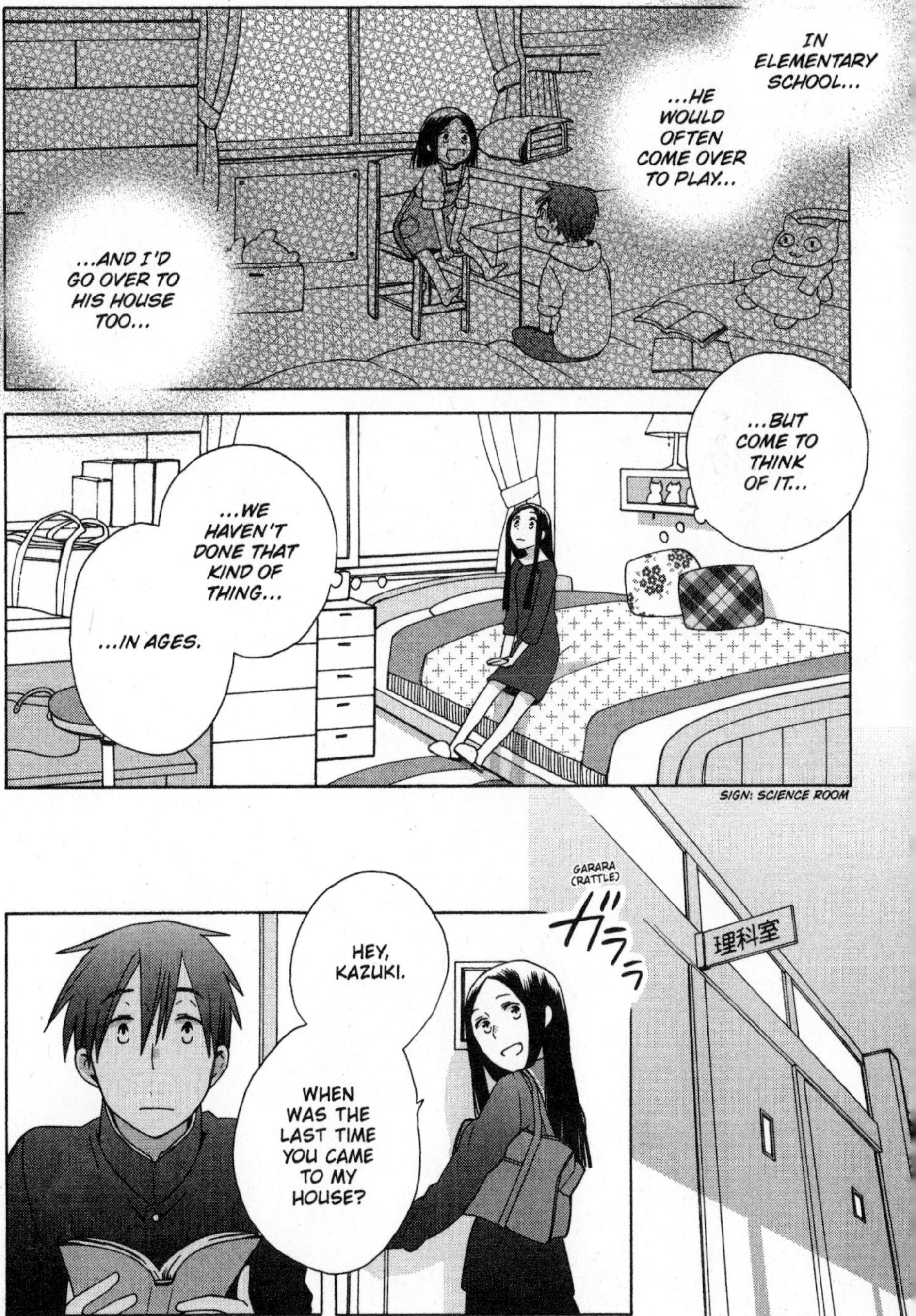
IN ELEMENTARY SCHOOL...
...HE WOULD OFTEN COME OVER TO PLAY...
...AND I'D GO OVER TO HIS HOUSE TOO...
...BUT COME TO THINK OF IT...
...WE HAVEN'T DONE THAT KIND OF THING...
...IN AGES.
SIGN: SCIENCE ROOM
GARARA (RATTLE)
ガララ
理科室
HEY, KAZUKI.
WHEN WAS THE LAST TIME YOU CAME TO MY HOUSE?

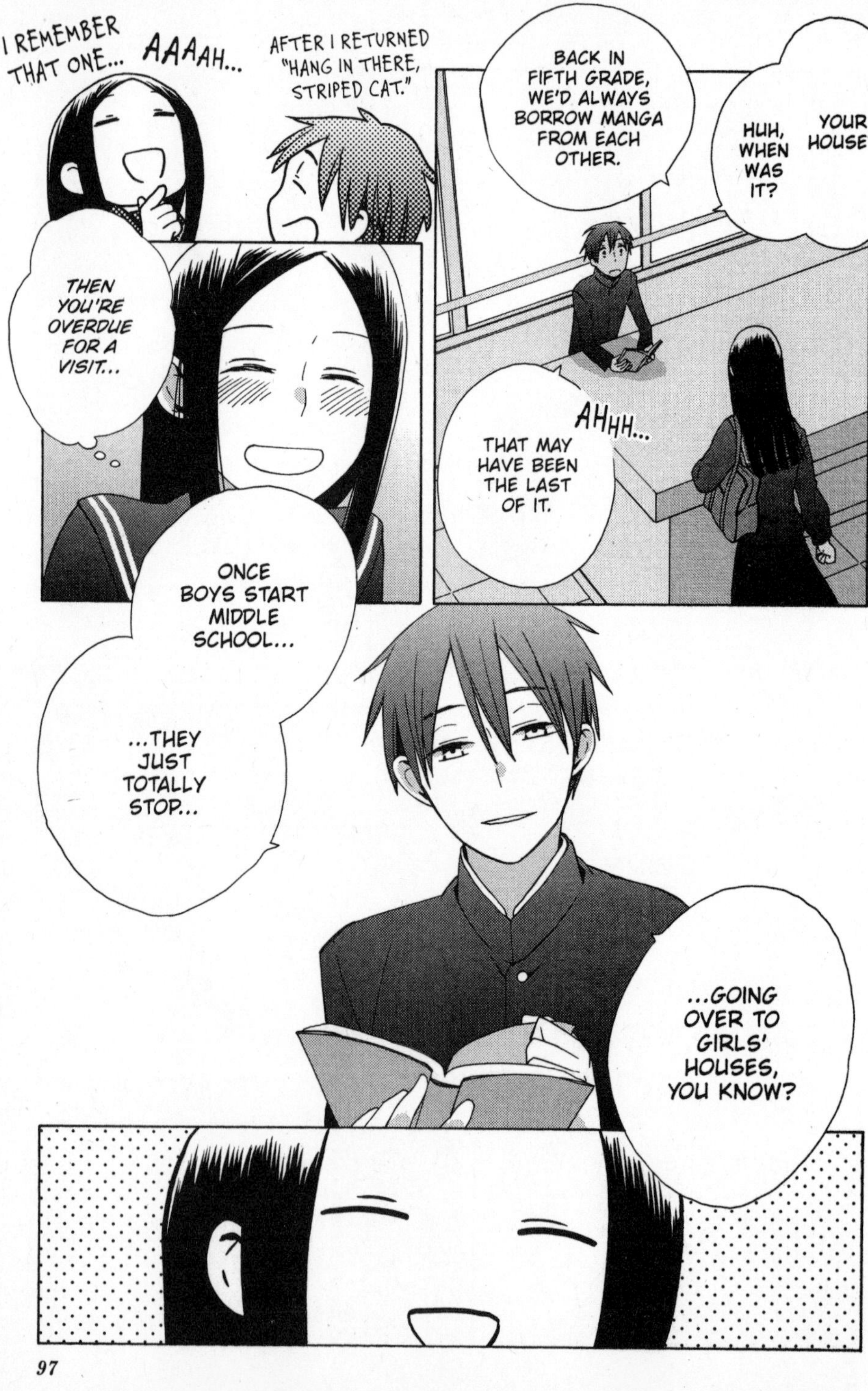
YOUR HOUSE? HUH, WHEN WAS IT?
BACK IN FIFTH GRADE, WE'D ALWAYS BORROW MANGA FROM EACH OTHER.
AHHH...
THAT MAY HAVE BEEN THE LAST OF IT.
AFTER I RETURNED "HANG IN THERE, STRIPED CAT."
I REMEMBER THAT ONE...
AAAAH...
THEN YOU'RE OVERDUE FOR A VISIT...
ONCE BOYS START MIDDLE SCHOOL...
...THEY JUST TOTALLY STOP...
...GOING OVER TO GIRLS' HOUSES, YOU KNOW?

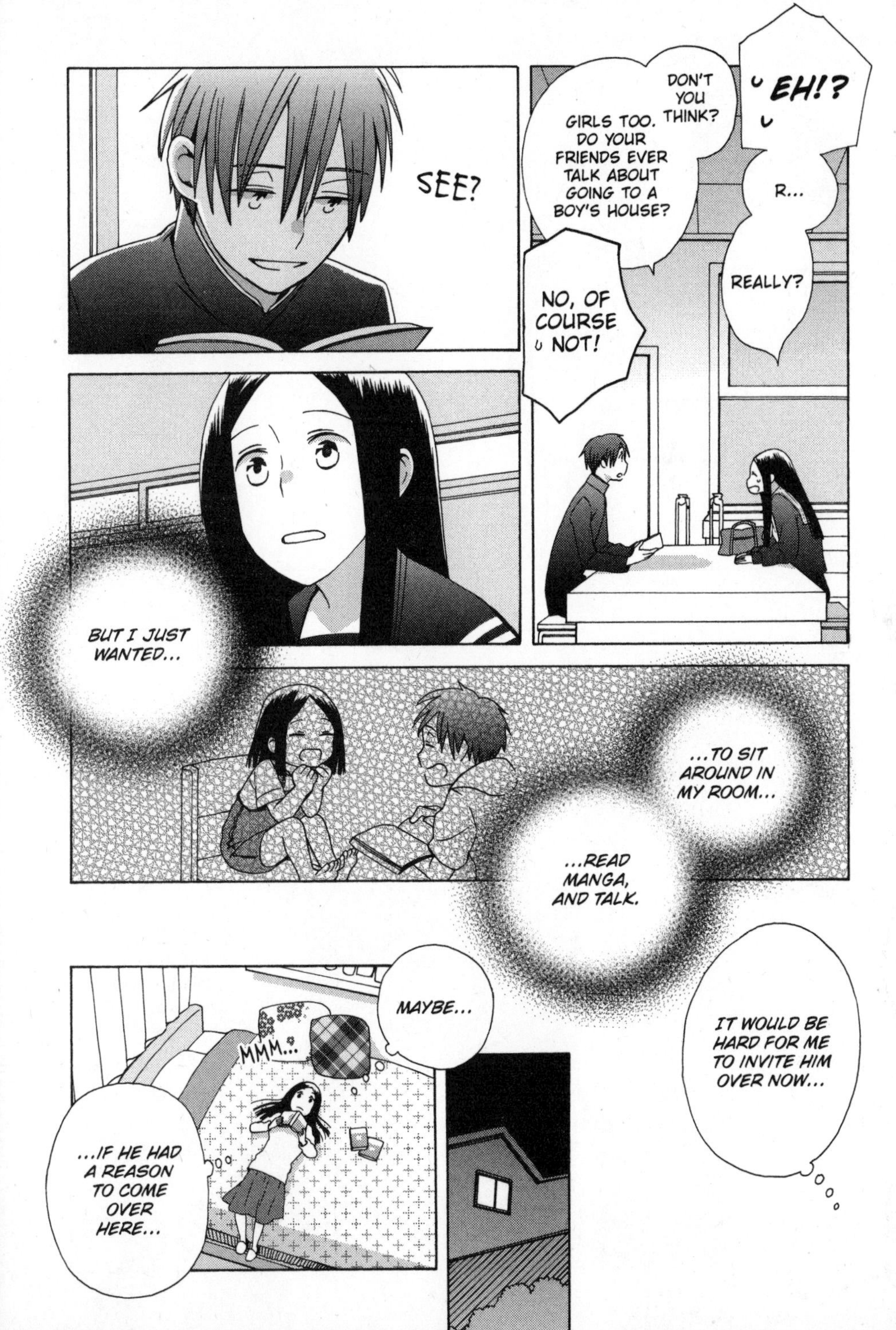
EH!?
GIRLS TOO. DON'T YOU THINK? DO YOUR FRIENDS EVER TALK ABOUT GOING TO A BOY'S HOUSE?
R...
REALLY?
NO, OF COURSE NOT!
SEE?
BUT I JUST WANTED...
...TO SIT AROUND IN MY ROOM...
...READ MANGA, AND TALK.
IT WOULD BE HARD FOR ME TO INVITE HIM OVER NOW...
MAYBE...
MMM...
...IF HE HAD A REASON TO COME OVER HERE...

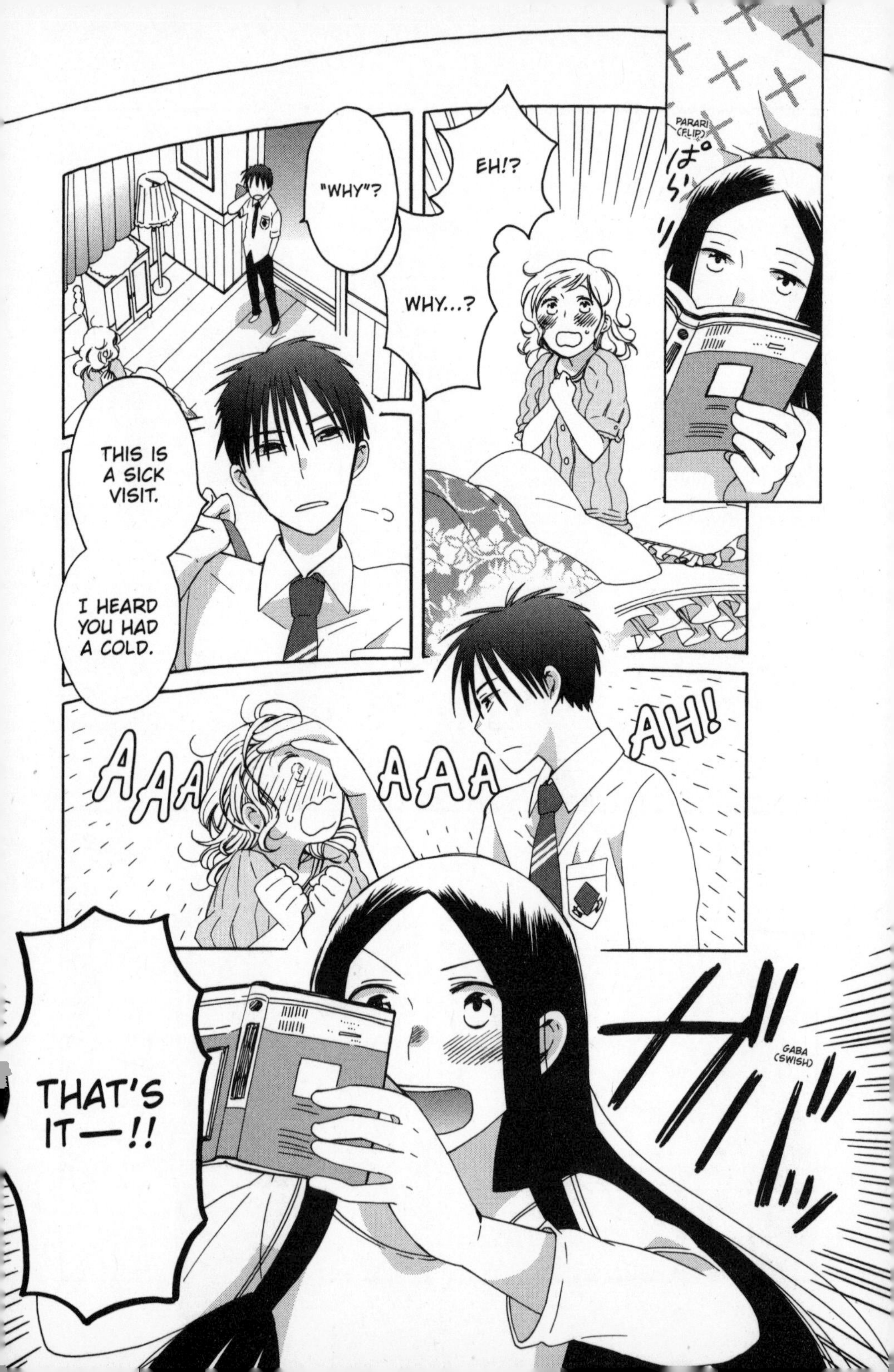

PARARI (FLIP)
ぱらり
EH!?
WHY...?
"WHY"?
THIS IS A SICK VISIT.
I HEARD YOU HAD A COLD.
AAAAAAAH!
GABA (SWISH)
ガバッ
THAT'S IT—!!

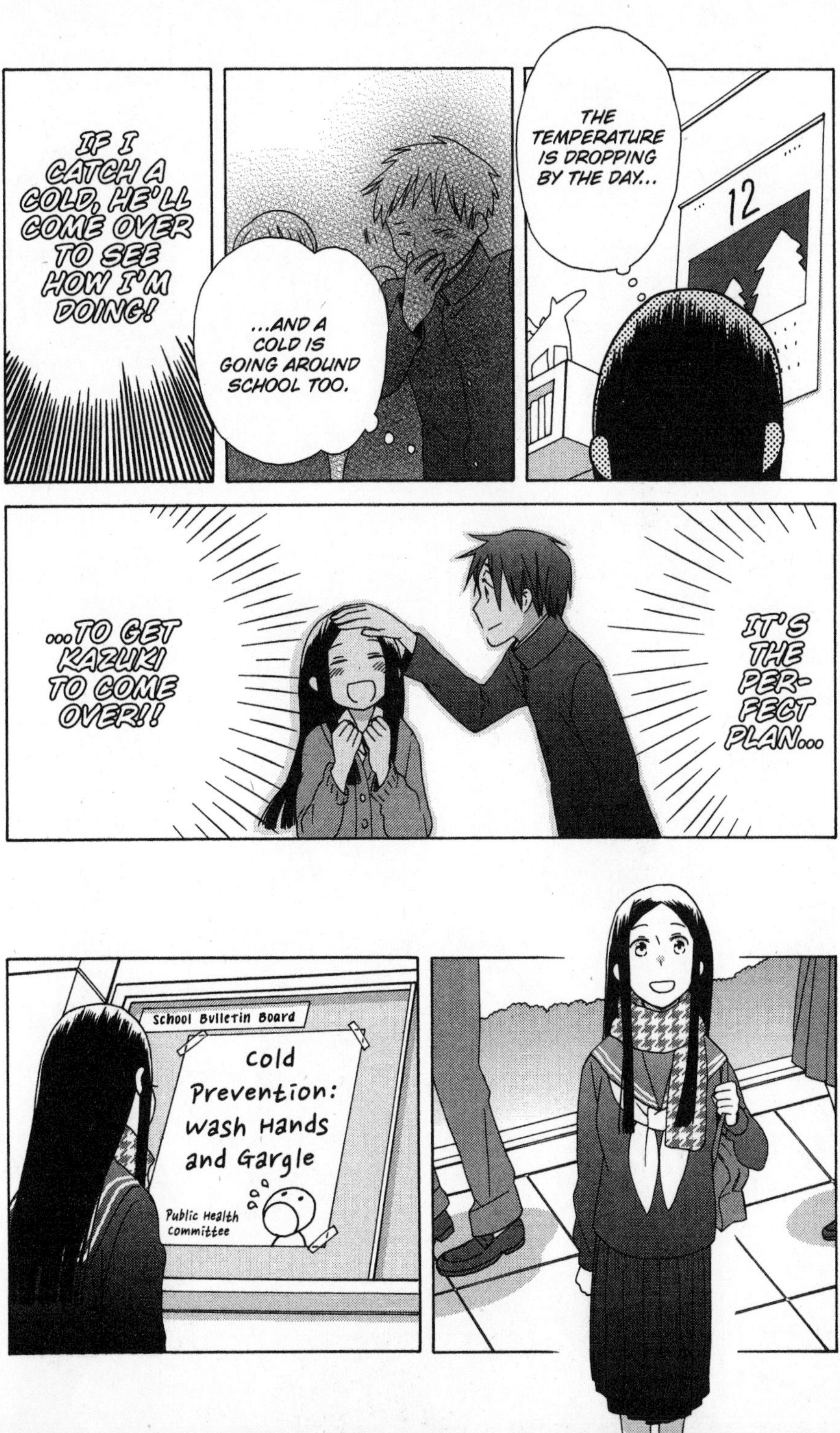
THE TEMPERATURE IS DROPPING BY THE DAY...
12
...AND A COLD IS GOING AROUND SCHOOL TOO.
IF I CATCH A COLD, HE'LL COME OVER TO SEE HOW I'M DOING!
IT'S THE PERFECT PLAN...
...TO GET KAZUKI TO COME OVER!!
School Bulletin Board
Cold Prevention: Wash Hands and Gargle
Public Health Committee

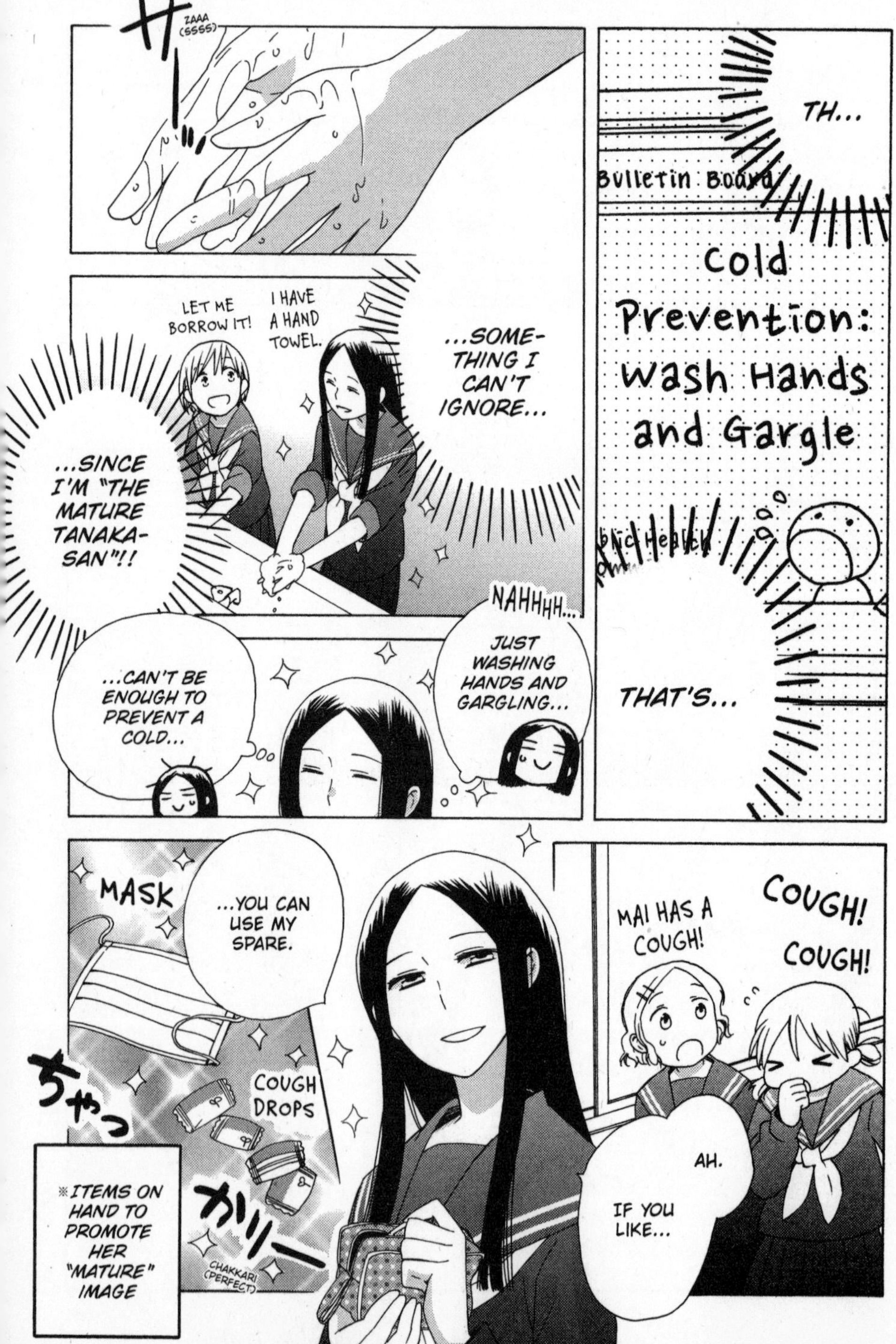
TH...
Bulletin Board
Cold Prevention: Wash Hands and Gargle
THAT'S...
ZAAA (SSSS)
...SOMETHING I CAN'T IGNORE...
I HAVE A HAND TOWEL.
LET ME BORROW IT!
...SINCE I'M "THE MATURE TANAKA-SAN"!!
NAHHHH...
JUST WASHING HANDS AND GARGLING...
...CAN'T BE ENOUGH TO PREVENT A COLD...
COUGH!
COUGH!
MAI HAS A COUGH!
AH.
IF YOU LIKE...
...YOU CAN USE MY SPARE.
MASK
COUGH DROPS
CHAKKARI (PERFECT)
※ITEMS ON HAND TO PROMOTE HER "MATURE" IMAGE

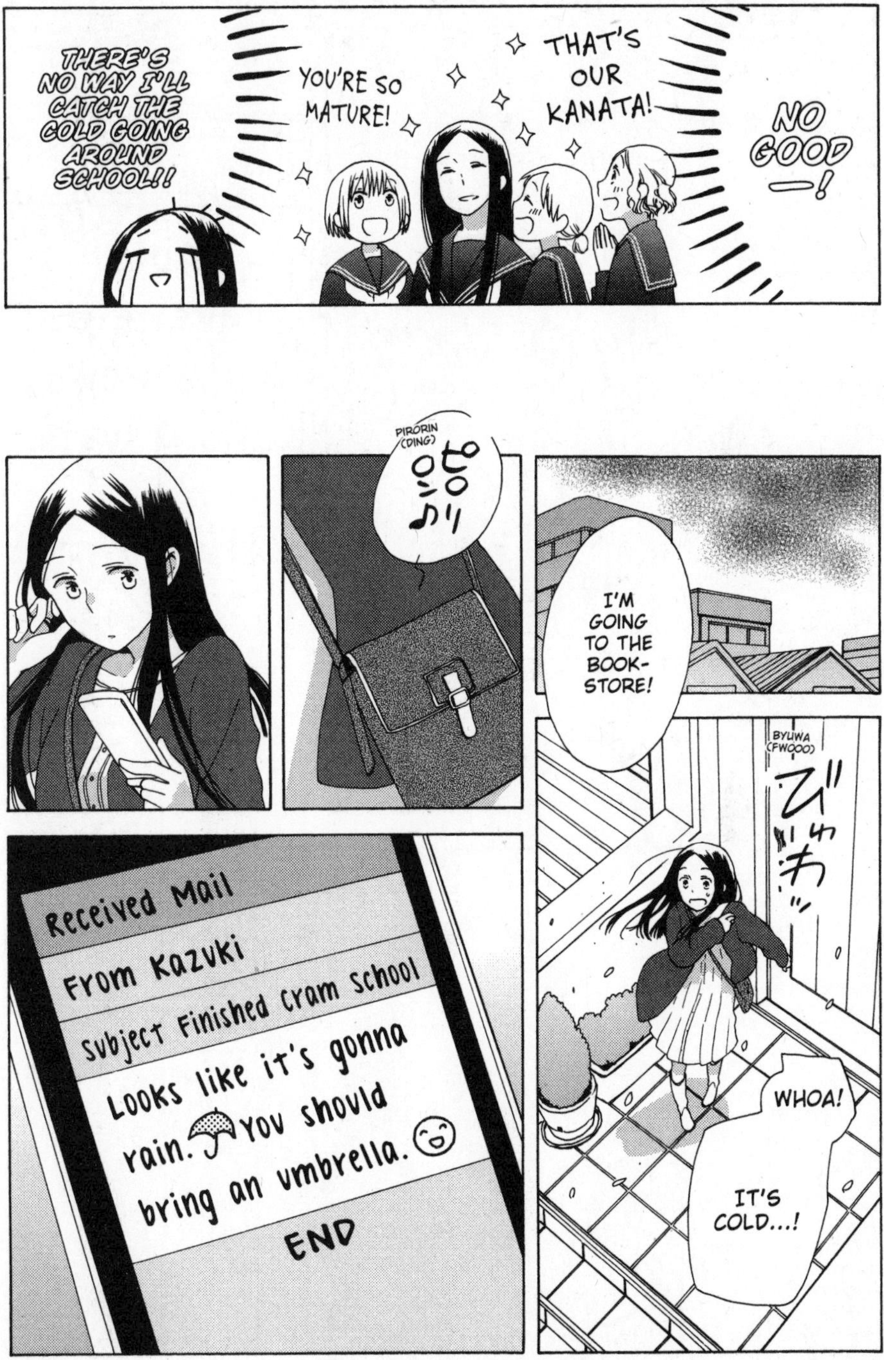
NO GOOD —!
THAT'S OUR KANATA!
YOU'RE SO MATURE!
THERE'S NO WAY I'LL CATCH THE COLD GOING AROUND SCHOOL!!
I'M GOING TO THE BOOK-STORE!
BYUWA (FWOOO)
WHOA!
IT'S COLD...!
PIRORIN (DING)
Received Mail
From Kazuki
Subject Finished Cram School
Looks like it's gonna rain. You should bring an umbrella.
END

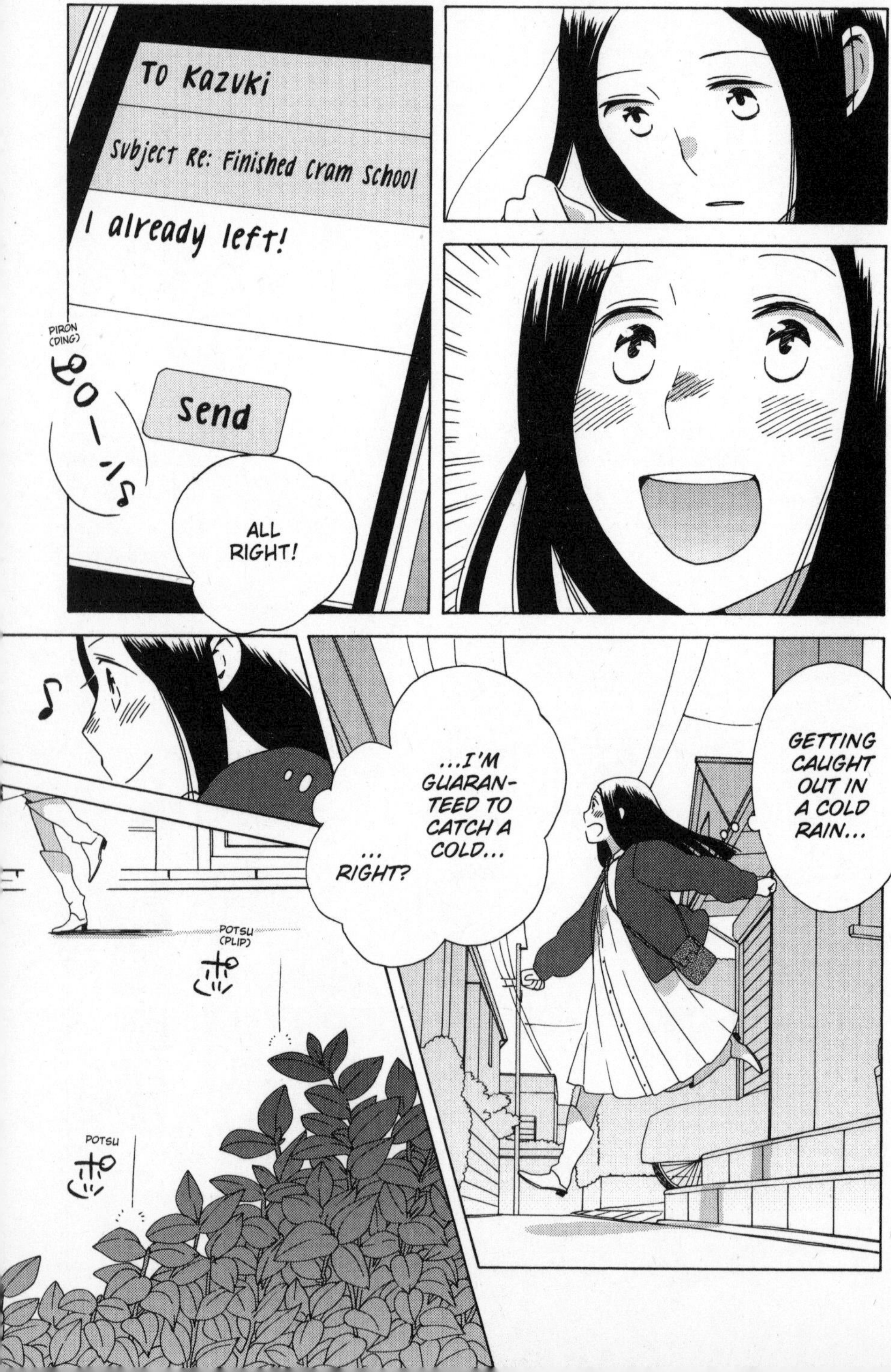
To Kazuki
Subject Re: Finished cram school
I already left!
Send
PIRON (DING)
ALL RIGHT!
GETTING CAUGHT OUT IN A COLD RAIN...
...I'M GUARANTEED TO CATCH A COLD...
... RIGHT?
POTSU (PLIP)
POTSU

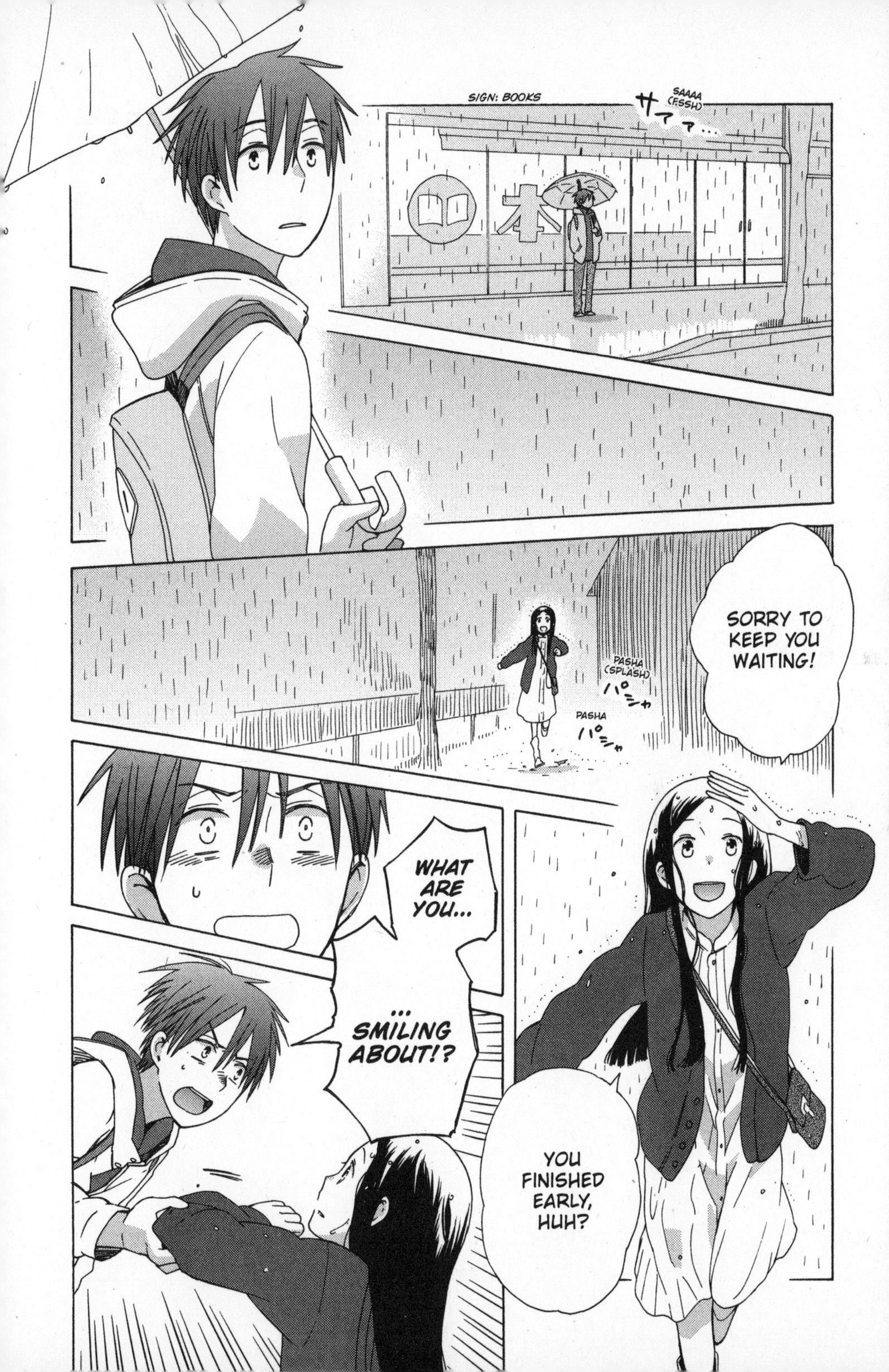
SIGN: BOOKS
SAAAA (FSSH)
SORRY TO KEEP YOU WAITING!
PASHA (SPLASH)
PASHA
YOU FINISHED EARLY, HUH?
WHAT ARE YOU...
...SMILING ABOUT!?

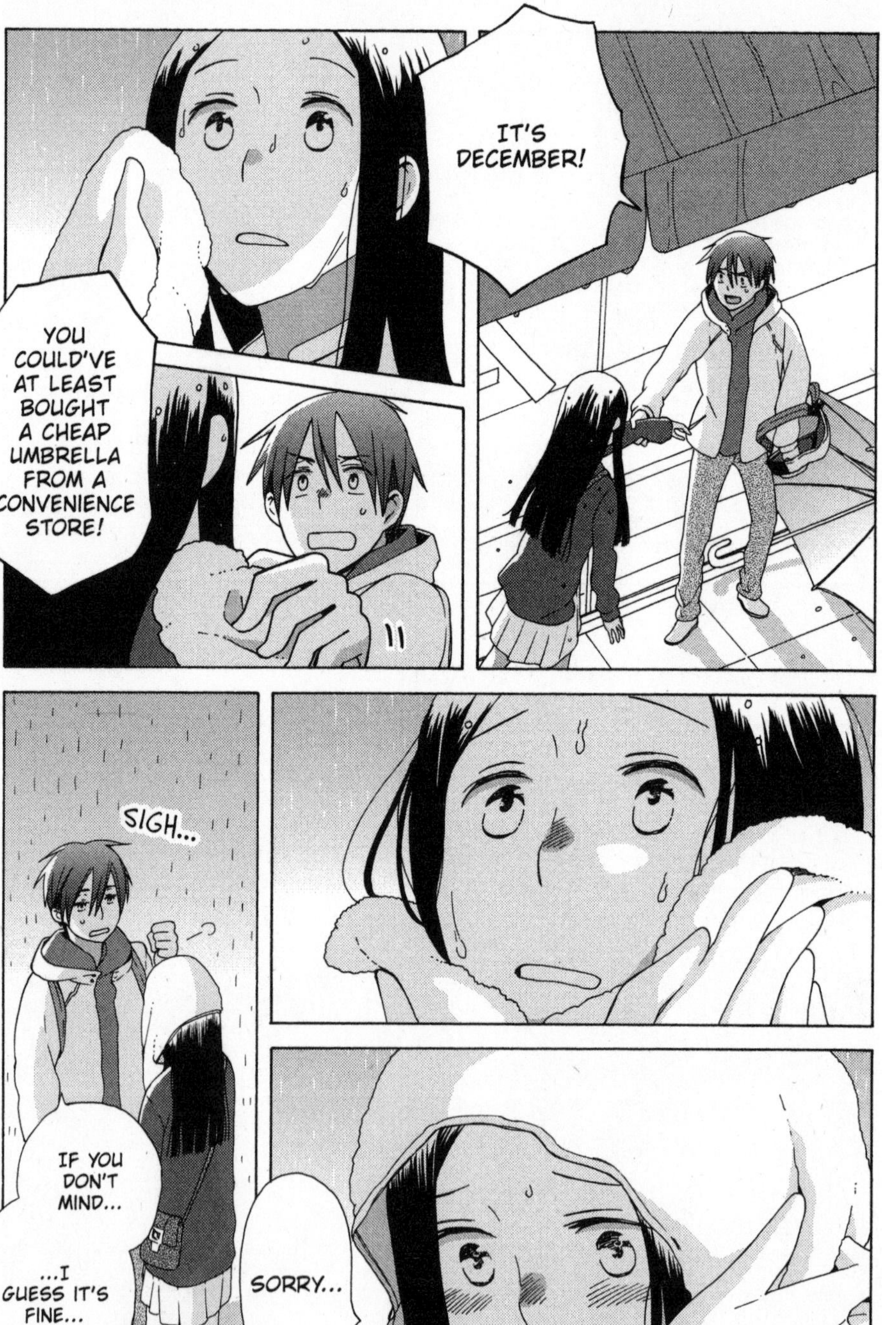
IT'S DECEMBER!
YOU COULD'VE AT LEAST BOUGHT A CHEAP UMBRELLA FROM A CONVENIENCE STORE!
SORRY...
SIGH...
IF YOU DON'T MIND...
...I GUESS IT'S FINE...

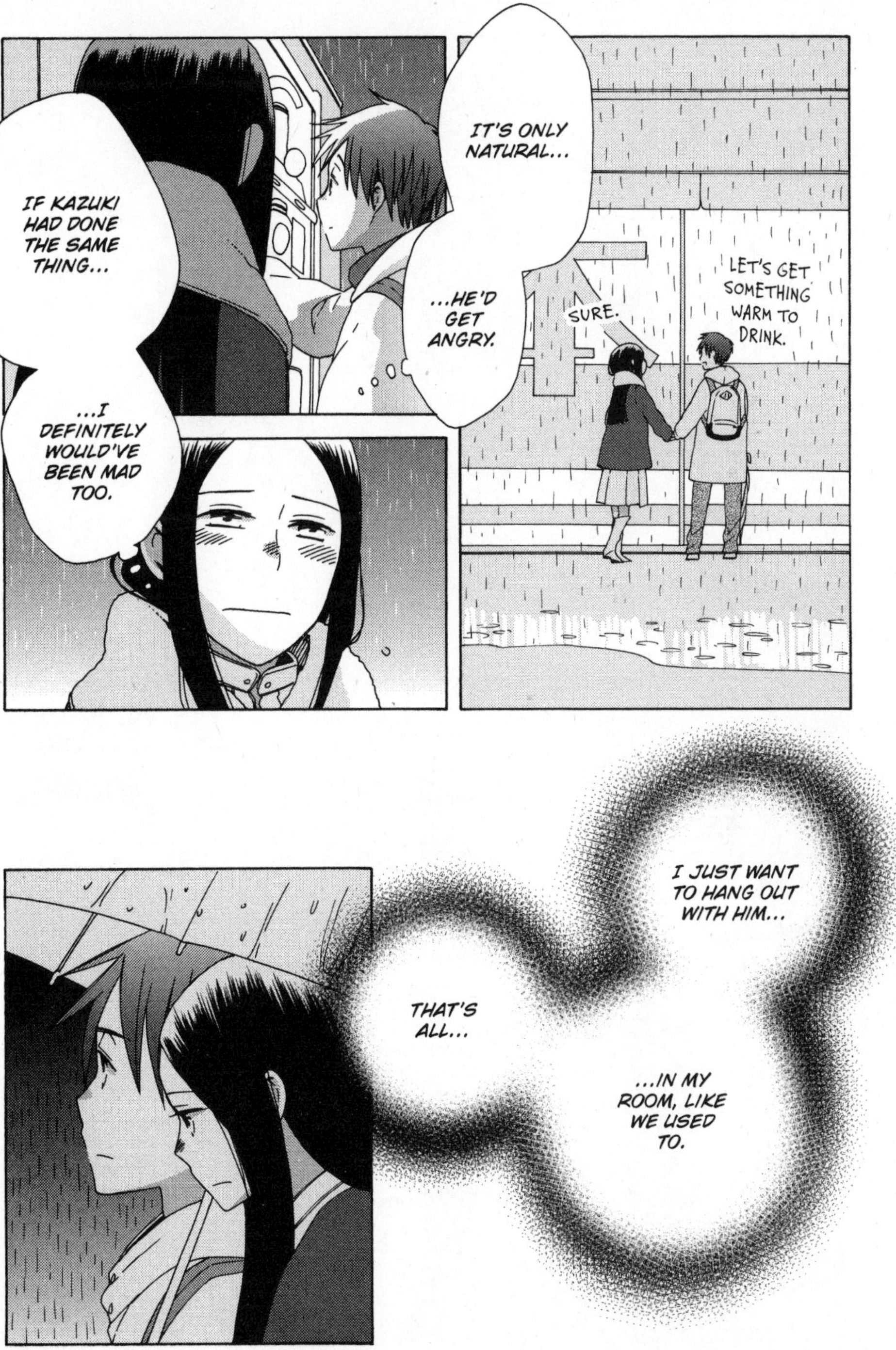
LET'S GET SOMETHING WARM TO DRINK.
SURE.
IT'S ONLY NATURAL...
...HE'D GET ANGRY.
IF KAZUKI HAD DONE THE SAME THING...
...I DEFINITELY WOULD'VE BEEN MAD TOO.
I JUST WANT TO HANG OUT WITH HIM...
...IN MY ROOM, LIKE WE USED TO.
THAT'S ALL...

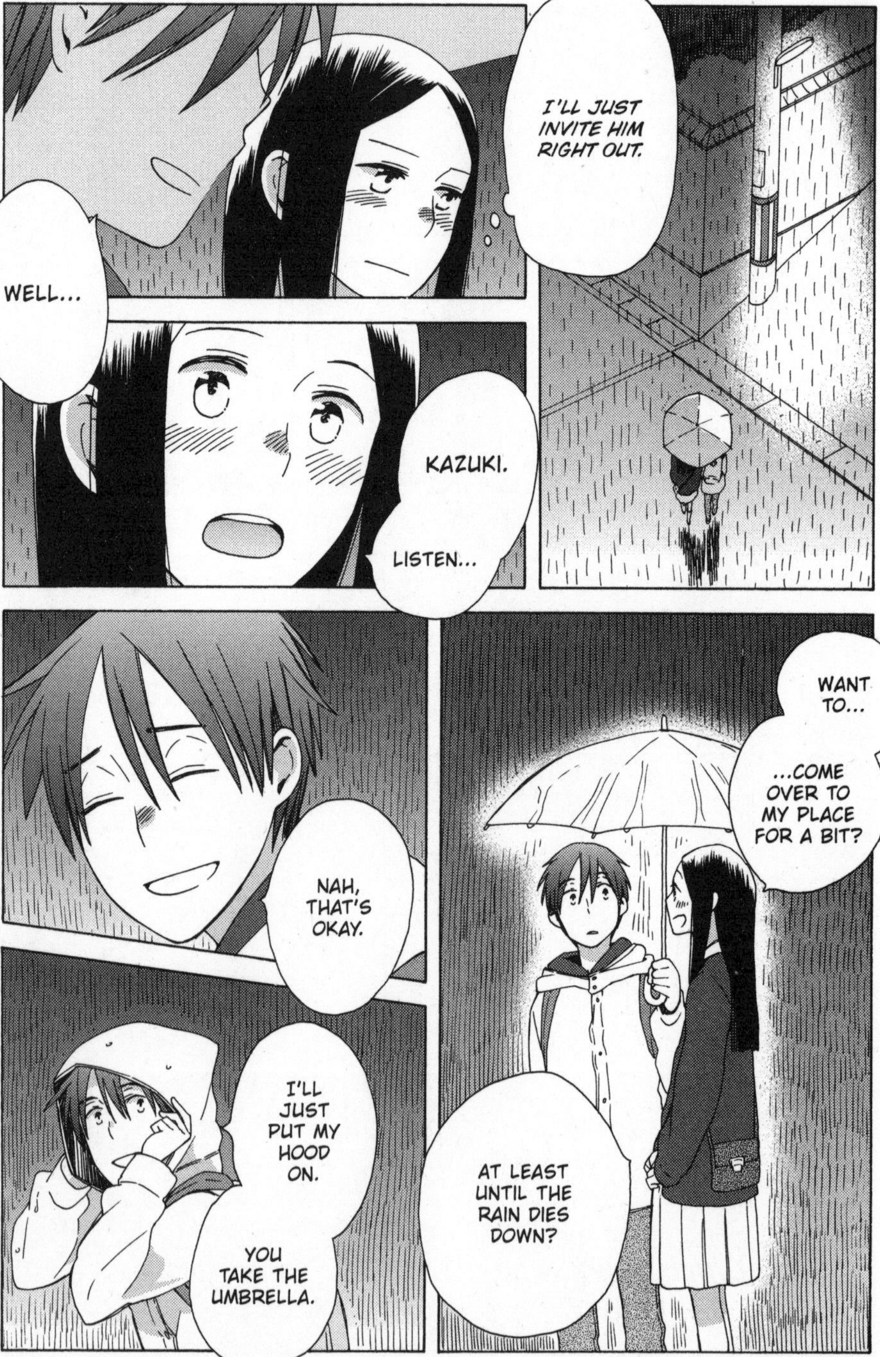
I'LL JUST INVITE HIM RIGHT OUT.
WELL...
KAZUKI.
LISTEN...
WANT TO...
...COME OVER TO MY PLACE FOR A BIT?
AT LEAST UNTIL THE RAIN DIES DOWN?
NAH, THAT'S OKAY.
I'LL JUST PUT MY HOOD ON.
YOU TAKE THE UMBRELLA.

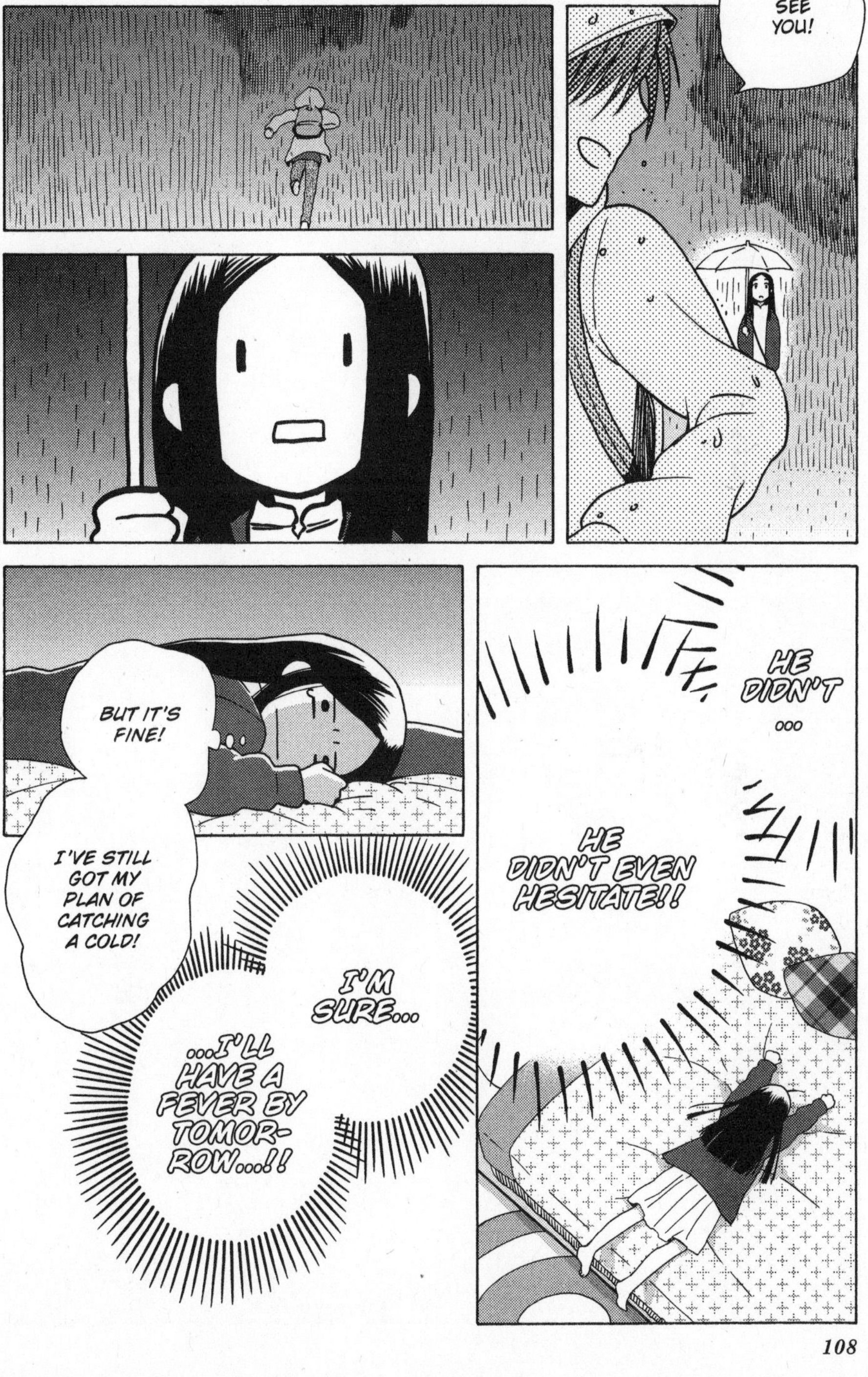
SEE YOU!
HE DIDN'T ...
HE DIDN'T EVEN HESITATE!!
BUT IT'S FINE!
I'VE STILL GOT MY PLAN OF CATCHING A COLD!
I'M SURE...
...I'LL HAVE A FEVER BY TOMOR-ROW...!!

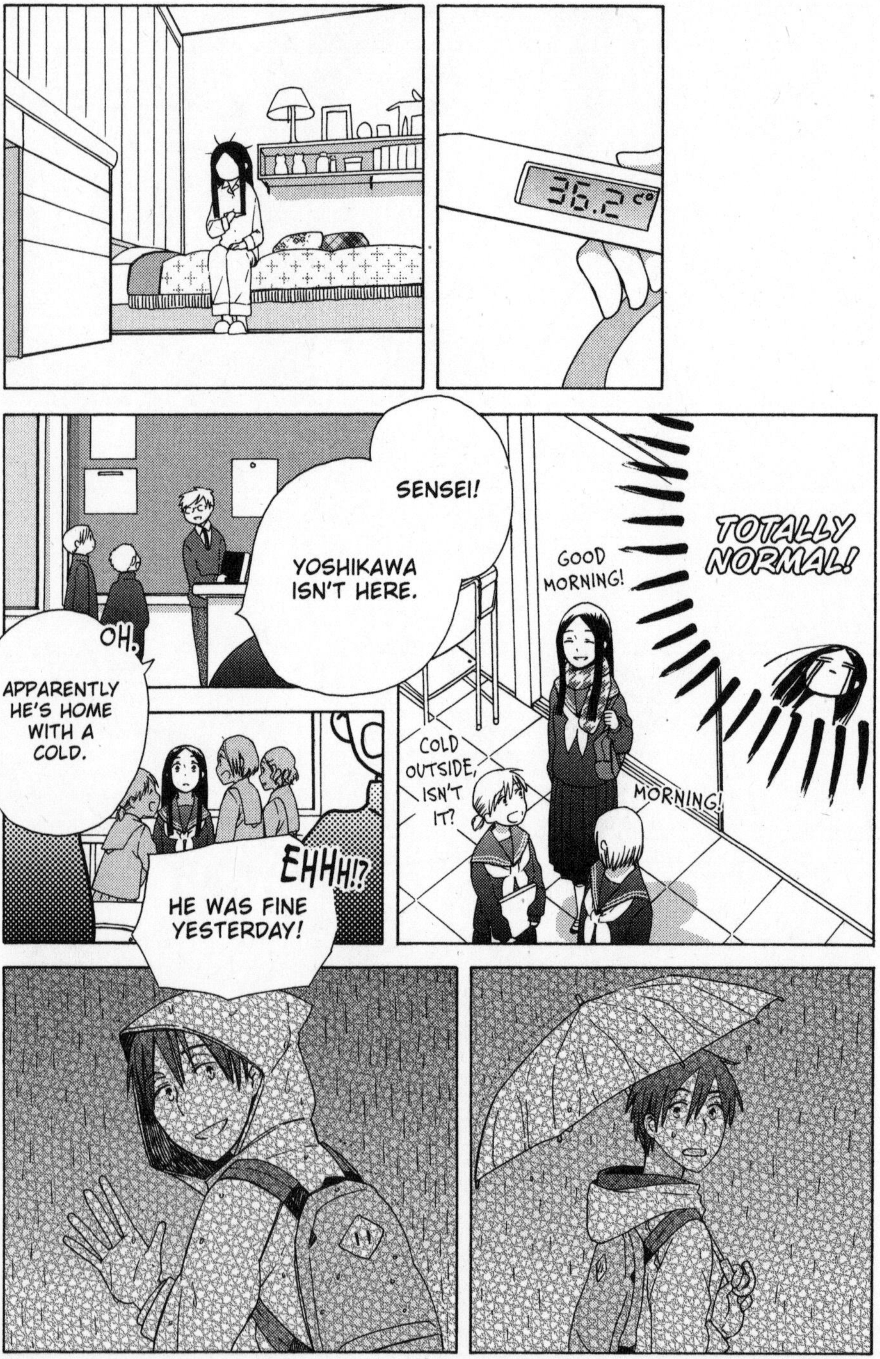
36.2°C
TOTALLY NORMAL!
GOOD MORNING!
MORNING!
COLD OUTSIDE, ISN'T IT?
SENSEI!
YOSHIKAWA ISN'T HERE.
OH,
APPARENTLY HE'S HOME WITH A COLD.
EHHH!?
HE WAS FINE YESTERDAY!

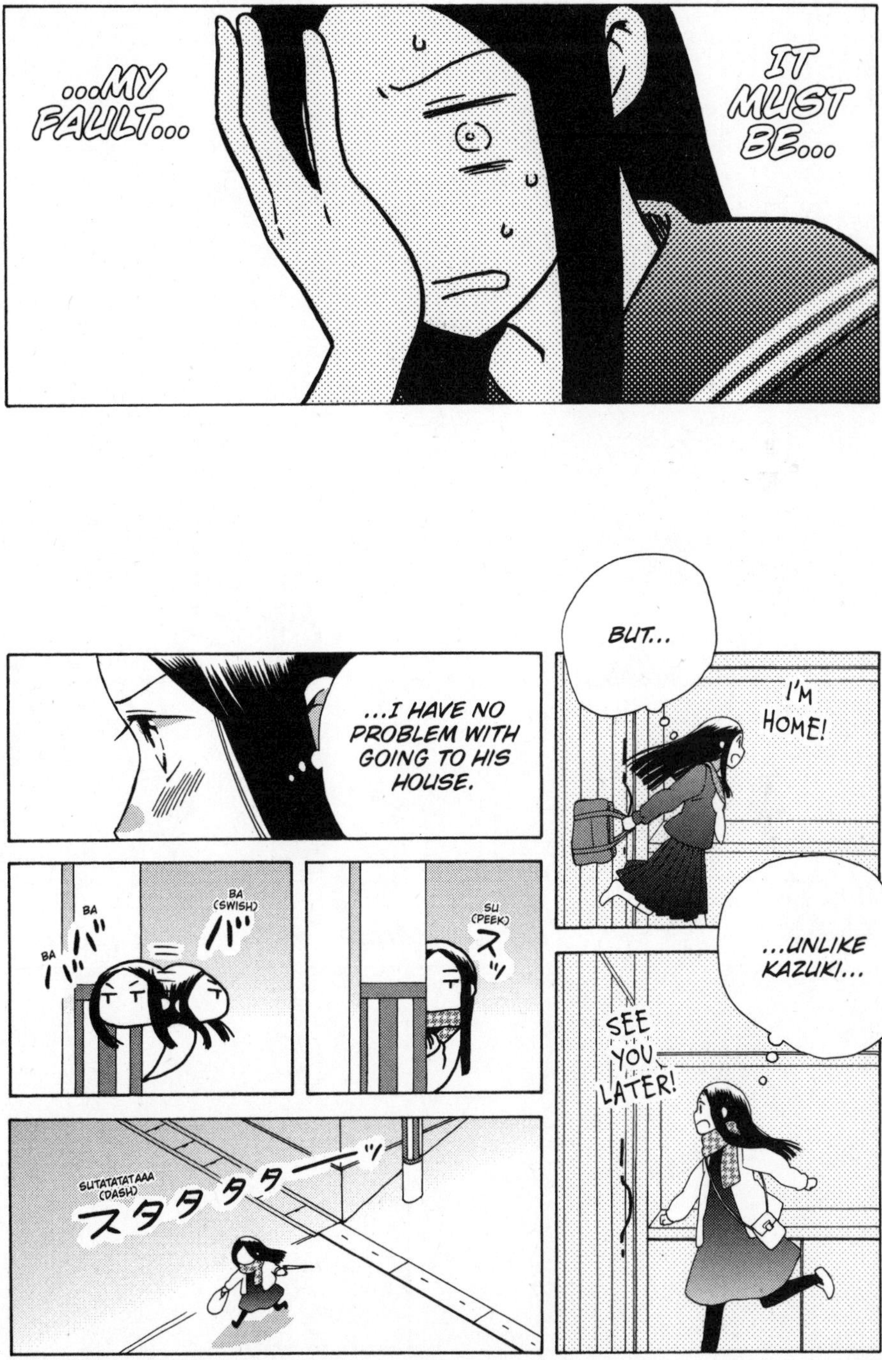
IT MUST BE...
...MY FAULT...
BUT...
I'M HOME!
...UNLIKE KAZUKI...
SEE YOU LATER!
...I HAVE NO PROBLEM WITH GOING TO HIS HOUSE.
SU (PEEK)
スッ
BA (SWISH)
バ
BA
バ
BA
バ
SUTATATATAAA (DASH)
スタタタターッ

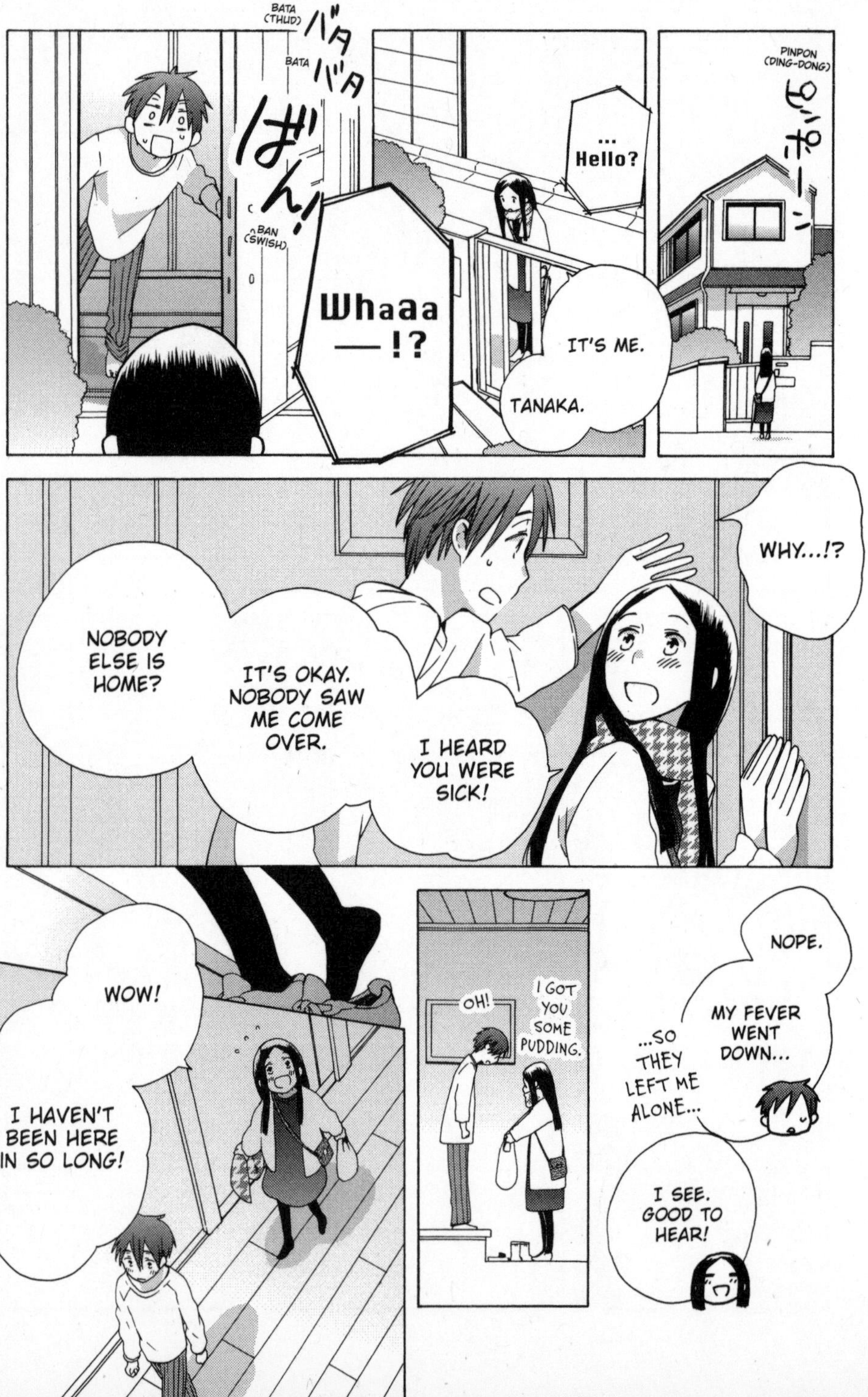
PINPON (DING-DONG)
ピンポーン
... Hello?
IT'S ME.
TANAKA.
BATA (THUD)
バタ
BATA
バタ
ばん!
BAN (SWISH)
Whaaa—!?
WHY...!?
I HEARD YOU WERE SICK!
IT'S OKAY. NOBODY SAW ME COME OVER.
NOBODY ELSE IS HOME?
NOPE.
MY FEVER WENT DOWN...
...SO THEY LEFT ME ALONE...
I SEE. GOOD TO HEAR!
I GOT YOU SOME PUDDING.
OH!
WOW!
I HAVEN'T BEEN HERE IN SO LONG!

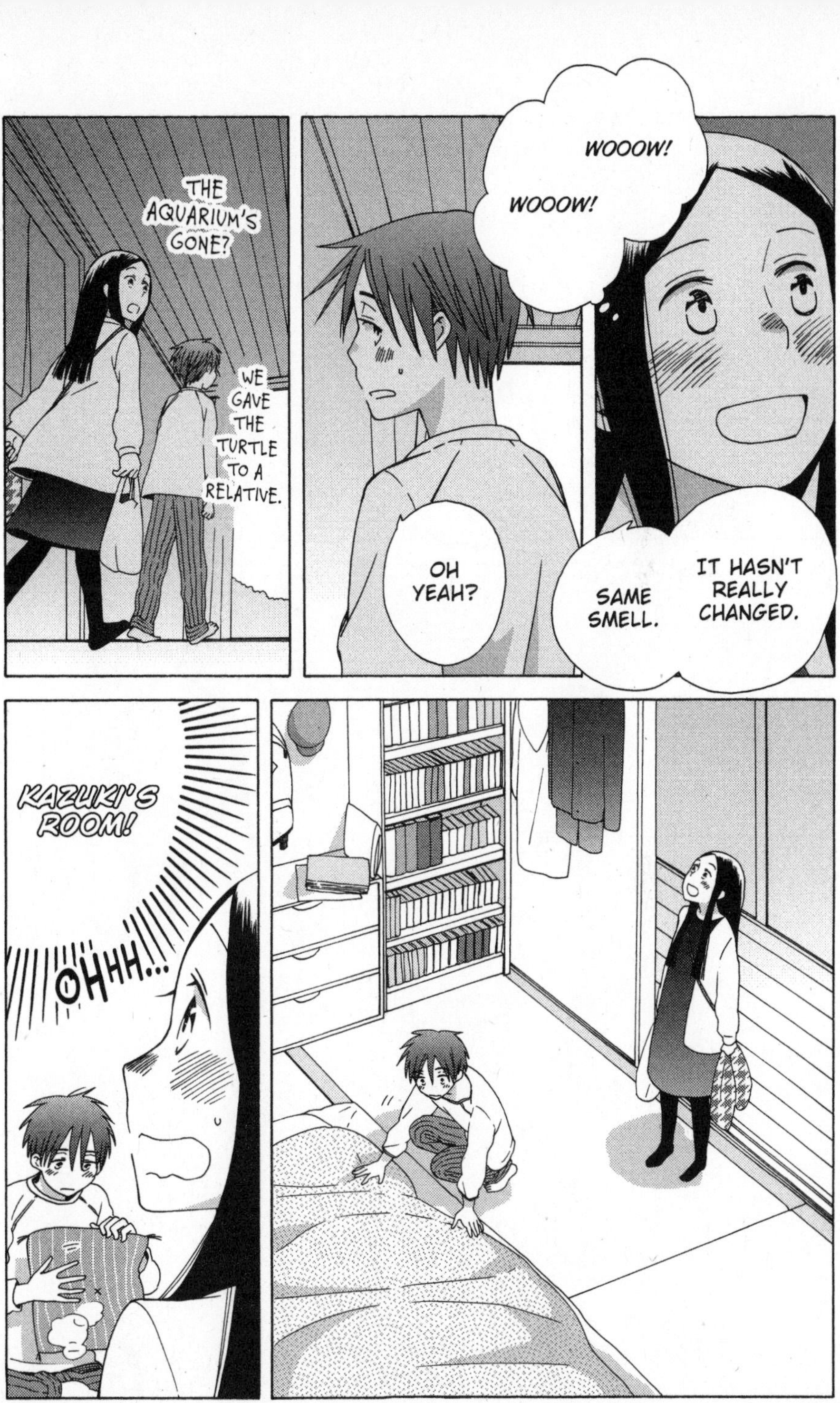
WOOOW!
WOOOW!
IT HASN'T REALLY CHANGED.
SAME SMELL.
OH YEAH?
THE AQUARIUM'S GONE?
WE GAVE THE TURTLE TO A RELATIVE.
KAZUKI'S ROOM!
OHHH...

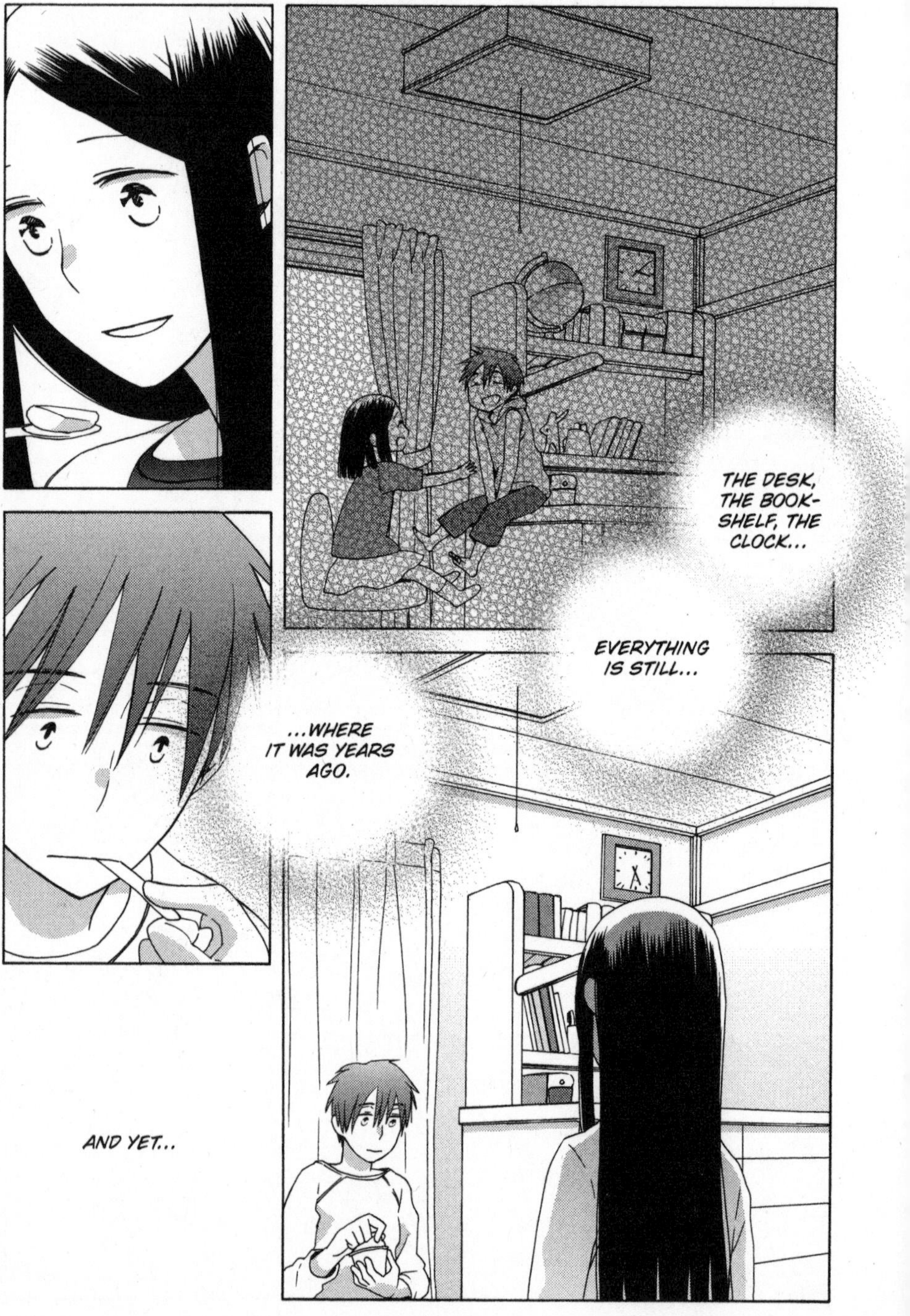
THE DESK, THE BOOK-SHELF, THE CLOCK...
EVERYTHING IS STILL...
...WHERE IT WAS YEARS AGO.
AND YET...

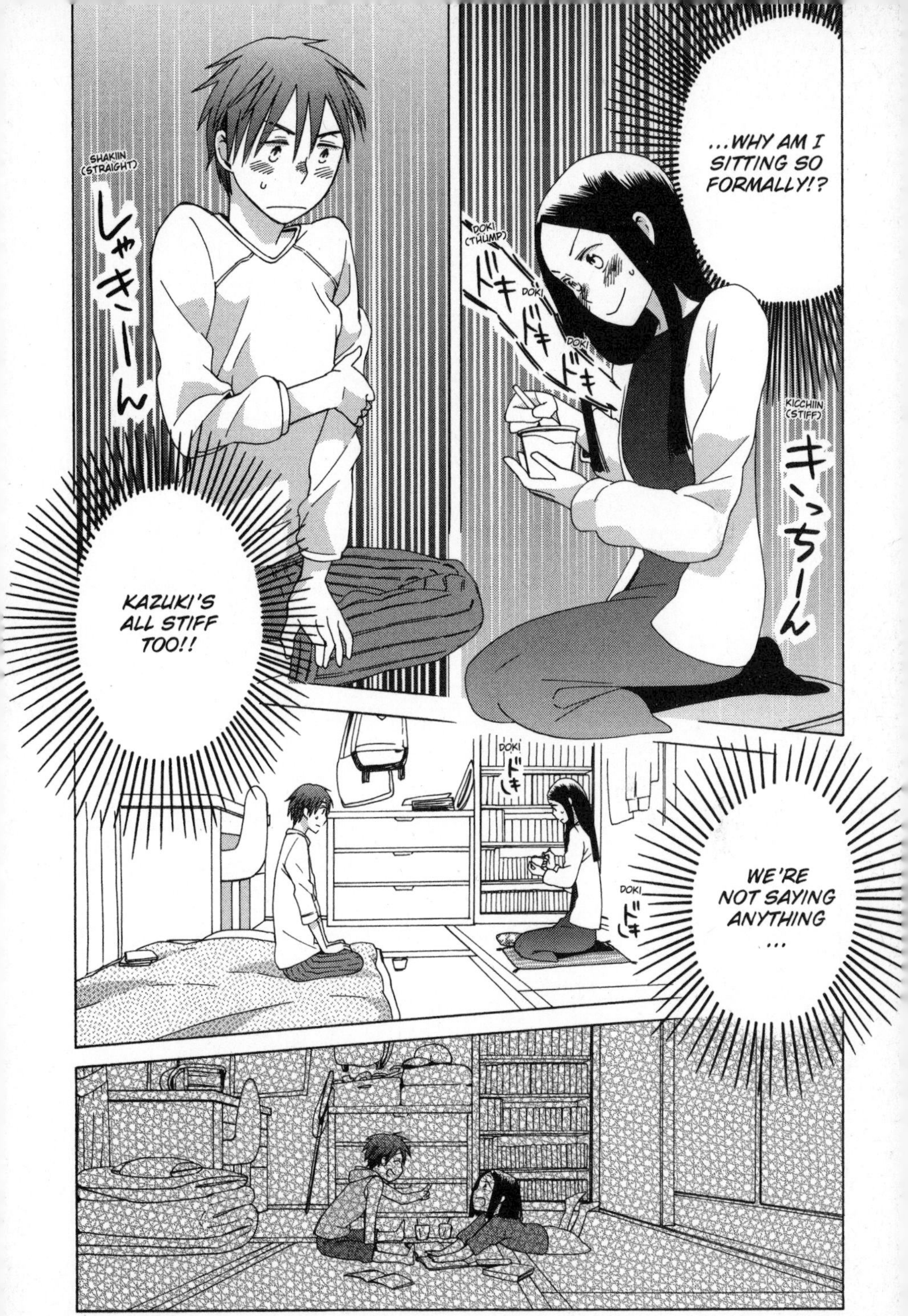
...WHY AM I SITTING SO FORMALLY!?
DOKI (THUMP)
ドキ
DOKI
ドキ
DOKI
ドキ
KICCHIIN (STIFF)
きっちーん
SHAKIIN (STRAIGHT)
しゃきーん
KAZUKI'S ALL STIFF TOO!!
DOKI
ドキ
DOKI
ドキ
WE'RE NOT SAYING ANYTHING ...

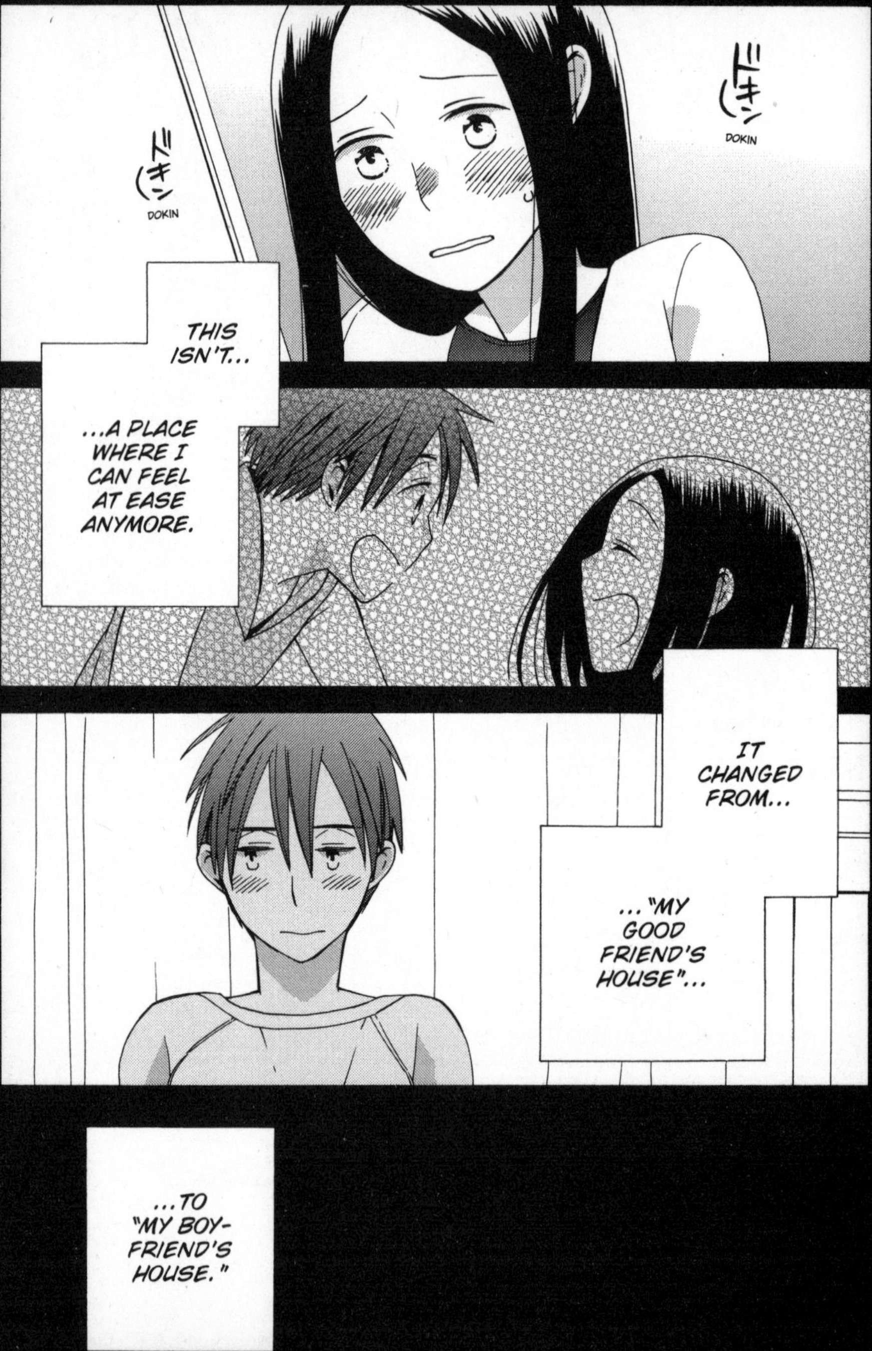
ドキン
DOKIN
ドキン
DOKIN
THIS ISN'T...
...A PLACE WHERE I CAN FEEL AT EASE ANYMORE.
IT CHANGED FROM...
..."MY GOOD FRIEND'S HOUSE"...
...TO "MY BOY-FRIEND'S HOUSE."

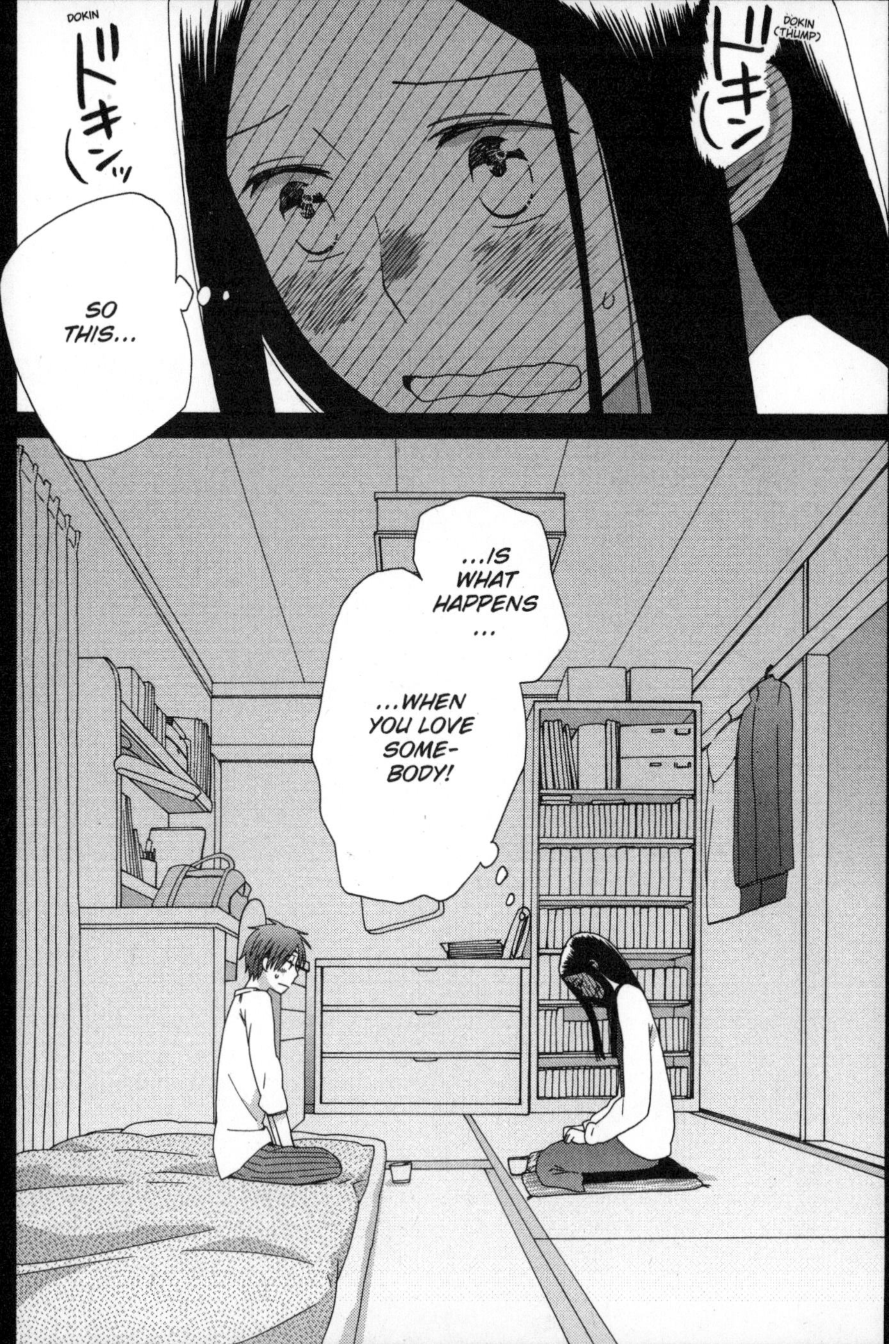
ドキン
DOKIN (THUMP)
ドキンッ
DOKIN
SO THIS...
...IS WHAT HAPPENS ...
...WHEN YOU LOVE SOME-BODY!

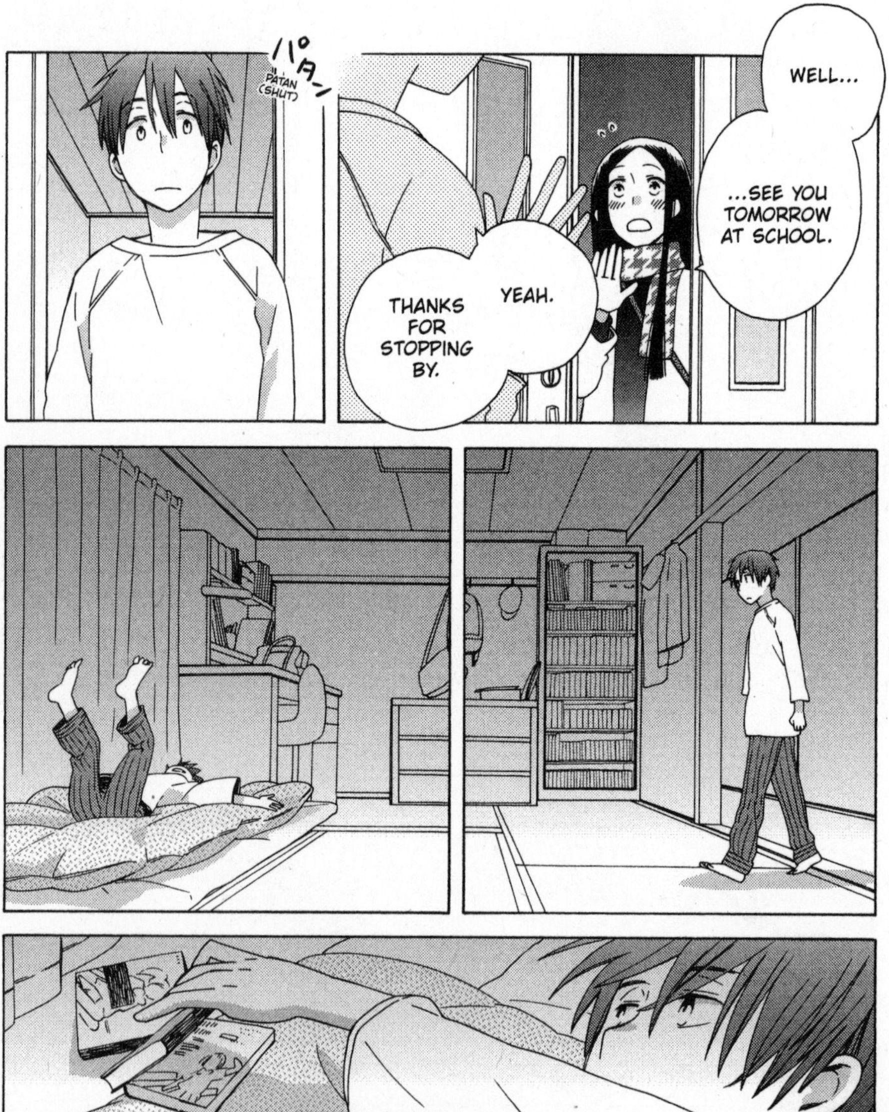
WELL...
...SEE YOU TOMORROW AT SCHOOL.
YEAH.
THANKS FOR STOPPING BY.
パタン
PATAN (SHUT)

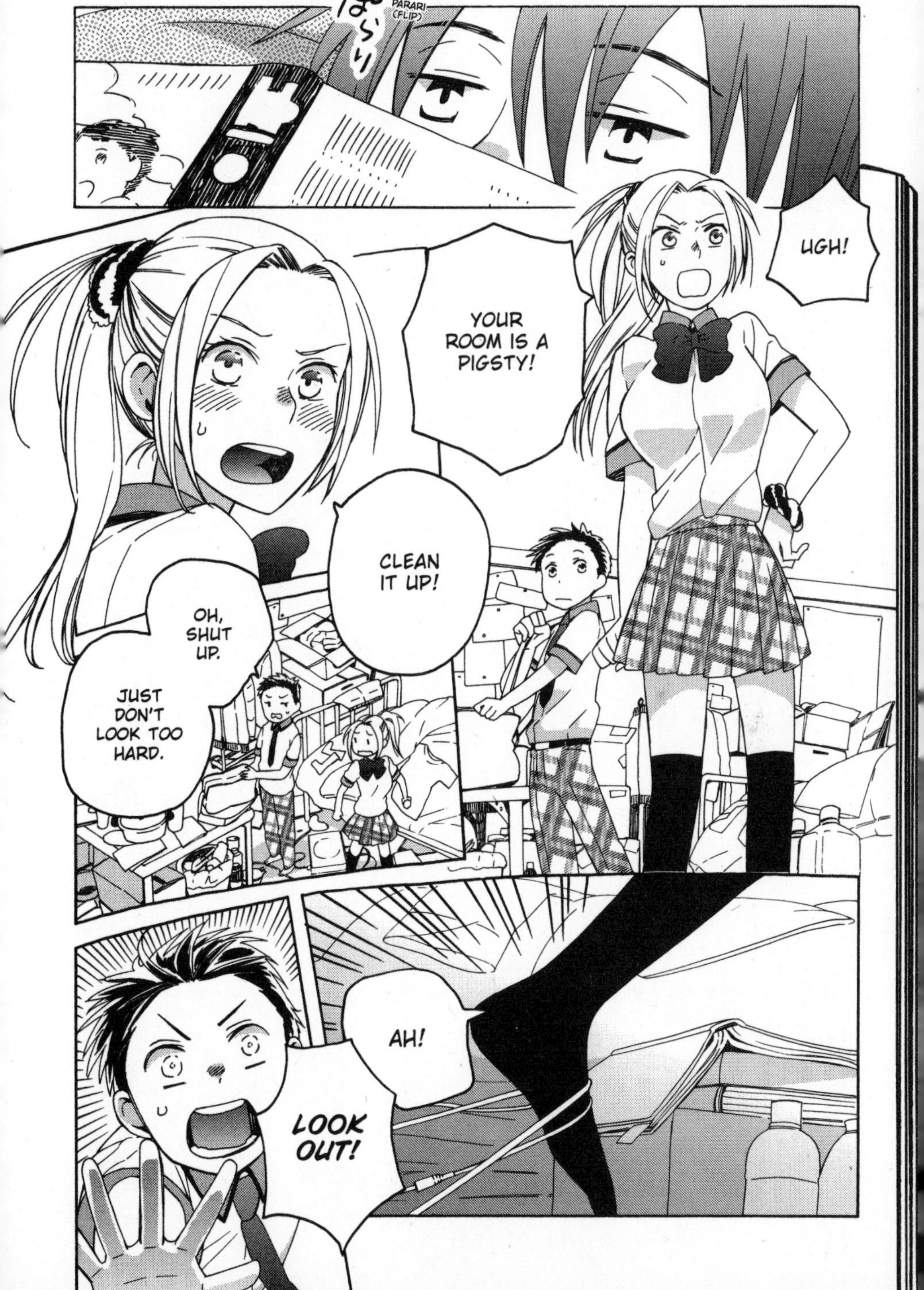
ぱらり
PARARI (FLIP)
UGH!
YOUR ROOM IS A PIGSTY!
CLEAN IT UP!
OH, SHUT UP.
JUST DON'T LOOK TOO HARD.
AH!
LOOK OUT!

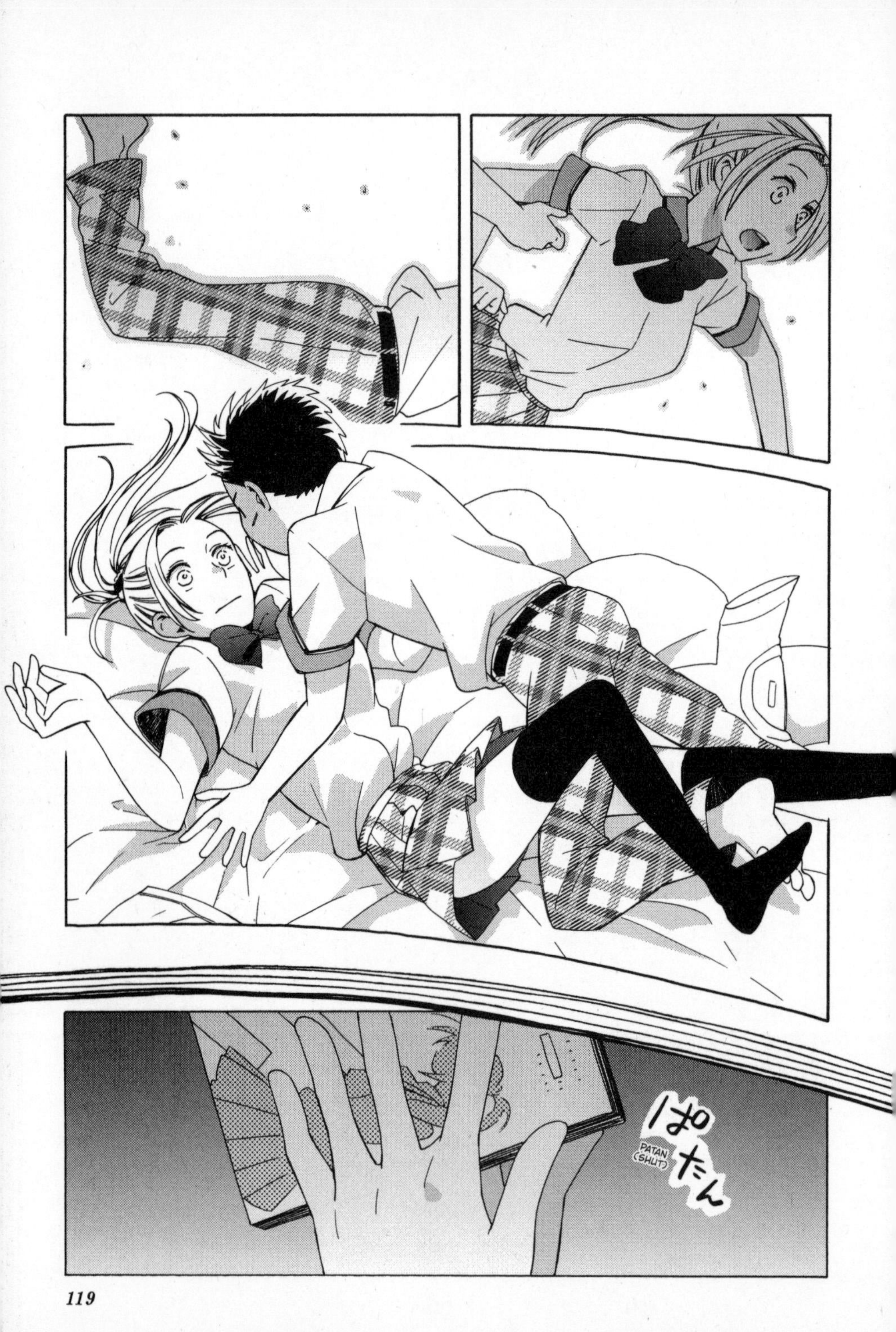
ぱたん
PATAN (SHUT)

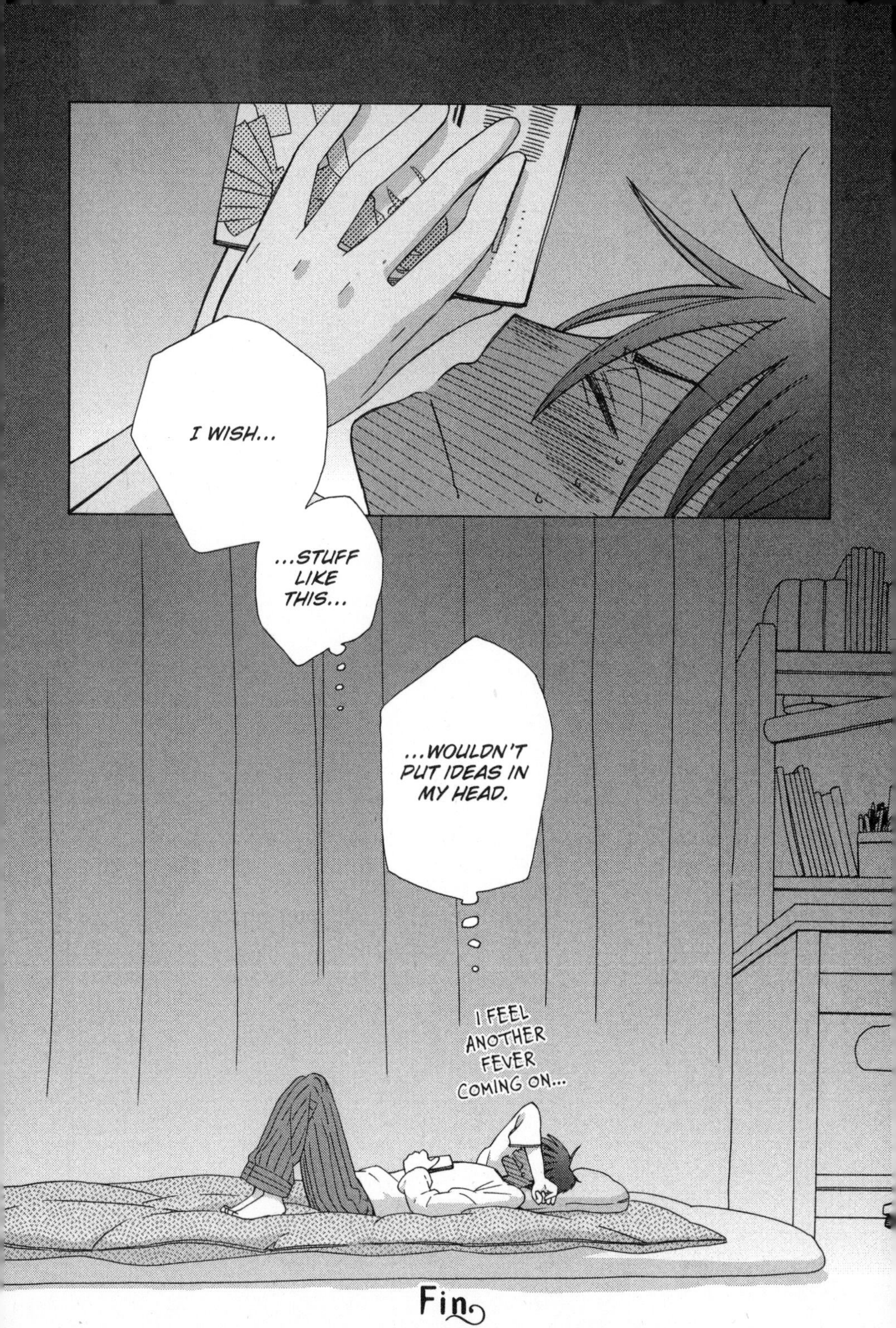
I WISH...
...STUFF LIKE THIS...
...WOULDN'T PUT IDEAS IN MY HEAD.
I FEEL ANOTHER FEVER COMING ON...

Fin

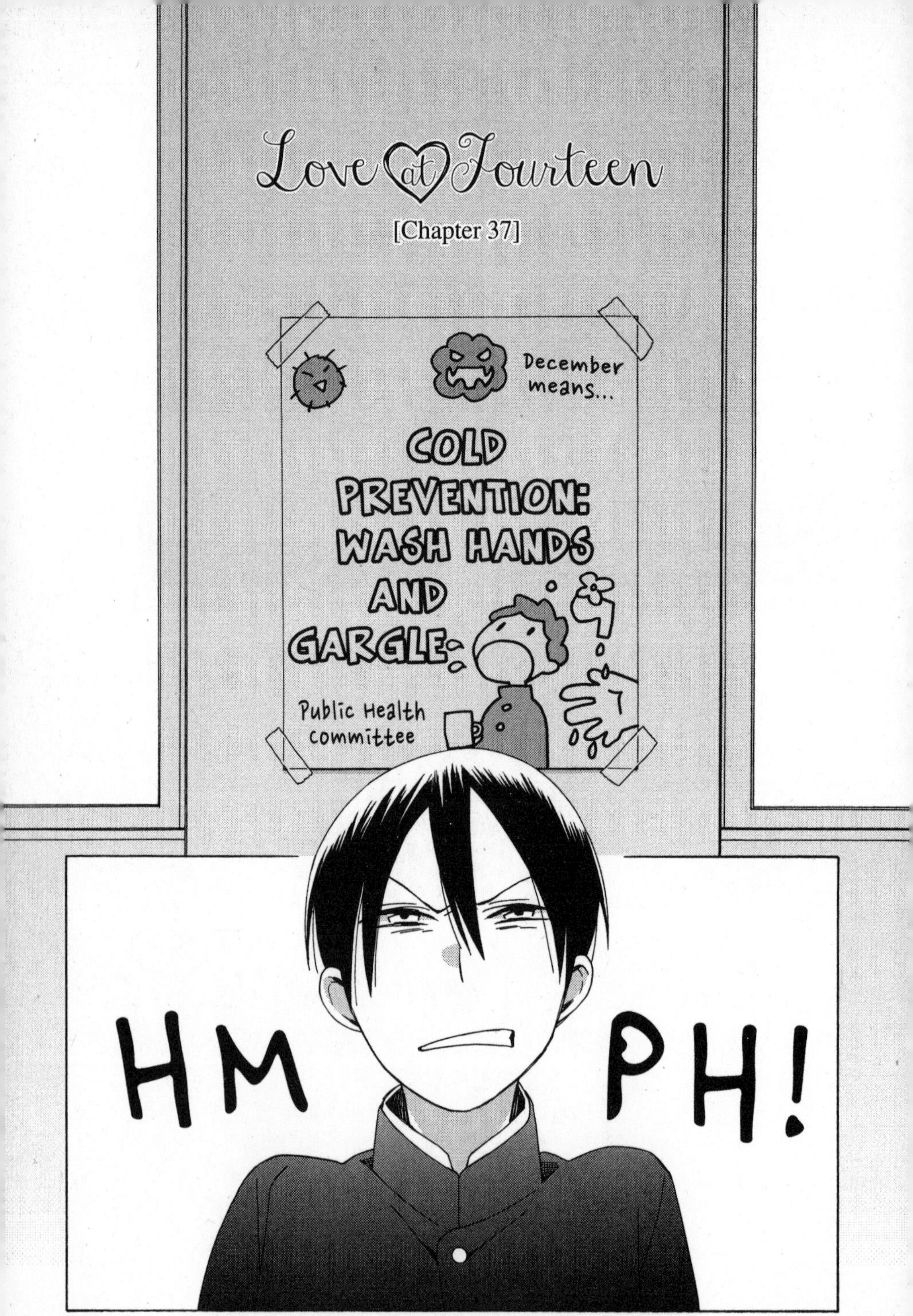
Love at Fourteen
[Chapter 37]
December means...
COLD PREVENTION: WASH HANDS AND GARGLE
Public Health committee
HMPH!

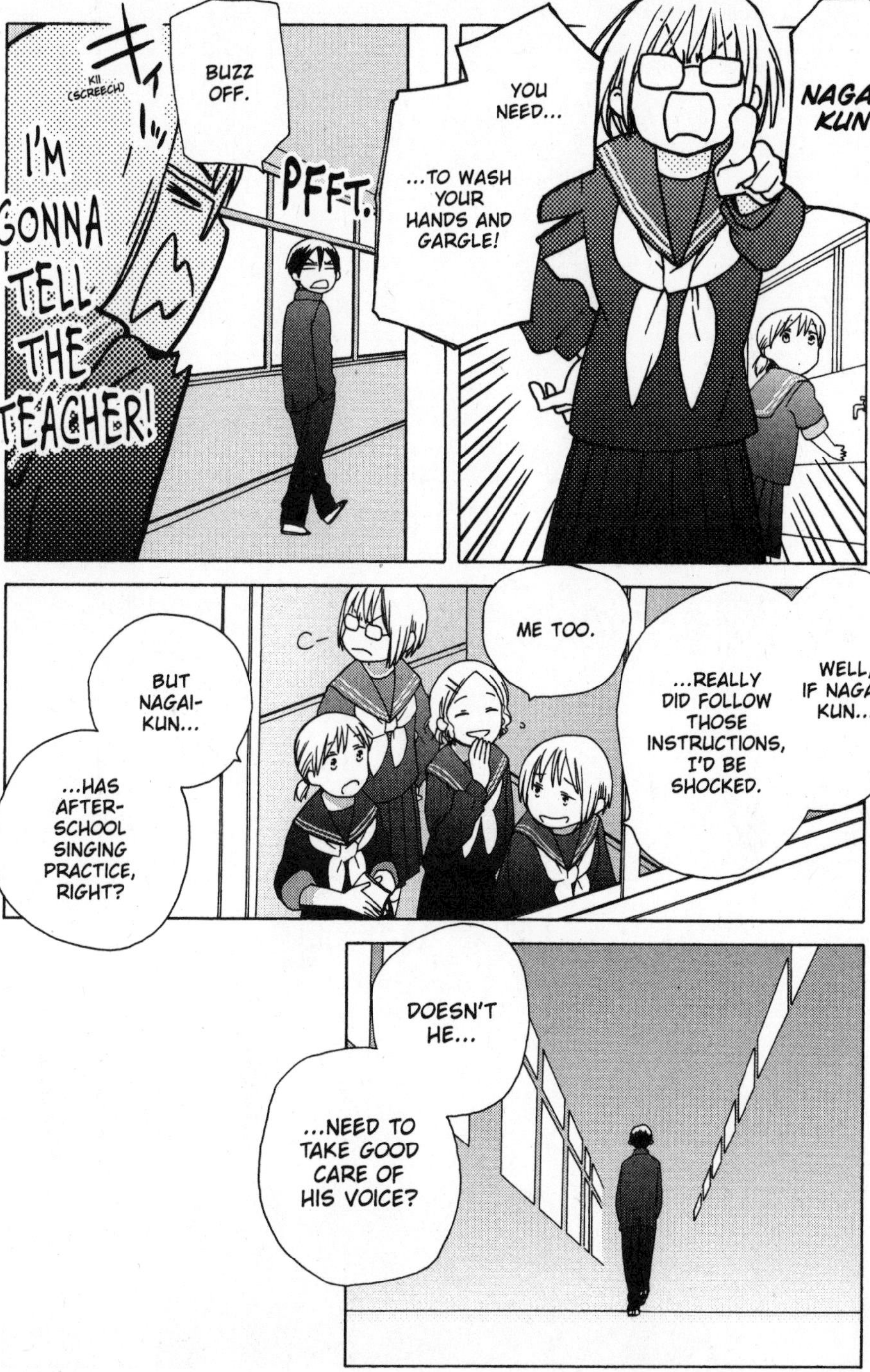
NAGAI-KUN!
YOU NEED...
...TO WASH YOUR HANDS AND GARGLE!
BUZZ OFF.
KII (SCREECH)
PFFT.
I'M GONNA TELL THE TEACHER!
WELL, IF NAGAI-KUN...
...REALLY DID FOLLOW THOSE INSTRUCTIONS, I'D BE SHOCKED.
ME TOO.
BUT NAGAI-KUN...
...HAS AFTER-SCHOOL SINGING PRACTICE, RIGHT?
DOESN'T HE...
...NEED TO TAKE GOOD CARE OF HIS VOICE?

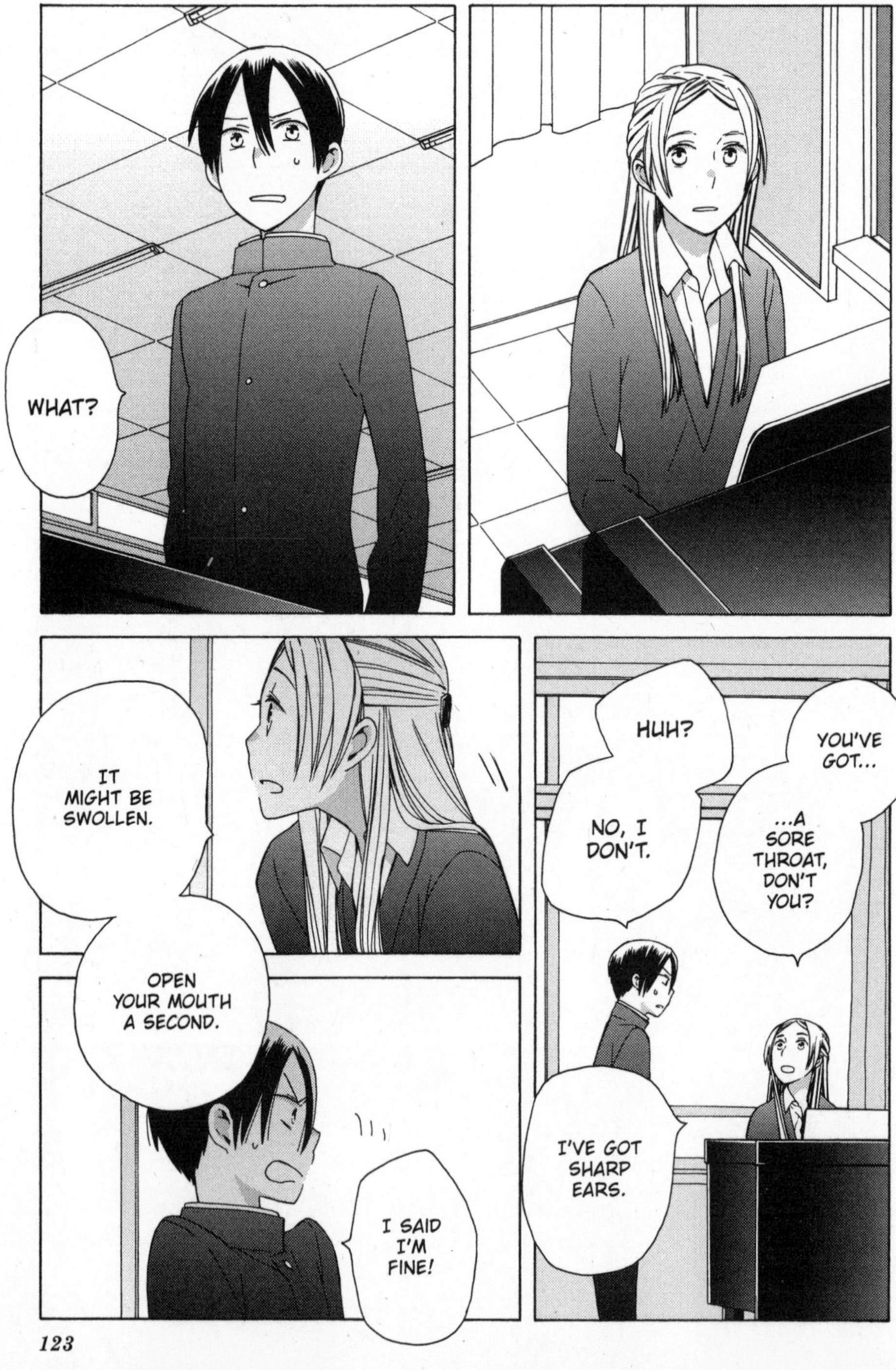
WHAT?
YOU'VE GOT...
HUH?
...A SORE THROAT, DON'T YOU?
NO, I DON'T.
I'VE GOT SHARP EARS.
IT MIGHT BE SWOLLEN.
OPEN YOUR MOUTH A SECOND.
I SAID I'M FINE!

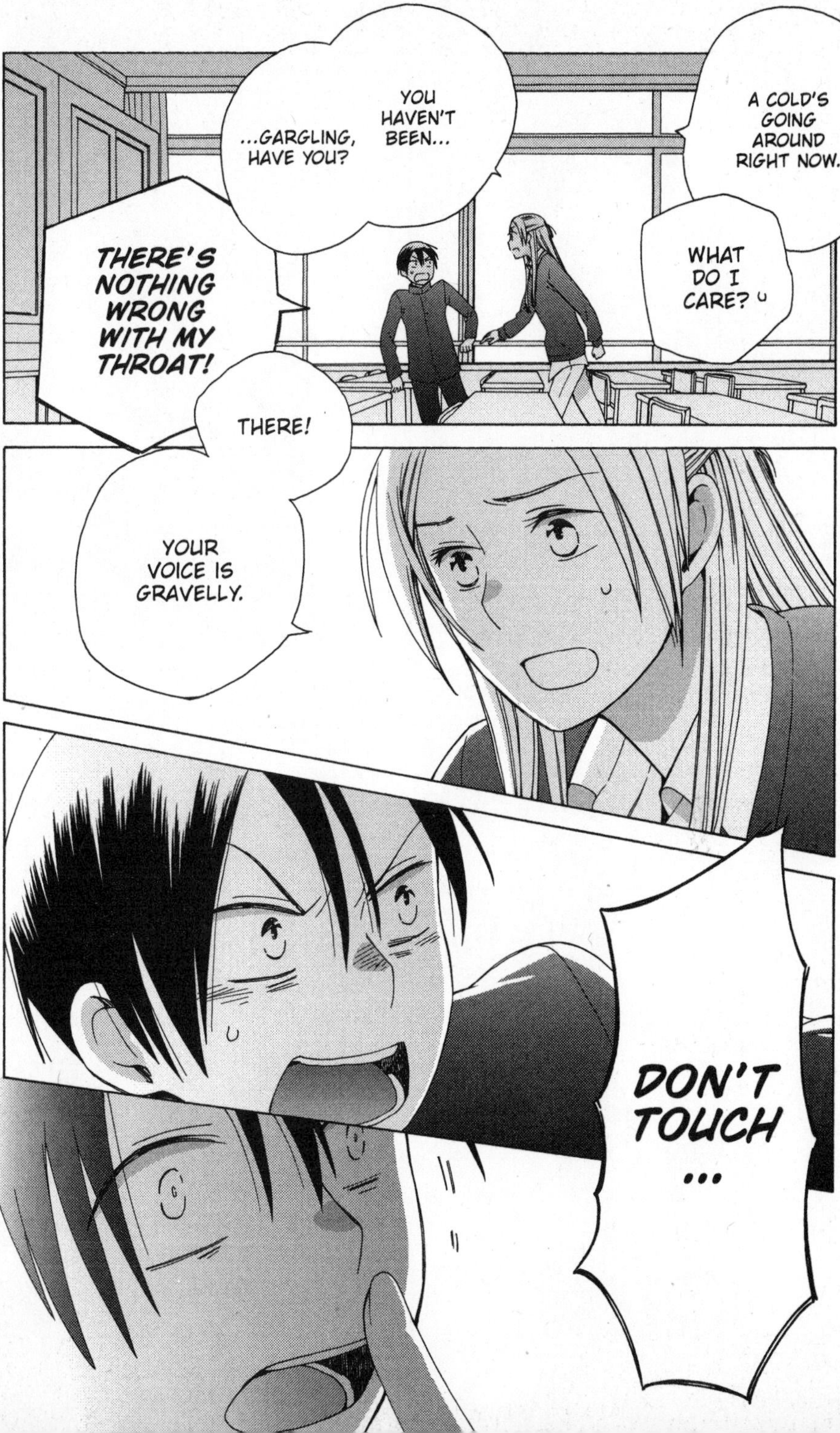
A COLD'S GOING AROUND RIGHT NOW.
YOU HAVEN'T BEEN...
...GARGLING, HAVE YOU?
WHAT DO I CARE?
THERE'S NOTHING WRONG WITH MY THROAT!
THERE!
YOUR VOICE IS GRAVELLY.
DON'T TOUCH ...

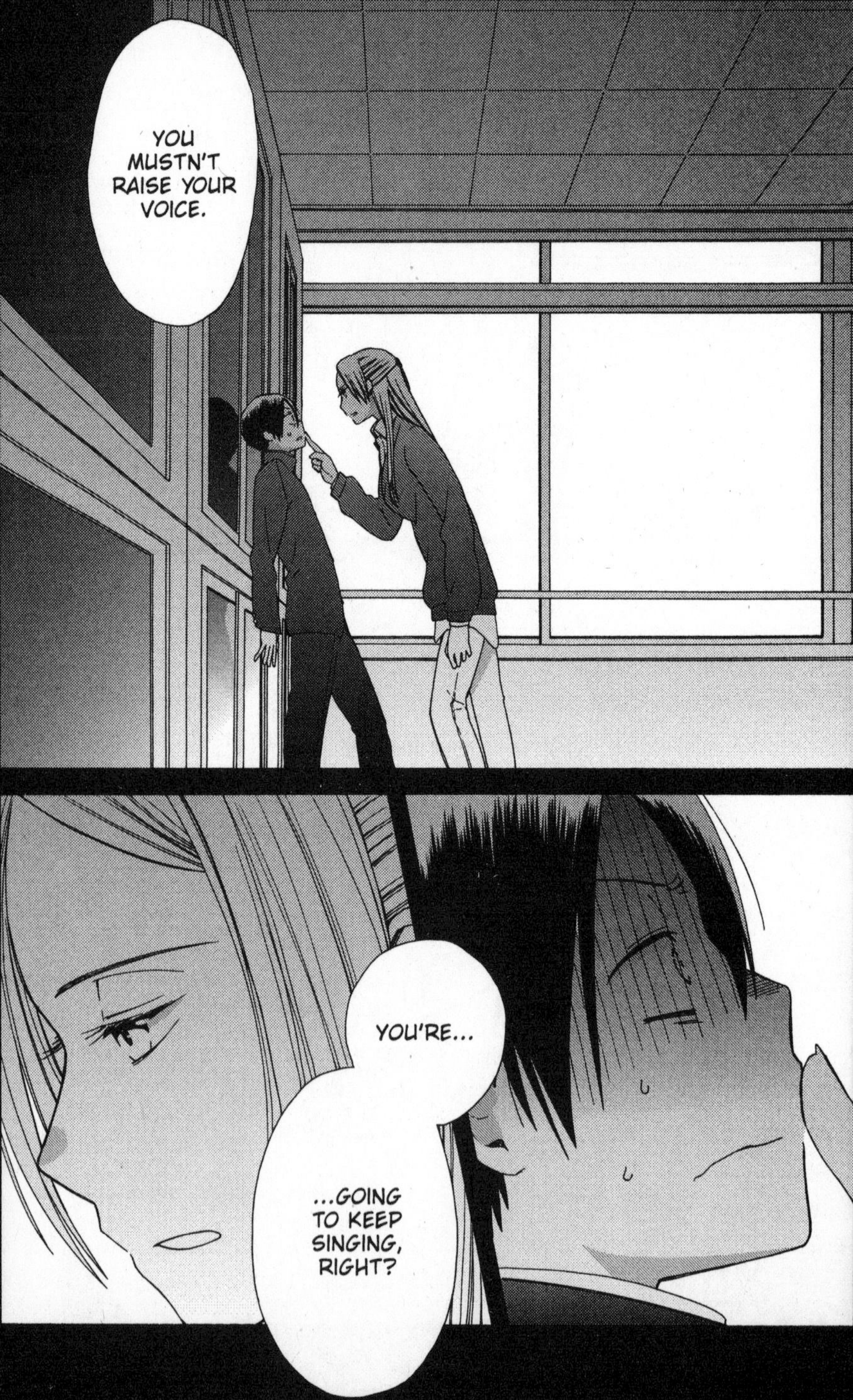
YOU MUSTN'T RAISE YOUR VOICE.
YOU'RE...
...GOING TO KEEP SINGING, RIGHT?

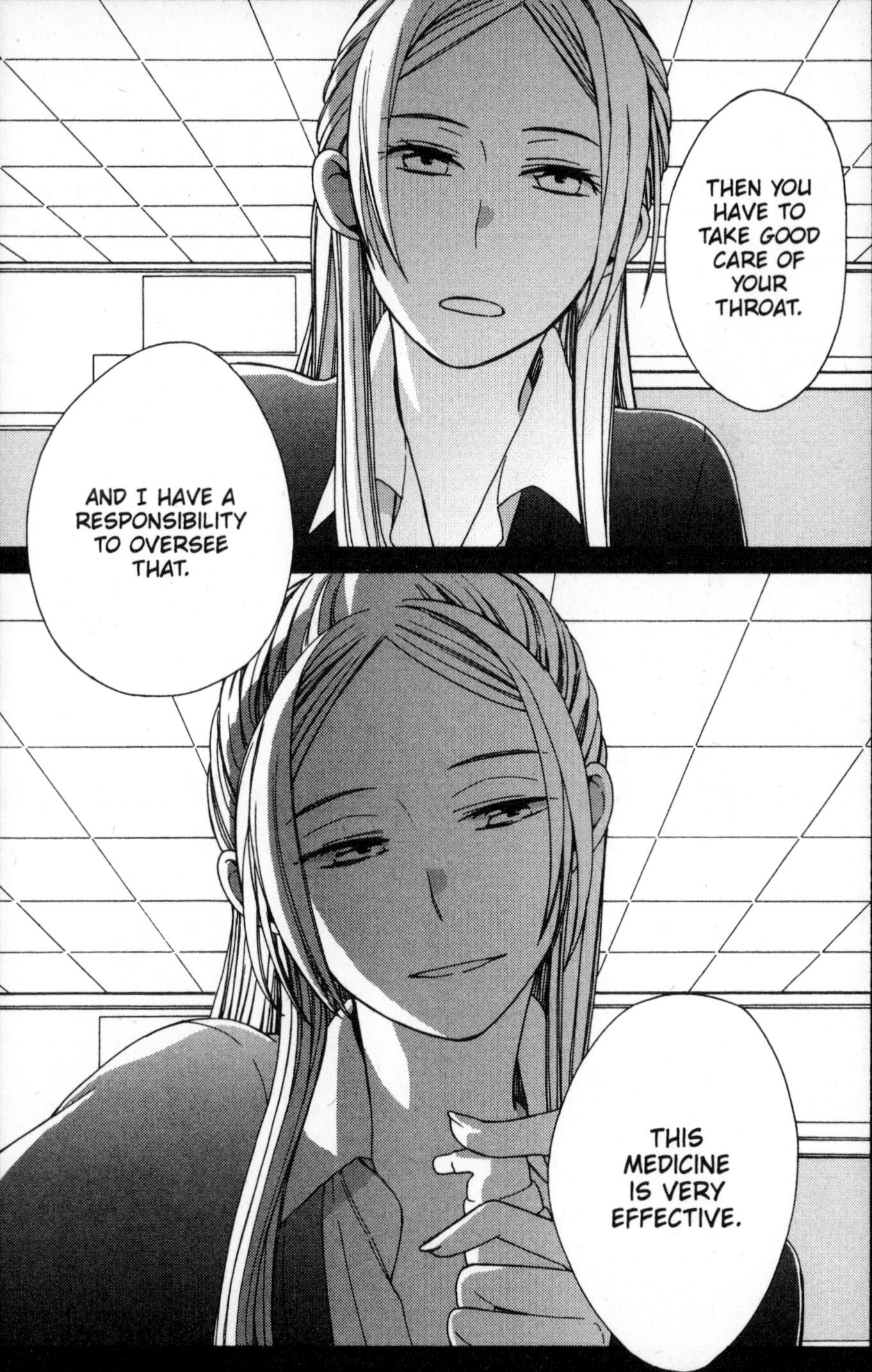
THEN YOU HAVE TO TAKE GOOD CARE OF YOUR THROAT.
AND I HAVE A RESPONSIBILITY TO OVERSEE THAT.
THIS MEDICINE IS VERY EFFECTIVE.

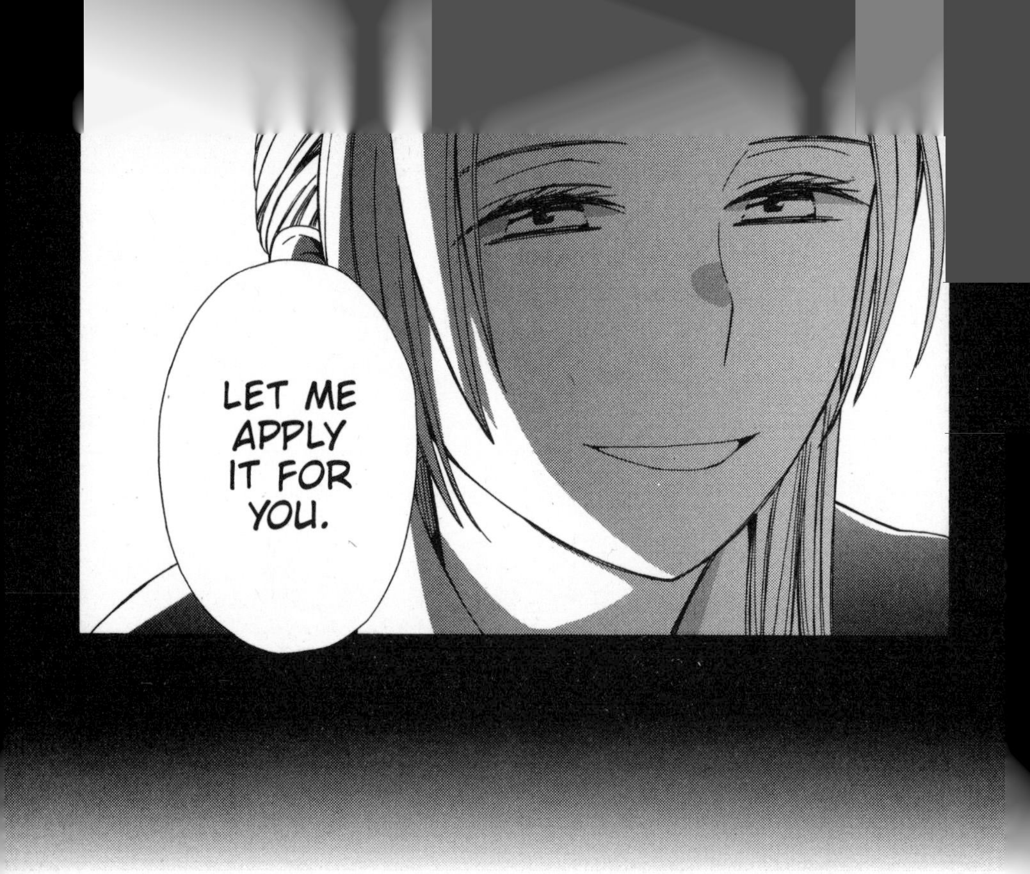
LET ME APPLY IT FOR YOU.

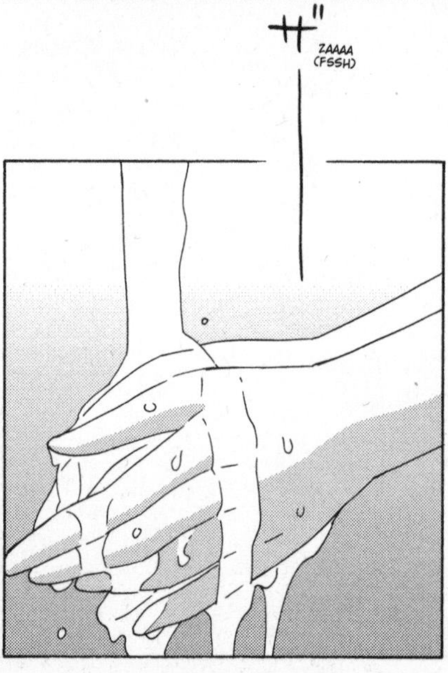
ザー
ZAAAA (FSSH)

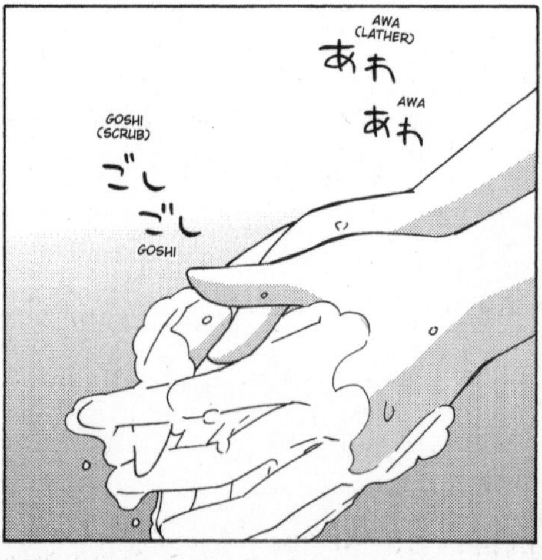
AWA (LATHER)
あわ
AWA
あわ
GOSHI (SCRUB)
ごし
ごし
GOSHI

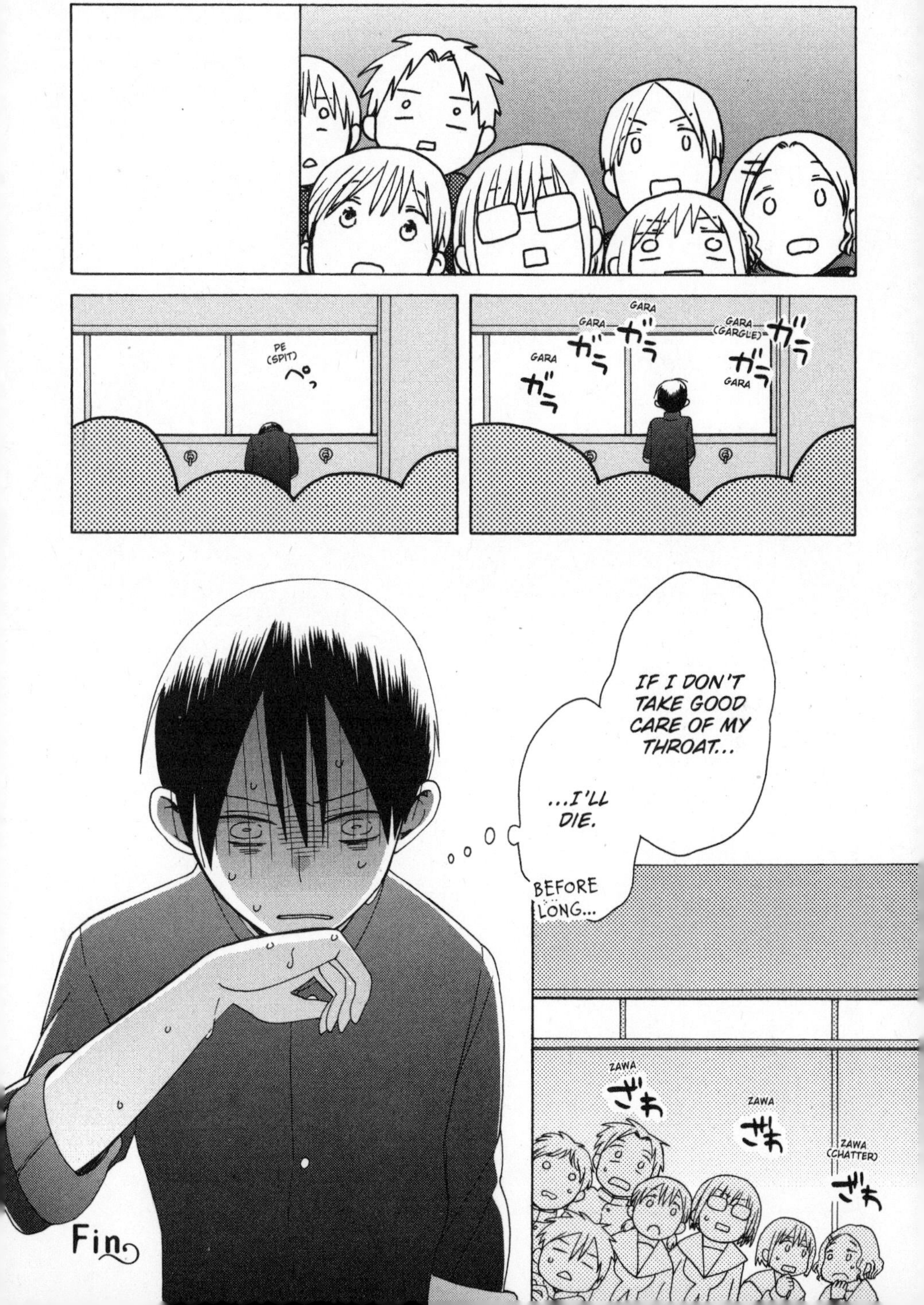
GARA (GARGLE) ガラ
GARA ガラ
GARA ガラ
GARA ガラ
GARA ガラ
PE (SPIT) ぺっ
IF I DON'T TAKE GOOD CARE OF MY THROAT...
...I'LL DIE.
BEFORE LONG...
ZAWA (CHATTER) ざわ
ZAWA ざわ
ZAWA ざわ
Fin

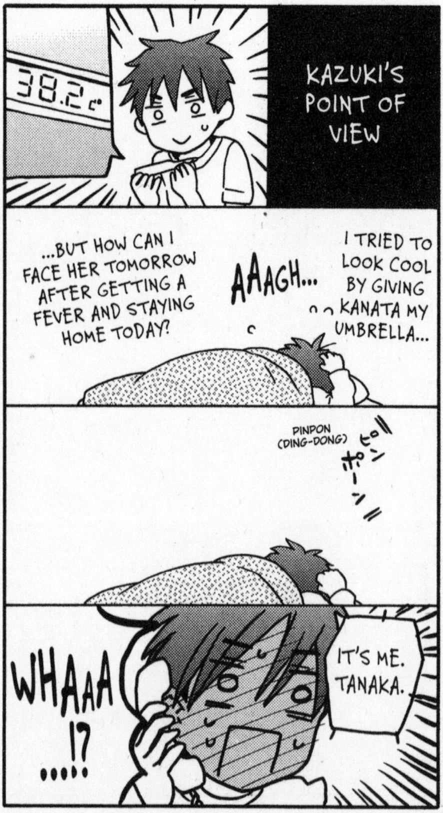
KAZUKI'S POINT OF VIEW
38.2°C
I TRIED TO LOOK COOL BY GIVING KANATA MY UMBRELLA...
AAAGH...
...BUT HOW CAN I FACE HER TOMORROW AFTER GETTING A FEVER AND STAYING HOME TODAY?
PINPON (DING-DONG)
ピンポーン
IT'S ME. TANAKA.
WHAAA...!?

Love at Fourteen

Fuka Mizutani

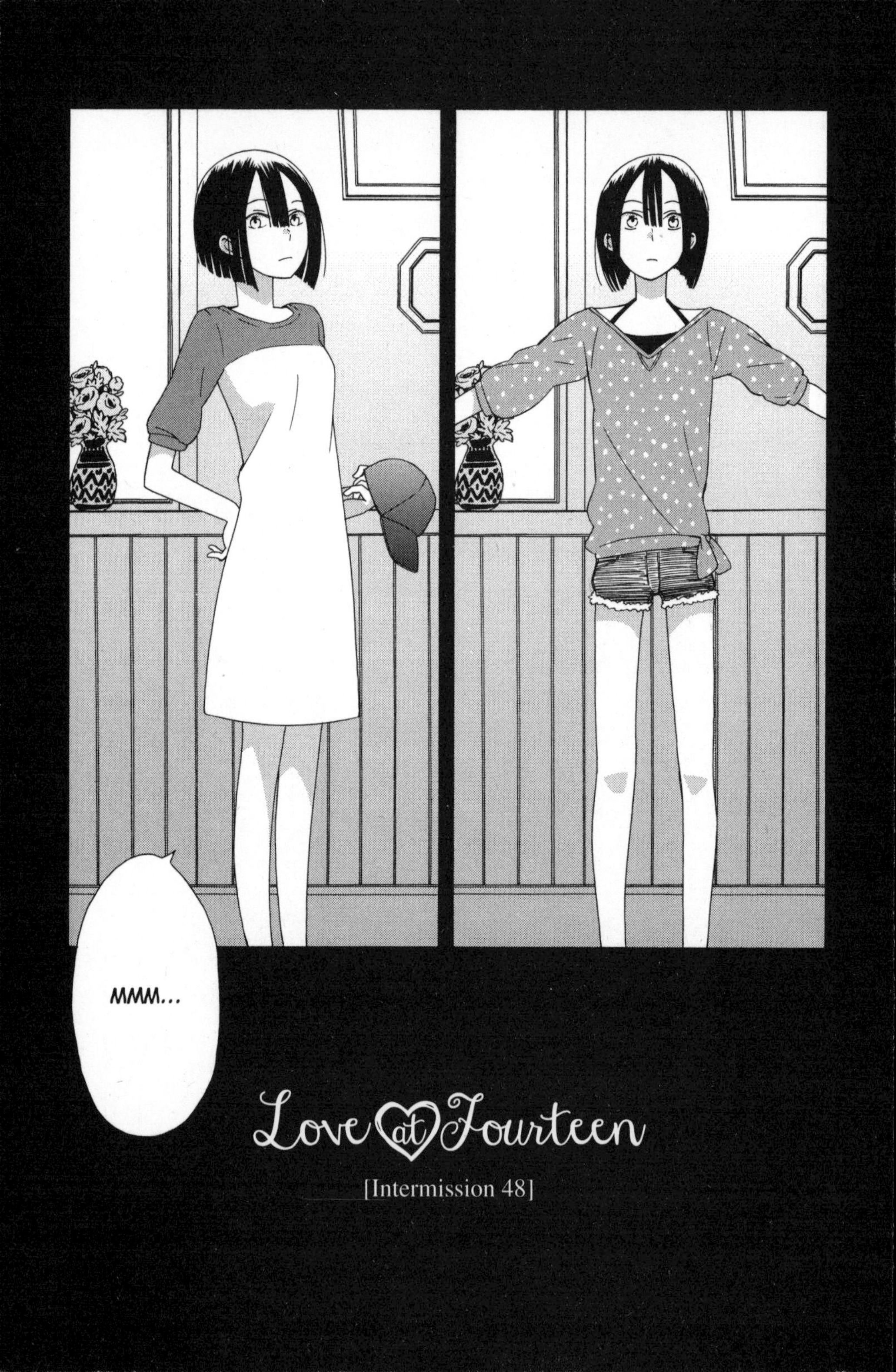
MMM...

Love at Fourteen

[Intermission 48]

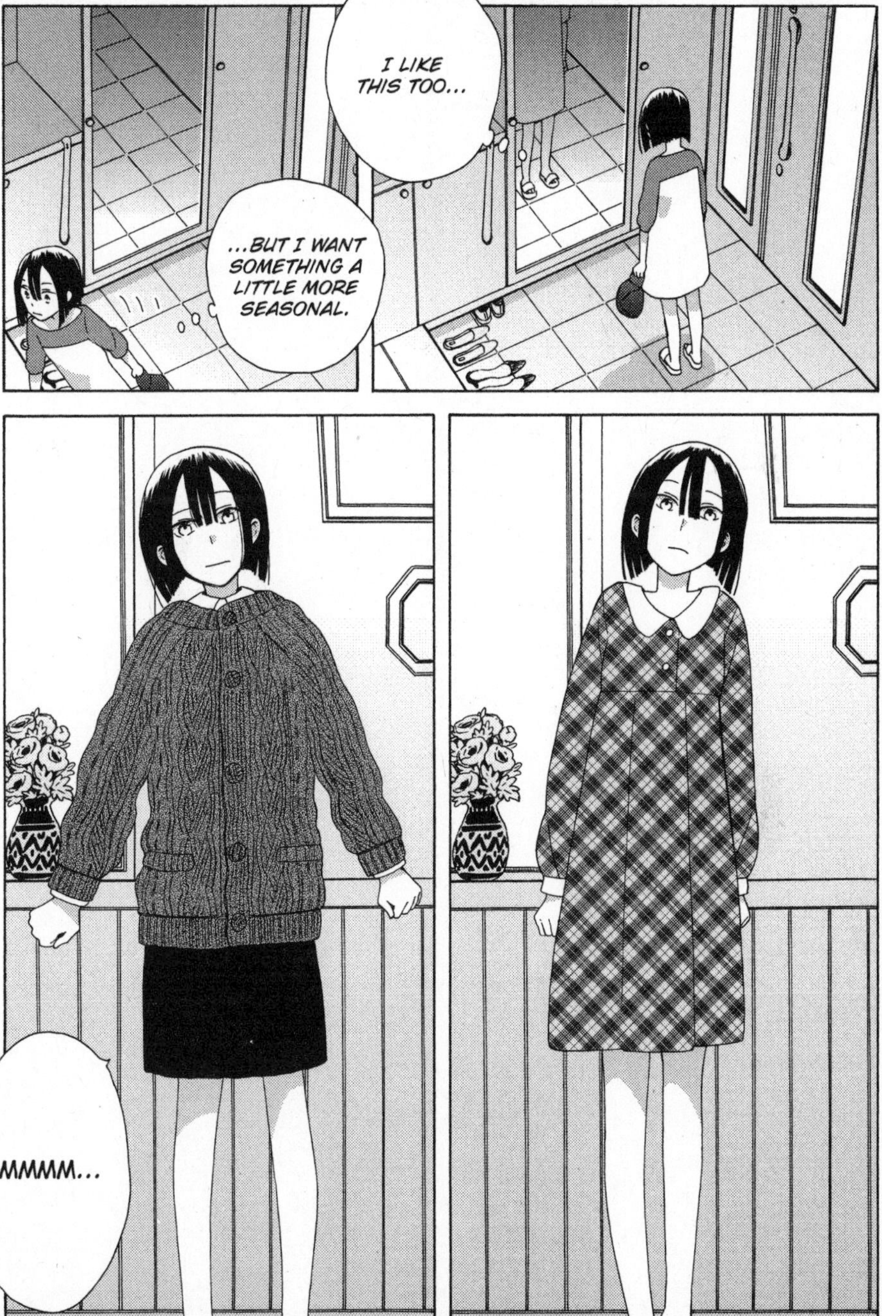
I LIKE THIS TOO...
...BUT I WANT SOMETHING A LITTLE MORE SEASONAL.
MMMM...

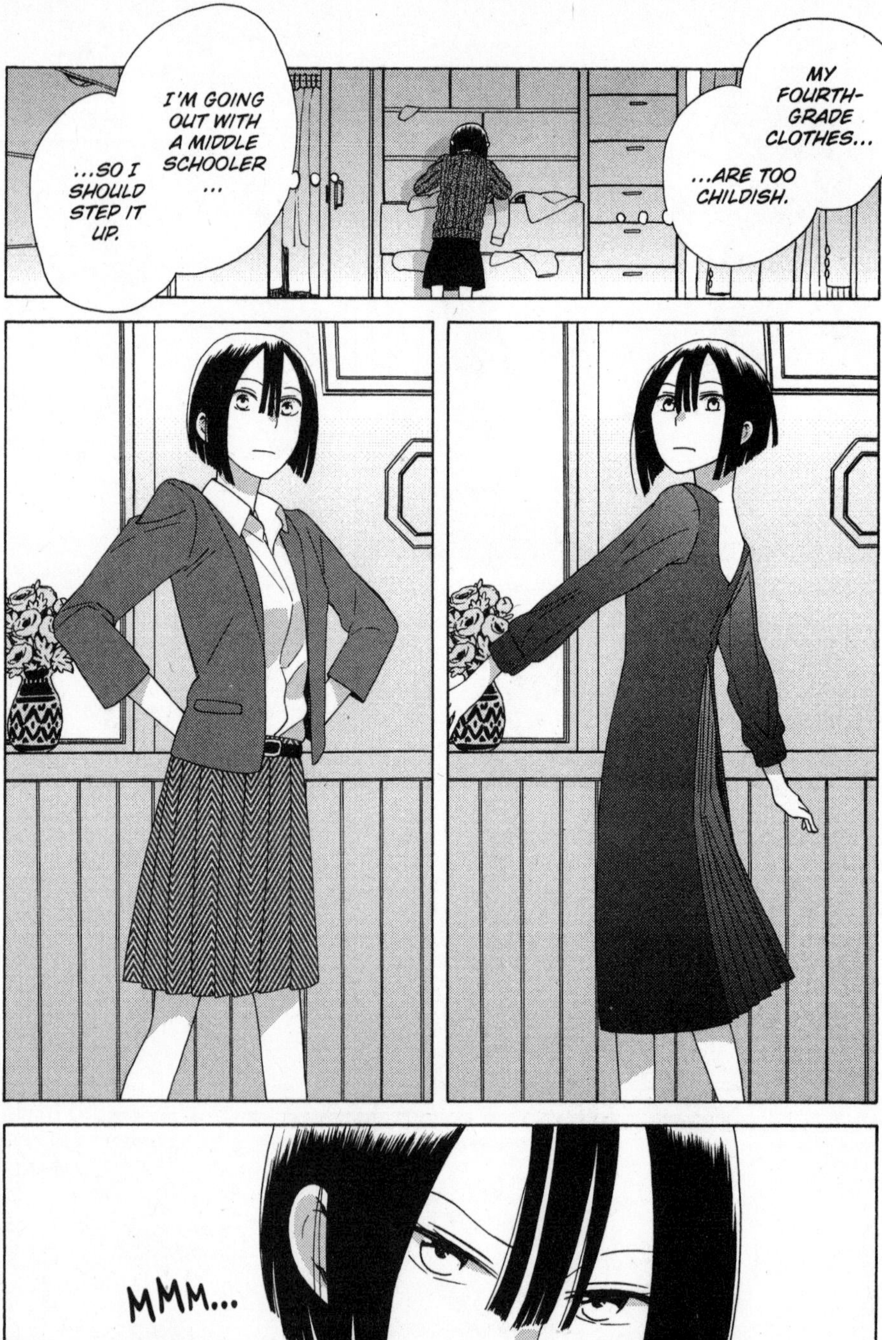
MY FOURTH-GRADE CLOTHES...
...ARE TOO CHILDISH.
I'M GOING OUT WITH A MIDDLE SCHOOLER...
...SO I SHOULD STEP IT UP.
MMM...

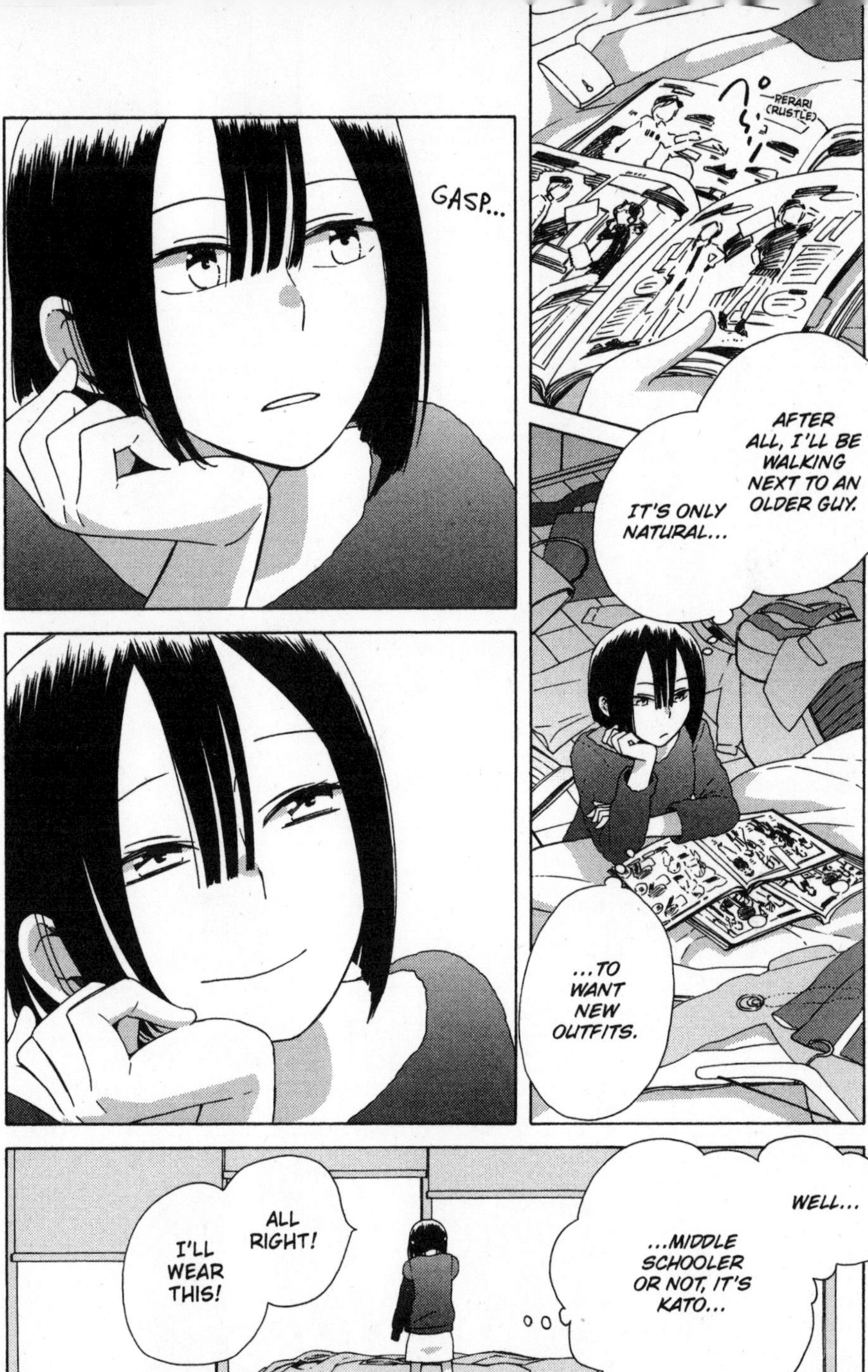
PERARI (RUSTLE)
AFTER ALL, I'LL BE WALKING NEXT TO AN OLDER GUY.
IT'S ONLY NATURAL...
...TO WANT NEW OUTFITS.
GASP...
WELL...
...MIDDLE SCHOOLER OR NOT, IT'S KATO...
ALL RIGHT!
I'LL WEAR THIS!

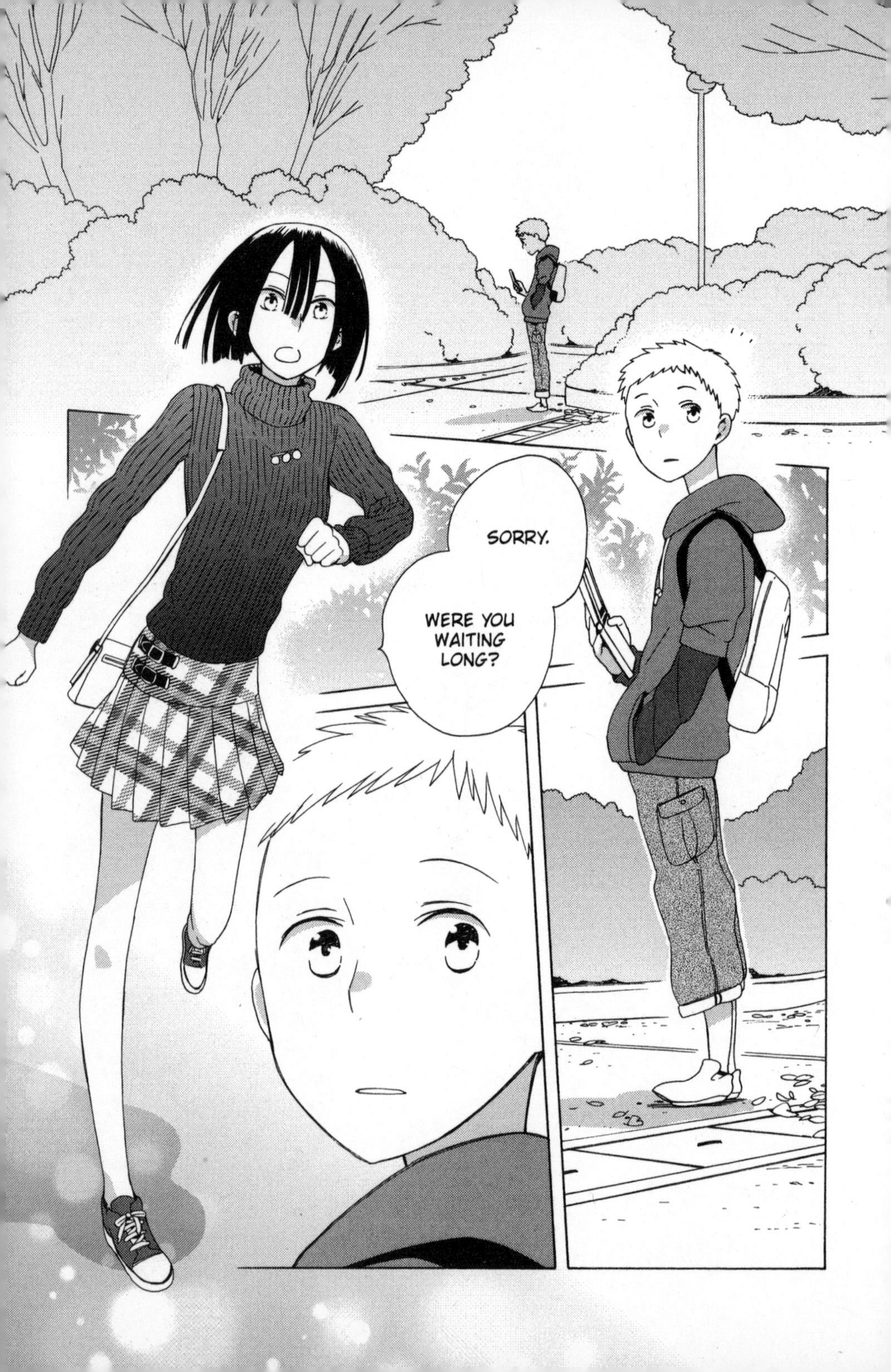
SORRY.
WERE YOU WAITING LONG?

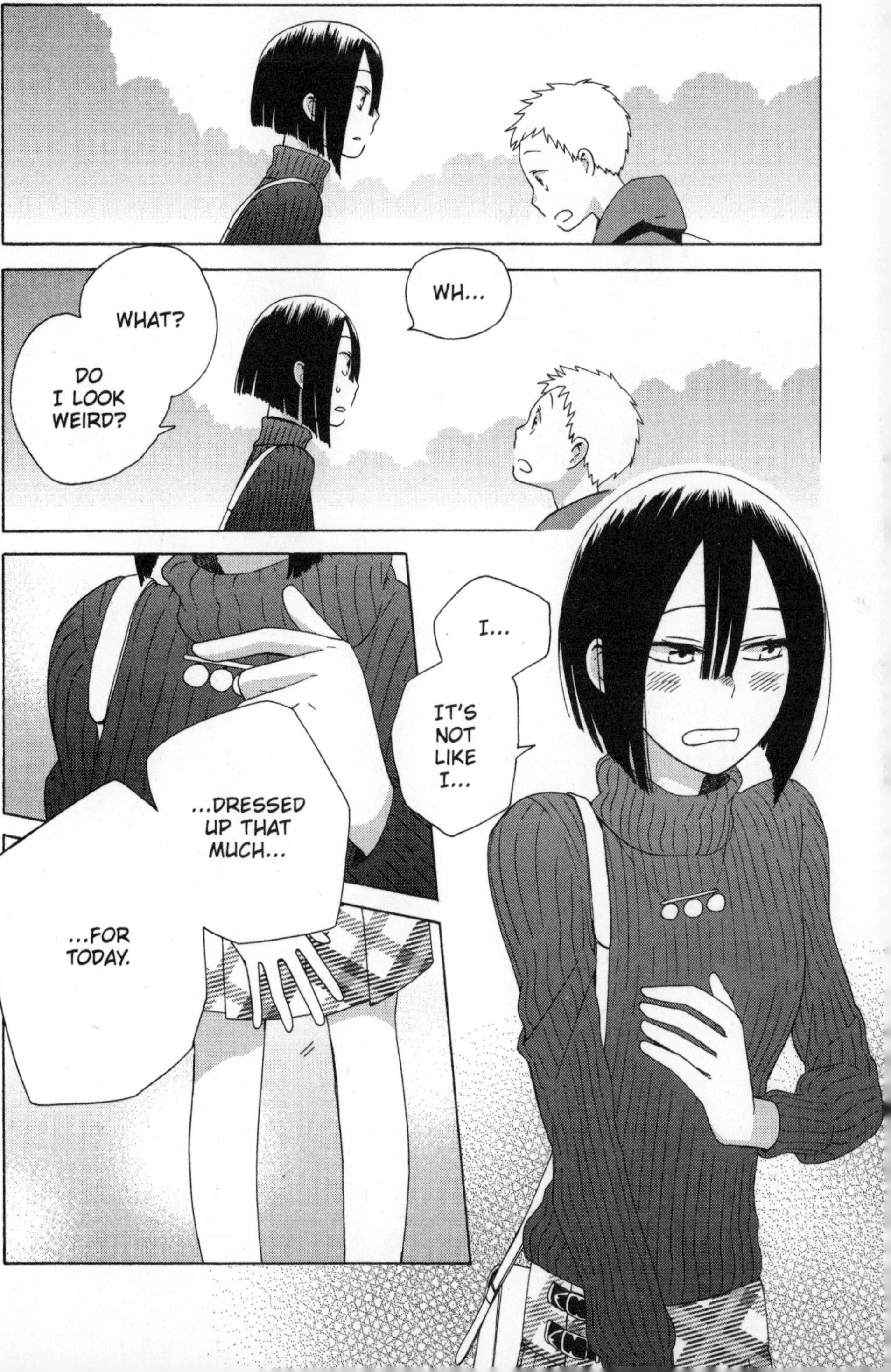
WH...
WHAT?
DO I LOOK WEIRD?
I...
IT'S NOT LIKE I...
...DRESSED UP THAT MUCH...
...FOR TODAY.

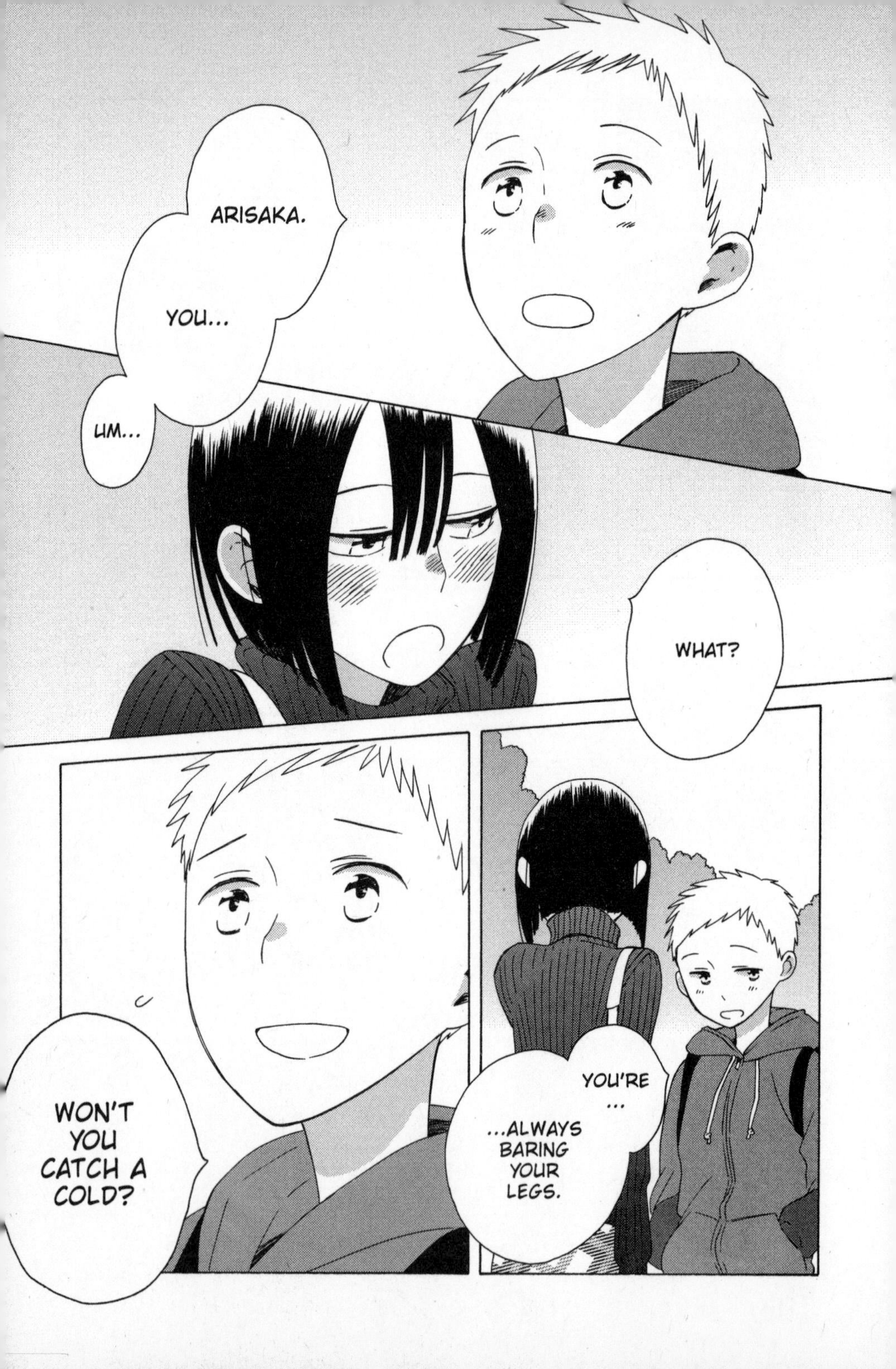
ARISAKA.
YOU...
UM...
WHAT?
YOU'RE ...
...ALWAYS BARING YOUR LEGS.
WON'T YOU CATCH A COLD?

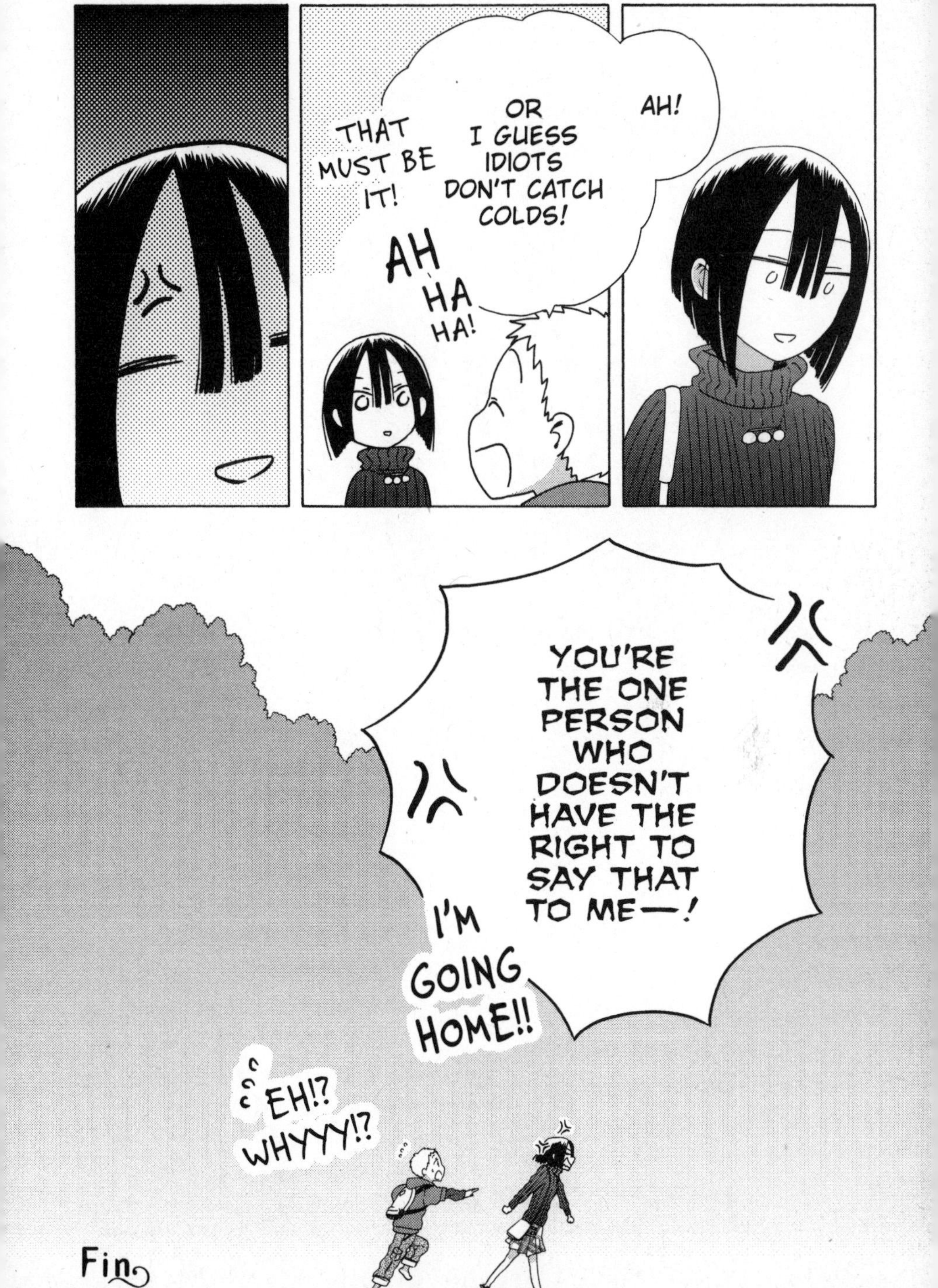
AH!
OR I GUESS IDIOTS DON'T CATCH COLDS!
THAT MUST BE IT!
AH HA HA!
YOU'RE THE ONE PERSON WHO DOESN'T HAVE THE RIGHT TO SAY THAT TO ME—!
I'M GOING HOME!!
EH!? WHYYY!?
Fin

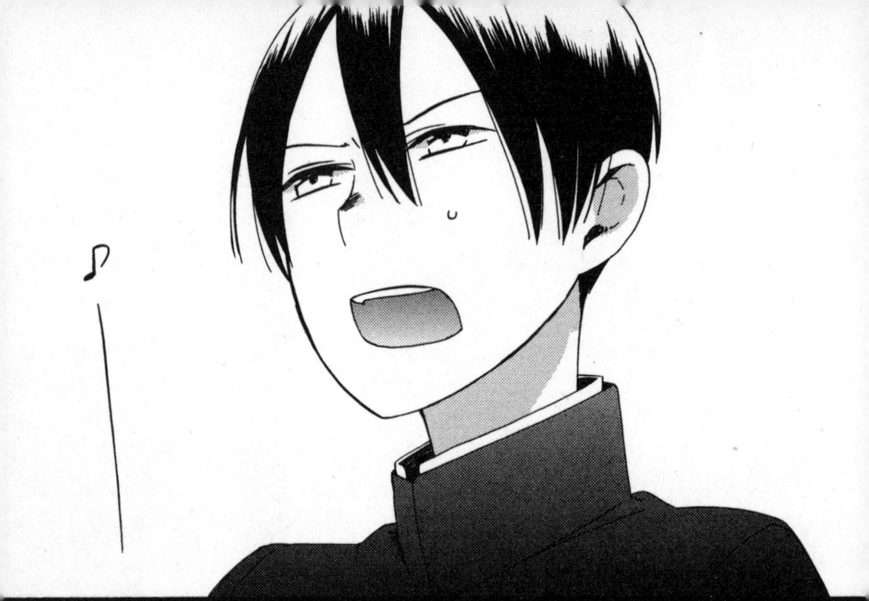

Love at Fourteen

[Intermission 49]

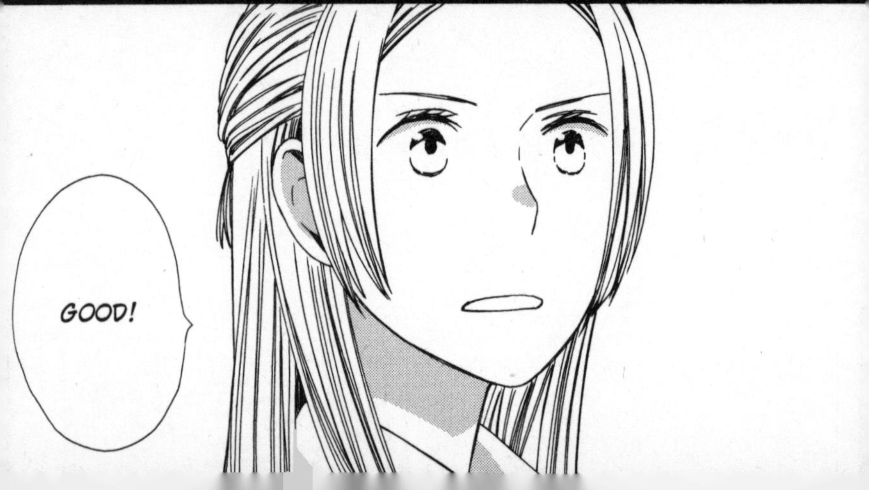
GOOD!

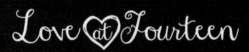

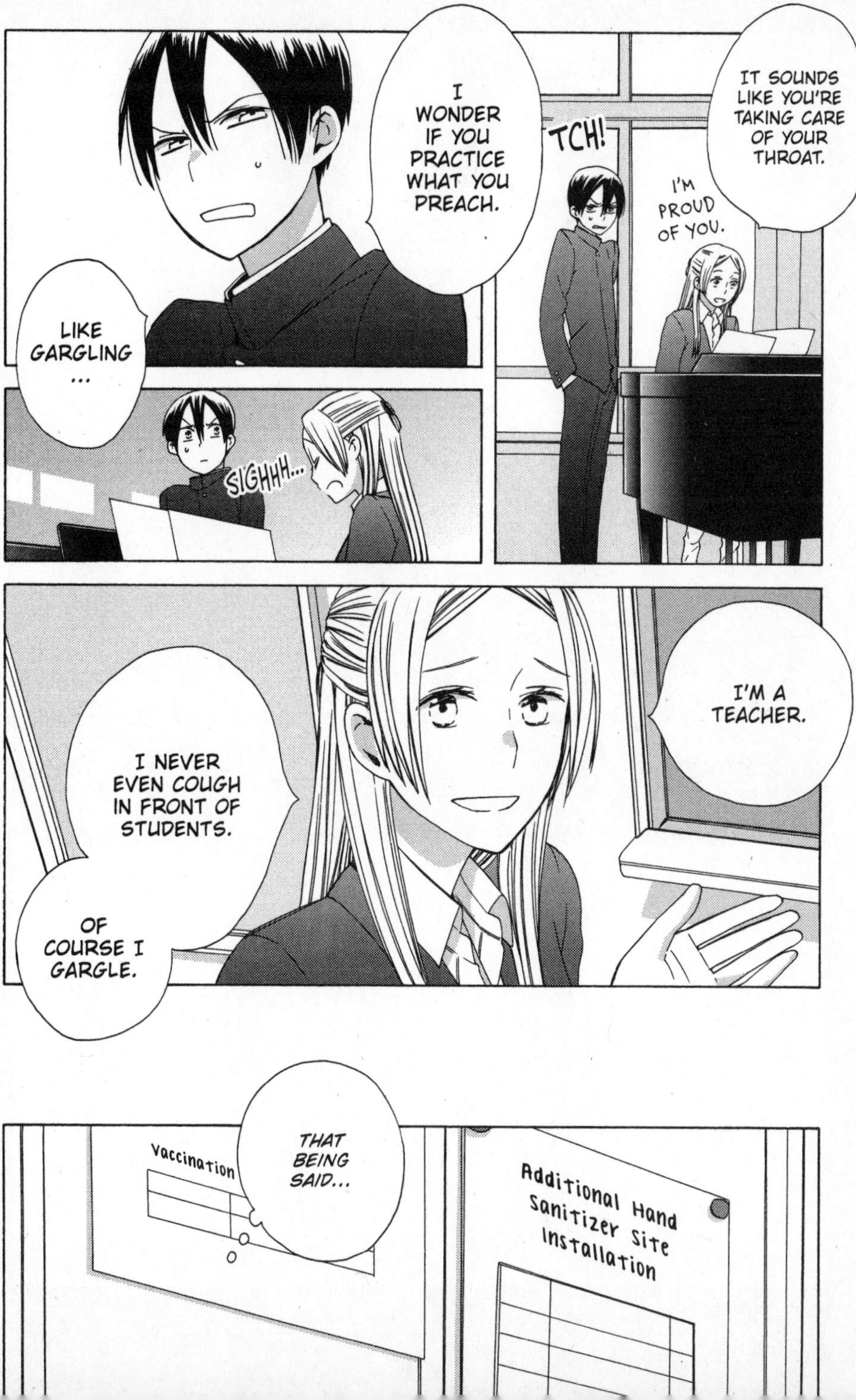
IT SOUNDS LIKE YOU'RE TAKING CARE OF YOUR THROAT.
I'M PROUD OF YOU.
TCH!
I WONDER IF YOU PRACTICE WHAT YOU PREACH.
LIKE GARGLING...
SIGHHH...
I'M A TEACHER.
I NEVER EVEN COUGH IN FRONT OF STUDENTS.
OF COURSE I GARGLE.
THAT BEING SAID...
Vaccination
Additional Hand Sanitizer Site Installation

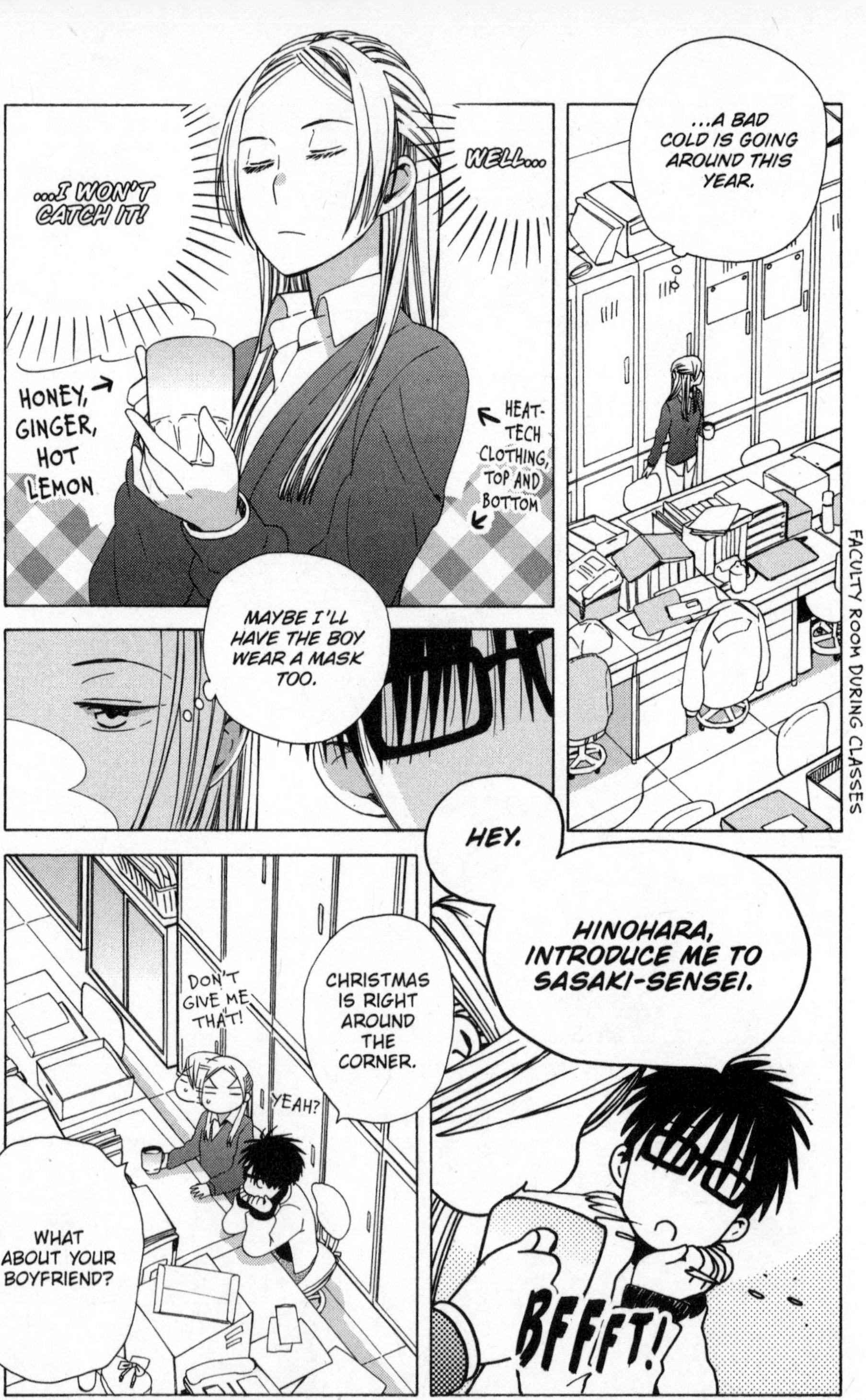
...A BAD COLD IS GOING AROUND THIS YEAR.
FACULTY ROOM DURING CLASSES
WELL...
...I WON'T CATCH IT!
HONEY, GINGER, HOT LEMON
HEAT-TECH CLOTHING, TOP AND BOTTOM
MAYBE I'LL HAVE THE BOY WEAR A MASK TOO.
HEY.
HINOHARA, INTRODUCE ME TO SASAKI-SENSEI.
BFFFT!
CHRISTMAS IS RIGHT AROUND THE CORNER.
DON'T GIVE ME THAT!
YEAH?
WHAT ABOUT YOUR BOYFRIEND?

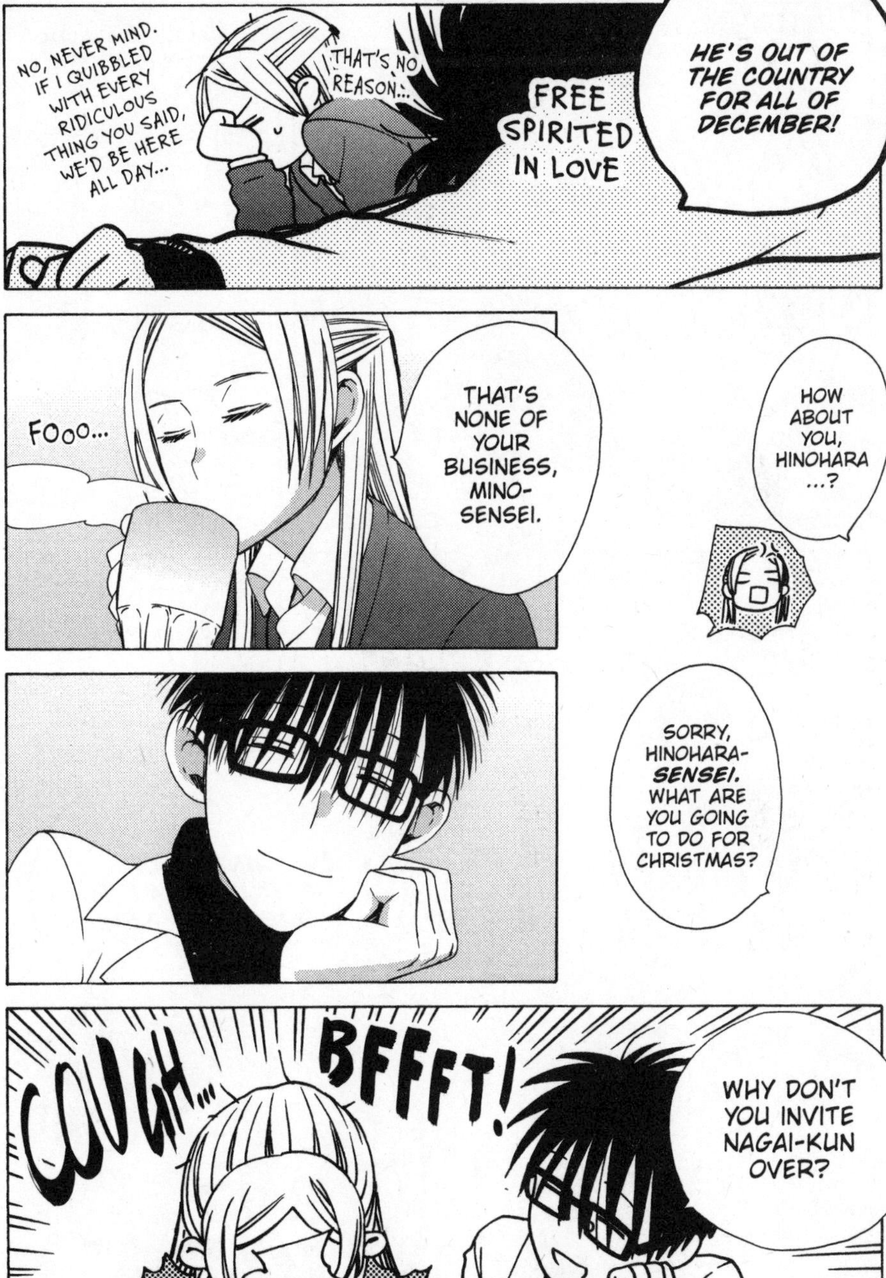
HE'S OUT OF THE COUNTRY FOR ALL OF DECEMBER!
FREE SPIRITED IN LOVE
THAT'S NO REASON...
NO, NEVER MIND. IF I QUIBBLED WITH EVERY RIDICULOUS THING YOU SAID, WE'D BE HERE ALL DAY...
HOW ABOUT YOU, HINOHARA ...?
THAT'S NONE OF YOUR BUSINESS, MINO-SENSEI.
FOOO...
SORRY, HINOHARA-SENSEI. WHAT ARE YOU GOING TO DO FOR CHRISTMAS?
WHY DON'T YOU INVITE NAGAI-KUN OVER?
BFFFT!
COUGH...

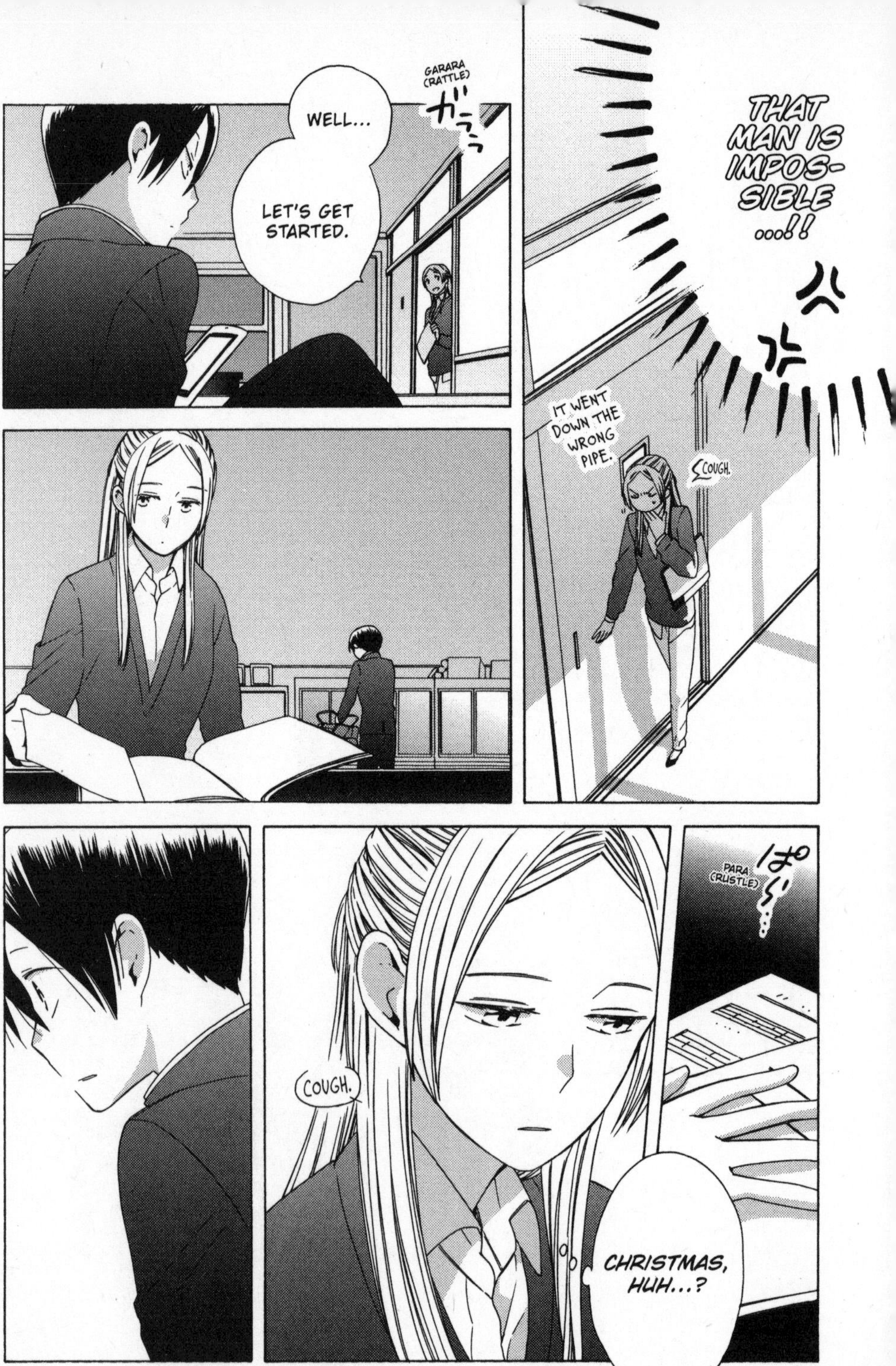
THAT MAN IS IMPOSSIBLE...!!
IT WENT DOWN THE WRONG PIPE.
COUGH.
GARARA (RATTLE)
WELL...
LET'S GET STARTED.
PARA (RUSTLE)
CHRISTMAS, HUH...?
COUGH.

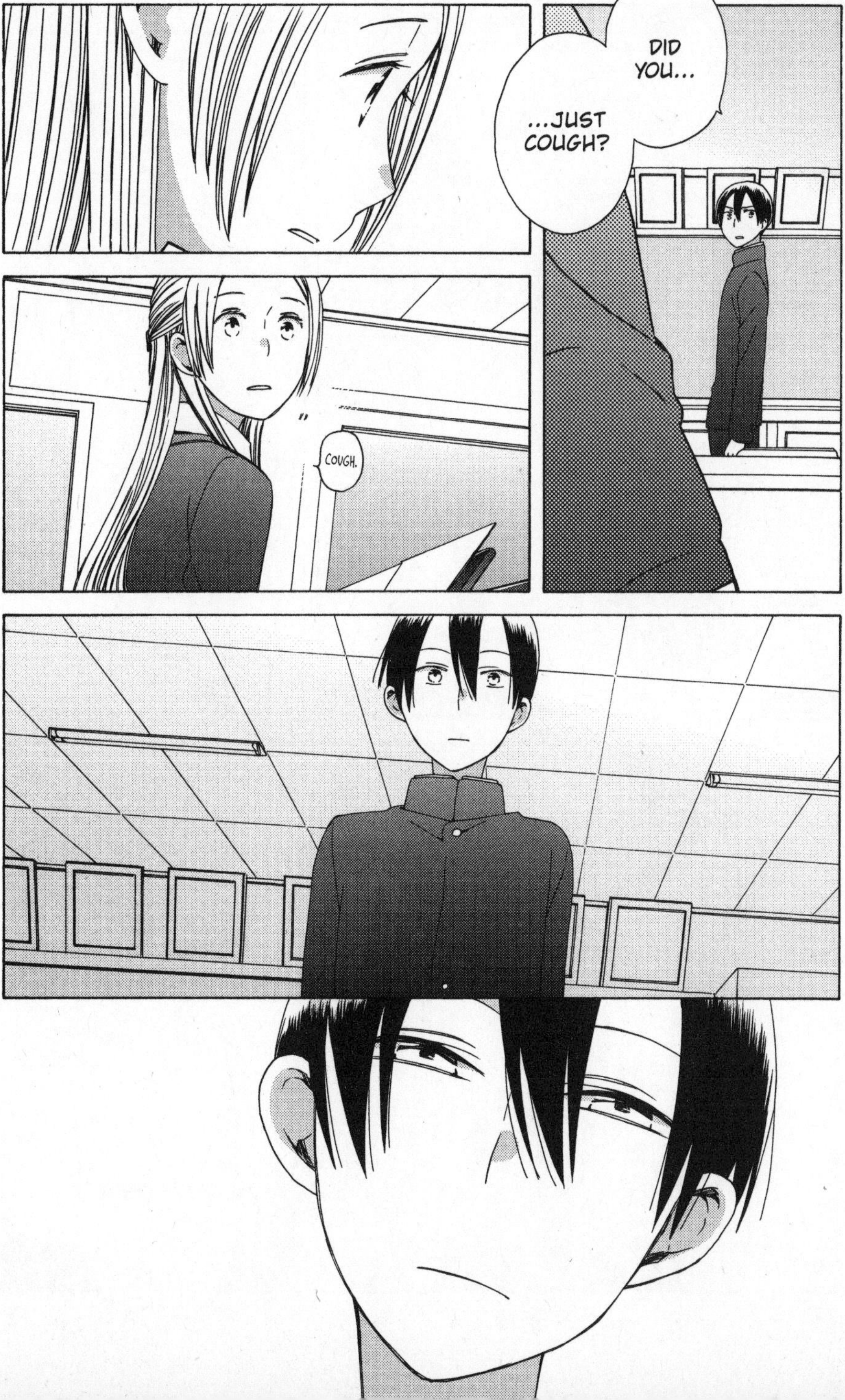
DID YOU...
...JUST COUGH?
COUGH.

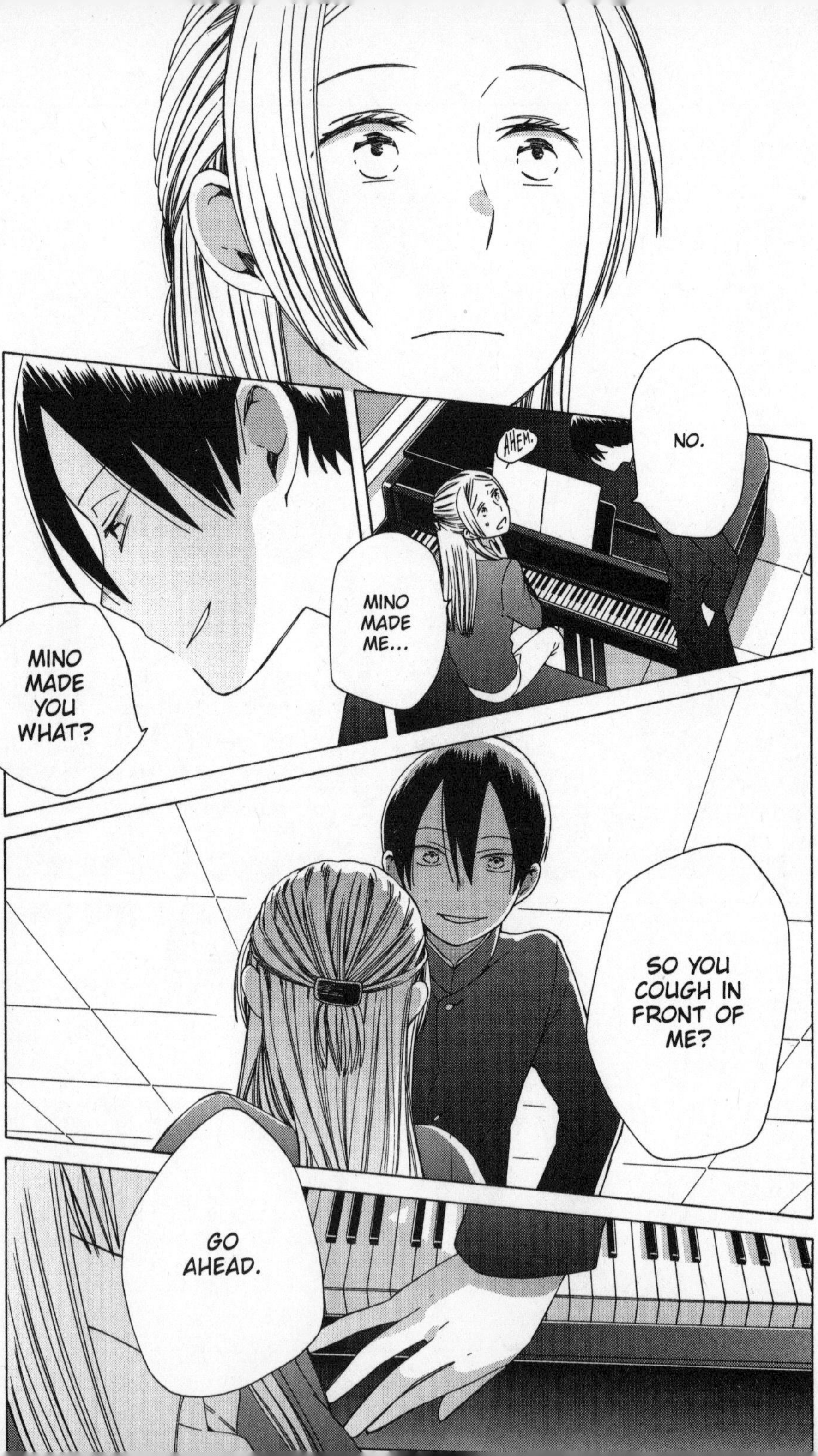
NO.
AHEM.
MINO MADE ME...
MINO MADE YOU WHAT?
SO YOU COUGH IN FRONT OF ME?
GO AHEAD.

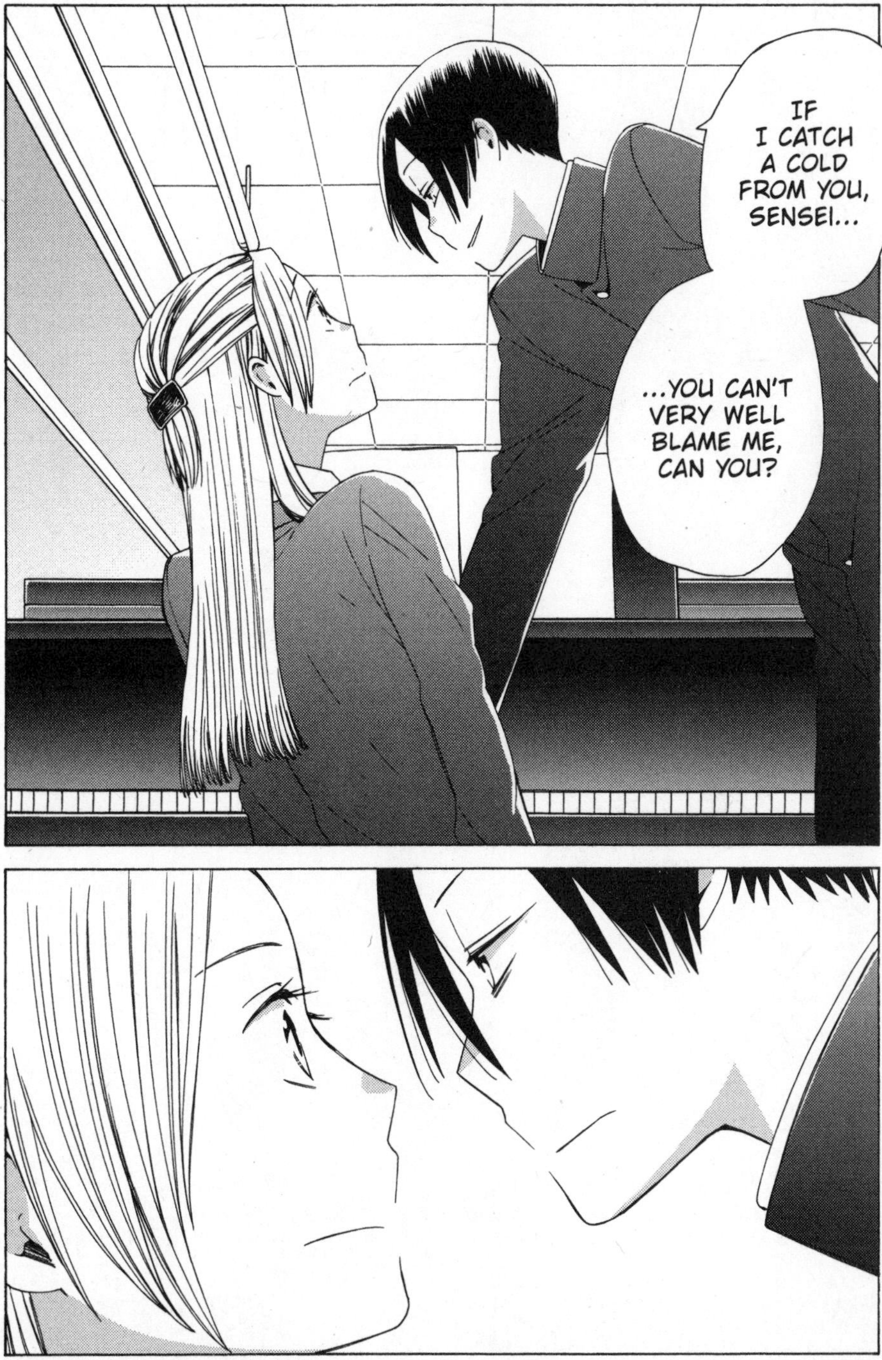
IF I CATCH A COLD FROM YOU, SENSEI...
...YOU CAN'T VERY WELL BLAME ME, CAN YOU?

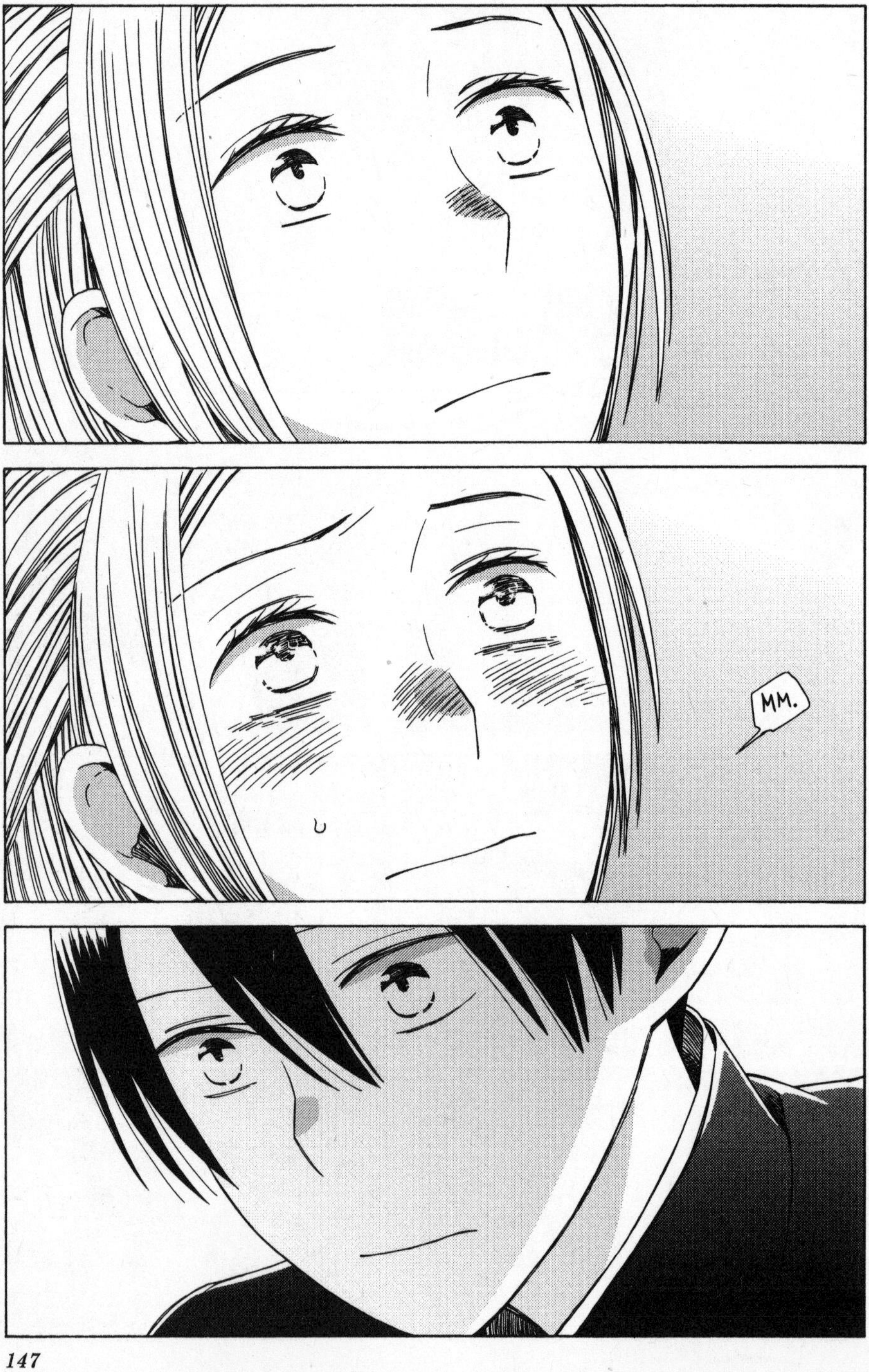
MM.

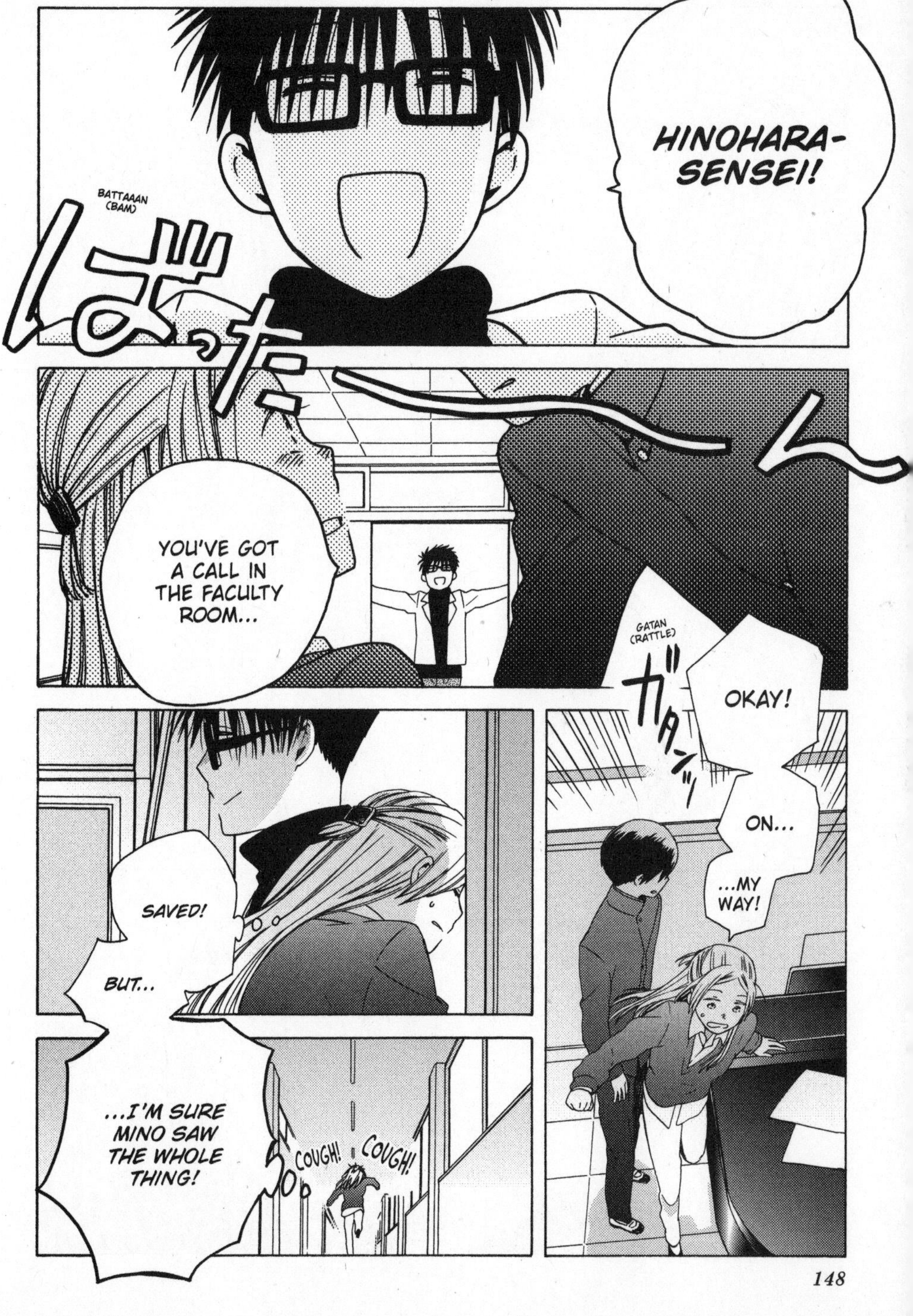
HINOHARA-SENSEI!
BATTAAAN (BAM)
YOU'VE GOT A CALL IN THE FACULTY ROOM...
GATAN (RATTLE)
OKAY!
ON...
...MY WAY!
SAVED!
BUT...
...I'M SURE MINO SAW THE WHOLE THING!
COUGH! COUGH!

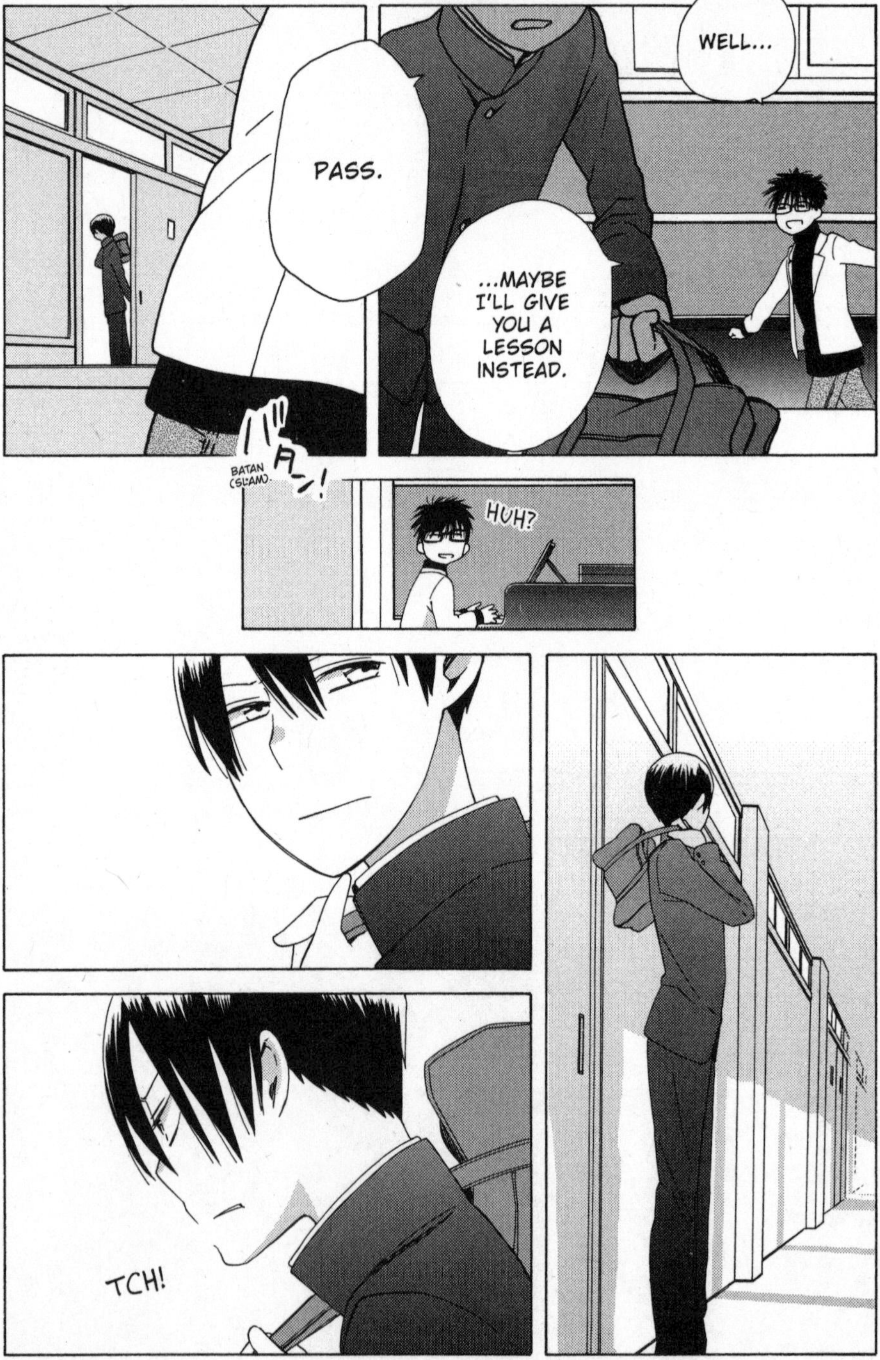
WELL...
...MAYBE I'LL GIVE YOU A LESSON INSTEAD.
PASS.
BATAN (SLAM)
HUH?
TCH!

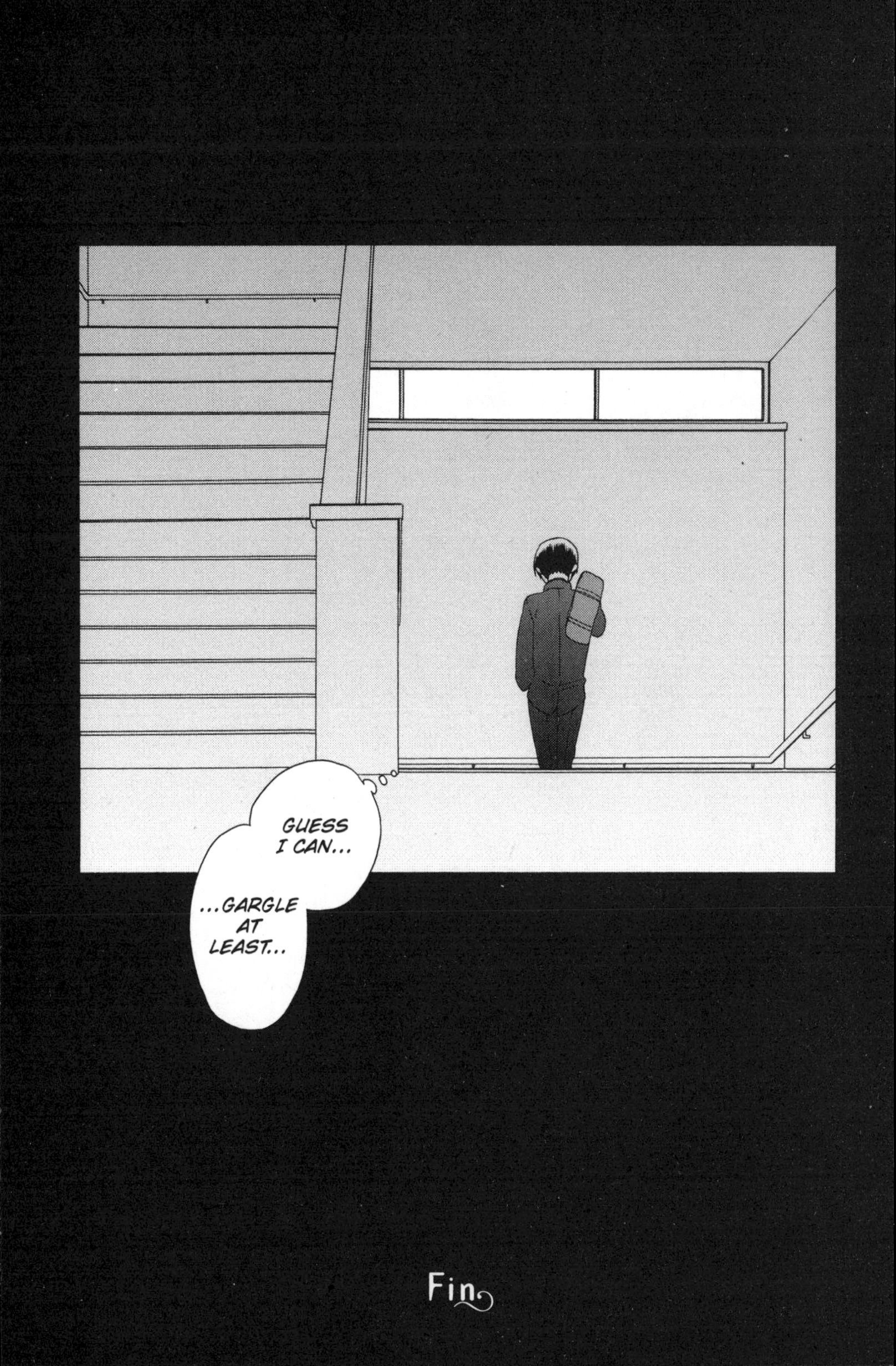
GUESS I CAN...
...GARGLE AT LEAST...

Fin

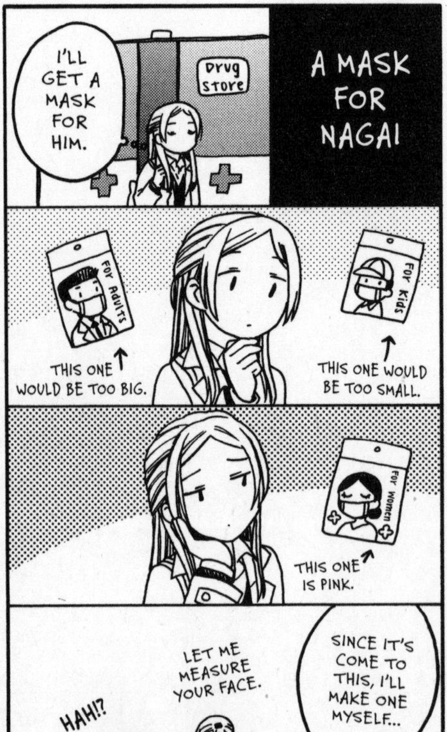
A MASK FOR NAGAI
Drug store
I'LL GET A MASK FOR HIM.
For Kids
THIS ONE WOULD BE TOO SMALL.
For Adults
THIS ONE WOULD BE TOO BIG.
For women
THIS ONE IS PINK.
SINCE IT'S COME TO THIS, I'LL MAKE ONE MYSELF...
LET ME MEASURE YOUR FACE.
HAH!?

Love at Fourteen

Fuka Mizutani

Love at Fourteen

[Chapter 38]

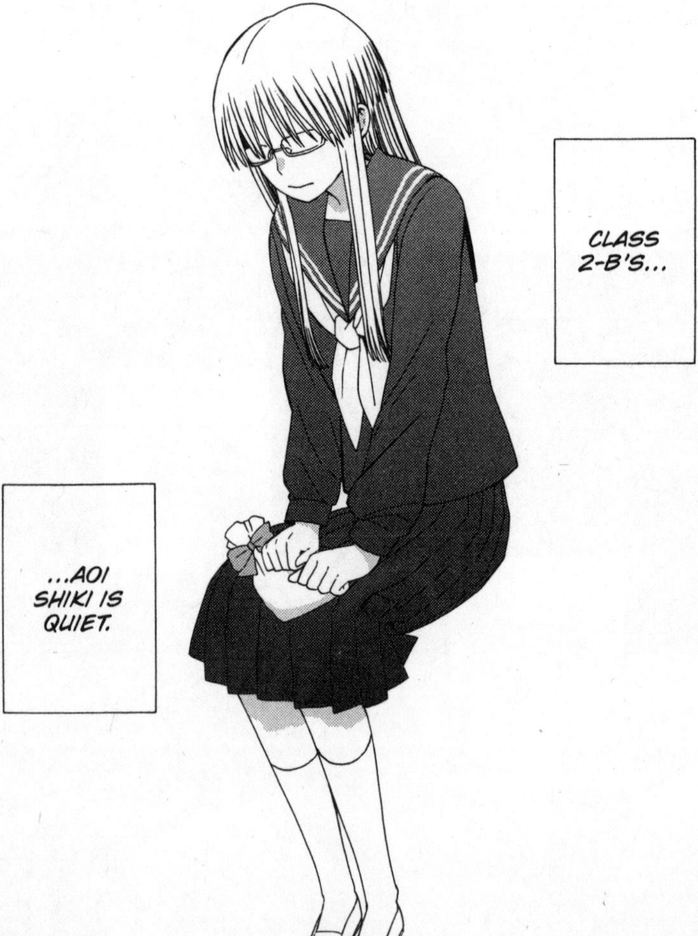
CLASS 2-B'S...
...AOI SHIKI IS QUIET.

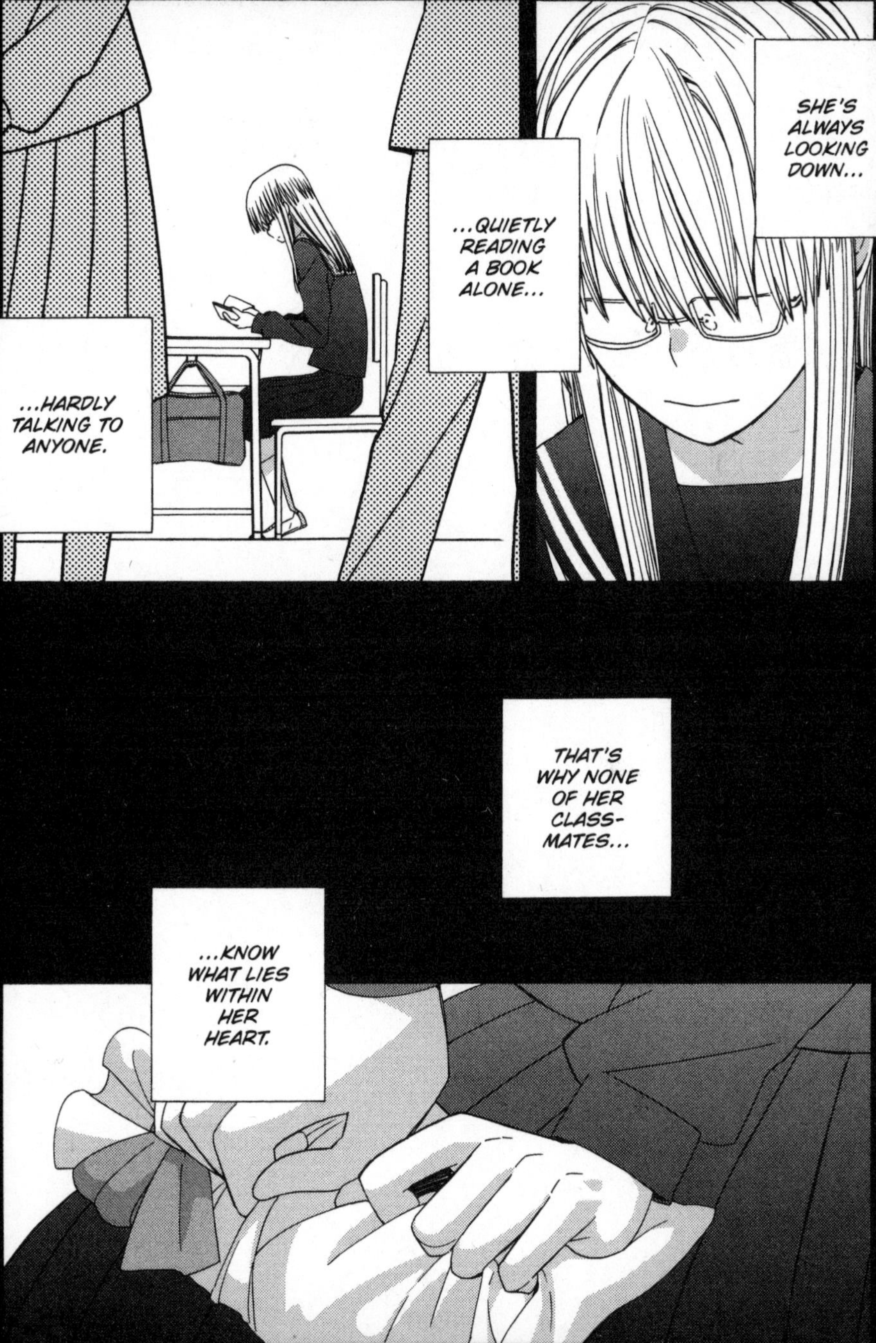
SHE'S ALWAYS LOOKING DOWN...
...QUIETLY READING A BOOK ALONE...
...HARDLY TALKING TO ANYONE.
THAT'S WHY NONE OF HER CLASS-MATES...
...KNOW WHAT LIES WITHIN HER HEART.

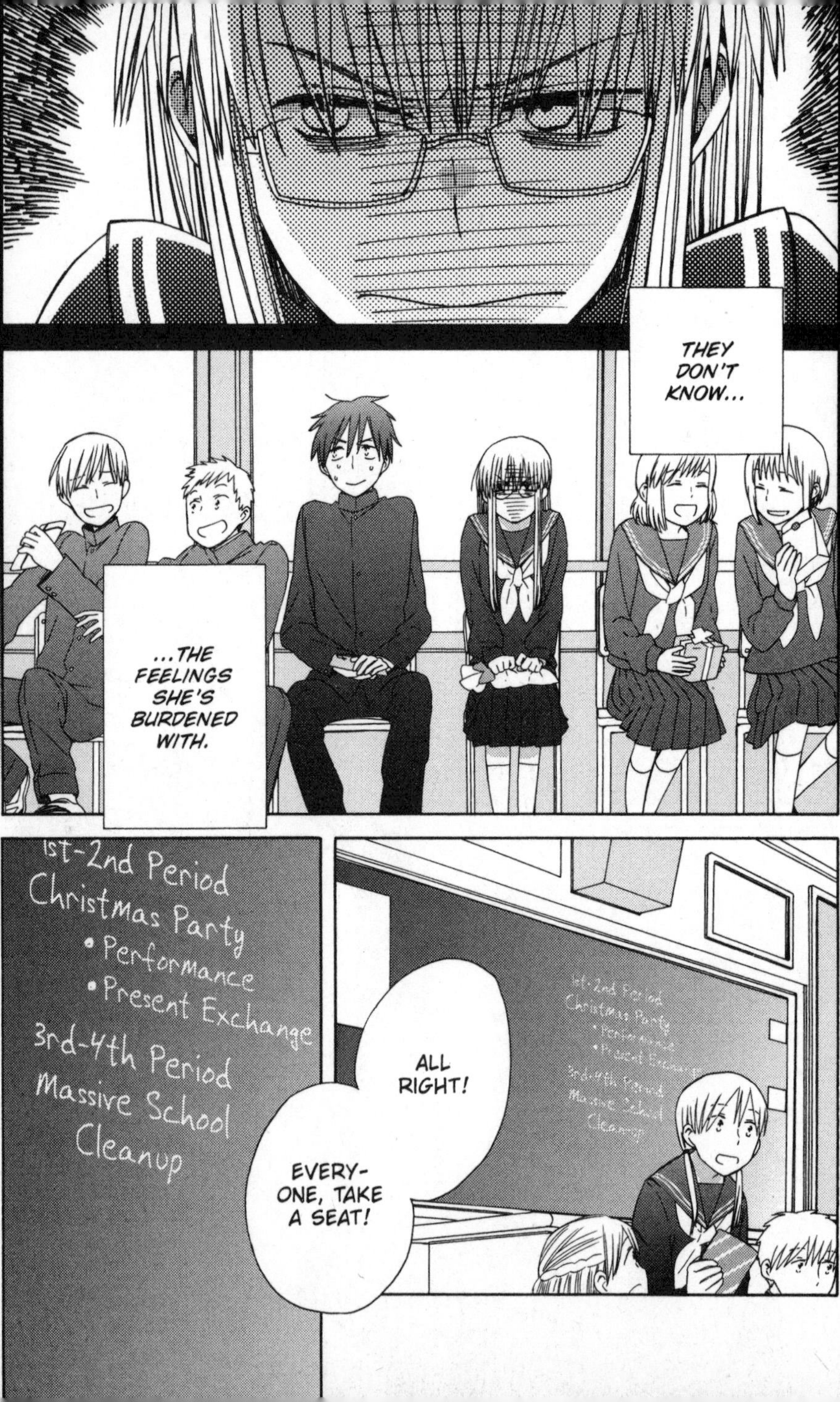
THEY DON'T KNOW...
...THE FEELINGS SHE'S BURDENED WITH.
ALL RIGHT!
EVERY-ONE, TAKE A SEAT!
1st-2nd Period
Christmas Party
• Performance
• Present Exchange
3rd-4th Period
Massive School Cleanup

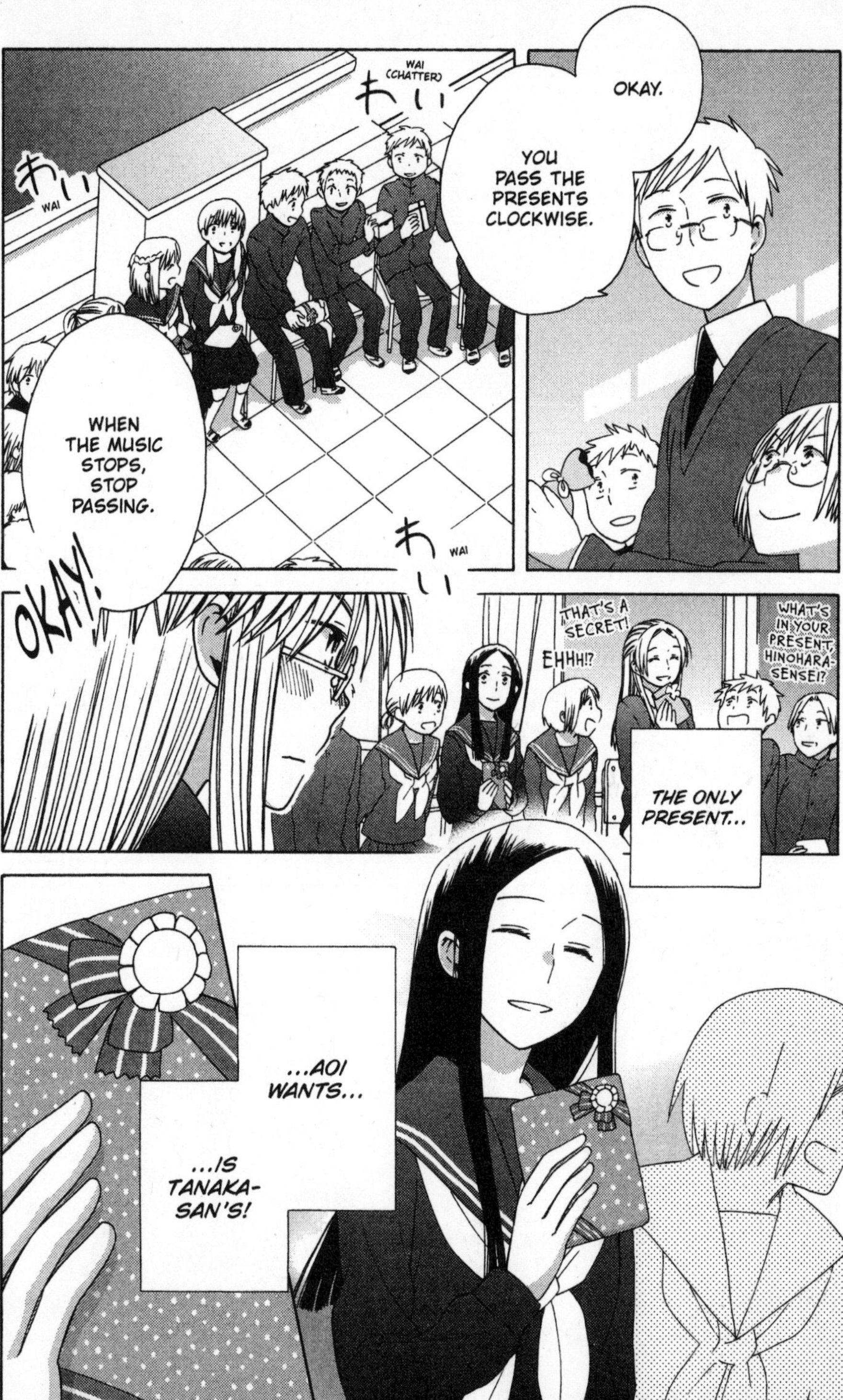
OKAY.
YOU PASS THE PRESENTS CLOCKWISE.
WAI (CHATTER)
わい
わい
WAI
WHEN THE MUSIC STOPS, STOP PASSING.
わい
WAI
OKAY!
WHAT'S IN YOUR PRESENT, HINOHARA-SENSEI!?
THAT'S A SECRET!
EHHH!?
THE ONLY PRESENT...
...AOI WANTS...
...IS TANAKA-SAN'S!

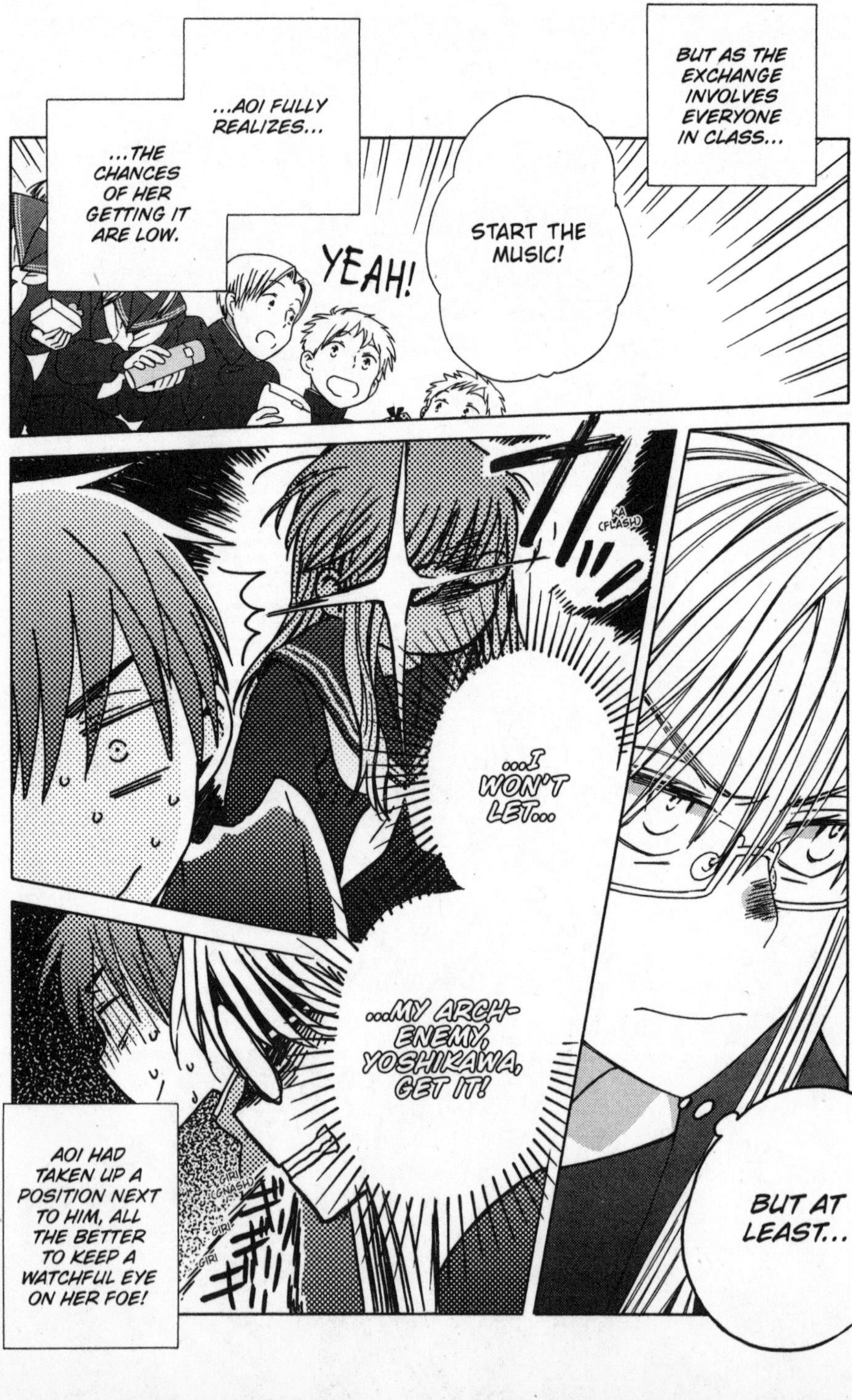
BUT AS THE EXCHANGE INVOLVES EVERYONE IN CLASS...
START THE MUSIC!
YEAH!
...AOI FULLY REALIZES...
...THE CHANCES OF HER GETTING IT ARE LOW.
BUT AT LEAST...
KA (FLASH)
...I WON'T LET...
...MY ARCH-ENEMY, YOSHIKAWA, GET IT!
GIRI (GNASH) GIRI GIRI
AOI HAD TAKEN UP A POSITION NEXT TO HIM, ALL THE BETTER TO KEEP A WATCHFUL EYE ON HER FOE!

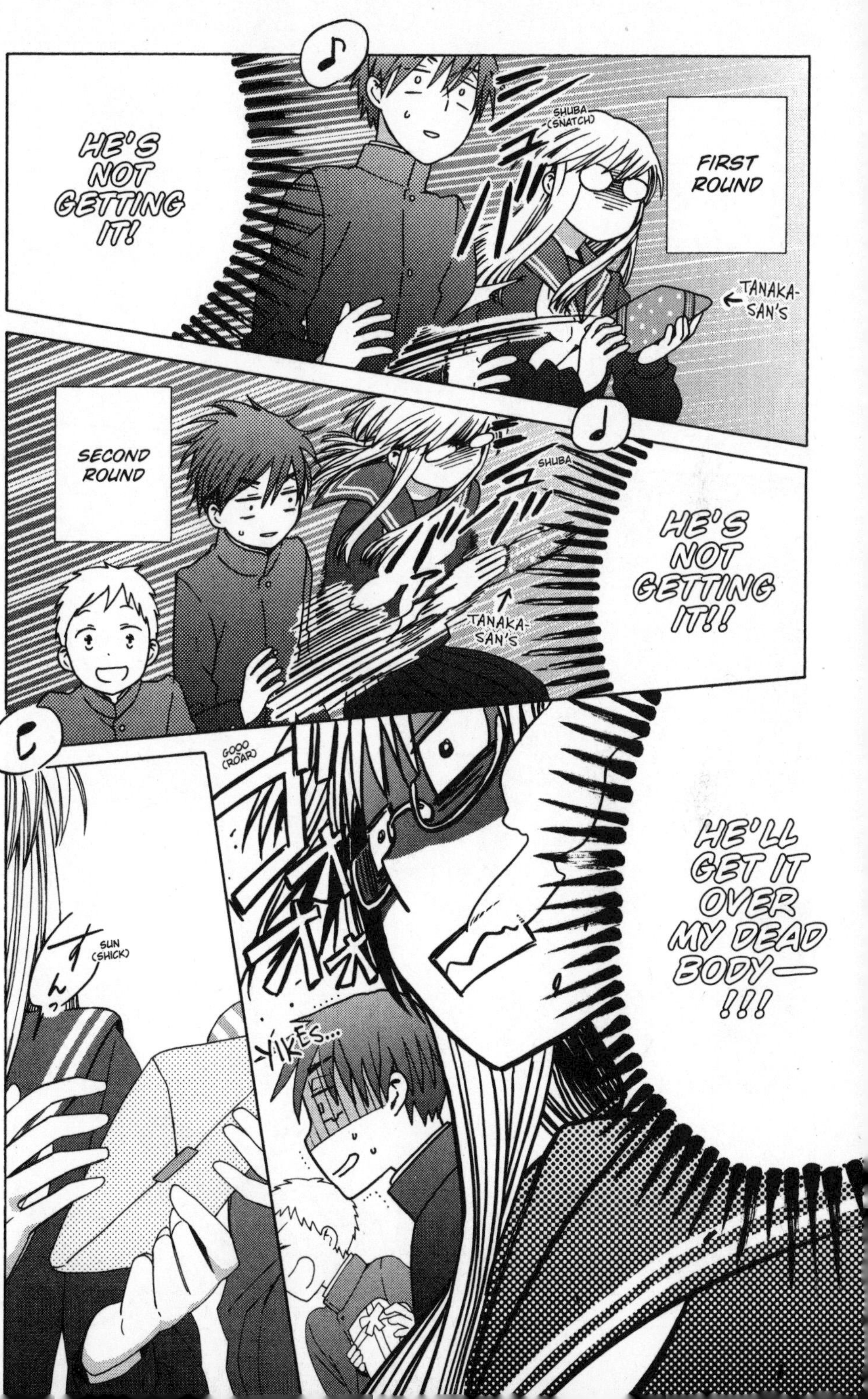
FIRST ROUND
SHUBA (SNATCH)
HE'S NOT GETTING IT!
← TANAKA-SAN'S
SECOND ROUND
SHUBA
HE'S NOT GETTING IT!!
TANAKA-SAN'S
HE'LL GET IT OVER MY DEAD BODY—!!!
GOOO (ROAR)
YIKES...
SUN (SHICK)

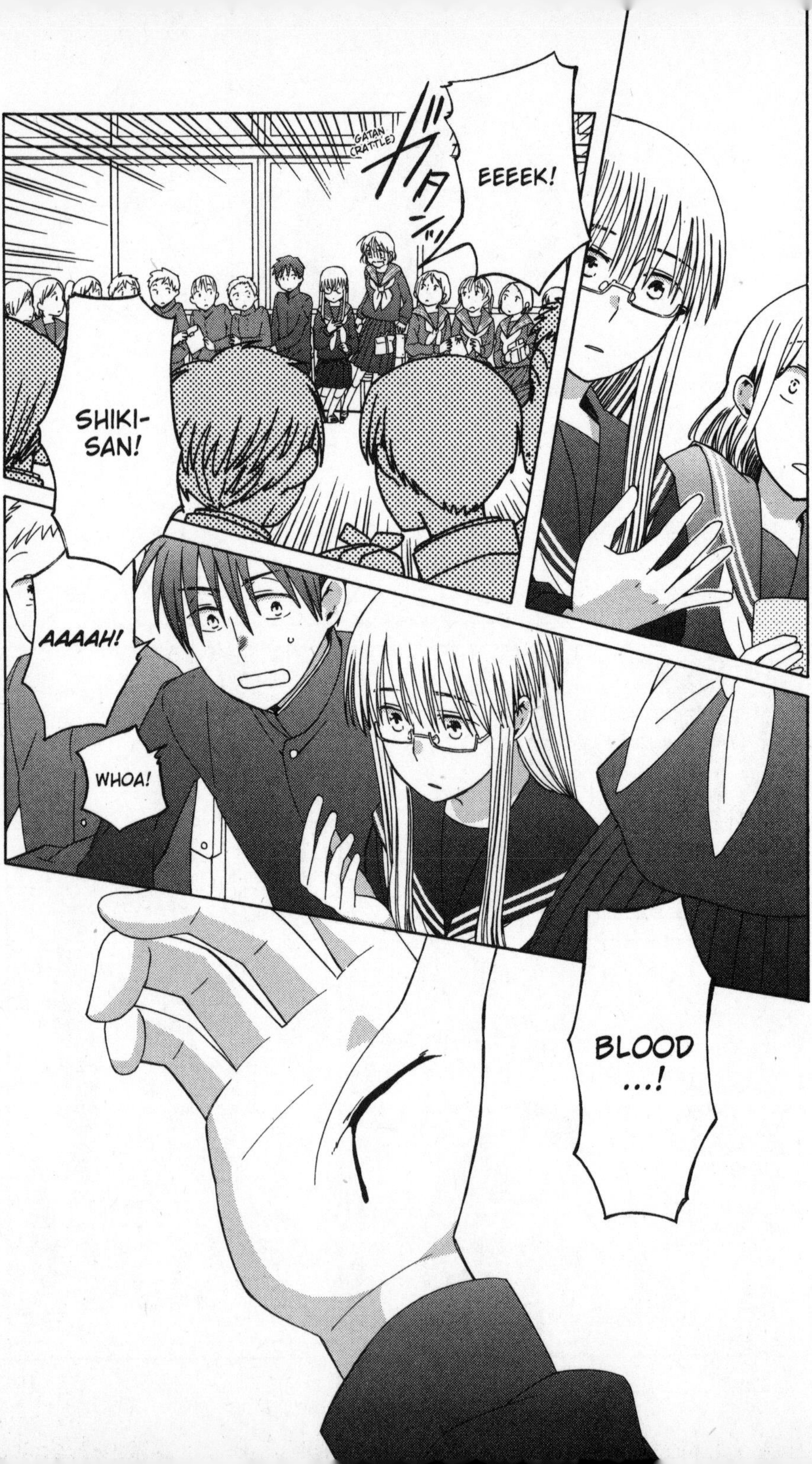
GATAN (RATTLE)
EEEEK!
SHIKI-SAN!
AAAAH!
WHOA!
BLOOD ...!

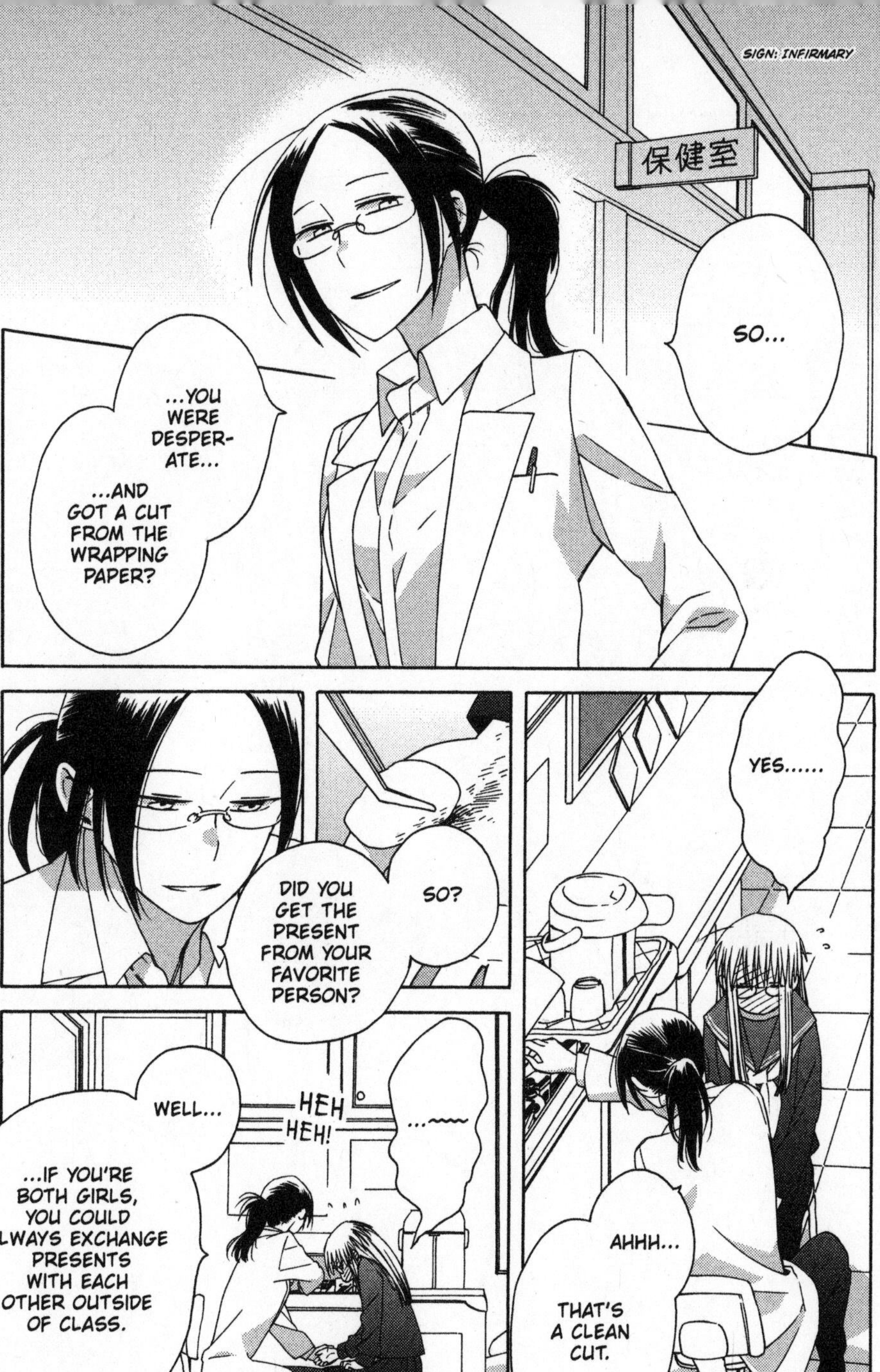
SIGN: INFIRMARY
保健室
SO...
...YOU WERE DESPERATE...
...AND GOT A CUT FROM THE WRAPPING PAPER?
YES......
AHHH...
THAT'S A CLEAN CUT.
SO?
DID YOU GET THE PRESENT FROM YOUR FAVORITE PERSON?
...~~~
HEH HEH!
WELL...
...IF YOU'RE BOTH GIRLS, YOU COULD ALWAYS EXCHANGE PRESENTS WITH EACH OTHER OUTSIDE OF CLASS.

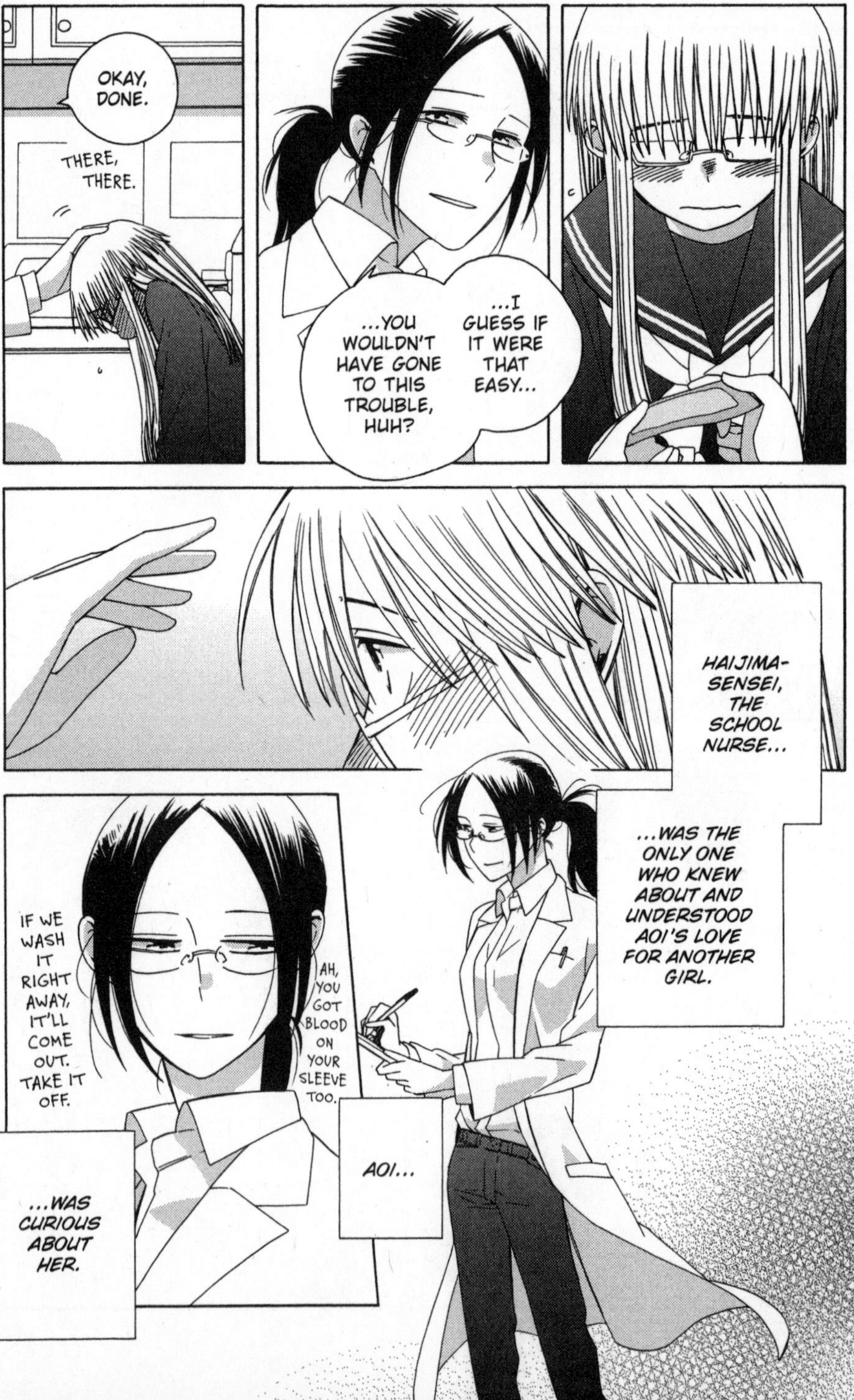
...I GUESS IF IT WERE THAT EASY...
...YOU WOULDN'T HAVE GONE TO THIS TROUBLE, HUH?
OKAY, DONE.
THERE, THERE.
HAIJIMA-SENSEI, THE SCHOOL NURSE...
...WAS THE ONLY ONE WHO KNEW ABOUT AND UNDERSTOOD AOI'S LOVE FOR ANOTHER GIRL.
AH, YOU GOT BLOOD ON YOUR SLEEVE TOO.
IF WE WASH IT RIGHT AWAY, IT'LL COME OUT. TAKE IT OFF.
AOI...
...WAS CURIOUS ABOUT HER.

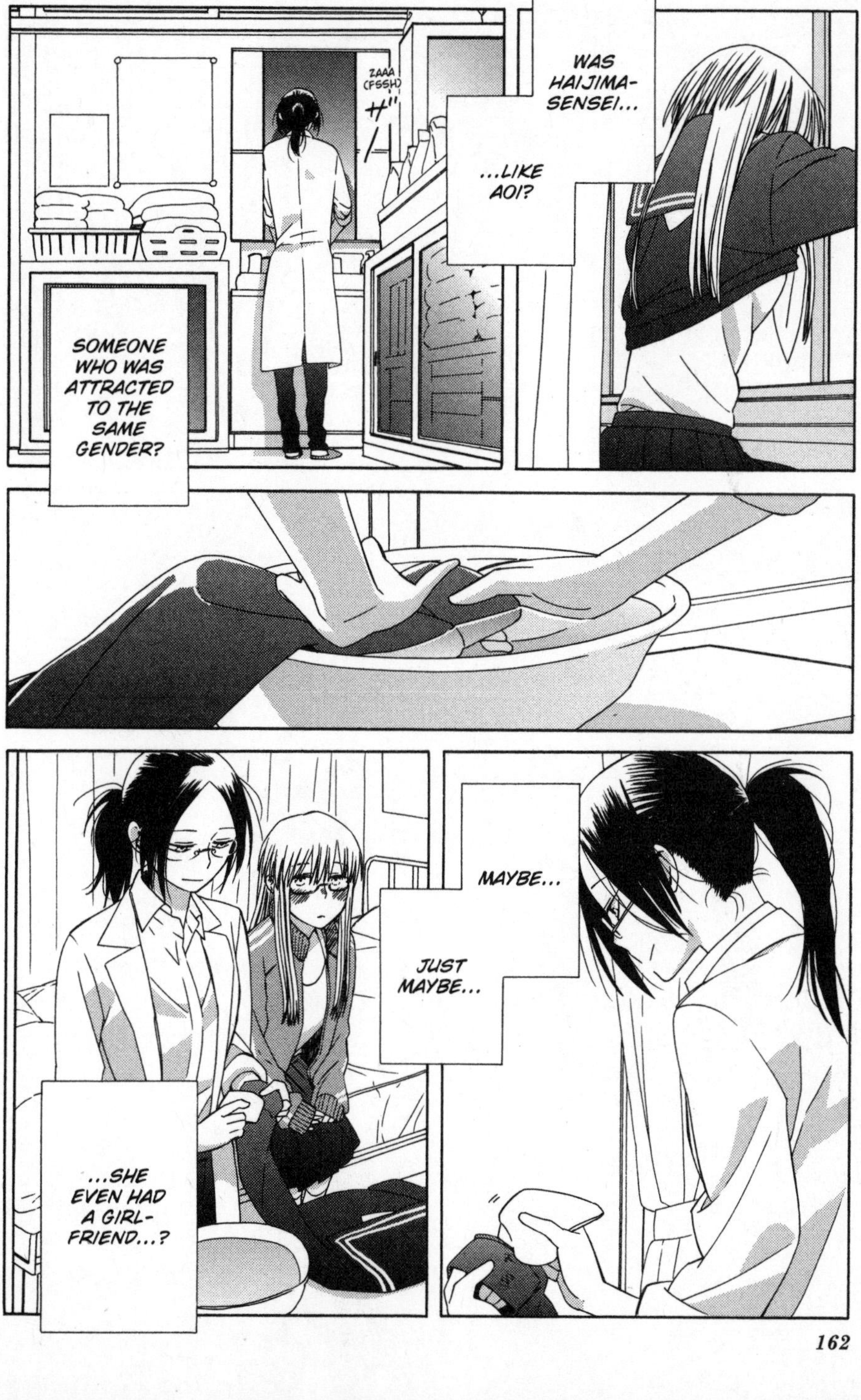
WAS HAIJIMA-SENSEI...
...LIKE AOI?
ZAAA (FSSH)
SOMEONE WHO WAS ATTRACTED TO THE SAME GENDER?
MAYBE...
JUST MAYBE...
...SHE EVEN HAD A GIRL-FRIEND...?

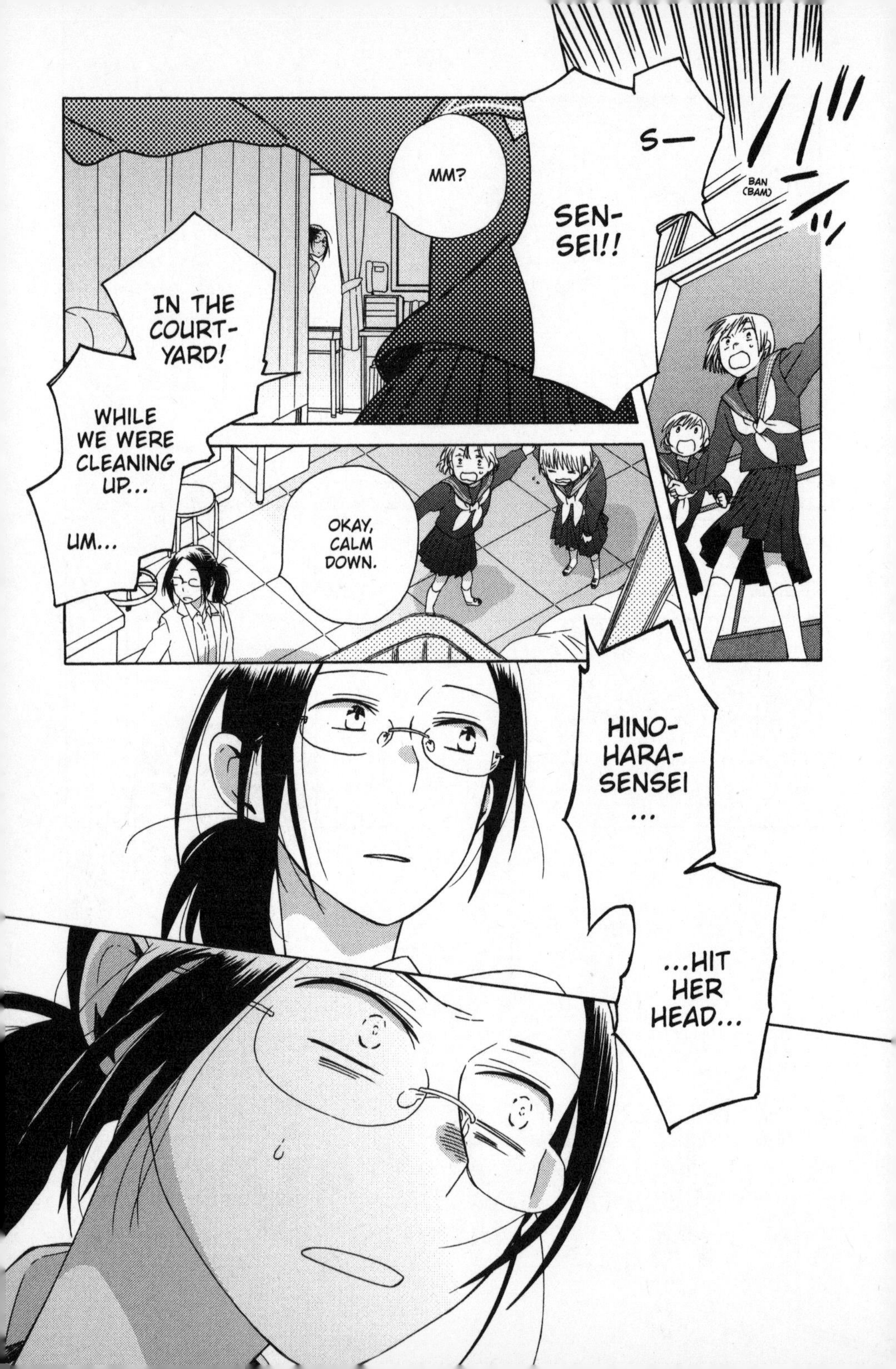
S—
BAN (BAM)
SEN-SEI!!
MM?
IN THE COURT-YARD!
WHILE WE WERE CLEANING UP...
UM...
OKAY, CALM DOWN.
HINO-HARA-SENSEI ...
...HIT HER HEAD...

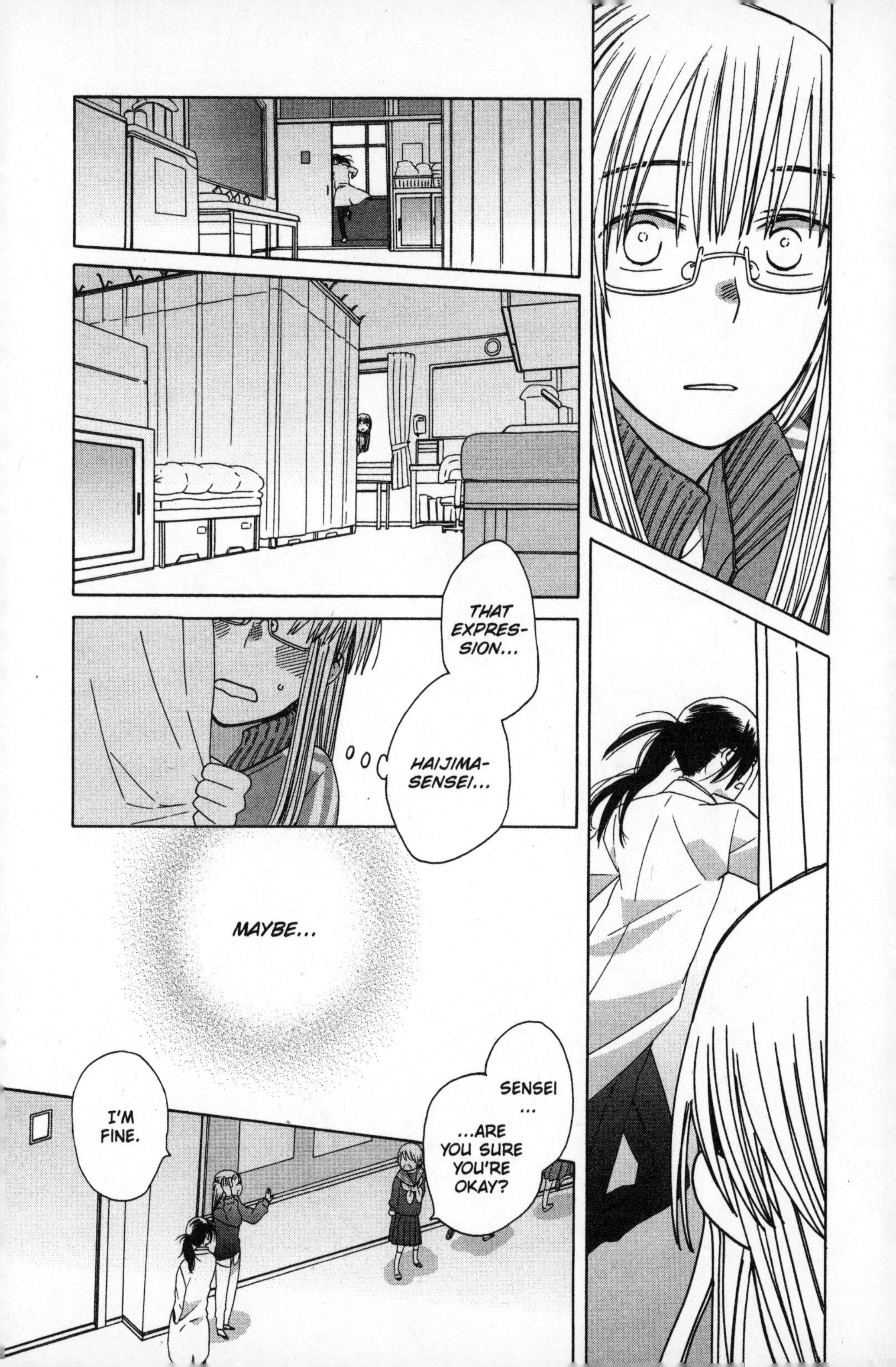
THAT EXPRESSION...
HAIJIMA-SENSEI...
MAYBE...
SENSEI ... ...ARE YOU SURE YOU'RE OKAY?
I'M FINE.

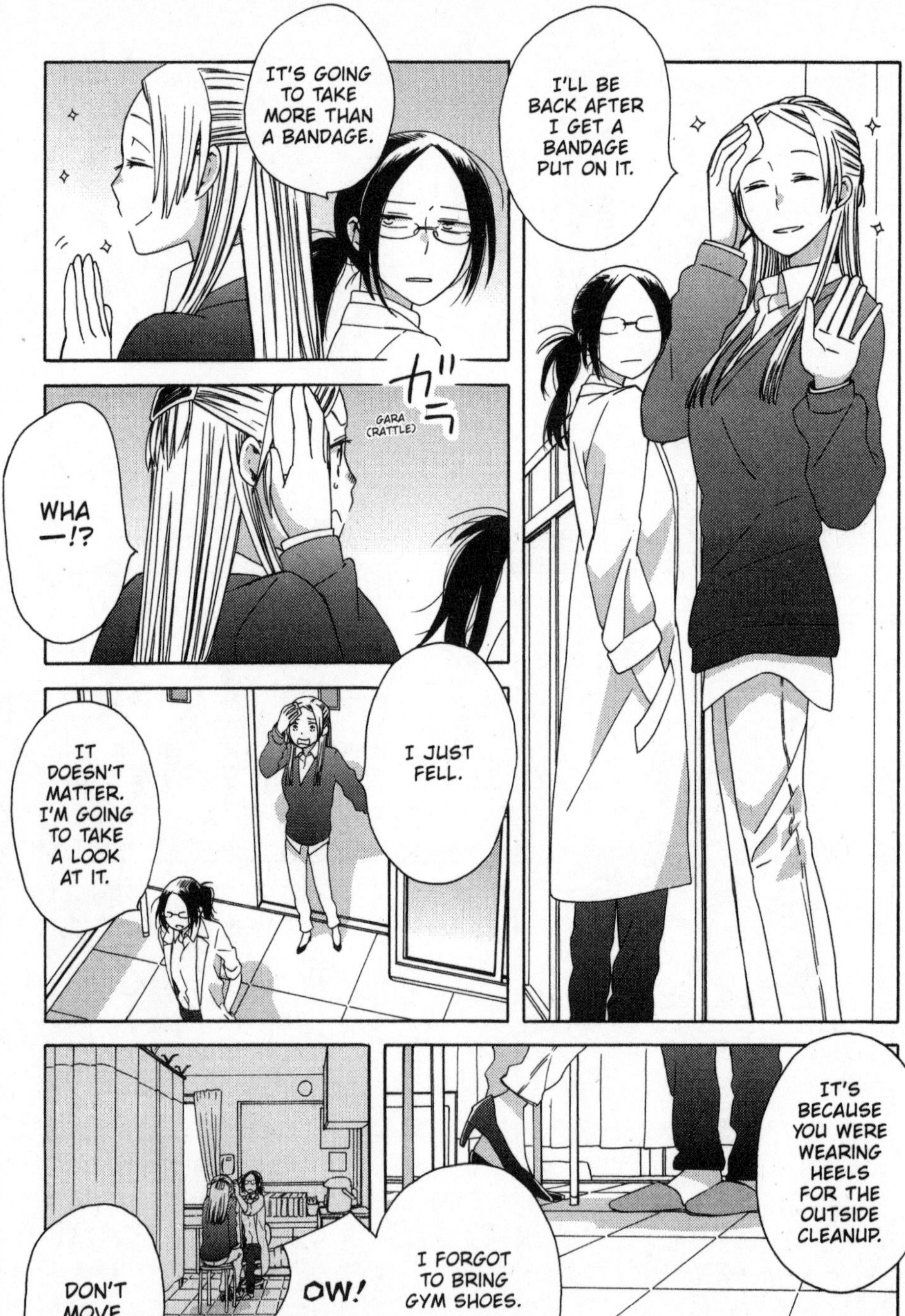
I'LL BE BACK AFTER I GET A BANDAGE PUT ON IT.
IT'S GOING TO TAKE MORE THAN A BANDAGE.
ガラ
GARA (RATTLE)
WHA—!?
I JUST FELL.
IT DOESN'T MATTER. I'M GOING TO TAKE A LOOK AT IT.
IT'S BECAUSE YOU WERE WEARING HEELS FOR THE OUTSIDE CLEANUP.
I FORGOT TO BRING GYM SHOES.
OW!
DON'T MOVE.

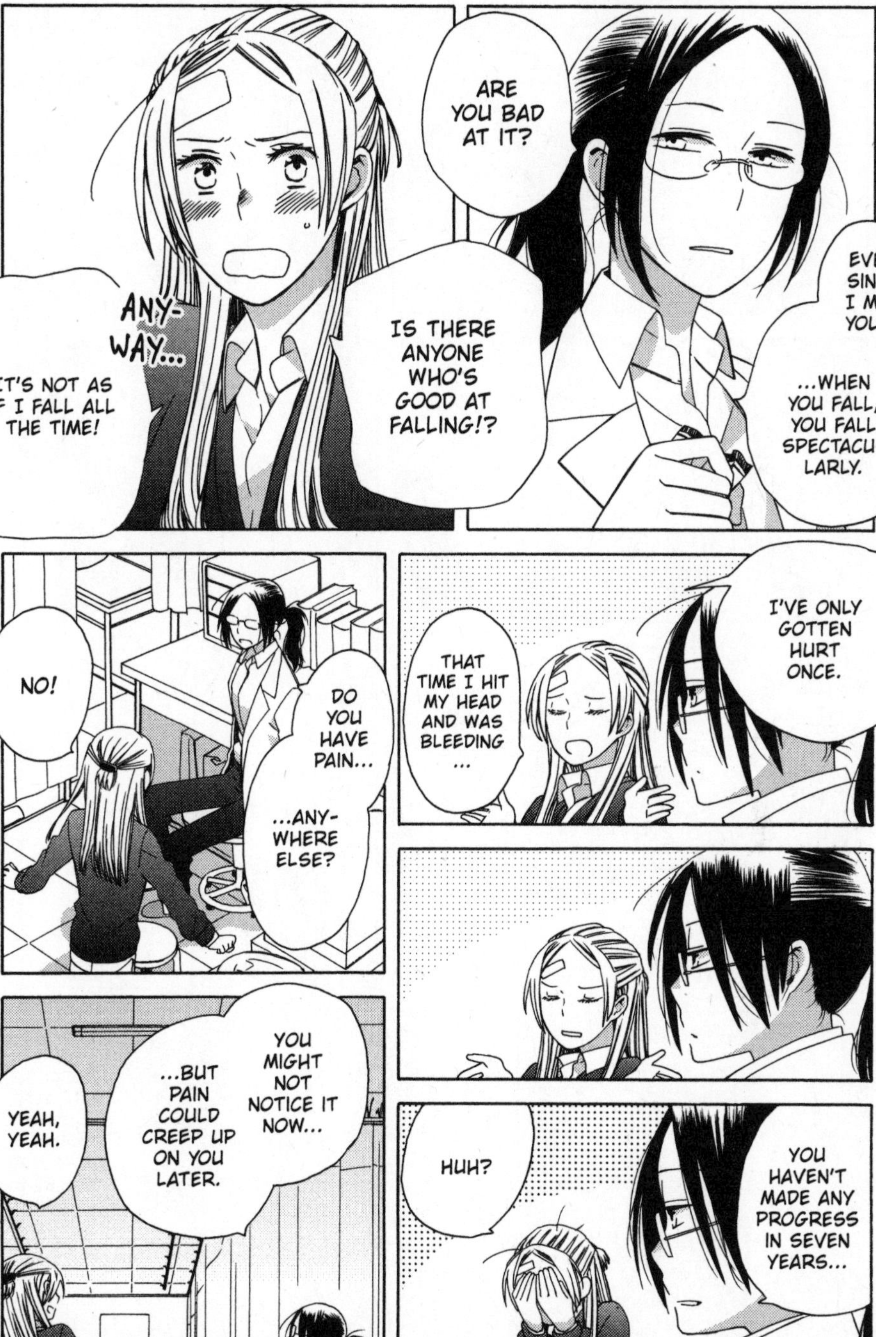
ARE YOU BAD AT IT?
EVER SINCE I MET YOU...
...WHEN YOU FALL, YOU FALL SPECTACULARLY.
IS THERE ANYONE WHO'S GOOD AT FALLING!?
ANY-WAY...
IT'S NOT AS IF I FALL ALL THE TIME!
I'VE ONLY GOTTEN HURT ONCE.
THAT TIME I HIT MY HEAD AND WAS BLEEDING...
DO YOU HAVE PAIN...
...ANY-WHERE ELSE?
NO!
YOU HAVEN'T MADE ANY PROGRESS IN SEVEN YEARS...
HUH?
YOU MIGHT NOT NOTICE IT NOW...
...BUT PAIN COULD CREEP UP ON YOU LATER.
YEAH, YEAH.

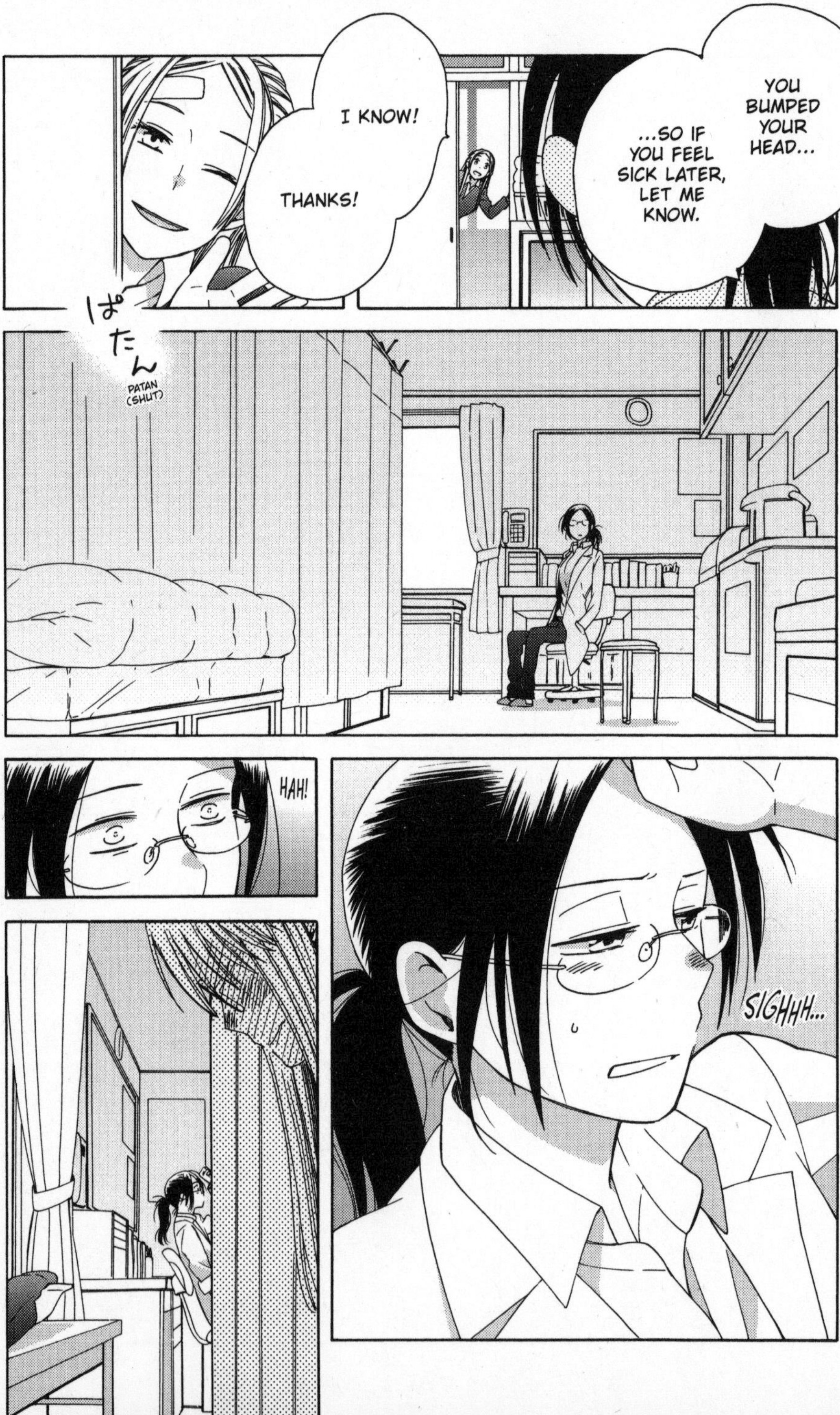
YOU BUMPED YOUR HEAD...
...SO IF YOU FEEL SICK LATER, LET ME KNOW.
I KNOW!
THANKS!
ぱたん
PATAN (SHUT)
SIGHHH...
HAH!

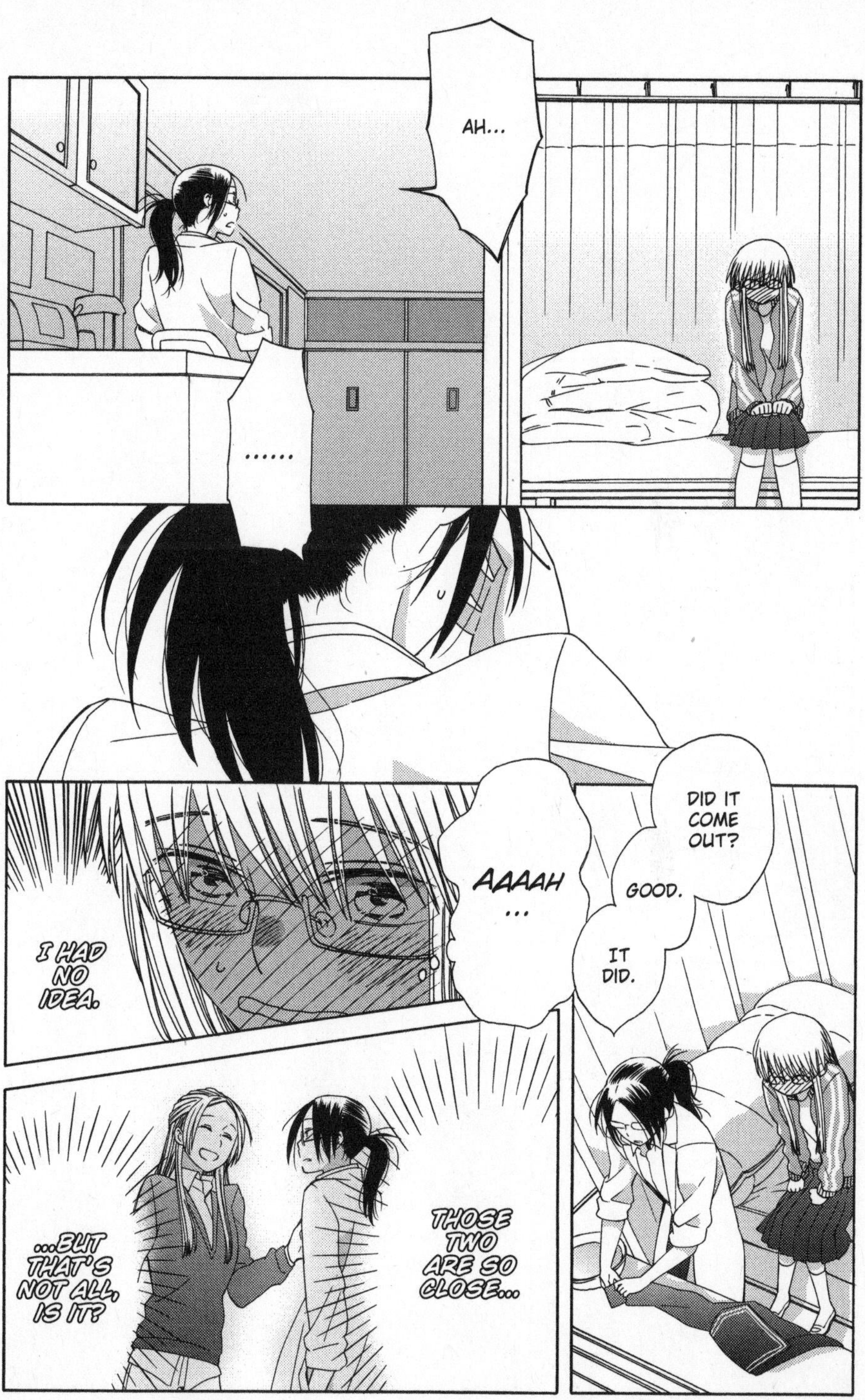
AH...
......
DID IT COME OUT?
GOOD.
IT DID.
AAAAH ...
I HAD NO IDEA.
THOSE TWO ARE SO CLOSE...
...BUT THAT'S NOT ALL, IS IT?

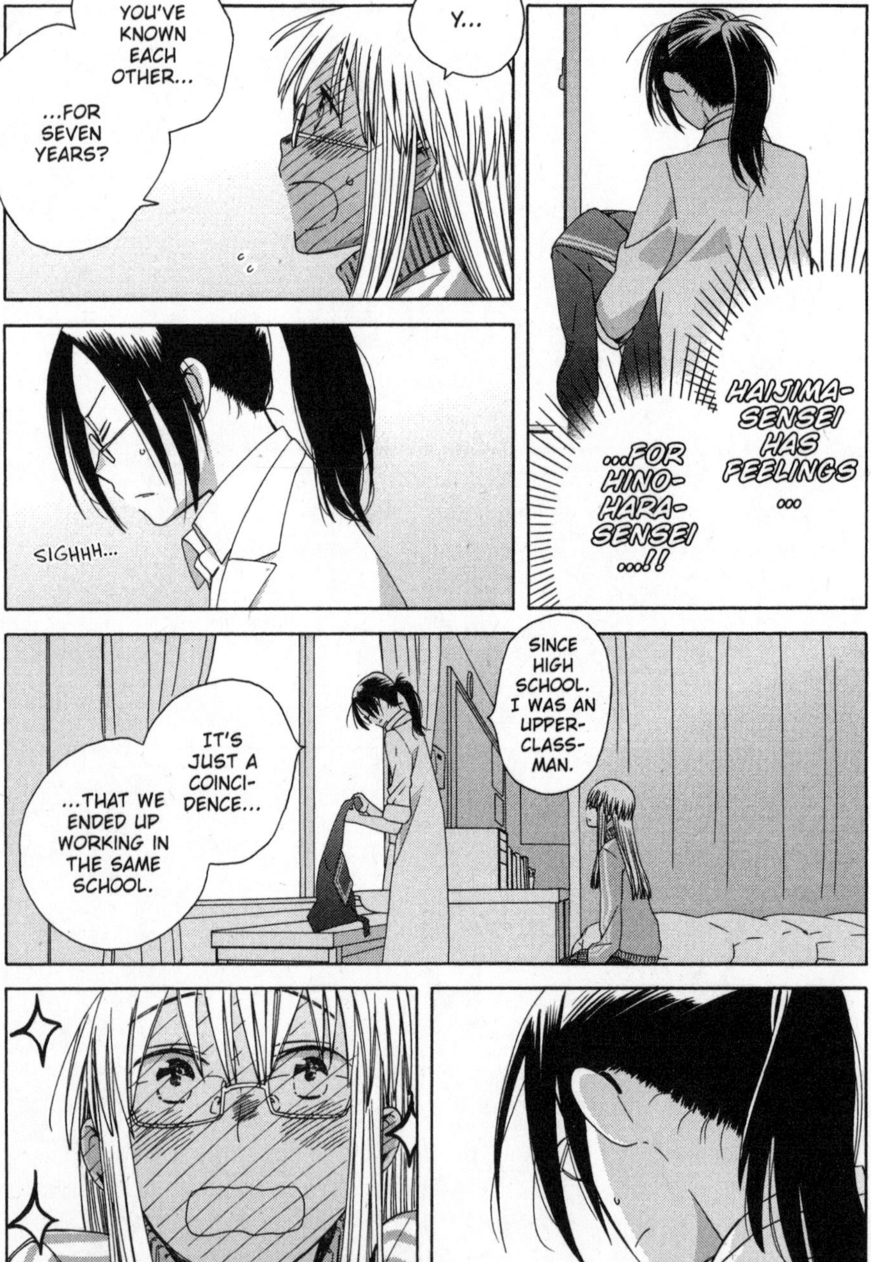
HAIJIMA-SENSEI HAS FEELINGS...
...FOR HINO-HARA-SENSEI...!!
Y...
YOU'VE KNOWN EACH OTHER...
...FOR SEVEN YEARS?
SIGHHH...
SINCE HIGH SCHOOL. I WAS AN UPPER-CLASS-MAN.
IT'S JUST A COINCI-DENCE...
...THAT WE ENDED UP WORKING IN THE SAME SCHOOL.

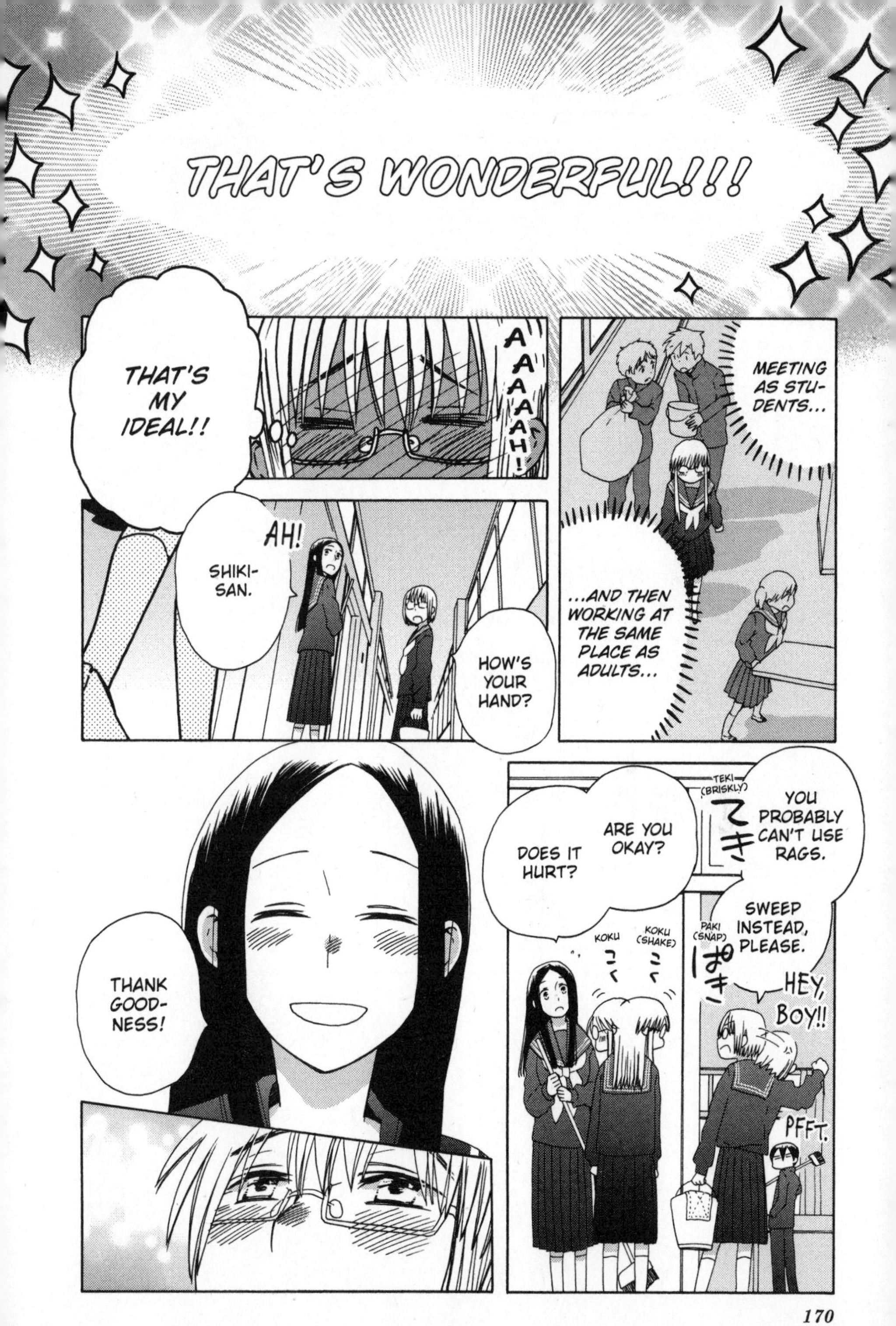
THAT'S WONDERFUL!!!
MEETING AS STUDENTS...
...AND THEN WORKING AT THE SAME PLACE AS ADULTS...
AAAAAH!
THAT'S MY IDEAL!!
AH!
SHIKI-SAN.
HOW'S YOUR HAND?
TEKI (BRISKLY) てき
YOU PROBABLY CAN'T USE RAGS.
ARE YOU OKAY?
DOES IT HURT?
SWEEP INSTEAD, PLEASE.
PAKI (SNAP) ぱき
KOKU (SHAKE) こく
KOKU こく
HEY, BOY!!
PFFT.
THANK GOODNESS!

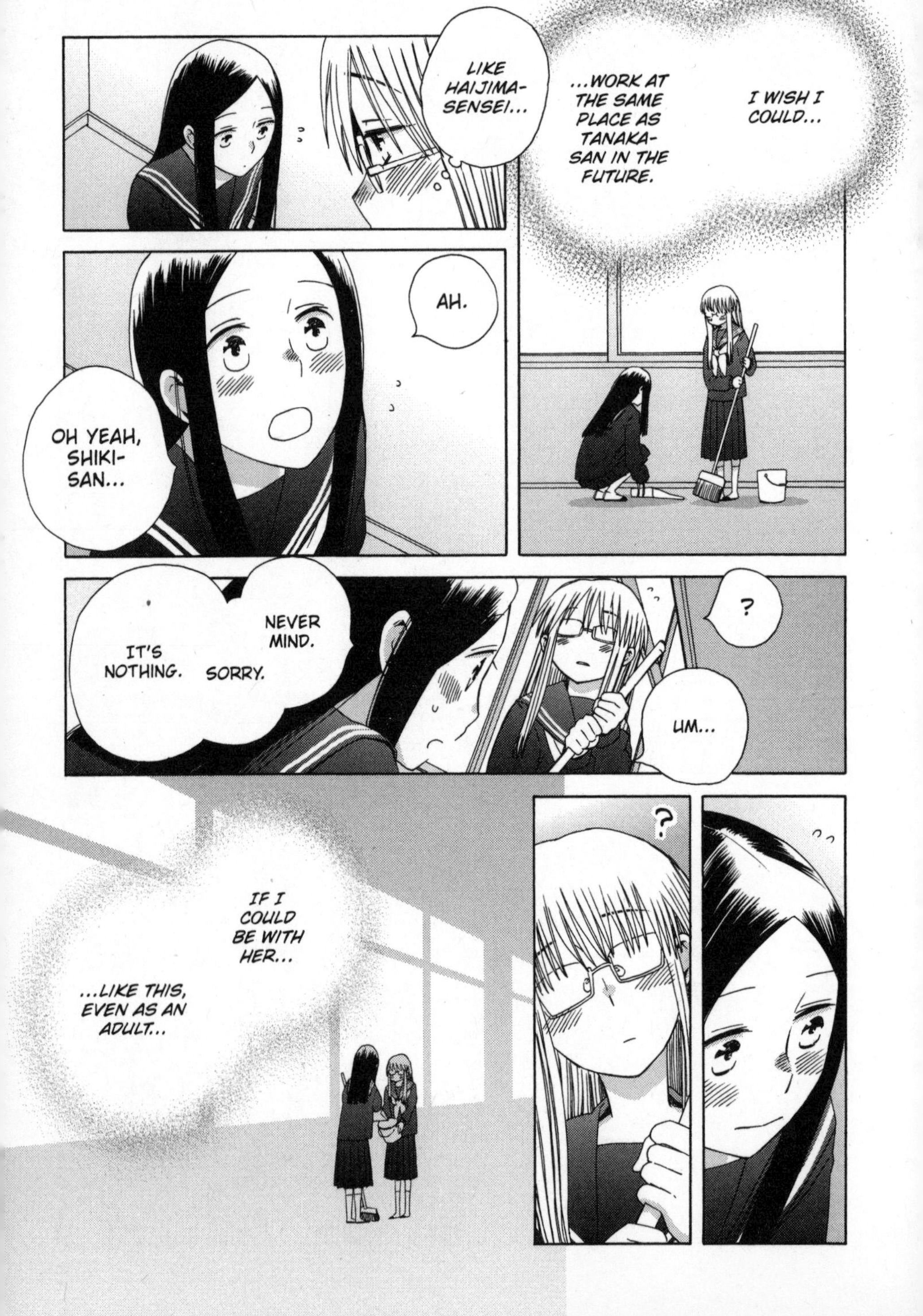
I WISH I COULD...
...WORK AT THE SAME PLACE AS TANAKA-SAN IN THE FUTURE.
LIKE HAIJIMA-SENSEI...
AH.
OH YEAH, SHIKI-SAN...
?
UM...
NEVER MIND.
SORRY.
IT'S NOTHING.
?
IF I COULD BE WITH HER...
...LIKE THIS, EVEN AS AN ADULT...

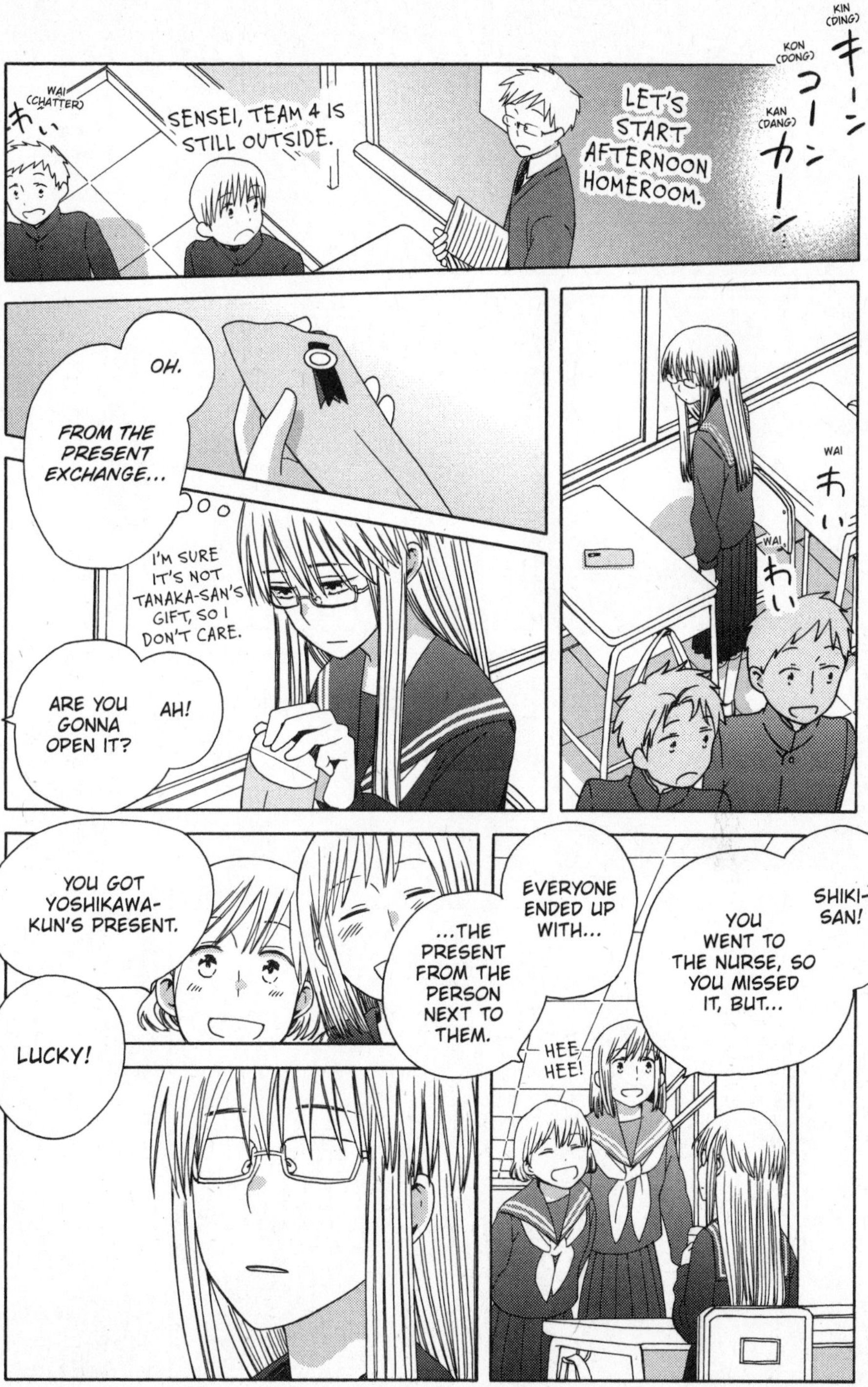
KIN (DING) キーン
KON (DONG) コーン
KAN (DANG) カーン
LET'S START AFTERNOON HOMEROOM.
SENSEI, TEAM 4 IS STILL OUTSIDE.
WAI (CHATTER) わい
WAI わい
WAI わい
OH.
FROM THE PRESENT EXCHANGE...
I'M SURE IT'S NOT TANAKA-SAN'S GIFT, SO I DON'T CARE.
AH!
ARE YOU GONNA OPEN IT?
SHIKI-SAN!
YOU WENT TO THE NURSE, SO YOU MISSED IT, BUT...
EVERYONE ENDED UP WITH...
...THE PRESENT FROM THE PERSON NEXT TO THEM.
HEE HEE!
YOU GOT YOSHIKAWA-KUN'S PRESENT.
LUCKY!

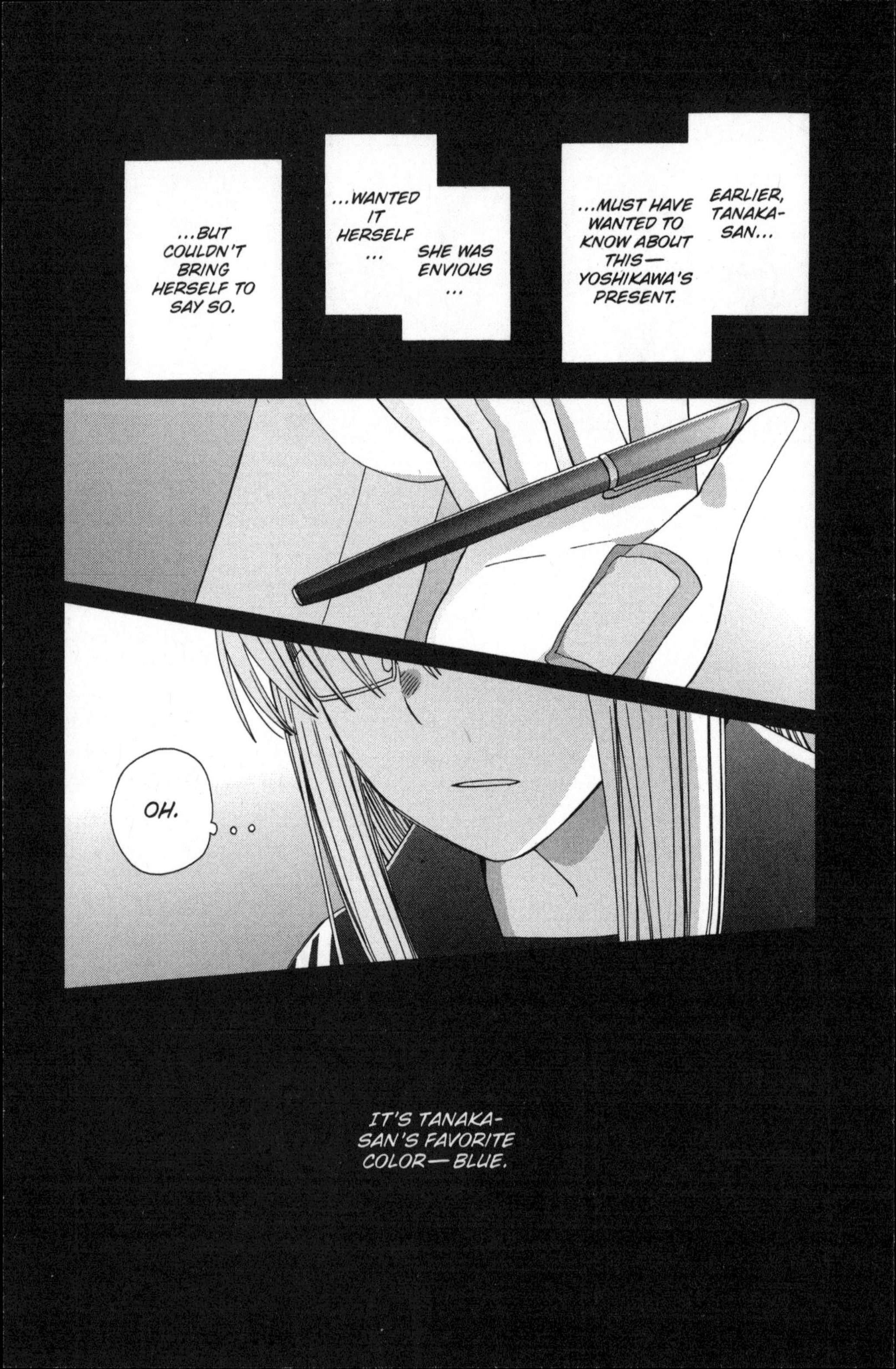
EARLIER, TANAKA-SAN...
...MUST HAVE WANTED TO KNOW ABOUT THIS—YOSHIKAWA'S PRESENT.
SHE WAS ENVIOUS...
...WANTED IT HERSELF...
...BUT COULDN'T BRING HERSELF TO SAY SO.
OH.
IT'S TANAKA-SAN'S FAVORITE COLOR—BLUE.

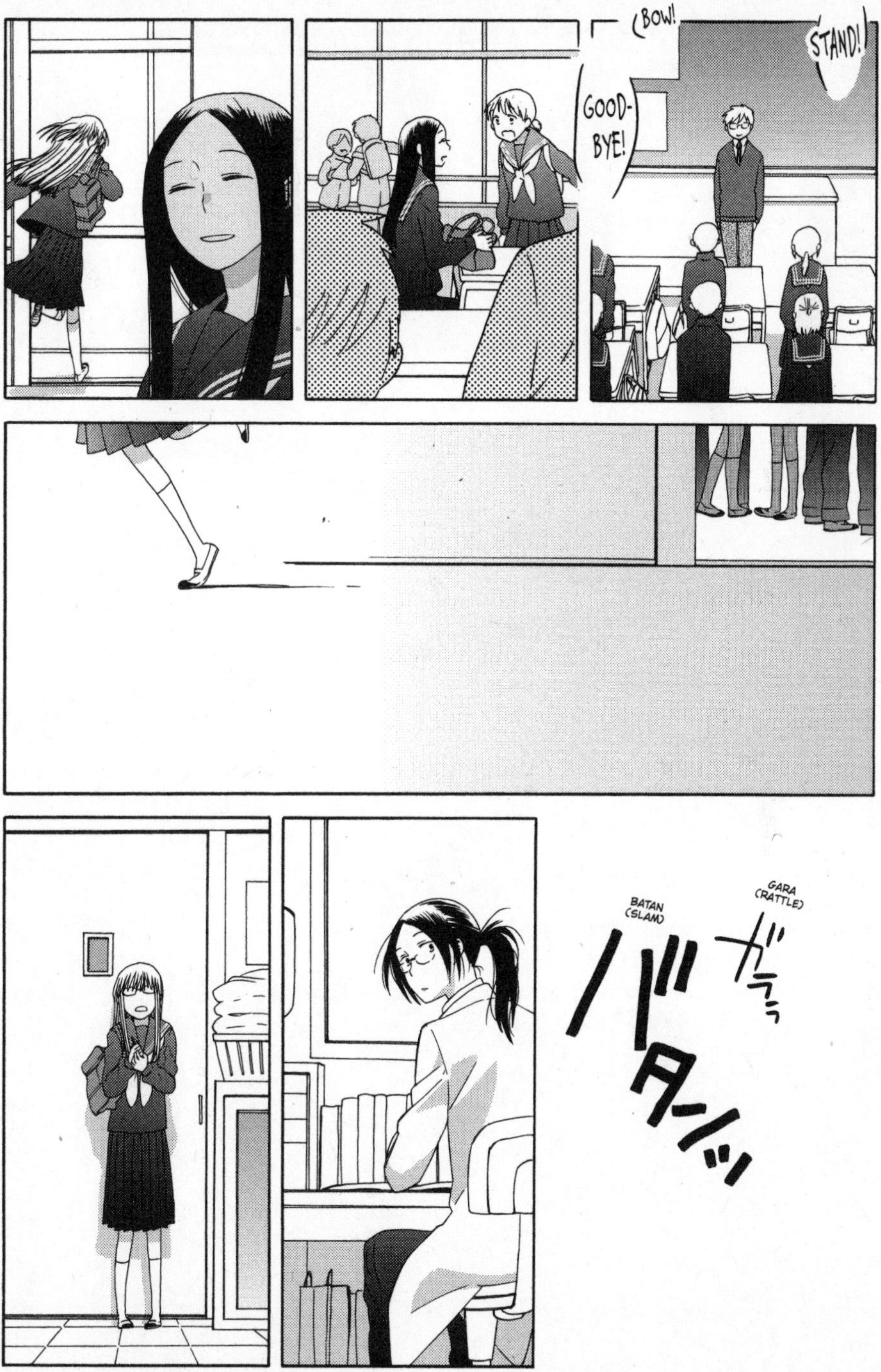
STAND!
BOW!
GOOD-BYE!
GARA (RATTLE)
ガラ
BATAN (SLAM)
バタンッ

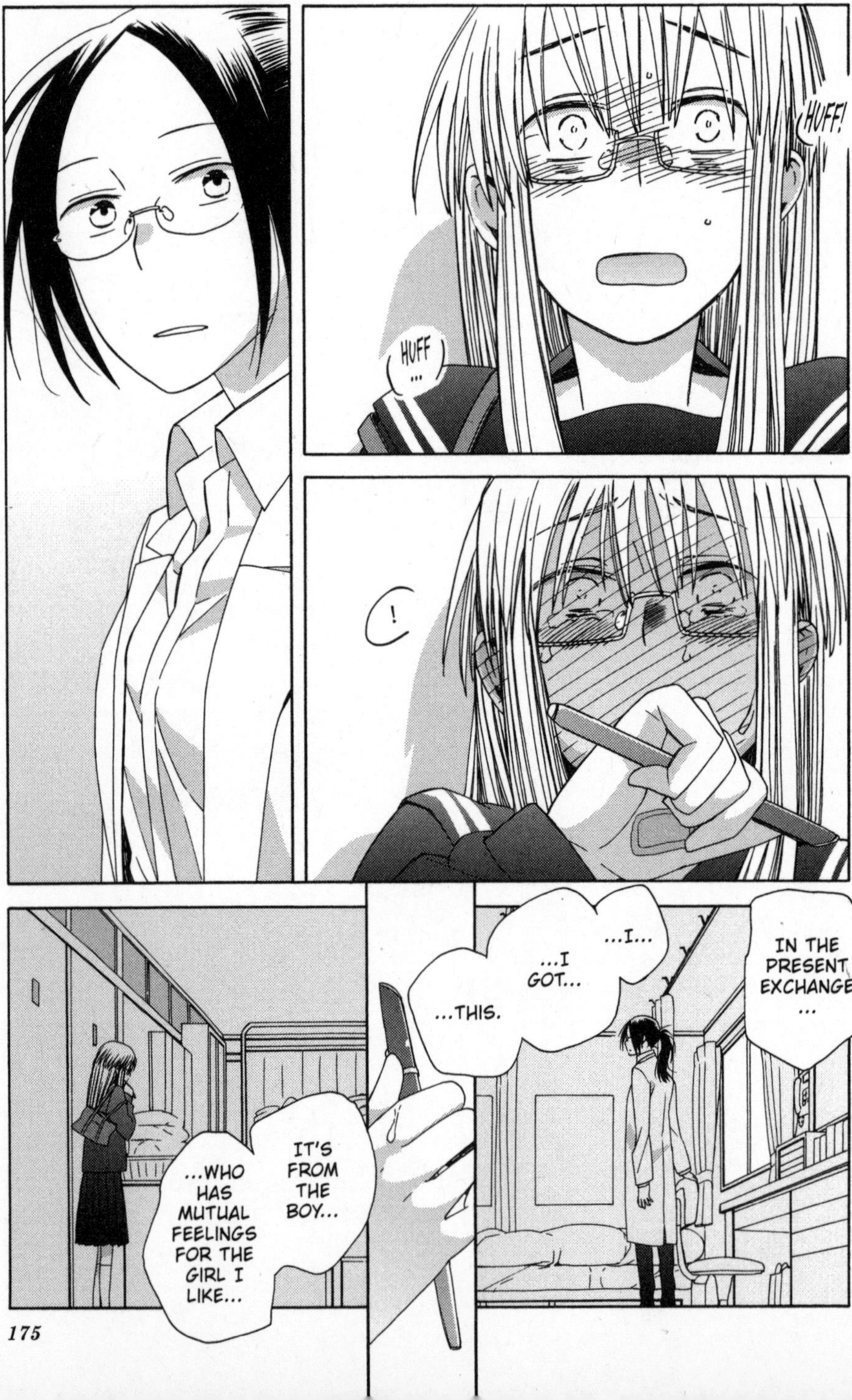
HUFF!
HUFF …
!
IN THE PRESENT EXCHANGE …
…I…
…I GOT…
…THIS.
IT'S FROM THE BOY…
…WHO HAS MUTUAL FEELINGS FOR THE GIRL I LIKE…

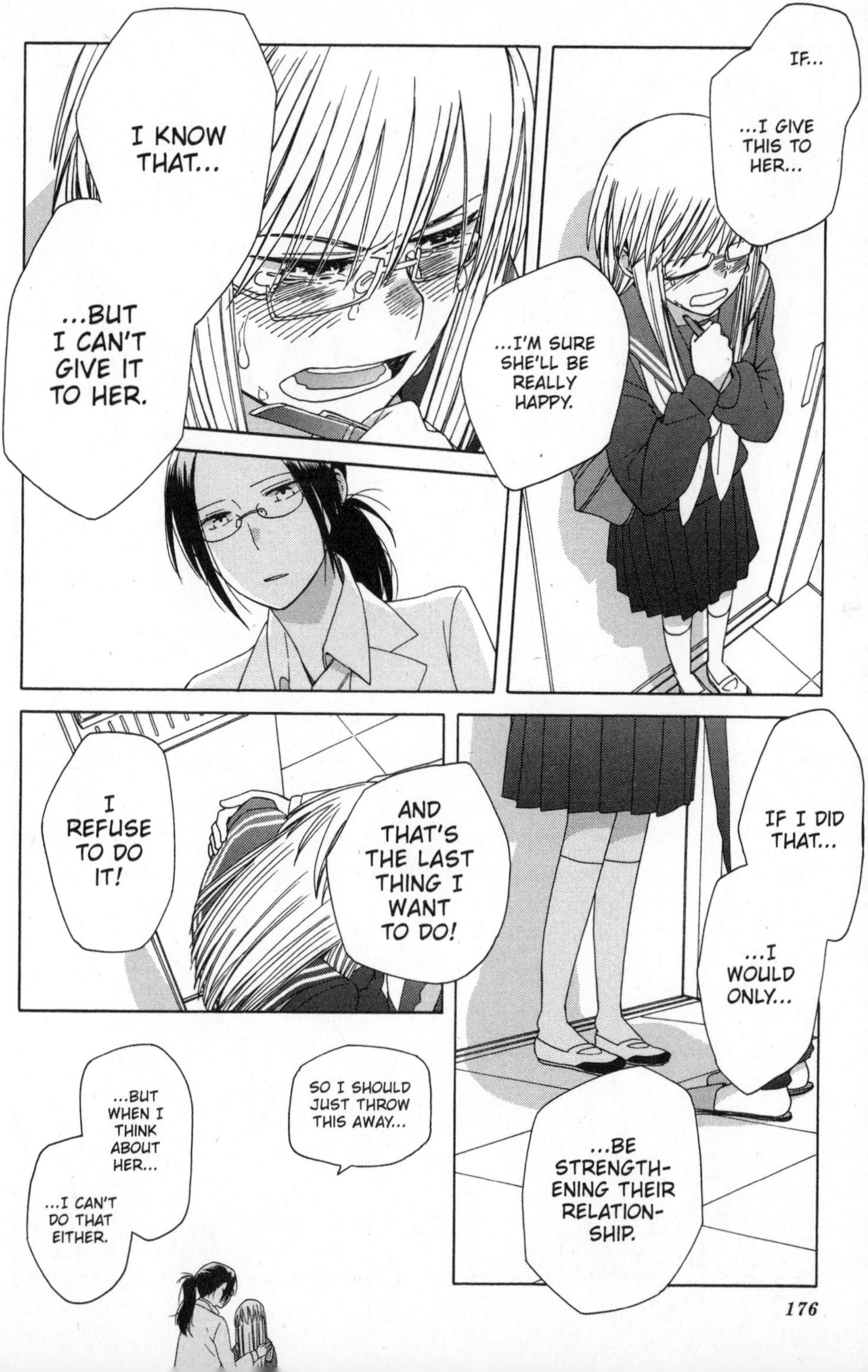
IF...
...I GIVE THIS TO HER...
...I'M SURE SHE'LL BE REALLY HAPPY.
I KNOW THAT...
...BUT I CAN'T GIVE IT TO HER.
IF I DID THAT...
...I WOULD ONLY...
...BE STRENGTH-ENING THEIR RELATION-SHIP.
AND THAT'S THE LAST THING I WANT TO DO!
I REFUSE TO DO IT!
SO I SHOULD JUST THROW THIS AWAY...
...BUT WHEN I THINK ABOUT HER...
...I CAN'T DO THAT EITHER.

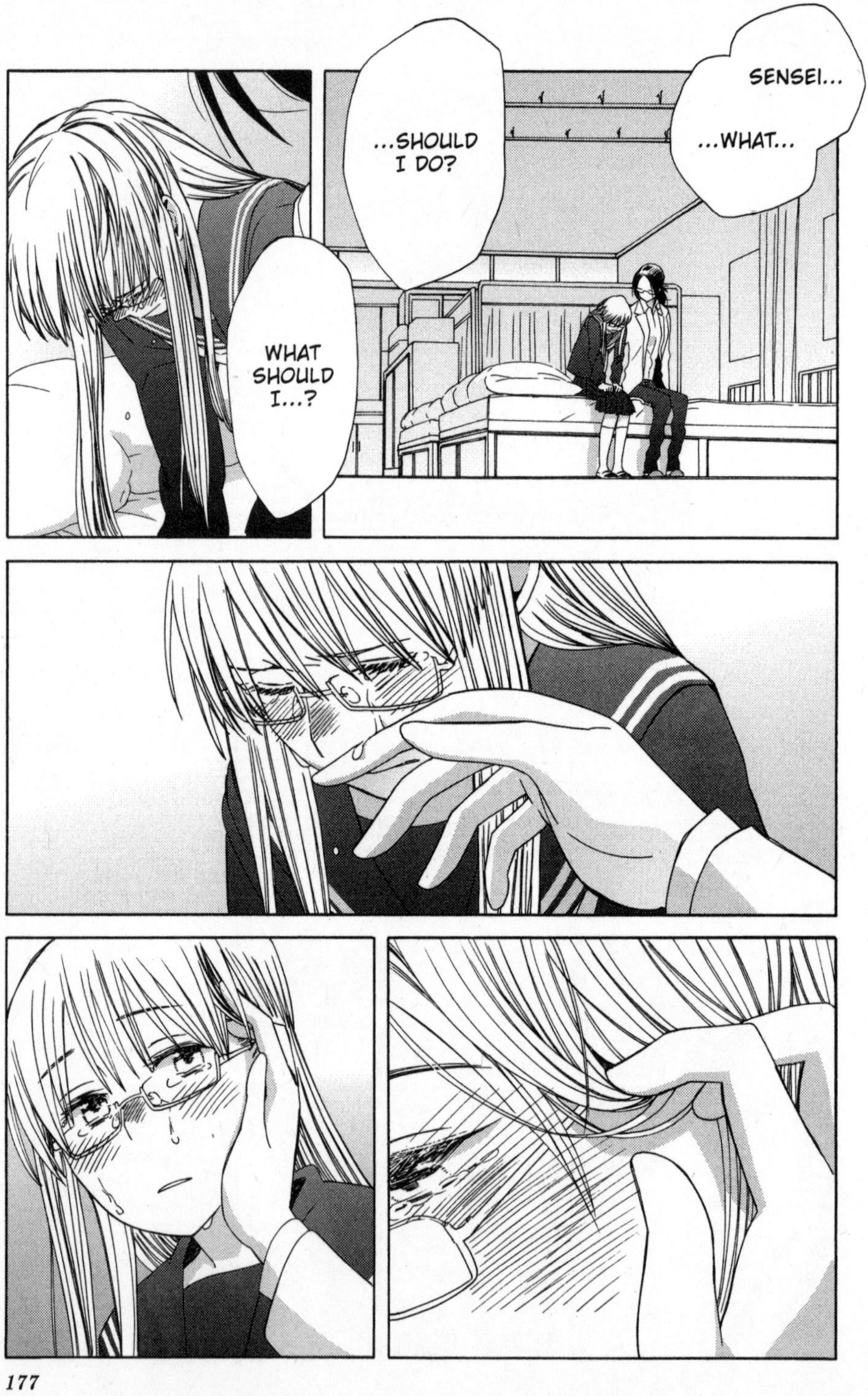
SENSEI...
...WHAT...
...SHOULD I DO?
WHAT SHOULD I...?

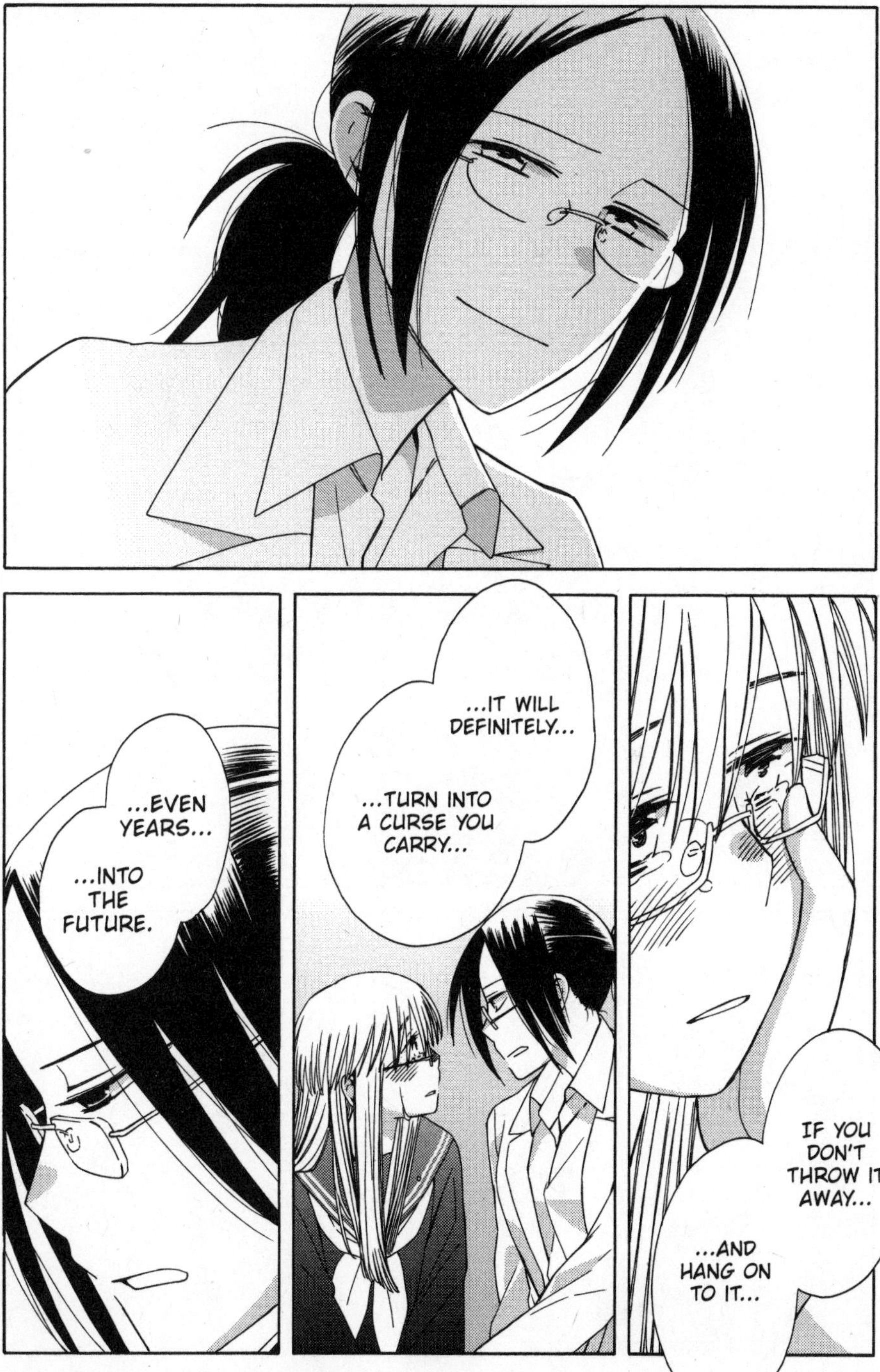
IF YOU DON'T THROW IT AWAY...
...AND HANG ON TO IT...
...IT WILL DEFINITELY...
...TURN INTO A CURSE YOU CARRY...
...EVEN YEARS...
...INTO THE FUTURE.

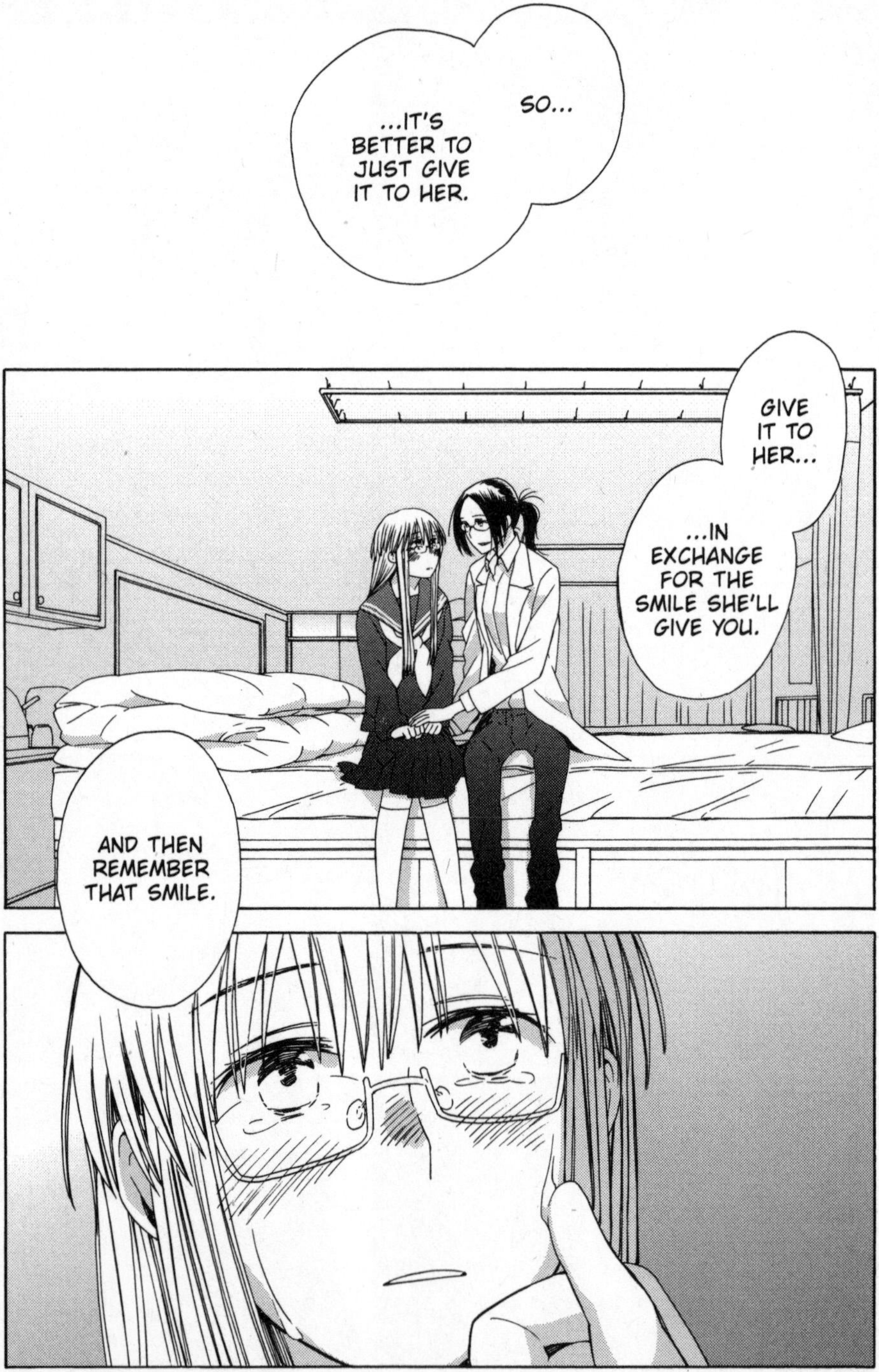
SO...
...IT'S BETTER TO JUST GIVE IT TO HER.
GIVE IT TO HER...
...IN EXCHANGE FOR THE SMILE SHE'LL GIVE YOU.
AND THEN REMEMBER THAT SMILE.

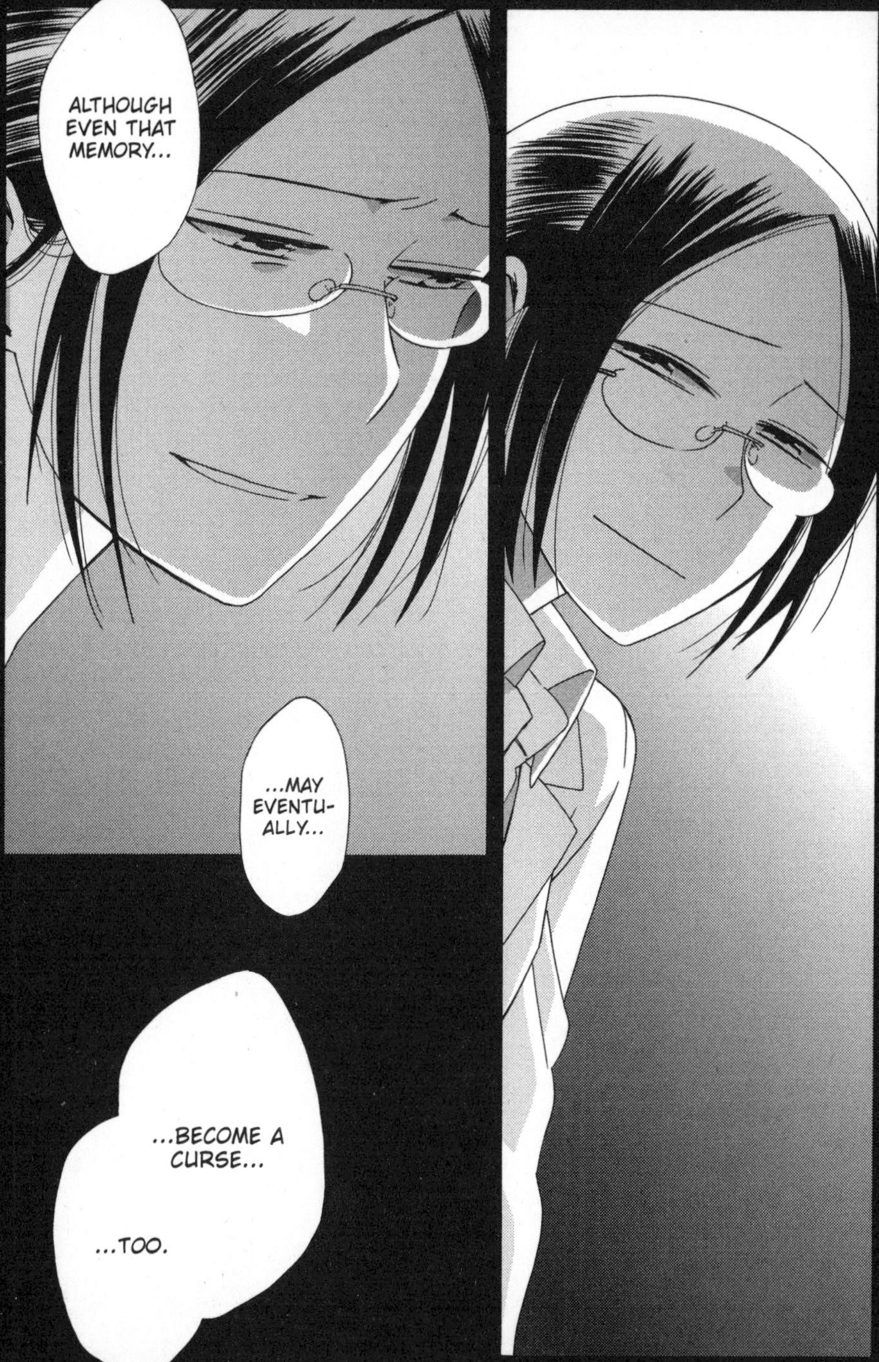
ALTHOUGH EVEN THAT MEMORY...
...MAY EVENTU-ALLY...
...BECOME A CURSE...
...TOO.

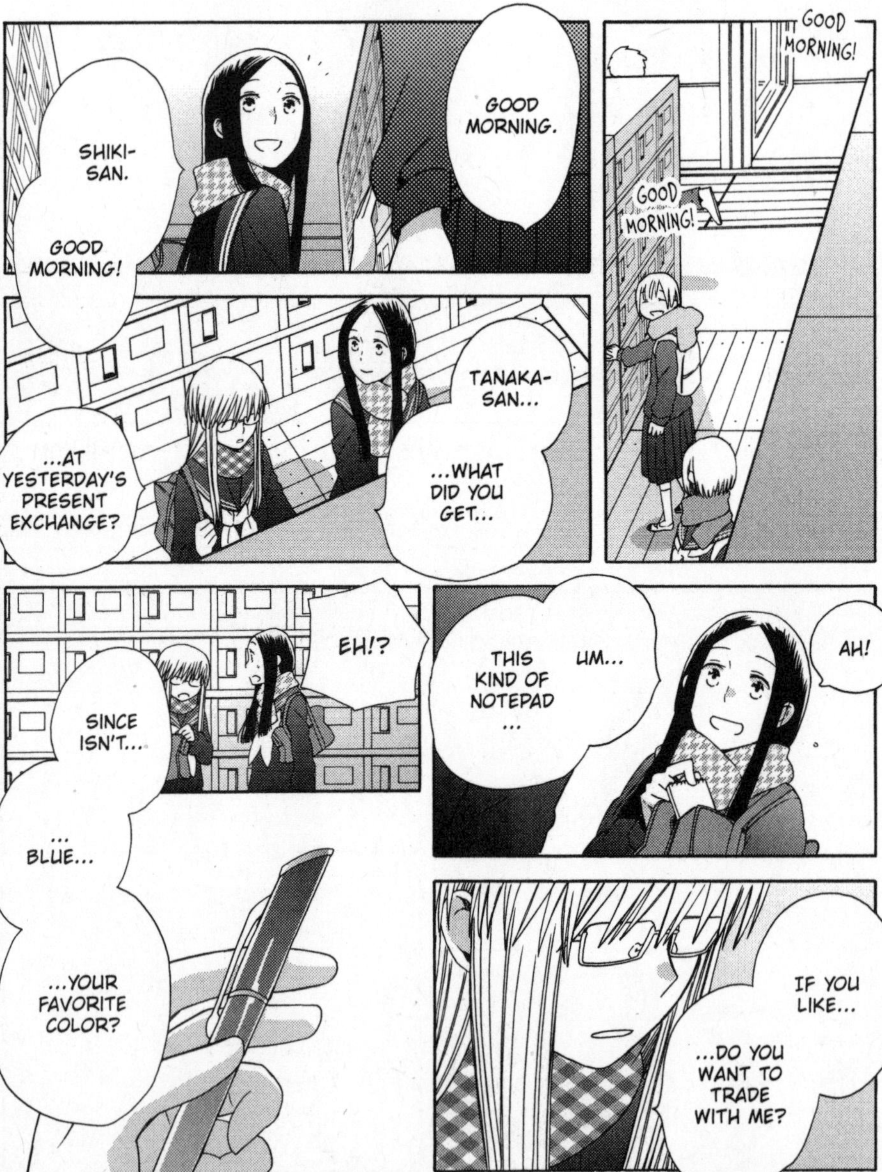
GOOD MORNING!
GOOD MORNING!
GOOD MORNING.
SHIKI-SAN.
GOOD MORNING!
TANAKA-SAN...
...WHAT DID YOU GET...
...AT YESTERDAY'S PRESENT EXCHANGE?
AH!
UM...
THIS KIND OF NOTEPAD ...
EH!?
SINCE ISN'T...
... BLUE...
...YOUR FAVORITE COLOR?
IF YOU LIKE...
...DO YOU WANT TO TRADE WITH ME?

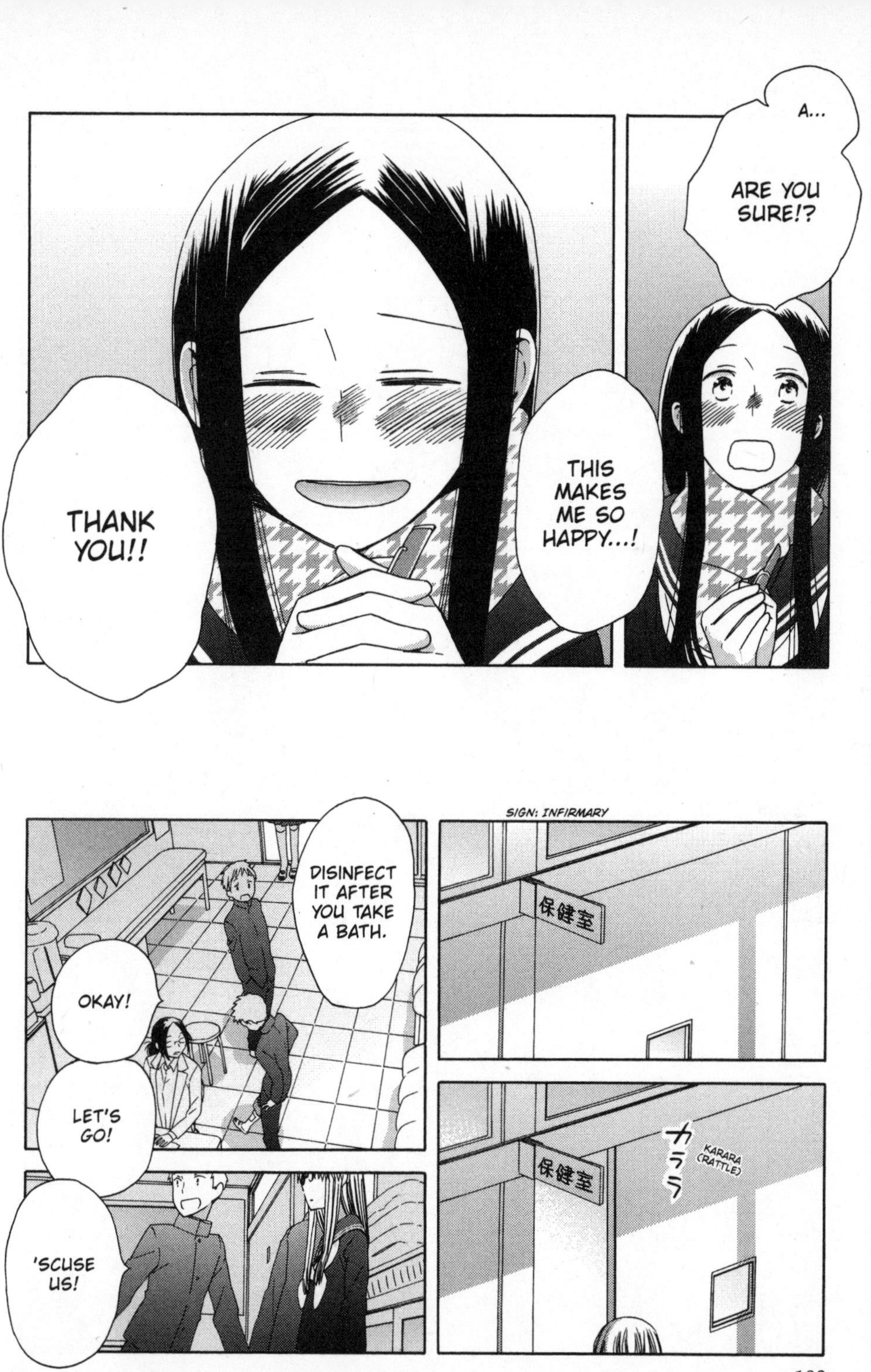
A...
ARE YOU SURE!?
THIS MAKES ME SO HAPPY...!
THANK YOU!!
SIGN: INFIRMARY
保健室
DISINFECT IT AFTER YOU TAKE A BATH.
OKAY!
LET'S GO!
カララ
KARARA (RATTLE)
保健室
'SCUSE US!

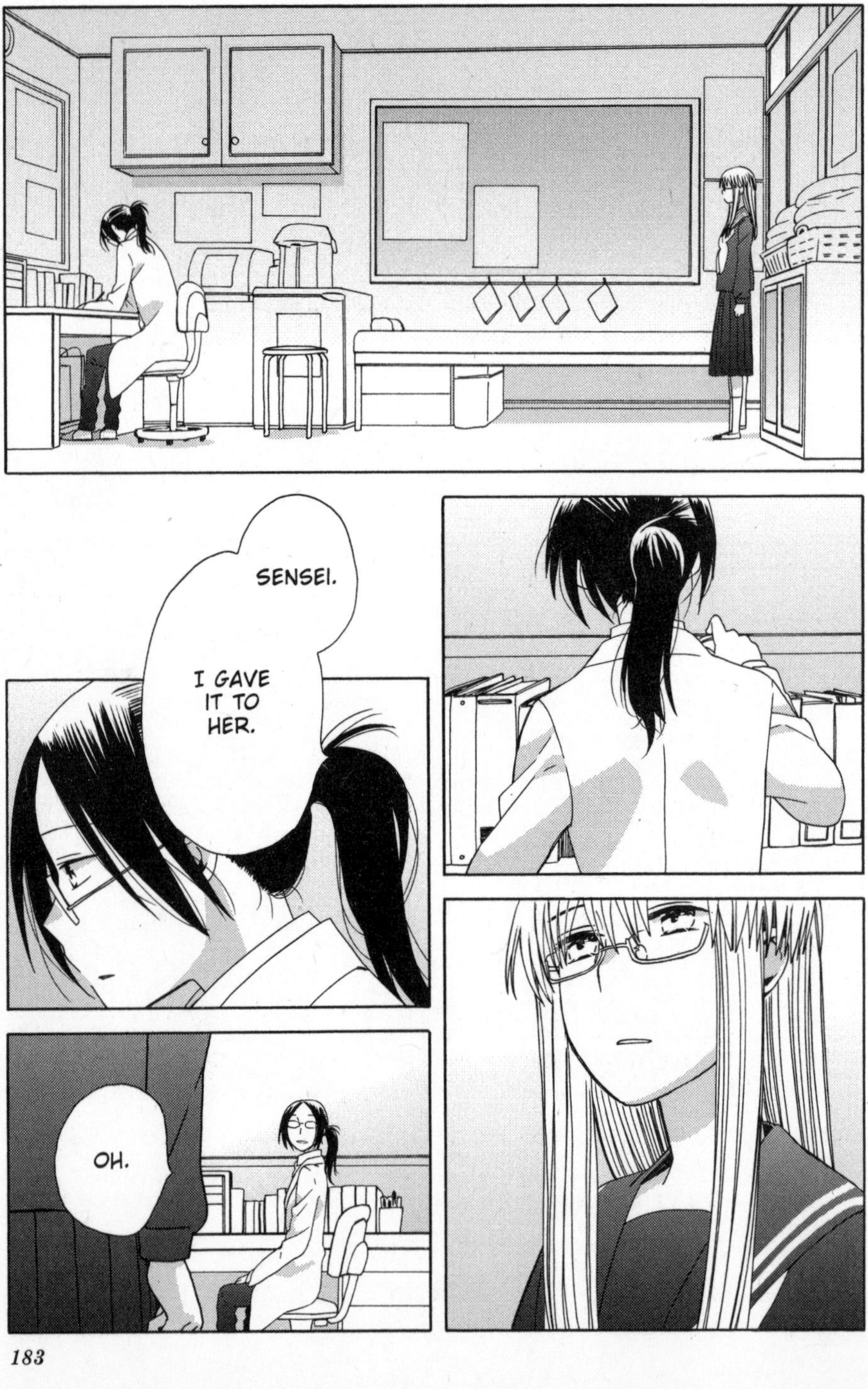
SENSEI.
I GAVE IT TO HER.
OH.

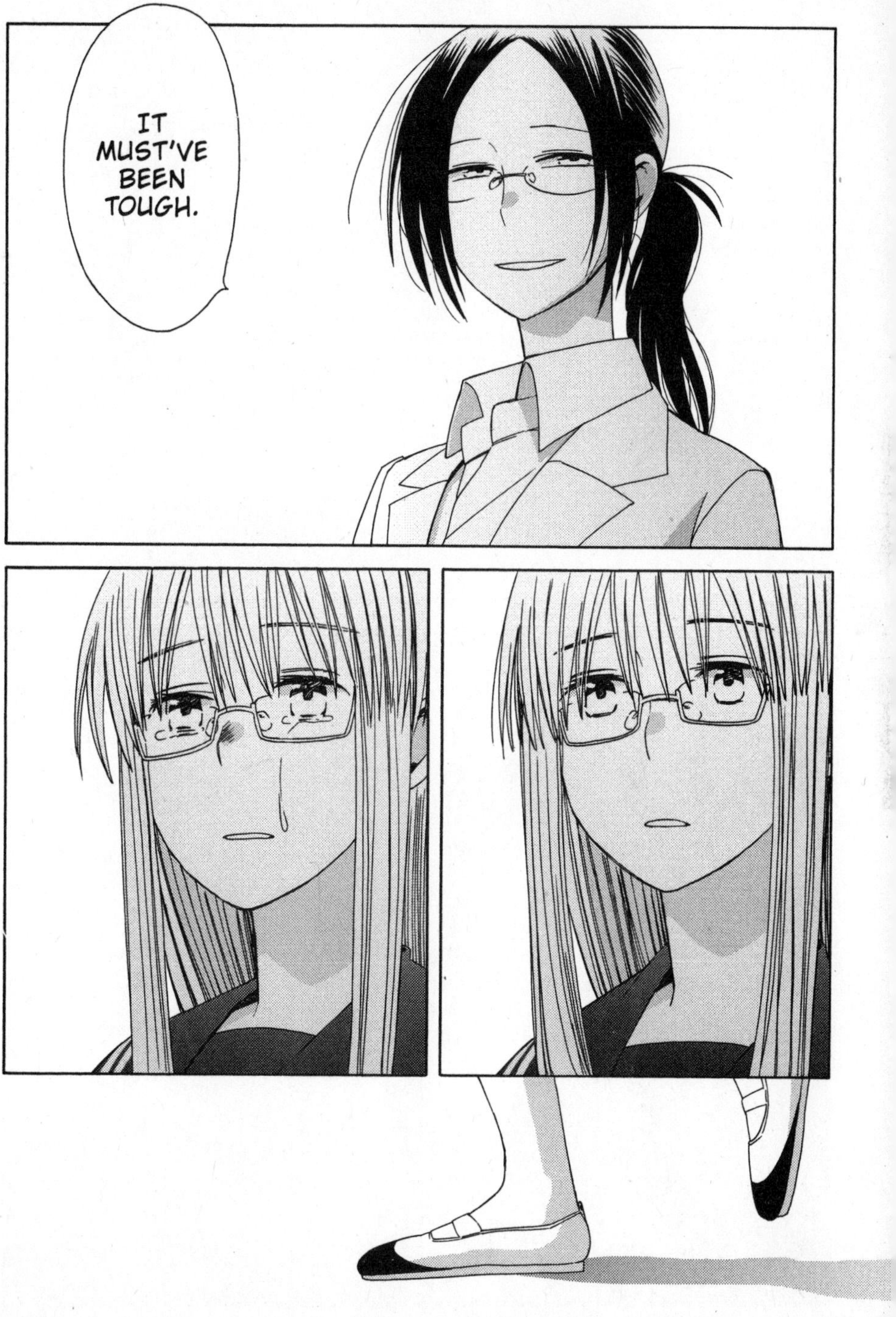
IT MUST'VE BEEN TOUGH.

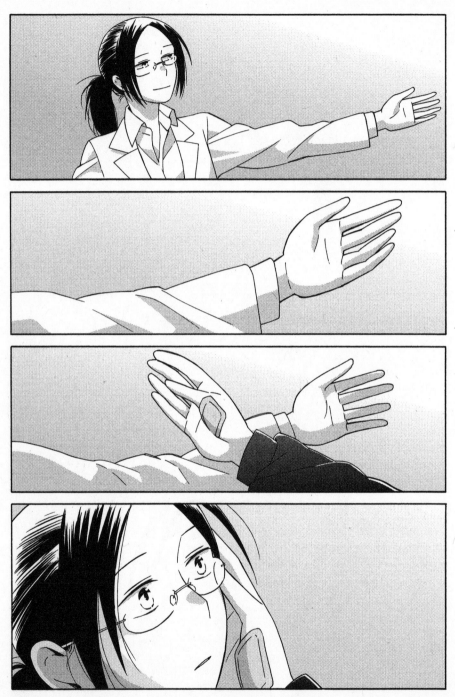

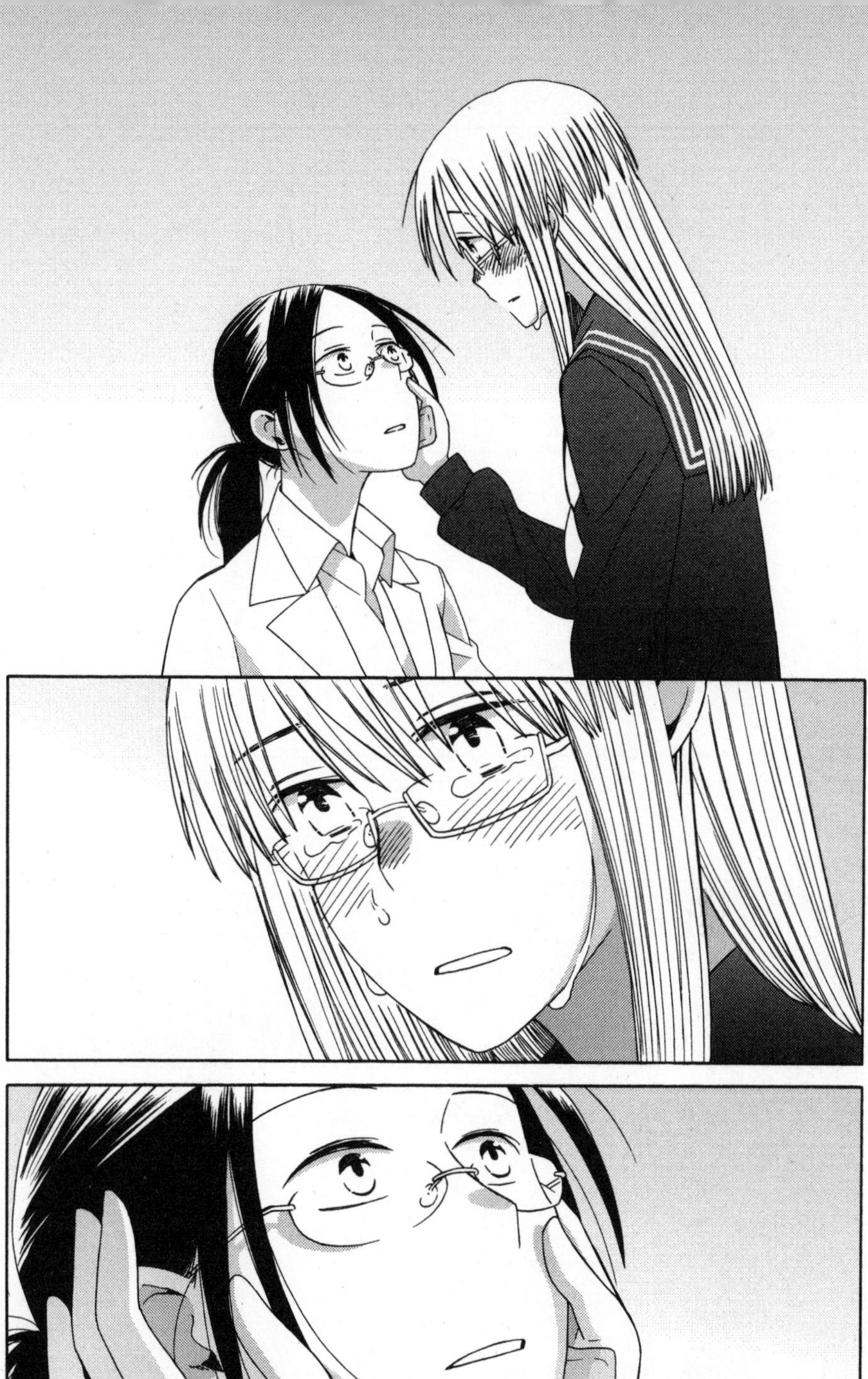

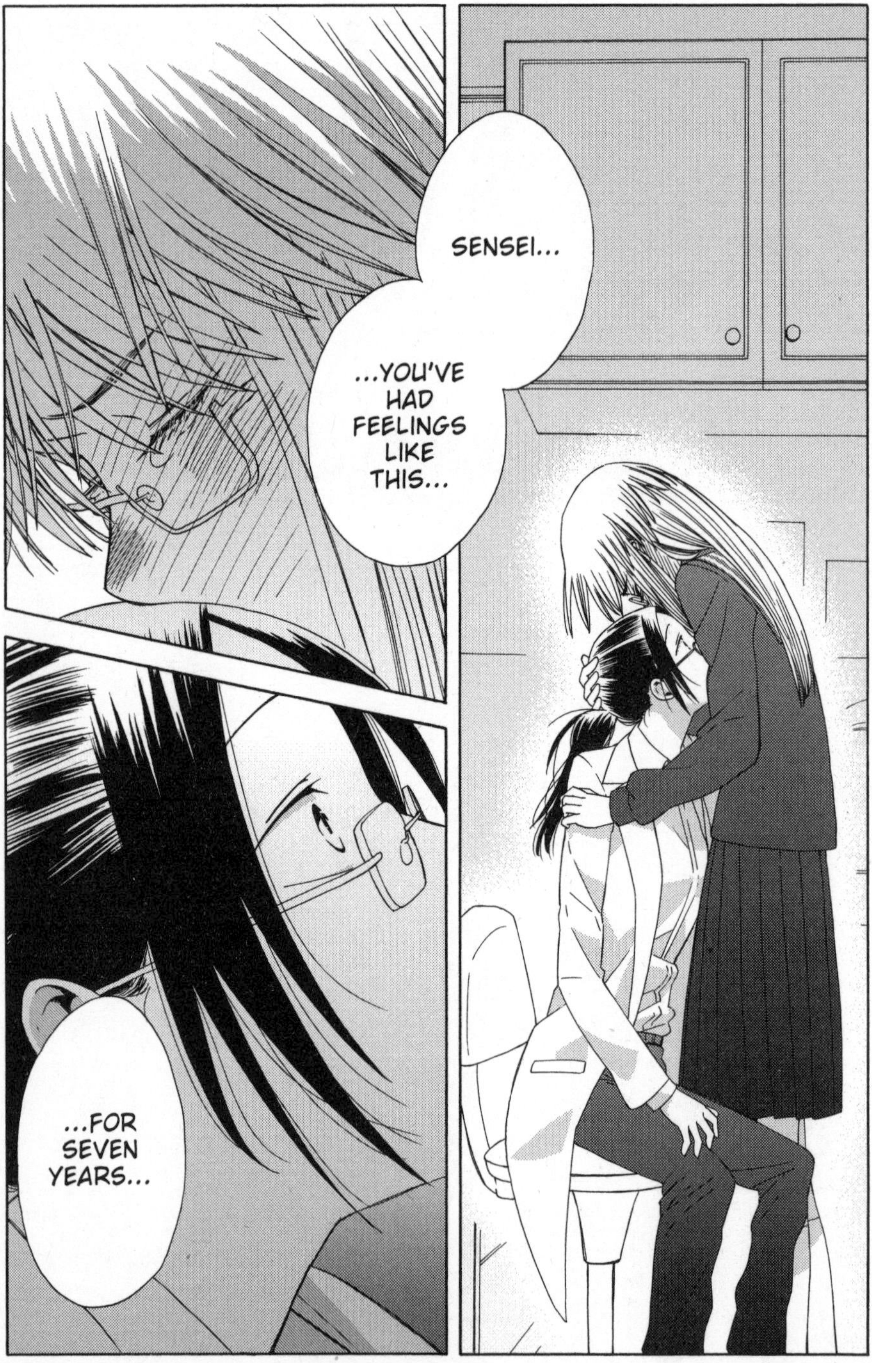
SENSEI...
...YOU'VE HAD FEELINGS LIKE THIS...
...FOR SEVEN YEARS...

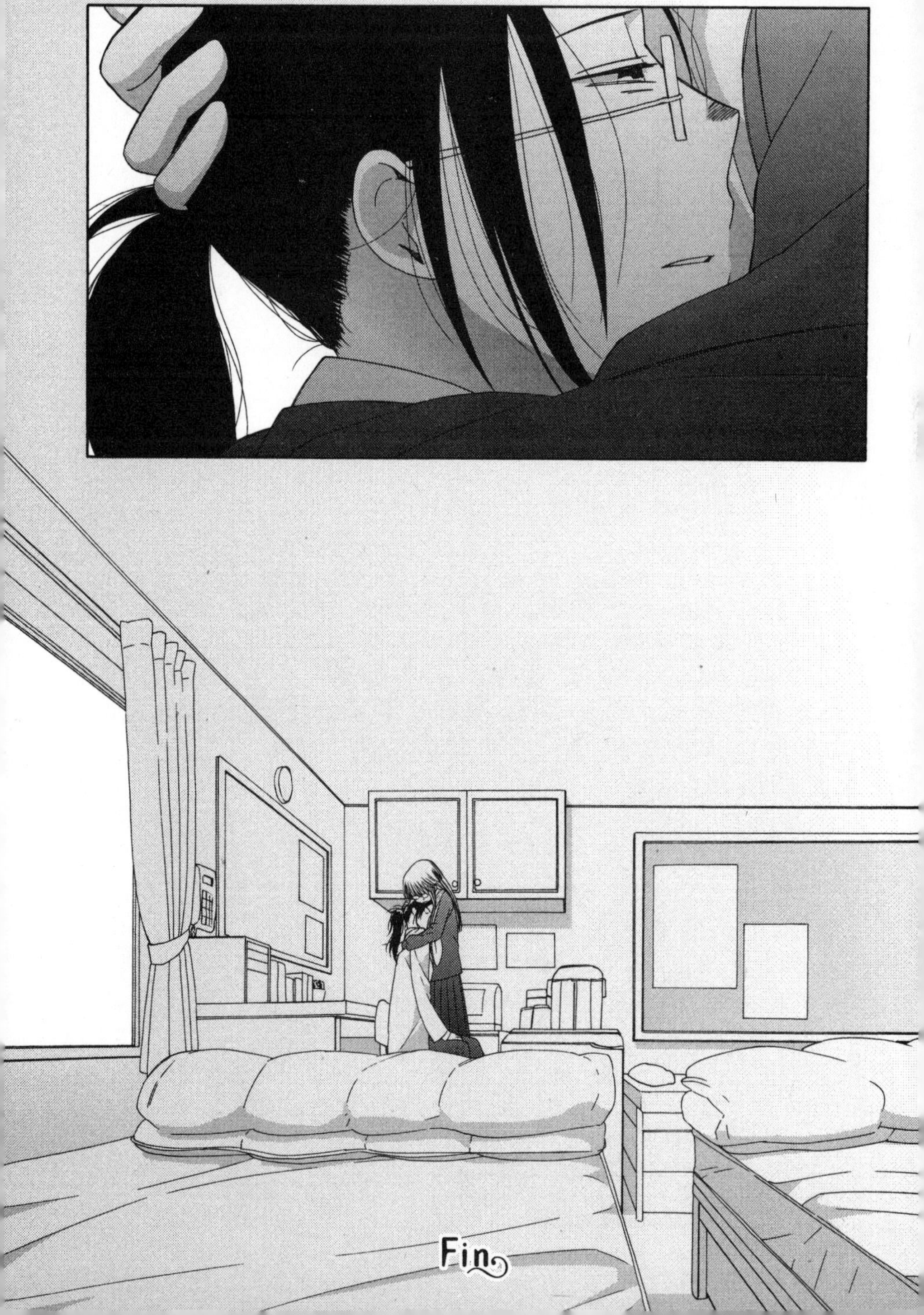
Fin

Love at Fourteen

Fuka Mizutani

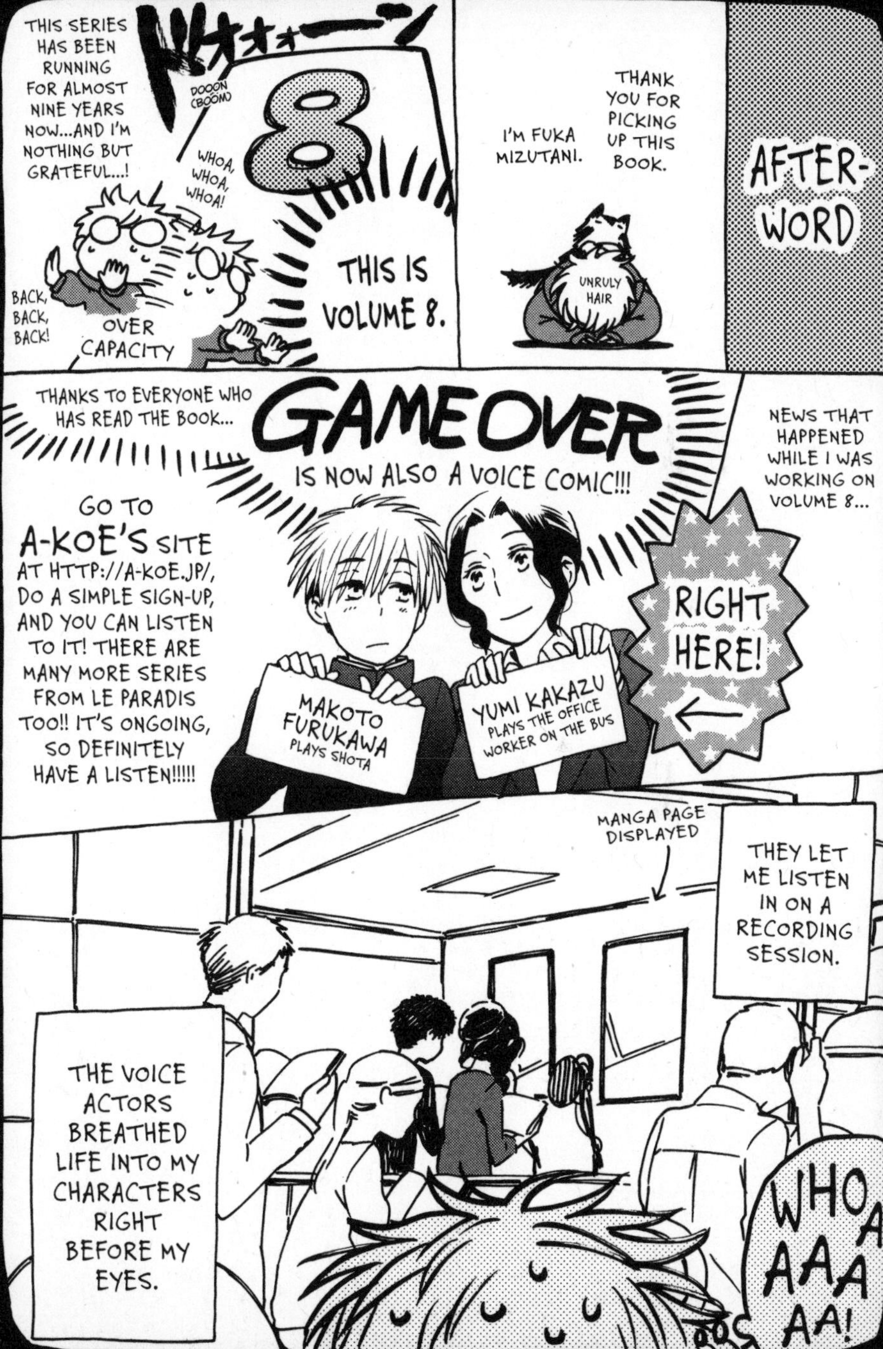

AFTER-WORD
THANK YOU FOR PICKING UP THIS BOOK.
I'M FUKA MIZUTANI.
UNRULY HAIR
ドオオーン
DOOON (BOOM)
8
THIS SERIES HAS BEEN RUNNING FOR ALMOST NINE YEARS NOW...AND I'M NOTHING BUT GRATEFUL...!
WHOA, WHOA, WHOA!
THIS IS VOLUME 8.
OVER CAPACITY
BACK, BACK, BACK!
NEWS THAT HAPPENED WHILE I WAS WORKING ON VOLUME 8...
RIGHT HERE!
GAME OVER
IS NOW ALSO A VOICE COMIC!!!
THANKS TO EVERYONE WHO HAS READ THE BOOK...
YUMI KAKAZU PLAYS THE OFFICE WORKER ON THE BUS
MAKOTO FURUKAWA PLAYS SHOTA
GO TO A-KOE'S SITE AT HTTP://A-KOE.JP/, DO A SIMPLE SIGN-UP, AND YOU CAN LISTEN TO IT! THERE ARE MANY MORE SERIES FROM LE PARADIS TOO!! IT'S ONGOING, SO DEFINITELY HAVE A LISTEN!!!!!
THEY LET ME LISTEN IN ON A RECORDING SESSION.
MANGA PAGE DISPLAYED
WHOAAAAAA!
THE VOICE ACTORS BREATHED LIFE INTO MY CHARACTERS RIGHT BEFORE MY EYES.

※ ONLY AVAILABLE IN JAPANESE.

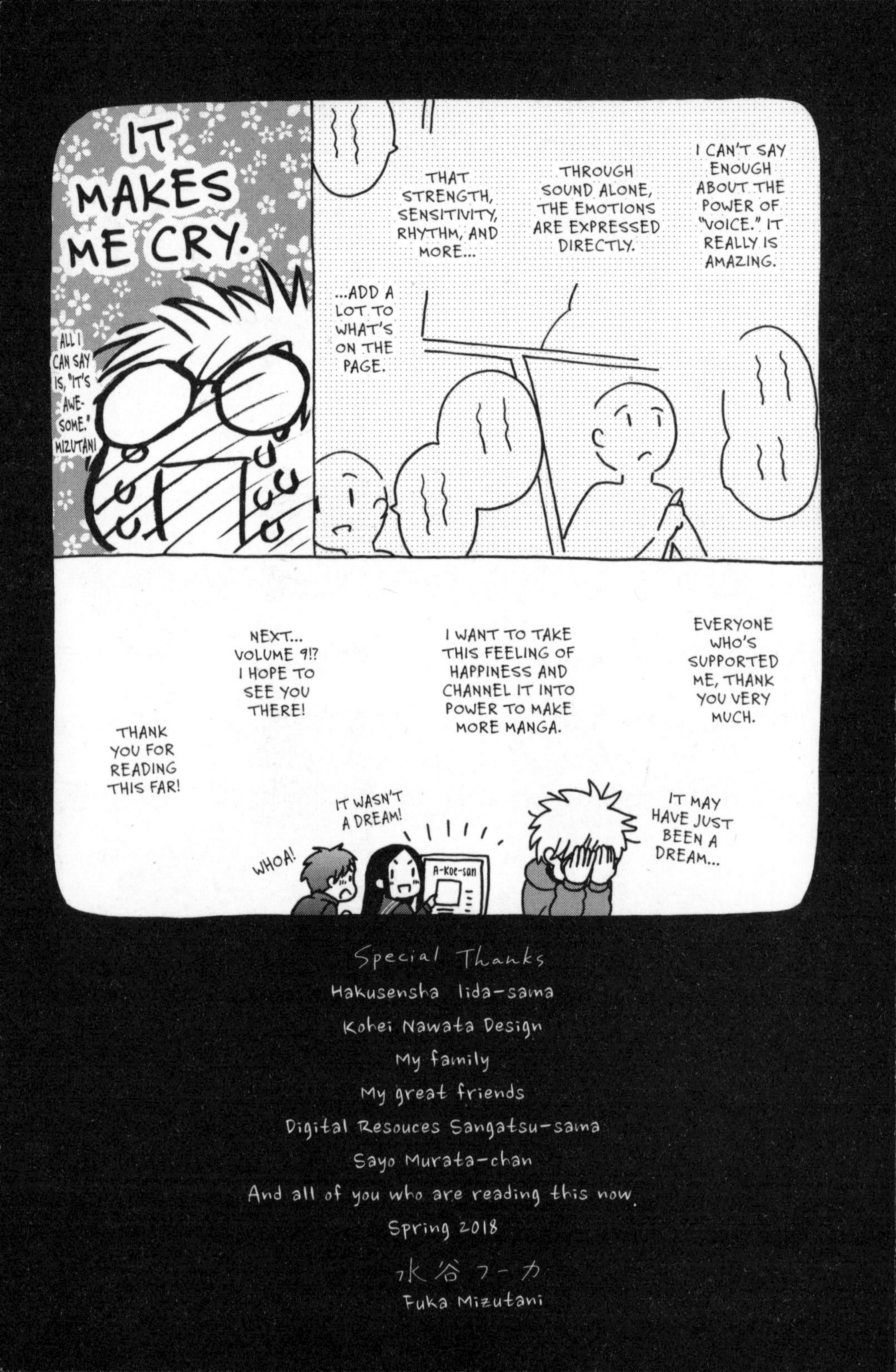
I CAN'T SAY ENOUGH ABOUT THE POWER OF "VOICE." IT REALLY IS AMAZING.
THROUGH SOUND ALONE, THE EMOTIONS ARE EXPRESSED DIRECTLY.
THAT STRENGTH, SENSITIVITY, RHYTHM, AND MORE...
...ADD A LOT TO WHAT'S ON THE PAGE.
IT MAKES ME CRY.
ALL I CAN SAY IS, "IT'S AWE-SOME." MIZUTANI
EVERYONE WHO'S SUPPORTED ME, THANK YOU VERY MUCH.
I WANT TO TAKE THIS FEELING OF HAPPINESS AND CHANNEL IT INTO POWER TO MAKE MORE MANGA.
NEXT... VOLUME 9!? I HOPE TO SEE YOU THERE!
THANK YOU FOR READING THIS FAR!
IT MAY HAVE JUST BEEN A DREAM...
IT WASN'T A DREAM!
A-Koe-san
WHOA!

Special Thanks

Hakusensha Iida-sama

Kohei Nawata Design

My family

My great friends

Digital Resouces Sangatsu-sama

Sayo Murata-chan

And all of you who are reading this now.

Spring 2018

水谷フーカ

Fuka Mizutani

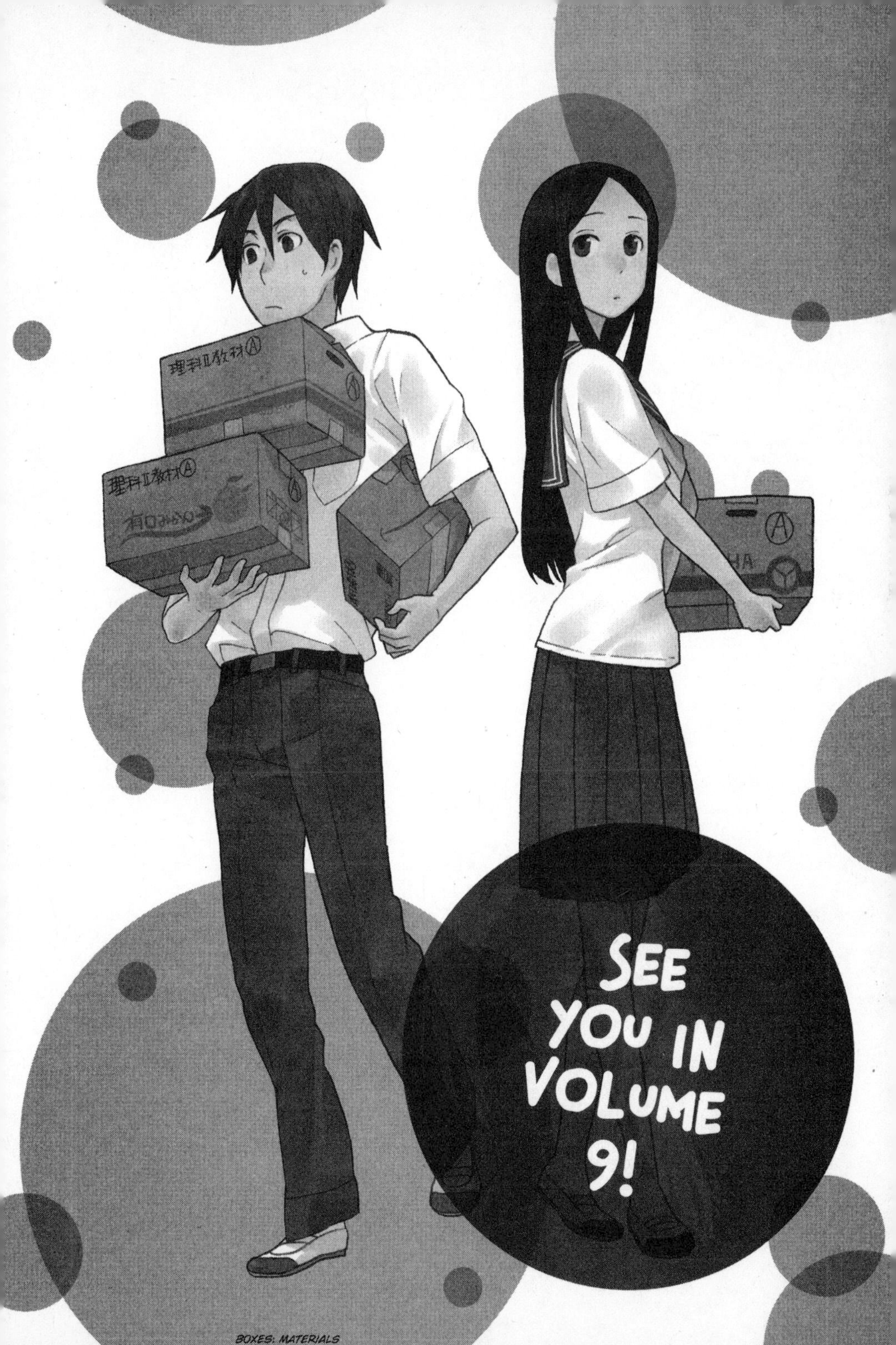
SEE YOU IN VOLUME 9!
BOXES: MATERIALS

TRANSLATION NOTES

COMMON HONORIFICS:
no honorific: Indicates familiarity or closeness; if used without permission or reason, addressing someone in this manner would constitute an insult.
-san: The Japanese equivalent of Mr./Mrs./Miss. If a situation calls for politeness, this is the fail-safe honorific.
-sama: Conveys great respect; may also indicate that the social status of the speaker is lower than that of the addressee.
-kun: Used most often when referring to boys, this indicates affection or familiarity. Occasionally used by older men among their peers, but it may also be used by anyone referring to a person of lower standing.
-chan: An affectionate honorific indicating familiarity used mostly in reference to girls; also used in reference to cute persons or animals of either gender.
-senpai: A suffix used to address upperclassmen or more experienced coworkers.
-sensei: A respectful term for teachers, artists, or high-level professionals.

PAGE 9
Visitor slippers: Students wear their own slippers at school in order to keep the floors pristine, stopping to switch them with their street shoes (kept in an assigned cubbyhole) upon going home. However, visitors to the school must also switch to slippers upon entering the school. There may be a barrel of generic slippers or a shelf full and if the visitor is lucky, they'll choose an approximately correct size the first time. This slipper system is also often used at temples and medical clinics.

PAGE 51
Backpack: This hard-sided style of backpack, called *ransel* in Japanese (from Dutch), is a staple of elementary school, hence the giveaway that Arisaka is years younger than Kato assumed.

PAGE 62
Toh-chan: Arisaka's given name sounds very similar to the Japanese word for "dad" (*otou*). As a young, elementary age girl, her classmates must find this hilarious, so she prefers to go by her family name instead.

PAGE 101
Washing hands: Schools often have a long communal sink for washing hands (and gargling in the winter) near the entrance. The idea is for students to wash their hands here upon entering, not after using the toilet (for which there are non-communal sinks in the restroom).

PAGE 109 & 129
Celsius: Tanaka's plan to get a fever after running in the rain has clearly not worked, as she wakes up with a 36.2°C temperature, which is a very healthy 97°F. Kazuki, on the other hand, has spiked a 38.2°C, or 100.7°F, fever and ends up staying home from school.

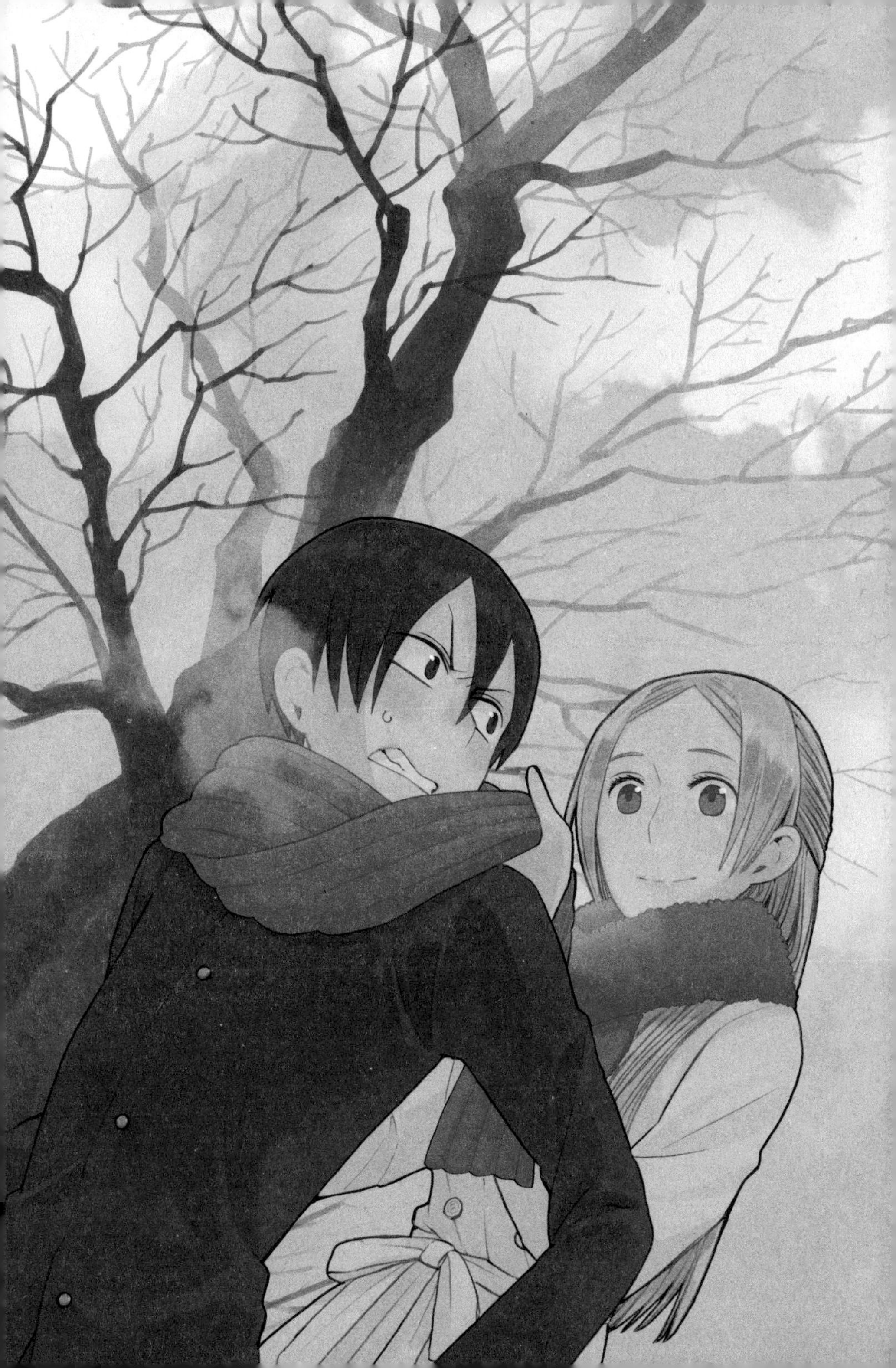

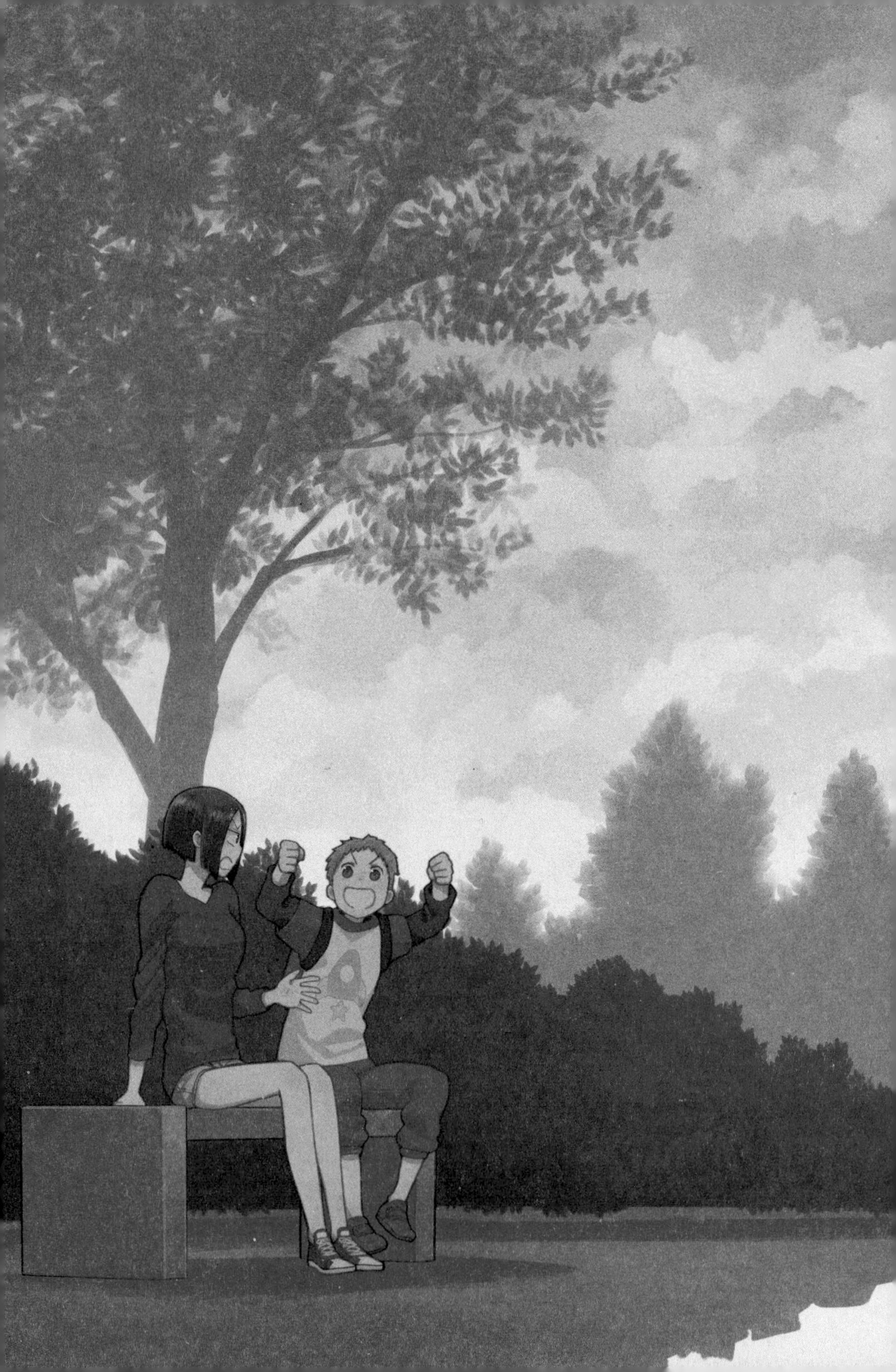

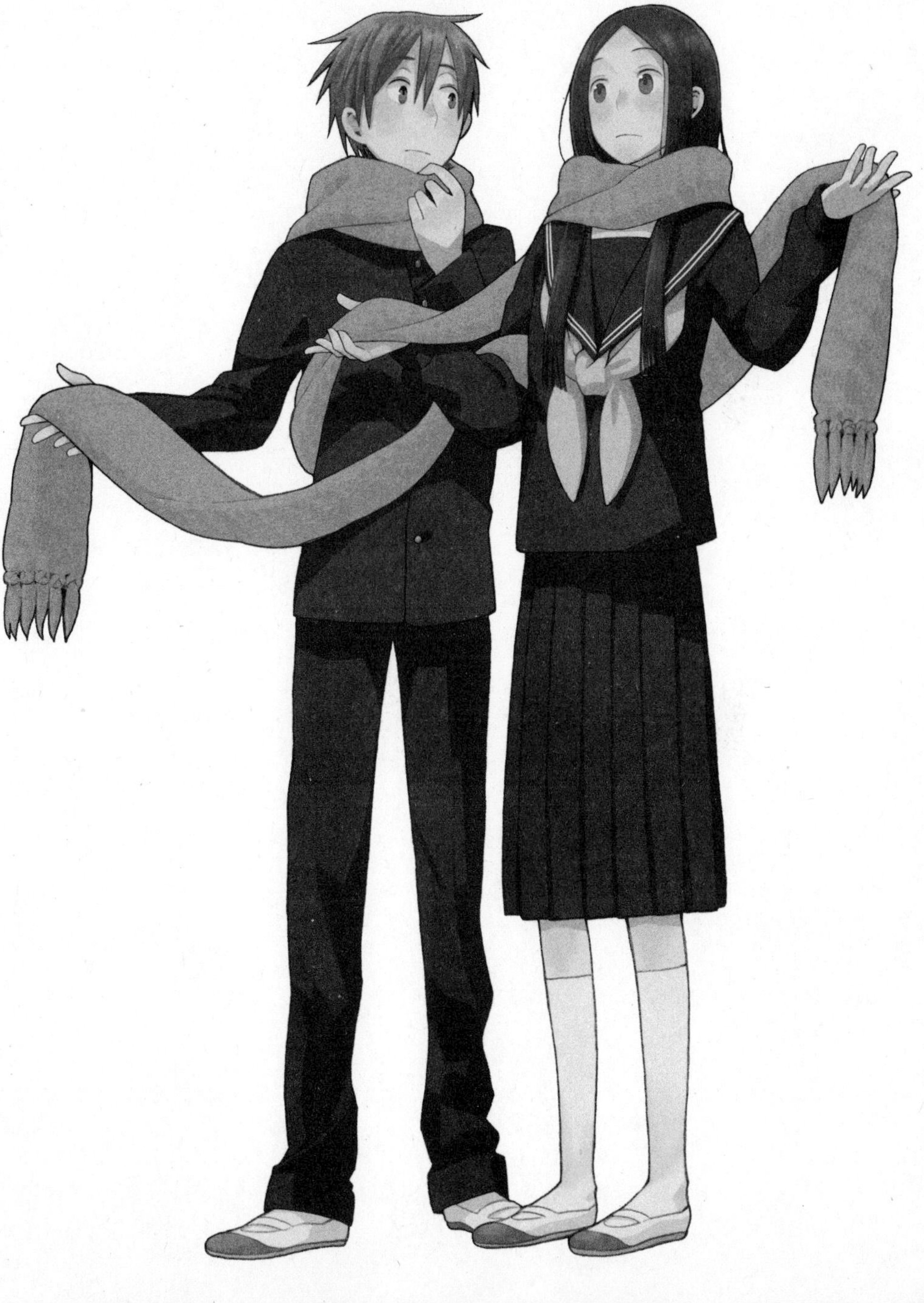

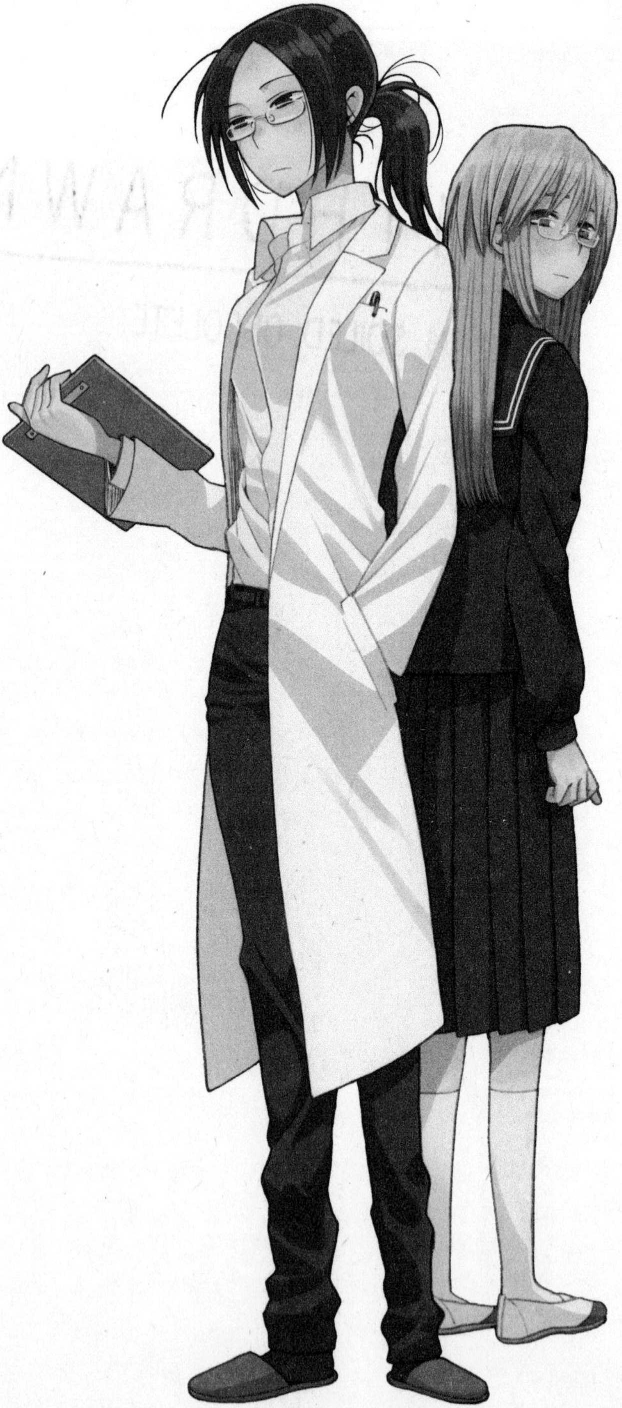

LOVE AT FOURTEEN
FUKA MIZUTANI

Translation: Sheldon Drzka

Lettering: Lys Blakeslee

JUYON-SAI NO KOI by Fuka Mizutani
© Fuka Mizutani 2018
All rights reserved.
First published in Japan in 2018 by HAKUSENSHA, INC., Tokyo.
English language translation rights in U.S.A., Canada and U.K. arranged with
HAKUSENSHA, INC., Tokyo through Tuttle-Mori Agency, Inc., Tokyo.

English translation © 2018 by Yen Press, LLC

Yen Press
1290 Avenue of the Americas
New York, NY 10104

Visit us at yenpress.com
facebook.com/yenpress
twitter.com/yenpress
yenpress.tumblr.com
instagram.com/yenpress

First Yen Press Edition: November 2018

Yen Press is an imprint of Yen Press, LLC.
The Yen Press name and logo are trademarks of Yen Press, LLC.

Library of Congress Control Number: 2016297684

ISBNs: 978-1-9753-2812-2 (paperback)
       978-1-9753-2906-8 (ebook)

10 9 8 7 6 5 4 3 2 1

WOR

Printed in the United States of America